VON SAVIGNY'S TREATISE

ON

POSSESSION;

OR THE

𝕵𝖚𝖘 𝕻𝖔𝖘𝖘𝖊𝖘𝖘𝖎𝖔𝖓𝖎𝖘 𝖔𝖋 𝖙𝖍𝖊 𝕮𝖎𝖛𝖎𝖑 𝕷𝖆𝖜.

———◆———

SIXTH EDITION.

TRANSLATED FROM THE GERMAN,

BY

SIR ERSKINE PERRY,

CHIEF JUSTICE OF THE SUPREME COURT AT BOMBAY.

THE LAWBOOK EXCHANGE, LTD.
Clark, New Jersey

ISBN 978-1-58477-289-7 (hardcover)
ISBN 978-1-61619-510-6 (paperback)

Lawbook Exchange edition 2003, 2017

The quality of this reprint is equivalent to the quality of the original work.

THE LAWBOOK EXCHANGE, LTD.
33 Terminal Avenue
Clark, New Jersey 07066-1321

*Please see our website for a selection of our other publications
and fine facsimile reprints of classic works of legal history:*
www.lawbookexchange.com

Library of Congress Cataloging-in-Publication Data

Savigny, Friedrich Karl von, 1779-1861.
    [Recht des Besitzes. English]
    Von Savigny's treatise on possession, or, The jus possessionis of the civil law /
    translated from the German by Sir Erskine Perry.
        p. cm.
    Translation of: Das Recht des Besitzes.
    Originally published: 6th ed. London: S. Sweet, 1848.
    Includes bibliographical references and index.
    ISBN 1-58477-289-1 (cloth: alk. paper)
        1. Possession (Roman law) 2. Possession (Law) I. Title: Treatise on possession, or,
    The jus possessionis of the civil law. II. Title: Von Savigny's treatise on possession. III.
    Title: Jus possessionis of the civil law. IV. Title.

    KJA2440 .S28 2002
    346.04—dc21   2002034068

Printed in the United States of America on acid-free paper

VON SAVIGNY'S TREATISE

ON

POSSESSION;

OR THE

𝕵𝖚𝖘 𝕻𝖔𝖘𝖘𝖊𝖘𝖘𝖎𝖔𝖓𝖎𝖘 𝖔𝖋 𝖙𝖍𝖊 𝕮𝖎𝖛𝖎𝖑 𝕷𝖆𝖜.

———◆———

SIXTH EDITION.

TRANSLATED FROM THE GERMAN,

BY

SIR ERSKINE PERRY,

CHIEF JUSTICE OF THE SUPREME COURT AT BOMBAY.

————————

LONDON:

S. SWEET, 1, CHANCERY LANE, FLEET STREET,

Law Bookseller and Publisher.

————

1848.

LONDON:
PRINTED BY RAYNER AND HODGES,
109, Fetter Lane, Fleet Street.

TO THE MEMBERS

OF

THE HONORABLE COMPANY'S SERVICE,

ENGAGED IN

THE ADMINISTRATION OF JUSTICE

IN

INDIA.

GENTLEMEN,

It is the privilege of an author, be it only of a humble translation, to dedicate his work to any quarter where he may desire to express esteem and regard. The members of the Honorable Company's Service, in all its branches, are engaged from time to time in the administration of justice to one hundred millions of British subjects, and the experience which I have acquired of the impartiality displayed, of the earnest desire to do right, and of the pains exhibited to acquire the requisite knowledge, in their exercise of judicial functions, has inspired in my bosom the sentiments which I have above stated.

The dispensation of justice, however, forms only a portion of the duties which fall to the lot of an Indian Official, who, like the Roman administrator of a Province, has frequently the whole burthen of government thrown upon him, and is called upon to act in some of the most difficult emergencies of life on the spur of the moment, and on his own responsibility. It necessarily follows, therefore, that your Service is not enabled to obtain the same scientific knowledge of the law which follows only upon deep study and exclusive attention to the subject, and I conceive that by placing before you in an English dress the most celebrated treatise of modern times on a very important title of the Law, I shall be rendering you a service of which you will not be slow to avail yourselves.

The Author has been characterised by a high authority (a) as the greatest master of Roman Law in Europe, and although the subject of his work is treated very technically, and solely with reference to Civil Law, an accurate knowledge of the distinction between Possession and Property, and of the legal protection afforded to the former in order to repress violence and breaches of the public peace, is essential in all systems of Jurisprudence, and will be found, I apprehend, most valuable to Indian Practitioners.

Independently of this feature of the work, it affords the most admirable model of strict legal

(a) The late Dr. Arnold.

reasoning, of interpretation of the language of the
law, and of that practical good sense in the treatment of legal questions, which the study of the
Roman Classical Jurists seems to engender, that
I have met with in any modern treatise, and as
such it appears to me to commend itself with
peculiar propriety to your distinguished Service.

I have the honor to be,
Gentlemen,
Your most obedient servant,

THE TRANSLATOR.

Bombay, May 15, 1848.

TRANSLATOR'S PREFACE.

"WHAT is it to possess? This appears a very simple question:—there is none more difficult of resolution, and it is in vain that its solution is sought for in books of law: the difficulty has not even been perceived. It is not, however, a vain speculation of metaphysics. Every thing which is most precious to a man may depend upon this question:—his property, his liberty, his honour, and even his life. Indeed, in defence of my possession, I may lawfully strike, wound, and even kill, if necessary. But was the thing in my possession? If the law trace no line of demarcation, if it decide not what is possession, and what is not, I may, whilst acting with the best intentions, find myself guilty of the greatest crime, and what I thought was legitimate defence, may, in the opinion of the Judge, be robbery and murder.

" This, then, is a matter which ought to be investigated in every code, but it has not been done in any.

" To prevent perpetual equivocation, it is necessary carefully to distinguish between physical and legal possession. We here refer to the former: it does not suppose any law, it existed before there were laws; it is the possession of the subject itself, whether a thing or the service of man. Legal possession is altogether the work of the law; it is the possession of the right over a thing, or over the services of man. To have physical possession of a thing, is to have a certain relation with that thing, of which, if it please the legislator, the existence may hold the place of an investive event, for the purpose of giving commencement to certain rights over that thing. To have legal possession of a thing, is already to have certain rights over that thing, whether by reason of physical possession, or otherwise.

" I have said, that to have physical possession of a thing, is to have a certain relation with that thing. This was all that I have said—this is all that I could say at first. What is that relation? It is here that the difficulty begins.

" To define possession, is to recall the image which presents itself to the mind when it is necessary to decide between two parties, which is in possession of a thing, and which is not. But if this image be different with different men—if many do not form any such image, or if they form a different one on different occasions, how shall a definition be found to fix an image so uncertain and variable.

" The idea of possession will be different according to the nature of the subject—according as it respects things or the services of man, or fictitious entities—as parentage, privilege, exemption from services, &c.

" The idea will be different, according as it refers to things moveable, or immoveable. How many questions are necessary for determining what constitutes a building a lodging; Must it be factitious? But a natural cavern may serve for a dwelling,—must it be immoveable? But a coach, in which one dwells in journeying, a ship, are not immoveables. But this land, this building,—what is to be done that it may be possessed? Is it actual occupation?—is it the habit of possessing it?—is it facility of possessing without opposition, and in spite of opposition itself?

" Other difficulties : In reference to exclusive possession, or possession in common—in reference to possession by an individual, or by everybody.

" Ulterior difficulties: In reference to possession by one's self, or possession by another. You are in the habit of occupying this manufactory, you alone occupy it at this hour : I say you are only my manager—you pretend to be my lessee : A creditor contends that you are my partner. This being the case, are you, or I, or are both, in possession of the manufactory ?

" A street porter enters an inn, puts down his bundle upon the table, and goes out. One person puts his hand upon the bundle to examine it ; another puts his to carry it away, saying it is mine. The innkeeper runs to claim it, in opposition to them both ; the porter returns or does not return. Of these four men, which is in possession of the bundle?

" In the house in which I dwell with my family is an escritoire, usually occupied by my clerk, and by what belongs to him : in this escritoire there is placed a locked box belonging to my son ; in this box he has deposited a purse entrusted to him by a friend. In whose possession is the bag—in mine, in my clerk's, in my son's, or his friend's ? It is possible to double or triple the number of these degrees ; the question may be complicated at pleasure.

" How shall these difficulties be resolved ?"—*Bentham.*

In the resolution of some of the difficulties here admirably indicated by Mr. Bentham, it is hoped that the following translation from a treatise which has been pronounced to be " of all books upon law, the most consummate and masterly" (a), will be found serviceable. It is singular enough

(a) Austin's Province of Jurisprudence Determined, App. xxxviii.

that an English law library does not contain a single
treatise on Possession, although as a term of univeral jurisprudence, it is constantly occurring in the system, and
distinct and clear ideas upon it are essential for the solution
of practical questions arising every day, I had intended,
when I commenced the translation of this Work, to have
accompanied it with an essay on the corresponding title in
English Law, but the difficulty which I have experienced in
obtaining sufficient leisure to prepare even this translation
for the press, has deterred me from undertaking the task,
and I leave it as one well worthy of being accomplished to
some younger and less employed member of the Profession.

I had also intended to have given a sketch of Roman
procedure, in order to make the text more intelligible to
English readers, and to induce them to get over the not
unnatural repugnance to enter upon a disquisition, in
which technical terms like vindicatim, Quiritarian property,
emphyteusis, summariissimum, interdicts, &c., require to be
understood; and the great light thrown upon the subject
by the researches of the illustrious modern school of German
civilians, and the newly discovered passages of Gaius, would
have made such a sketch not uninteresting. But here, also,
I have been deterred by the same press of business to which
I allude above.

I would take this opportunity, however, of pointing out
that all the principal notions as to Possession which run
through the English system, are directly traceable through
Bracton to the Roman Law, and if these notions are not so
clear, and have not been carried out so logically, amongst
ourselves, as with our continental neighbours, I think the
cause may be found in the neglect of the study of the Civil
Law, which has been a matter of observation and regret by
many of the ablest of the Profession for several years past.

The highest name which the English Common Law can

boast of, Sir Matthew Hale, may perhaps be usefully called in aid here, in order to induce a few hours' patient study being given to a work, which, if my own experience does not deceive me, is calculated to prove as useful to the practical Lawyer as to the philosophical Jurist.

" He (Sir Matthew Hale), set himself much to the study of the Roman Law; and though he liked the way of judicature in England, by juries, much better than that of the Civil Law, where so much was trusted to the Judge, yet he often said, that the true grounds and reason of law were so well delivered in the Digests, that a man could never understand law as a science so well as by seeking it there, and therefore lamented much that it was so little studied in England." *Bishop Burnet's Life of Sir Matthew Hale, p.* 10.

In conclusion, I have only to crave the indulgence of the reader for many imperfections which no doubt have crept into the translation. The greater portion of it was executed during Vacation months on a mountain range in India, where I had no access to books, not even to a Dictionary, and in the careful revision of it, and correction for the Press, which I have subsequently made, I have been so frequently sensible of my want of accurate knowledge of the procedure in Civil Law, that I think it probable I may have mistaken the purport of many technical passages.

CONTENTS

OF

VON SAVIGNY'S RIGHT OF POSSESSION.

———◆———

BOOK I.

NOTION OF POSSESSION.   Page.

Sect. 1. Introduction to the Inquiry   .   .   1
—   *Detention*—difference of jus *possessionis*, and
     jus *possidendi*.
— 2. Juridical meaning of term,   5—7
     In relation to { 1. Usucaption.
                  2. Interdicts.
— 3. Refutation of other relations   .   .   8
     Delivery and Occupancy, &c.
— 4. Passages containing the doctrine in the Roman
     law   13
— 5. Is Possession a right ? .   .   .   16
— 6. To what class of rights does it belong   .   21
— 7. Terminology of the Roman law   .   .   38
     Civilis and *naturalis* possessio.
     Possessio ad interdicta and naturalis possessio.
— 8. Terminology *continued* .   .   .   65
     Possessio *justa, injusta.*
— 9. Essential (*material*) notion of Possession .   71
— 10. Literary History of the Notion   .   .   96
— 11. All Possession exclusive   .   .   112
     Compossessio.
     Possessio justa, injusta.
— 12. Review of the contents of Treatise   .   129
     Possession only possible of things corporeal.
     Jura and jura in re.
     Juris quasi possessio.
     Errors of Jurists.
— 13. Account of Possession on historical grounds   135

Page.

BOOK II.

ACQUISITION OF POSSESSION, MODE OF ACQUIRING.

Sect. 14. General view 142
        Factum, first condition (Prehension).
— 15. Ficta apprehensio examined . . 143
— 16. Prehension of immoveables . . 149
        Corporeal presence.
— 17. Prehension of moveables . . 152
        Presence.
        Delivery of Keys.
— 18. Continuation of last chapter . . 160
        Prehension without presence.
— 19. More precise definition of prehension . 169
— 20. Acquisition of Possession, where the physical
        relation had previously existed . 174
        Traditio brevi manu.
        Conditional delivery.
        Mode of acquiring Possession.
— 21. *Animus,* second condition for acquiring Pos-
        session . . . 177
— 22. Persons, incapable of *animus* . . 179
        Juridical persons.
        Lunatics, wards, infants.
— 23. Possession of a part of a thing . . 189
— 24. Acquisition of profits . . . 199
        1. By the owner of the principal thing
        2. By tenants, fructuaries.
        3. By bonæ fidei possessor.
        4. In cases of emphyteusis.
        5. By Pledge-creditors.
— 25. Derivative Possession . . . 205
        Three classes of transfer of custody without
        change in the property.
— 25. 1st Class—where the right of Possession does
        not pass . . . 205
— 26. 2nd Class—where the right of Possession
        passes with the custody . 215

Page.

Sect. 27. 3rd Class—where the right of Possession sometimes passes, sometimes not . · 221

— 28. Acquisition by means of an agent . . 224
Peculiarity of this mode.
Act of the agent.

— 29. Constitutum possessorium . . 236
Meaning of constitutum.

— 30. Results of this Book . . 241
Mere juridical acts do not give possession.
Succession—Mancipation.

BOOK III.

LOSS OF POSSESSION.

— 31. Introduction . . . 245
Continuance and loss of Possession equivalent
terms.
Rule as to loss derived from the notion of
Possession, *factum* and *animus*.

— 32. Historical investigation of this rule . 247

— 33. Loss by external events. (*Factum*) . 253
Moveables held by another.
Immoveables.
Mere absence does not lose Possession.

— 34. Loss by *Animus* . . . 266

— 35. Continuance of Possession by an Agent . 272
What must be done by the Possessor ?
What by the Agent ?
Loss by act of the Agent himself.
Loss by act of another towards the Agent.

BOOK IV.

REMEDIES FOR PROTECTION OF POSSESSION, INTERDICTS.

Sect. 36. Notion of Interdicts . . . 285
Not a summary procedure.

— 37. Possessory Interdicts . . . 289
Notion.
Interdicta *adipiscendæ* possessionis.

Page.

Sect. 38. Possessory Interdicts not provisional vindica-
              tions   .   .   297
— 39. Interdicta *retinendæ* Possessionis   .   301
      Requisites for them.
      Object.
— 40. Interdictum, uti possidetis   .   .   310
      Requisites.
— 41. Interdictum, Utrubi   .   .   .   314
— 42. Interdictum De Vi   .   .   .   322
— 43. Interdictum de clandestina possessione   .   348
— 44. Interdictum de precario   .   .   354
— 45. New right given by the constitutions ?   .   360
      Common opinion.
      Refutation of it.

BOOK V.

JURIS QUASI POSSESSIO.

— 46. Introduction   .   .   .   366
— 47. Personal easements (easements in gross)   .   367
— 48. Real easements (easements appurtenant)   .   372
— 49. Superficies   388

BOOK VI.

MODIFICATIONS OF THE ROMAN LAW.

— 50. Introduction   390
— 51. Notion of Possession   .   .   .   391
— 52. Spoliatory suits   .   .   .   395
— 53. Possessorium Summariissimum   .   .   406
— 54. Results of the Sixth Book   .   .   417

ERRATA.

Page 23, line 10, for *malificiis*, read *maleficiis*.
Pages 33, 35, and 37 (head line), for POSSESSIONE, read POSSESSIONIS.
Page 55, note (*p*), for *esse in potestate*, read *esse in possessione*.
  „   203, line 20, after *example*, insert *is*.
  „   265, line 1, for *nundinnæ*, read *nundinas*.
  „   288, line 9, for *restipilutations*, read *restipulations*.
  „   299, line 1, for *then*, read *than*.

VON SAVIGNY'S

RIGHT OF POSSESSION.

BOOK I.

ON THE NOTION OF POSSESSION.

—◆—

SECTION I.

DETENTION.

WHEN a series of authors take up the same subject successively, a set of traditionary general remarks very soon arise, which are sure to meet the reader always in the same place, even in works of the most different character.

Thus, in inquiries into the nature of Possession, it is usual to commence with complaints as to the extraordinary difficulty of the subject. Some, indeed, have been so serious with their complaints, as to have been driven by it into a sort of despair (*a*). With the greater number, however, all this means no more than an indirect encomium on their own work, which is to satisfy the reader on the difficulties sug-

(*a*) Two of the authors who counsel their readers to seek assistance in any other way than by a hopeless endeavour to base the subject on principle, are Leyser, Sp. 451, med. 1—4; and Sibeth, Vom Besitz, p. 61; "Amidst the numerous crotchets and actual contradictions of the Roman law, it is quite impossible on such subjects to arrive at any conclusion with certainty. We may, therefore, well ask whether there can be any *right of possession* at all, &c."

gested. I willingly refrain, at the commencement of this work, from attempting to prove the difficulty of my task; but it will be less easy to prevent its suggesting itself to the reader at several points of the inquiry through my mode of treatment.

All definitions of Possession, however much they may differ from one another in terms and even in substance, contain the same general principle as their basis, from which every inquiry into the subject must proceed. By the possession of a thing, we always conceive the condition, in which not only one's own dealing with the thing is physically possible, but every other person's dealing with it is capable of being excluded (b). Thus the seaman possesses his ship, but not the water in which it moves, although he makes each of them subserve his purpose.

This condition, which is called *Detention*, and which lies at the bottom of every notion of possession, is not by itself in any way an object for legislation, and the notion of it is not a juridical notion (c) but there springs from it immediately a relation to a juridical notion, by which it becomes in itself an object for legislation. For, as property consists

(b) I first of all adopted the expression, "but every other person's dealing with it is impossible." It was rightly however objected to this, that such impossibility excluded the conception of a disturbance of Possession; besides, if it even might be admitted with respect to the commencement of Possession, it would not at all suit the much looser and more remote relation of a continuing Possession. The expressions now chosen do not appear to me to be open to these objections. For if we adopt the mere power of defence as an element of the notion, the ultimate result thereupon remains indeterminate; besides which there are several grades in this power which could not be distinguished in the first selected expression. (Add. to 6th ed.)

(c) The German *juristisch*, which is formed from the low Latin word *jurista*, with a Gothic affix in *isch*, is not translatable by legal, or lawful, or rightful, but denotes a legality arising out of positive law, out of the *jus proprium ipsius civitatis;* see Hugo's Lehrbuch eines civilistischen Cursus, B. 1, p. 14, 8th ed. In English we do not distinguish between an act which is lawful from having a definite legal character attached to it, and an act

in the legal power of dealing with a thing at will, and of excluding every one else from its enjoyment, the exercise of property takes place by means of detention, which thus is the condition of *fact*, corresponding to property as the condition of *law*.

If this juridical relation of Possession were the only one, all that need be predicated of it in juridical terms might be comprehended in the following proposition:—The owner has the right to possess; he also, whom the owner permits to possess, has the same right; no one else has this right.

But the Roman Law defines the modes of acquiring and of losing Possession, as well as of property; it treats Possession, therefore, not merely as the consequence of a right, but as the foundation of rights. We have therefore in a juridical theory of Possession to consider only the rights of Possession (*jus possessionis*), not the right to possess, (the *jus possidendi* of modern jurists), which forms part of the theory of property (*d*).

We have now proceeded from the notion of simple detention to that of (juridical) Possession, which is the subject of the present treatise. The first book, as the ground-work of the whole inquiry, endeavours to define the notion in form and in substance (*e*); *in form*, by describing the rights which require possession for their foundation, and thus giving the

which is lawful from being simply not contrary to law. But as the distinction is an important one, and is essential to an understanding of the text, I have ventured to appropriate the term juridical to the former meaning, as that word was already floating in the language, though without any precise notion. [Transl.]

(*d*) This distinction is too evident to need its being dwelt upon longer, and Donellus Comm. lib. 9, c. 9, has elucidated it so satisfactorily, that it is inconceivable how several writers should have gone astray upon it.

(*e*) This is the Aristotelian distinction of *matter* and *form* which plays so considerable a part in German philosophy. Mr. Whewel observes of it, that it is "one of the most comprehensive and fundamental antitheses with which philosophy has to do;—the opposition of the sense and reason, of impressions and laws." Hist. of the Inductive Sciences, Vol. i. p. 55. [Transl.]

meaning which the non-juridical notion of detention acquires in jurisprudence, so as to allow it to be understood as a legal entity— as Possession; *in substance,* by enumerating the conditions which the Roman Law itself prescribes for the existence of Possession, and thus pointing out the precise modifications under which detention operates as Possession.

The formal definition of the notion, by which it becomes a real subject for jurisprudence, divides itself into two parts:

First of all, those passages in the system of Roman Private Law must be sought out which apply to Possession in this system as a legal relation.   Next, the rights must be ascertained which the Roman Law recognizes as flowing from Possession, and at the same time those rights must be analysed, which are erroneously put forward as rights of Possession. It will then be easy to answer the famous question, whether Possession is to be considered as a right, and whether it is a *jus in re.*   As, moreover, the first and simplest form which Possession presents in jurisprudence, consists in the owner's right to possess, but in the present inquiry Possession independent of property is to be treated as the source of peculiar rights, the question first above mentioned may be expressed thus : In what sense is it that Possession has been severed from property; which mode of putting the question has been adopted by many writers (*f*).

Secondly, it must be inquired how the different meanings, in which Possession is used in the Roman Law, are distinguishable from one another by the form of expression; and especially what it is the Roman Jurists mean by *possessio* simply, by *naturalis possessio,* and *civilis possessio.* This inquiry into terminology will, in the first place, afford a confirmation of that which precedes, and it will besides enable a complete interpretation to be given, upon which the whole of the following Essay may be made to rest.

(*f*) By Cuperus; for instance, De Nat. Poss. p. 1, c. 2.

SECTION II.

RIGHTS OF POSSESSION.

Throughout the whole Roman law, there are only two rights which can be ascribed to bare naked Possession independent of all property; namely Usucaption, and Interdicts (*a*).

Usucaption is founded on the rule established by the Twelve Tables: whoever possesses any thing for one or two years, becomes the owner of it. Here, mere Possession, independent of all right, is the foundation of property itself. It is true that, to have such effect, the Possession must have begun in a particular way, but still it remains, what in all other respects it is, a mere Fact, without any other right than that which flows out of the abovementioned effect. The same Possession indeed, which formed ground for Usucaption, was subsequently regarded as a peculiar legal relation by means of the *Actio Publiciana;* but the origin of Usucaption cannot be found in that form of procedure which was introduced long after. It is therefore on simple Possession independently of any other legal relation, that Usucaption, and therewith the acquisition of property, depended. Usucaption received an extension in the *longi temporis præscriptio,* which was a bar to the *rei vindicatio,* and the requisites of which were, for the most part, the same as those of Usucaption, so that Possession operated in the same way, and accordingly it is unnecessary, so far as

(*a*) It has been contended lately, with great force, in objection to my view, that even these consequences cannot be deemed absolute and immediate, because, to admit of interdicts an act of violence also must occur, and for Usucaption a good title; accordingly, Possession by itself is followed by no consequences at all. Sintenis, p. 252. This writer, however, concedes that the most important practical relations of Possession occur with Interdicts and Usucaption, and it is only in reference to them that Possession receives a juridical definition (p. 258). As I had previously laid down the same doctrine, the above author has merely proved that which neither I nor any one else had ever called in question. (Add. to 6th Ed).

the older law is concerned, to consider the possession of the *præscriptio longi temporis* in a different point of view from the possession of Usucaption. Justinian in all these cases, and indeed, where *bona fides* exists, even in the case of the thirty years' prescription, established a true property, so that in the later law we may always use the term Usucaption, whether it be of three, ten, twenty, or thirty years' duration. The word Usucaption, indeed, is never used for the thirty years' prescription, but it is quite logical to do so, because that prescription, like all the others, confers good title. Undoubtedly no other word for it is to be found even in the writings of the lawyers under Justinian.

The right of possessory Interdicts is a second consequence flowing from Possession. The connection between them is as follows: As mere Possession is not a legal relation, disturbance of it is not a breach of the law, and it only becomes so, when some other right is violated at the same time. But if a disturbance of Possession is effected by force, a breach of the law *is* committed, because all violence is illegal, and this is an injury against which redress may be obtained by an interdict.

It is in this respect that all possessory interdicts correspond; they all presuppose an act illegal in point of form. This is clear in all proceedings accompanied with force, especially in those of a graver nature, but it is equally true of all such cases in the Roman law as admitted of possessory Interdicts. Thus for instance, the *interdictum de precario* is founded neither on the contract, nor on the plaintiff having a better right to recover than the defendant, but solely on its being illegal to abuse the confidence of the plaintiff, just as it is tortious even in the owner of a chattel to seize it by violence. Accordingly the three modes in which Possession may be unlawfully acquired (*vitia possessionis*) are always to be found associated together (*b*). As possessory Interdicts,

---

(*b*) "Hanc tu mihi vel *vi* vel *clam*, vel *precario* fac fradas." Terence, Eunuch. Act 2, Sect. 3;   and so in innumerable passages of the Pandects.

therefore, are founded on an act illegal in point of form, it is clear how Possession in this case also without reference to its own lawfulness may become the foundation of rights. If an owner brings an action of vindication, it is quite immaterial in what mode the defendant has come into possession, because the plaintiff has the right to exclude him from possession. And, as in vindication, so also with the interdict by which the *missio in possessionem* is protected (c); for this is not a possessory interdict, the *missio* itself not giving any possession (d), but it gives a right to detention, and this right may be made available in the same way as if property existed. Whoever on the other hand has merely the possession of a thing does not obtain thereby any right to detention, but he has the right of demanding that no one else shall use force against him; and, in such case, if his possession is forcibly invaded, he may protect himself by interdicts. Possession is the foundation of these interdicts, and thus, as in the case of Usucaption the foundation of rights generally.

Most writers, wholly dissenting from these views, look upon a disturbance of Possession as a substantive breach of the law, upon Possession itself as a right, namely as presumptive property, and on possessory actions as provisional vindications (e). As the latter part of this doctrine has a practical bearing it shall be discussed hereafter (§ 38).

(c) "Nec exigitur, ut vi fecerit qui prohibuit." L. 1, Sec. 3, *ne vis fiat ei, qui in poss.*

(d) Creditores missos in possessionem rei servandæ causa, interdicto uti possidetis uti non posse : et merito : *quia non possident.* Idem que et in ceteris omnibus, qui custodiæ causa missi sunt in possessionem, dicendum est. L. 3, Sec. 8, *uti possidetis.* This passage will be discussed at length in the second book.

(e) I need only cite the latest advocate of this doctrine, Hufeland; Vom Besitz, p. 43—45. In the third edition of this work I endeavoured to place this view on a right foundation. But at the end of the sixth Section, I have shown why I have now been constrained to give up this attempt.

SECTION III.

RIGHTS OF POSSESSION.—*Continued.*

It appears, then, that Usucaption and Interdicts presuppose Possession as a condition precedent, and make it necessary to define the notion of Possession juridically : and so far, all are agreed.   But I maintain further, that, except these two rights, no other can be found, which avails as a consequence of Possession, and in this I am opposed by all the text writers, except one or two.

My conclusion is founded principally upon this, that the Roman Jurists never seek to define *the existence of Possession* (*a*) in any other relation, except in the two above named. But as this argument can only be made to stand out clear by subsequent terminological investigations, nothing remains here but to expose the want of foundation of the other consequences ascribed to Possession.   I do not mean, however, to go through the catalogues which many authors have given of the fruits of Possession (*b*): and shall only apply myself to those writers who on examination present any error of moment, or from whom any new light on the nature of Possession itself can be extracted.

1. In the later Roman law there are two cases in which property is always acquired simultaneously with Possession, so that Usucaption is neither necessary nor possible; viz.,

(*a*) I say, advisedly, the *existence of Possession* as of a continuing relation.   For, no doubt, the acquisition of Possession is constantly inquired into, merely on account of the property arising from it, and I shall have subsequently to examine this combination more closely.

(*b*) One writer has enumerated as many as seventy-two of these advantages ; (Car. Tapia in Auth. ingressi C. de SS. Eccl.)   But even in Frider also (De nat. poss. C. 8, 9), and Claudius (Res quotid. C. 1), the confusion is so complete, that it is impossible to add to it.   In addition to these writers all those essays must be reckoned with titles such as, *Beati possidentes ;* or *De commodis Possessionis.*   It need not be observed that in each catalogue the same thing is repeated under different names.

Occupancy of a subject which has no owner, and *delivery* from the hand of the owner. In both cases, it is true, the obtaining of Possession is the true ground of the property itself (c), which is what the later Jurists call *modus adquirendi;* but Possession as a special continuing condition is in no way the ground of this acquired right, because the possession and the property both begin at the same moment. Therefore there can be no question here as to any right which accrues to the possessor, as such, and it is only introducing into the learning of property that portion of the theory of Possession which relates to *prehension.* But although no special juridical character of Possession can here be recognized, still the relation thus indicated is important for the theory of Possession itself. For, as in these cases the acquisition of Possession and the acquisition of Property, in so far as concerns the nature of the act of acquiring, are inseparably connected (d), it follows thereupon as a rule of construction that all precedents relating to occupancy and delivery, whenever they relate to the *form of the act,* may be used as authorities for Possession, although perhaps they never mention Possession itself; and this rule has been already alluded to in the list of authorities.

2. The *Actio Publiciana* is based on that sort of Possession which is capable of Usucaption (that of thirty years excepted), and therefore no practical error need be apprehended, in regarding this sort of property like Usucaption as a consequence of simple Possession. But as the *Actio Publiciana,* even in the early Roman law, and still more in the later system, was extremely like the procedure in vindication, the proper question in each case no longer turned on simple Possession, but a similar relation arose, as where by occupancy and delivery true Property had been acquired

(c) That is *per possessionem dominum quærere,* L. 20, § 2, *de adq. ver dom.* Sec. 5, I. *per quas pers.*

(d) The passage in the code must be so explained, " per pro-curatorem utilitatis causa Possessionem, *et si proprietas ab hac seperari non possit,* (i. e. when valid occupancy or delivery is in question), "dominium etiam quæri placet." L. 8, C. de poss.

simultaneously with Possession. Accordingly every Usucaption-possession has a double aspect; in respect of the
property, which subsequently arises out of it, it is, as mere
Possession, a subject for jurisprudence; in respect of the
Publician right of action, which is now combined with it, it
enures in itself as property. And in this last view most Jurists
hitherto have treated it, not as Possession, but as Property.

3. Whoever possesses the property of another in such
wise that he may hold it as his own on a juridical ground,
(*bona fides* and *justa causa*), acquires an actual property in
the profits (*fructuum perceptio*). This right is generally
considered as something quite peculiar, and is reckoned one
of the most important emoluments arising from bare Possession. But it is easy to prove that this right is nothing
more than the Publician ownership, founded on the universal rule of accession, and the demonstration shall be
given at length subsequently (§. 23); so much being pro-
mised, all that has been said above, on the last mentioned
right (No. 2), applies here also, and it is wholly inconsistent
to exclude that from amongst the consequences of simple
Possession, whilst the *fructuum perceptio* is enumerated in
them.

4. In every contest as to property, the possessor has the
benefit of the burden of proof being thrown on his adversary,
and of being entitled to succeed if no proofs are offered on
either side (*e*). But that here also no right of Possession
is to be found, by which Possession itself may receive a new
juridical signification, appears from this, that the same proposition is universally applicable to all defendants (*f*). It is,
accordingly, merely the natural privilege of a defendant

(*e*) Sec. 4, I. *de Interdictis.*
This right, moreover, is an-
nounced by German Jurists under a variety of expressions, each
of which again is specially enumerated as a *beatitudo Possessionis;* for instance, " a possessor
needs no evidence;" " it will be
presumed that he has the property;" " on any doubt it will be
decided in his favour;" " he is
not called upon to show the origin
of his Possession," &c.

(*f*) ...... Semper necessitas
probandi incumbit illi, qui agit,
L. 21, *de probat.*

applied to the case of vindication, because in that suit none other but a possessor can be the defendant.

A point of practical interest in this doctrine, however, distinguishes it from the preceding. If the last mentioned right is a consequence of juridical Possession, no one can have it who is not recognized as a legal possessor, although he may have the custody of the article ; it follows that such person never could be a defendant in an action touching the property, for otherwise the universal right of a defendant would be denied him. If, on the other hand, this right is not a privilege of Possession, it must be affirmed also of mere detention, which does not enure as Possession. Now the Roman law expressly lays down that vindication may be maintained, whether the defendant is a juridical possessor or not (g). But as, without doubt, the plaintiff must always be cast, if he does not establish his case, the right now in question is just as much a right belonging to mere detention, as to Possession, and, consequently, is not such a right as can be characterized as a special juridical result of Possession.

5. A party may use force in defending his Possession (h). This like the preceding cannot be brought forward as a consequence of Possession, for this reason, that the passage on which it rests does not belong to Private Law (i). For as the protection of the Court is certainly not referred to in the passage, the meaning of it as a legal proposition must be this : whoever in the case supposed uses force is not subject to the penalty applicable to all other forcible proceedings. This

(g) L. 9, de rei vind.

(h) Recte possidenti, ad defendendam Possessionem, quam sine viti is tenebat, inculpatæ tutelæ moderatione illatam vim propulsare licet. L. 1, C. unde vi.

(i) Modern civilians, like the jurists of ancient Rome, divide their whole Corpus Juris into public and private law ; the provinces of the two are not very distinctly defined, nor are opinions upon the subject concordant, but the basis of the division very much corresponds on the whole with our English division, into civil and criminal law. See Prof. Austin's Province of Jurisprudence, App. x. [Transl.]

proposition belongs in part to criminal law on the ground of the public penalty, in part to civil law on account of the private penalty against parties taking the law into their own hands. But in neither relation can it be admitted as a consequence of simple Possession, because such defence is just as likely to occur, and is as much permitted, in the case of mere detention as with juridical Possession. This construction may seem to contradict the passage cited in the note from the code; self-defence is there permitted to the possessor, whose Possession has had a legal commencement, and consequently is denied to every one else, and amongst others to him who has but the bare custody.

But this mode of construction, which in all cases must be used with the greatest caution is nearly altogether inapplicable to the Rescripts of the Code, and a case may at once be conceived in which the position in the text applies without militating indirectly with our rule. Whoever for instance is forcibly ejected from his Possession may use force to reinstate himself, and it will be even held that his Possession had never been interrupted (*k*); if then the intruding party repels this attack with force, the latter cannot shelter himself under a plea of self-defence, because he is not to be looked upon as one defending his Possession. But where a party simply shews that he was in a possession which had commenced legally, this objection could not be taken, and the words *recte possidenti* have sense and meaning, without contradicting the above rule.

Such defence therefore, cannot in any way be looked upon as a privilege of Possession.

6. The right of Retainer (*l*).

That this is not one of the characteristic consequences of Possession follows from this, that other parties also enjoy it, to whom nevertheless all juridical Possession whatever must be expressly denied. In fact, this right is nothing but an *exceptio doli* which is only accidentally distinguished

(*k*) *L.* 17, *de vi*.   Sec. 311. Hufeland Vom Besitz,
(*l*) Thibaut Pandekten, 5 ed. Sec. 34.

from other employments of this exception by accidental circumstances.

SECTION IV.

RIGHTS OF POSSESSION.— *Continued.*

It has thus been established that Possession as a legal relation refers only to Usucaption and Interdicts; and this view is confirmed by the place in the system attributed to Possession by Roman legislators and lawyers.

1. In the Institutes (*a*) it is to be found in the midst of possessory Interdicts, because the right to use these Interdicts can only be supported on Possession; with Usucaption (*b*) it is assumed provisionally as a matter understood.

2. In the Digest throughout the whole of the 41st book, the acquisition of property is treated of; in the first title, the natural modes of acquiring; in the third and following, Usucaption. In the second title Possession is discussed, evidently as a step towards Usucaption, which is principally founded upon it, and cannot be understood without a thorough knowledge of Possession. Interdicts follow at some distance, and it is therefore quite natural why, in treating of them, no further mention should be made of Possession.

This view of the arrangement of the Digest is so simple, that most lawyers from the earliest times have given the same explanation of the subject (*c*). Some have supposed a converse relation, as they contend, that the whole learning of property has been only accidentally associated with Possession, and that Possession itself merely finds a place as a preliminary to interdicts (*d*) or to execution (*e*).

(*a*) *Lib.* IV. *tit.* 15.
(*b*) *Lib.* II. *tit.* 6.
(*c*) Duarenus in *tit. de possess. proem. p. m.* 823.

(*d*) Cujacius in paratit. Dig. lib. 41, tit. 2.
(*e*) Giphanius, in Œconomiâ juris, p. 162, et in lecturâ Althorph. p. 394.

3. In the Code, Possession stands between Usucaption (*f*), and the *longi temporis præscriptio* (*g*) evidently because both are founded on it in the same way. Here also a remote reference to execution is asserted (*h*).

The Basilica (*i*) correspond on the whole with the order of the titles in the Digest, and the titles in the Code are merely intercalated, still it is remarkable that here, immediately after Usucaption and just before the title *pro emptore* (*k*), possessory interdicts are inserted (*l*).

4. In Paulus (*m*) Possession is only treated of as the condition for Usucaption. But, as throughout the whole title which bears the latter heading, besides Possession itself, the *longi temporis præscriptio* is discussed, but Usucaption is never mentioned, it is most probable that the Gothic compilers have made many alterations under this head (*n*).

5. The Edict, although older than all the preceding sources, is mentioned last, because we know so little about its arrangement. In the commentaries upon it, the places in which Possession is discussed never coincide. In Ulpian's commentary, interdicts are mixed up with Possession, and Usucaption is mentioned long subsequently; whereas in the commentary of Paulus, it is just the other way. The following table may be useful as a review of the whole.

(*f*) Lib. 7, tit. 26—31.

(*g*) Lib. 7, tit. 33—38.

(*h*) Giphanius in Œconom. juris, p. 162.

(*i*) Lib. 50, tit. 42, in Meermanni Thes. T. 5, p. 42—50. Only a portion of the possessory interdicts are here given, the remainder are in the 58th and 60th books.

(*k*) L. c. p. 58.

(*l*) L. c. p. 57.

(*m*) Recept. Sentent. Lib. 5, tit. 2, *de Usucapione*.

(*n*) Schulting, *In Rubr. tit. cit.*

Ulpianus ad Edictum lib. 11.	*Possession.*	*Interdicts.*	*Usucaption.*
lib. 12.			l. 6. de usurp.
lib. 15.			l. 1. pro derelicto.
lib. 16.			l. 1. pro suo.
lib. 19.	l. 10. de poss.	l. 3. de interdict.	l. 10 de usurp.
		l. 1. 3. de vi.	
		l. 1. 3. uti poss.	
lib. 70.	l. 2. de poss.	l. 4. uti poss.	
	l. 6. de poss.	l. 1. de superfic.	
	l. 12. de poss.	l. 1. de itin.	
		l. 1. de aqu. quod.	
		l. 1. 3. de rivis.	
lib. 71.		l. 1. de fonte.	
		l. 1. de cloac.	
lib. 72.	l. 13. de poss.	l. 2. 4. 6. 8. de prec.	
lib. 73.	l. 16. de poss.	l. 1. utrubi.	
PAULUS. ad Ed.			l. 2. 4. de usurp.
lib. 54.	l. 1. de poss.		l. 2. pro emp.
	l. 3. de poss.		l. 1. pro don.
	l. 7. de poss.		l. 2. pro cred.
			l. 2. 4, pro leg.
			l. 2. pro dote.
			l. 2. pro suo.
lib. 65.		l. 2. 9. de vi.	
		l. 2. uti poss.	
		l. 2. 6. de itin.	
lib. 66.		l. 2. de rivis.	
		l. 4. de interd.	
lib. 67.		l. 6. 16. quod vi.	

From this very discrepancy it becomes highly probable that Possession itself was not even mentioned in the Edict, and therefore the commentators who could not pass it over in their systematic treatises, introduced it just where it suited them best. But besides this, the thoroughly practical scope of the Edict, which confined itself to laying down legal remedies, does not allow us to suppose that propositions as to the notion, the acquisition, and the loss of Possession would be found there; and thus it happened that each commentator on the Edict introduced the subject according to his own good pleasure (*o*).

It may be shewn still more easily that the rights, which have been denied above [Sec. 3] to be the results of Posses-

(*o*) The first of these observations I owe to Heisse, the second
to Hugo (Gött. Anz. 1818, S.
1558), and I first introduced it
in the 4th ed. of this work.

sion, are not to be found associated with it in the sources of the Roman law.

Occupancy and Delivery are every where classed amongst those cases in which property is acquired independent of the *jus civile.*

The *Actio Publiciana* occurs in the Institutes (*p*) amongst the prætorian remedies, and in the Digest (*q*) with the *rei vindicatio.*

The *fructuum perceptio* is treated of as a natural mode of acquiring under the head of property, and indeed in the Institutes (*r*) immediately after accretion.

The advantage as to the *onus probandi* is indeed mentioned in the Institutes (*s*) as a *commodum Possessionis,* but not so much for the purpose of enumerating all that belongs to the doctrine of Possession, as to explain the frequent use and importance of the *interdictum retinendi Possessionis* (*t*).

The right of self-defence, properly enough, is not treated of as a peculiar law provision, for which a proper place in the system of civil rights needed to be ascertained, but is only casually mentioned in connection with some other subject.

Lastly, the right of retainer has no separate place.

SECTION V.

POSSESSION A QUESTION OF LAW AND OF FACT.

The meaning of Possession in the Roman law is now established: Possession always has reference to Usucaption, or to Interdicts, and all legal propositions which mention

(*p*) Lib. 4, tit. 6.
(*q*) Lib. 6, tit. 2.
(*r*) S. 35, *de rer div.*
(*s*) S. 4, I. *de interdictis*

(*t*) For this, namely, first appears in the passages immediately following.

Possession in its juridical sense have no other object than to express the availability of Usucaption or Interdicts.

No difficulty will now be found in answering two questions upon which, hitherto, opinions have been much divided; first whether Possession is to be looked upon as a Right or as a Fact; secondly, if it is a Right, under what class of Rights should it be enumerated?

With respect to the first question, it is clear, that Possession in itself, according to the original notion of it, is a simple fact; it is just as certain that legal consequences are bound up with it. Therefore, (a) it is at the same time both a right and a fact, namely, fact according to its nature, and equivalent to a right in respect of the consequences by which it is followed, and this double relation is a very important one to keep in view throughout.

For as Possession in its origin is a mere fact, its existence does not depend on any of the rules which the *Jus Civile* or even the *Jus Gentium* has established for the acquisition or loss of property (b). Thus Possession may be acquired or lost

---

(a) The *jus possessionis*, which hitherto has been only cursorily pointed out as the object of our inquiry, now begins to assume, through the legal consequences above described, a distinct meaning. The expression itself occurs in several passages;

L. 44, pr. de poss.
L. 2, Sec. 38, ne quid in loco pub.
L. 5, Sec. 1, ad L. Jul. de vi publ.
L. 5, c. de lib. causa.

The same meaning cannot be ascribed to Possessionis *dominium* and *dominus*, which some have construed to be a peculiar sort of right.

L. 7, D. de incendio.
Cod. Gregor. III. 4 Const. 1.

L. 2, C. Just. ubi in rem actio (III. 19.)
Cod. Theodos. VIII. 18 Const. 2.

In the three first passages, *possessio* means a possession, a close, *dominus possessionis* the owner of the close. In the passage in the Theodosian Code, the expression has a much looser meaning; it denotes custody and enjoyment without property, without, therefore, the right of alienation, and therefore properly only *ususfructus*; consequently not even true *possessio*. In a later constitution, moreover, *jus possessionis* stands for *jus possidendi*, (legality of the possession), *L. 10, c. de poss.*

(b) This is the meaning of the following passages:— " Ofilius quidem et Nerva filius, etiam

by violence, although violence never can avail as a juridical proceeding; so, likewise, the invalidity of a law proceeding, for instance, the failure of a large donation for want of notice (*insinuatio*) will not operate to prevent the transfer of the Possession. So, also, according to the original notion of Possession, a strict transfer of it is not possible, *i. e.*, no possessor is to be looked upon as the successor of the previous possessor, but he acquires for himself an entirely new Possession, independent of the previous one (*c*).

But this rule is not without exceptions. There are cases in which we are required to admit the rights of Possession, where the fact of Possession does not exist, or to deny them where it does (*d*). In all these instances it is not merely the effect of Possession which, as in all other cases, erects it into a substantive right, but the Possession itself, as the cause of that effect, acquires in such instances juridical attributes (*e*).

sine tutoris auctoritate possidere incipere posse pupillum aiunt: *eam enim rem facti non juris esse.*" L. 1, Sec. 3, *de poss.*—"Possessio autem *plurimum facti habet*," L. 19, *ex quibus causis majores.* . . . "quod naturaliter adquiriter, *sicuti est possessio*, per quem libet. . . adquirimus.*" *L. 53, de adq. rer. dominio.* Acquisition of possession is not here opposed to all juridical acquisition generally, but to that of the *jus civile*, for this antithesis was all that was required for the scope of the above passages.

(*c*) Duarenus de Poss. L. 1838—9, has already made this remark, which is not without its consequences. It serves, indeed, to explain a controversy between Bulgarus and Martinus Rogerius de Dissention. Dominorum ed.

Haubold. Lips. 1821, 800. "Differunt in eo an quis a me possidere valeat salva materia possessionis."

(*d*) The Possession thus recognized in the eye of the law, although the physical detention is wanting, is termed, by German jurists, Possessio *ficta, impropria, interpretativa.* Albericus was probably the first who used these expressions. Azonis *summa in cod. tit. de poss. num.* 15. [The *constructive* possession of English lawyers. Transl.]

(*e*) "*Plurimum ex jure Possessio mutuatur*," L. 49, *pr. de poss.*—"*Possessio non tantum corporis sed et juris est*," L. 49, Sec. 1, *de poss.* These passages, therefore, are not to be confounded with those cited above, which speak of the *jus Possessionis*,

It is well to be acquainted with these modifications of the original notion of Possession, *i. e.*, it is necessary to know in what cases generally Possession is to be recognized or not: it is not difficult, when once the original notion of Possession is clearly embraced, to detect the excepted cases as departures from the rule, and to distinguish them from the cases included in the rule itself; but such an inquiry is of no practical interest. Cuperus introduced the very inconvenient method of making a list of all these cases, and he himself enumerates seventy-three of them (*f*). Such a catalogue may be well enough to glance over by one previously acquainted with the subject, but is very little calculated to convey information upon it. For this reason each of these positive modifications of Possession shall be introduced in its place, namely, wherever the rule itself is discussed as to which any exception occurs.

The above twofold nature of Possession may be made still clearer by the following instance:—*No one can purchase his own property*, i. e., the contract in such case is a nullity (*g*). The same is true as to contracts of renting, of *precarium, depositum*, and *commodatum* (*h*). But there is an exception to this rule, namely, where the owner makes such a contract with reference to the *possession* of the vendor. In such case the *emptio possessionis* (*i*), *conductio*

although the juridical nature, which Possession itself contains, relates to that *jus Possessionis.* Zachariæ (De poss. p. 13) interprets the *ex jure* by *e servitute, ex usufructu.* Thus *Possessio ex usufructu aliquid mutuatur* means, Possession borrows a rule from *ususfructus*, i. e., a rule is applied to Possession which was laid down originally for *ususfructus.* According to this, Papinian's reasoning must be as follows. The slave of whom I have the *usus-* *fructus* is capable of acquiring a *ususfructus* for me, but Possession is often governed by the same rules as *ususfructus*, and therefore such slave may also acquire Possession.

But Papinian undoubtedly did not reason in this wise.

(*f*) De Natura poss. p. 1, c. 6.

(*g*) L. 21, *de usurp.*

(*h*) L. 21, *de usurp.*; L. 4, Sec. 3, *de precario* L. 15, *depositi.*

(*i*) L. 34, Sec. 4, *de contrah. emt.*; L. 28, *de poss.*

c 2

possessionis (*k*), *precarium possessionis* (*l*), and according to analogy the *possessionis depositum*, and *commodatum*, also are valid. But these expressions do not at all mean that juridical possession is transferred *by means* of those contracts; for the *emptor possessionis* does not acquire the Possession without actual prehension, and by prehension he would have acquired it even without purchase. On the other hand, the *conductor possessionis* never obtains juridical Possession, and so also with the *commodator*. Lastly, the *precarium* and *depositum* are governed in the matter, sometimes according to the rules of buying and selling, and sometimes according to the rules of hiring. The meaning of the above expressions is, that those contracts obtain validity by reference to the previous possession of the vendor, &c., rather than by any juridical relation recognised in positive law, and except for such possession they would have had no juridical foundation. But the whole of the above is most clearly connected with the twofold nature of Possession previously alluded to.

For, Possession is a fact, in so far as it consists of a mere non-juridical condition of fact (detention), therefore in the above cases, a contract of purchase or hiring would not have the slightest effect on the acquisition of Possession. But Possession is a right, in so far as rights are bound up with the mere existence of that condition of fact; and therefore contracts of sale or other contracts with reference to such right are just as valid as if they referred to property.

Thus Possession (in the sense defined above) is at the same time both a fact and a right. It would be both useless and uninstructive to quote the numerous discussions upon this question, which may be found in the text writers.

Cuperus (*m*) has discussed the whole subject thoroughly

(*k*) L. 28, 37, *de poss.*; L. 35, Sec. 1, L. 37, *de pign. act.*

(*l*) L. 28, *de poss.*; L. 6, Sec. 4,

L. 22, *pr. de precario*; L. 35, Sec. 1, *de pign. act.*

(*m*) *De nat. poss.* P. 1, c. 5.

and correctly, and since his time not a doubt has ever been
raised upon the point (*n*).

———◆———

SECTION VI.

JUS POSSESSIONIS CLASSIFIED.

The second question was; to what class of rights does
Possession belong?

With respect to the possession which enables Usucaption,
this question does not arise. No one thinks of asking to
what class of rights the *justa causa* belongs, without which
a delivery is not capable of passing the property. It is not
a right at all, but only part of a transaction, by which property is acquired. Possession stands just in the same relation
with respect to Usucaption.

The only object for our inquiry, therefore, is the possession
on which interdicts are founded. This question may be fully
discussed, without troubling ourselves with a classification of
the whole system of civil rights, which would interfere
considerably with the course of our inquiry. For it may be
shewn that possession belongs to the law of obligations,
which view may be assumed to be distinctly expressed in
the Roman law; whoever then divides the law of property
into the law of obligations and the law of things, is thereby
obliged to separate possession from the law of things; and
those who object to this division must establish for the law
of obligations a special place of its own, to which possession
must at the same time be allocated.

Now that the right of possessory interdicts belongs to the
law of obligations follows simply from this, that the same

(*n*) Zachariæ (p. 11), indeed,   but he has not added anything
has treated the question anew,   original.

proposition may be affirmed of all interdicts universally (*a*). But it may be even more clearly proved that they found themselves on *obligationes ex maleficio*. There is no doubt about this as to the *interdictum de vi* (*b*). The *interdictum uti possidetis* is not only always associated with the *interdictum de vi*, but like it only lies in the first year (*c*), and consequently not against an heir absolutely (*d*), which latter point arises from the general rule limiting the liability of heirs in all *actiones ex delicto* (*e*). All the other interdicts except that *de precario*, are exactly like the *interdictum uti possidetis*, and even in the excepted case the liability of the heir is just as limited as in every *obligatio ex maleficio* (*f*).

But if *obligationes ex maleficio* are the foundation of pos-

---

(*a*) L. 1, § 3, *de interdictis.* "Interdicta omnia, licet in rem videantur concepta, vi tamen ipsa personalia sunt." The words "licet in rem videantur concepta," must be construed "even those not excepted which," &c., for they do not refer to all interdicts, for instance, not to possessory interdicts, but only to a small class such as the *Interdictum quorum bonorum.* Feuerbach (Civilistische Versuche, 1st Th. § 249) refers these words to all interdicts generally, and therefore classes interdicts improperly under *actiones in rem* in the extended sense of the term. The personal character of all interdicts is well explained by Hasse, Rhein. Museum, VI. 196—7; but he seems to have misunderstood the meaning of the parenthesis, licet in rem videantur concepta ; see page 198 ; compare also Bentheim über Dominium, p. 160. (Add. to 6th ed.)

(*b*) In L. 19, *de vi*, the term *delictum* is used; in L. 1, § 14,

Cod. *maleficium*, in L. 1, § 15, C. a *moral* action. Moreover the interdict lies only against the heir in id, *quod pervenit*, which is expressly laid down as the consequence of one universal rule for all *obligationes ex delicto, L.* 3, *pr. de vi*; lastly, in the *exceptio facti* the interdict is classed with other *delicta, L.* 27, § 4, *de pactis.* (*Vide post*, § 40).

(*c*) "Intra annum...." L. 1, pr. uti poss.

(*d*) Honorariæ autem actiones (in which interdicts are included) quæ post annum non dantur, nec in hæredem danda sunt; ut tamen lucrum ei extorqueatur sicut fit in.... interdicto unde vi," &c. L. 35, pr. *de oblig. et act.*

(*e*) L. 38, 44, *de reg. jur.* L. un. C. *ex delictis defunct.* C. Uerm. tit. 2; see further, *post*, § 37.

(*f*) Hoc interdict. hæres ejus qui precario roguit tenetur ... ex dolo. .defuncti hactenus, qua tenus ad eum pervenit," L. 8, § 8, prec.

sessory interdicts, why are the two subjects not classed together in the Roman law? (g) Simply because the classification of the Romans has reference to principles of procedure. They class under the heading "obligations" merely those cases which give rise to an *actio* proper (h). Interdicts therefore are separated from that class of obligations merely because a particular kind of procedure was appliable to the former; if the Edict had permitted actions in all such cases, interdicts without doubt would have been placed among the *obligationes ex malificiis,* although the nature of the substantive right itself would not have been thereby altered. Now as German procedure knows nothing of the actions and interdicts of the Romans, the meaning of the distinction disappears before us, and therefore, according to the views of the Roman law itself, there is no doubt that we ought to class possessory interdicts with *obligationes ex delictis.*

The right of possessory interdicts therefore belongs to the law of obligations, and with respect to such right, possession itself only comes in question in so far as it presents the condition without which interdicts cannot be conceived. Thus, the *jus possessionis,* i. e. the right which bare possession confers, consists only in the claim which the possession has to interdicts whenever a certain form of disturbance occurs (i). Abstracted from such disturbance, mere possession gives no rights, neither a *jus obligationis,* as is self evident, nor even a right to the subject-matter, for no act of dealing with a subject is to be deemed legal merely because the acting party has the possession of the subject.

The question now before us is one upon which much

(g) The *obligationes ex delictis* occur in the Institutes, B. 1, tit. 1, 4; in the Pandects, B. 47; interdicts are in B. 4, tit. 15, of the Institutes, in B. 43 of the Pandects.

(h) Accordingly the heading runs *de obligationibus et actionibus.* 1 Dig. lib. 44, tit. 7.

(i) Sintenis (Zeitschrift von Linde, B. 7, p. 259) struggles in vain against this explanation of the *jus possessionis.* The expression does not denote the right flowing from possession (for then it should have been *jura possessionis*) but rather the legal consequences and relations of possession.

controversy has existed from early times; but the greater part
of it is very uninstructive, and, indeed, is out of place here,
because nearly all the disputants content themselves with
framing a definition of the *jus in re* (or *in rem*), and *ad rem*,
and then proceed either to class Possession, like every other
right in, or to exclude it from, the definition, without bringing
forward anything new or important as to the nature of those
rights themselves. All come back to the same point in the
end, by treating the exclusive relation of possession to usucaption and interdicts as indisputable. Donellus (*i*) alone
of all the civilians has pointed out the true connection of
possession with the rest of the system; and, indeed, in support of it, he has indicated briefly the greater portion of the
reasoning which must be now given more in detail. Merenda appears by a casual remark to have nearly approached
the right conclusion (*j*), although his special theory occupied him too exclusively to enable him to make proper use
of it.

Baldus first of all recognized four kinds of *jus in re ;*
ownership, servitude, pledge-right, and the right of inheritance. Subsequently, possession (*k*), *dos, emphyteusis,* and
many other matters were included under the same title.
Hahn finally fixed the number at five, the above-mentioned
four namely, and possession (*l*) : his worthless treatises,
moreover, have obtained the honour of being the text-books
of a very numerous party (*m*). Some have endeavoured to
get rid of the difficulty by placing the *jus possessionis* in the
law of things under a special title subordinate to the *jus in*

(*i*) Comm. lib. 5, c. 6, 13, (as
the ground of usucaption); lib.
15, c. 32, (possessory interdicts).

(*j*) Controv. lib. 12, c. 28,
"Ubicunque de possessione agitur, ad interdicta respicimus, vel
usucapionem."

(*k*) Alciati Resp L. 5, cons.
112, n. 4.

(*l*) Diss. inaug. de jure in re
He mst. 1639 ; best ed. Helmst.

1664, 4to. He repeats his opinion
in several treatises on Possession.

(*m*) This doctrine is controverted in the following essay, in
which it is clearly shewn that
Possession is not a *jus in re;* H.
G. Scheidemantel resp. T. F.
Rappolt, diss. de numero specie-
rum juris in re, et præsertim, an
possessio sit illis numeranda.
Stutt. 1786.

re and *ad rem* (*n*), a view which could only have been adopted because no better solution presented itself.

The writers who have treated the Roman law systematically have found themselves in great difficulty when they had to assign a place to possession. Connanus (*o*), and Ayliffe (*p*), discuss it quite correctly under usucaption, as the foundation of that institute; but then the other juridical *phase* of possession, the right of interdicts, nowhere appears in their systems. Domat (*q*) divides the whole of Private Law into *Engagemens and Successions;* under the first head he treats, amongst other things, of the consequences of an *engagement,* by which the latter may itself be limited, and amongst these consequences, possession and prescription occur (*r*). This classification itself shows, that he did not know what possession meant in the Roman law: accordingly, throughout his work he is continually confounding three distinct ideas, which must be carefully distinguished

---

(*n*) L. B. Friessen Resp. Sturm. de genuina poss. indole, Jenæ, 1725. Reprinted in Gottlieb Sturmii disputationes Jenenses. Vitemb. s. a. 4, Num. 1. Höpfner follows him (Commentar. über die Inst. § 280, vol. 2).

(*o*) Comm. J. civ. L. 3, c. 8—20 (tit. 1, pp. 173—189). ed. Neap. 1724, fol.

(*p*) A new Pandect of Roman Civil Law, London, 1734, fol. Book 3, tit. 10, pp. 336—344. Usucaption is placed in the 8th title, and in the 9th, Donations are intercalated, in order to adhere as much as possible to the titles in the Institutes.

(*q*) Loix Civiles, Prem. partie (Des engagemens et de leurs suites) Livre 3, (Des suites qui ajoutent aux engagemens ou qui les affermissent) Titre 7, (*De la*

possession et des prescriptions,) p. 258—276, *Paris,* 1713, fol.

(*r*) Strictly speaking, Domat does not use engagement as synonymous with *obligation*, as he includes in the former marriage and paternal authority (Traité des lois, ch. 3, 4). But in the work itself he leaves out the latter relations, and treats of obligations simply, without, it is true, any clearly conceived notion of an obligation to start from. Possession, therefore, merely obtains notice from him as the fulfilment and completion of an obligation, as where, for instance, the purchaser by the transfer of the possession acquires the property, that is, acquires that for which he contracted. See Traité des lois, ch. 14, § 12.

from one another, unless the whole doctrine of possession is to be made a mass of confusion ; viz. *possessio, possessio civilis,* and *jus possidendi.*

Many modern jurists have striven to relieve themselves by classing Possession under a general title in their system, although Possession contains nothing more general in its character than property or any other right (*s*).

There is another error more important than all of these relating to the juridical nature of possession, but it is so little connected with the present question, that it is to be found in writers of all sides. Namely, possession has been regarded not as a special right, but as provisional ownership, and interdicts as provisional vindications, which were introduced merely for the purpose of regulating the practice in suits respecting the right of property. This error, which, perhaps, has led to more practical results than all the rest, cannot be completely refuted till the nature of interdicts is explained. The following passages to the contrary can only be cited here, as they properly belong to this place from their having the nature of possession itself as their subject matter : " *nec possessio et proprietas misceri debent*" (*t*), and " *nihil commune habet proprietas cum possessione*" (*u*). That something more is meant here than the trite remark, an owner is not to be confounded with a possessor, is shown by the following words of the second passage:—" *et ideo non denegatur ei interdictum uti possidetis qui cepit rem vindi-*

(*s*) See Urfacher (Princ. jur. civ. lib. 3, § 2). The above objection requires a slight explanation to prevent it from being misunderstood. If a general title is found necessary, it is no objection to it that possession should be there introduced, because such a title is usually adopted only because, from the nature of the matters contained in it, they cannot be classed scientifically elsewhere. But it is essentially necessary, in this mode of treating the difficulty, that it should not be forgotten to point out and describe the connection of Possession with the other titles, i. e. with the whole system of the Law.

(*t*) L. 52, pr. de poss.

(*u*) L. 12, § 1, de poss.

care. Non enim videtur possessioni renuntiasse, qui rem vindicavit" (*v*).

[Add. to 6th ed.] Since the appearance of the fifth edition of this work, several writers have criticised, in different ways, the general description I have given of the nature of Possession in the second, fifth, and sixth sections. In order to make an examination of these conflicting opinions as short and clear as possible, it will be desirable to repeat here my own view in a little more detail, and corrected by a slight modification.

Possession appears to us, in the first instance, as the mere dominion in fact over a subject, and, therefore, as a non-legal condition (in distinction to illegal), as a matter wholly indifferent in law. Nevertheless it is protected against certain sorts of disturbance, and, in respect of this protection, certain rules as to the acquisition and loss of possession have been established, just as if it were a right. The ground of the above protection, and of this condition similar to a right, is to be ascertained : such is the problem. Now, this ground lies in the connection between the above condition of fact and the party possessing, the inviolability of whose person extends to those sorts of disturbance by which the person might, at the same time, be interfered with. For the person must, at all times, be secured against violence ; if violence occurs, it is illegal, but this illegality may have various results. In this view let us consider, first, the two extreme cases which may occur. First, violence to the person, and to the person only ; second, violence to the person, and, at the same time, to a right inherent in the person ; for instance, to a thing belonging to him. The first case would lead to no other result in civil

(*v*) L. 12, § 1, cit. No passage in the whole title has undergone so much and such copious discussion as this; the first printed treatise on Possession is a commentary upon it by Bolognin (Bononiæ, 1494, fol.) But all the treatises referred to have scarcely any bearing here, they merely take this passage as a text for discussing the question of practice, whether the *petitorium* may be cumulatory with the *possessorium*.

law than some kind of action *ex delicto* (we are not now
speaking of criminal law). In the second case, violence is
not essential towards the calling forth of protection to the
violated property, which by itself, without any violence, is
entitled to protection; but the occurrence of a double
injury may, nevertheless, have peculiar results, amongst
which the *actio vi bonorum raptorum* is to be classed.
Between these extremes, the case occurs where the violence
offered to the person disturbs or puts an end to possession.
An independent right is not, in this case, violated with the
person, but some change is effected in the condition of the
person to his prejudice; and if the injury, which consists
in the violence against the person, is to be wholly effaced
in all its consequences, this can only be effected by the
restoration or protection of the *status quo*, to which the
violence extended itself. This is the true ground of possessory suits, and a closer consideration of the nature of the
above condition will make this still more manifest. It has
been said that possession becomes similar to a right,
because it gives rise to a presumption of property, and
therefore it has a claim to protective suits (*w*). But this
presumption has, in fact, no legal foundation, for in naked
possession, it is no more probable that the possessor has the
property than that he has it not. This appears most clearly
by a comparison of naked possession with *bonâ fide possessio*.
With the latter, property is, in fact, feigned, and this
fiction is nothing but a presumption, as it is invalidated by

---

(*w*) I admitted this presumption in the third, fourth, and fifth
editions, at the close of ch. 2, but
I now reject it. What gives it
some plausibility is, the circumstance that, in vindication, the
onus probandi is on the plaintiff,
and that he is cast, if neither
party brings any evidence. But
the ground of this does not lie in
a presumption of property in the
defendant, but in that the Judge
generally can only give his assistance to that party who makes
out his title, and in other cases
he remains passive. In a personal suit also the plaintiff must
prove his case, yet the ground of
that does not lie in a presumption against the existence of all
disputed debts.

a *dominii exceptio*. The ground of the fiction or presumption consists therefore, here, solely in the legal title, and as none such occurs in bare possession, the above ground is wanting to it for a legal presumption as to property. On the other hand, the possibility of property even in a bare possession cannot be denied, and in reference to this possibility Possession confers upon him several important benefits, both in respect of being sued, and in matters of fact, which benefits must be maintained, or restored to him, if the consequences of violence are to be effaced. The first of these advantages consists in the possessor being entitled to the position of defendant in a suit upon property, which relieves him from the burden of proof (§ 3). Further, he may as possessor, profit by various rules as to the custody of the subject itself and the perception of profits, which possibly he may never be made answerable for to his opponent in a suit for mesne profits. Even indeed without reference to the above undoubted possibility of property, the possessor has unquestionably the advantage in fact of being able to use the subject exactly like an owner, in cases where the actual owner does not think proper to sue him. All these advantages make up the whole of what is considered as an *interest* in law, when violence has been committed, and by which Possession itself becomes capable of bringing forward such results as if it were a right, although in truth it is not so (*x*). The objection, therefore, that thus a wrong is made

(*x*) The above construction, upon which all depends, may be explained by the following analogy. In the earlier law, the Int. *de vi* applied only to land, not to moveables. But if, at the moment of ouster from land, moveables were at the same time taken away or injured, the Interdict extended to this latter injury also, as *the interest affected in the ejectment from the land* (§. 42). In this case, moveables, which in themselves are not objects of the Interdict, are comprised in the Interdict, merely on account of their connection with the ouster from the land. Just so the disturbance of possession, although the latter is in itself no right, is the foundation of a suit, merely on account of the connection of this disturbance with the illegal violence directed against the person.

to engender a right, has no ground, because possession itself
is not treated as a right, but only as the interest growing out
of the disturbance of another previously existing right. A
different objection might be more plausibly made, viz.; that
the above practical advantages are likewise conceivable of
mere detention, and that, therefore, in accordance with the
above view, the manager also of another person's possession
should be allowed Interdicts. The answer to this is; either
we must suppose this manager to be acting *for* the true
possessor, or *against* him. In the first case he does not need
Interdicts, as those of the possessor are sufficient to protect
him. But in the second case, if he should desire to use them
contrary to the will of the possessor, either against the latter
himself or against a third party, he cannot do so, because he
thereby would infringe the obligatory relation from which
his detention springs, and which is sufficient to protect every
conceivable interest he may have. If then we inquire as to
the place of possession in the system of law, we must always
come back to the same conclusion—Possession itself, as a
right, has no place at all, because it is not a right; the right
however which it gives rise to, and on whose account it presents most similarity to a right, and requires accordingly
special rules for its acquisition and loss—this right is the
right to possessory Interdicts, and therefore an obligatory
right.

The question here discussed has often been confused by
several changes of the terms. Firstly, many ask as to the
systematic place of possession in the following sense: if a
systematic work upon the Roman law were to be written, in
what part should possession be treated of? The answer to
this question must be founded only in part on the nature of
Possession, but in much greater part on the particular
arrangement of the work in question; as it might easily
happen that individual portions of the learning of possession
should be treated of in widely different departments of the
work, as in fact has been always the case with most authors
of systems of law.—Secondly, an historical inquiry may lead

to the conclusion that possession originally had a totally different signification to that which it presents in modern law (§ 13). But such historical view can have no immediate influence on the meaning of the doctrine of possession in modern law. For if its basis has been altogether altered, its basis in modern law is to be treated and explained just as independently as if it were the original, and indeed the only one: this is what I, in fact, have done; and this is the reason why the historical inquiry should not be placed at the commencement here, as in other titles of the law.

I now apply myself to describe the views of some modern writers on the question above discussed, and I put them down in the order of time:

Gans, System des Römischen Civilrechts im Grundrisse, Berlin, 1827, s. 201—216.

Puchta im Rheinischen Museum, B. 3, s. 289—308; 1829.

Rudorff in der Zeitschrift fuer geschichtl. Rechts wissenschaft, B. 7, s. 90—114; 1830.

Thaden, Ueber den Begriff des Römischen Interdictenbesitzes, Hamburg, 1833.

Hasse der juengere, im Rheinischen Museum, B. 6, s. 183; 1833.

Rauh, Geschichte der Lehre vom Besitz, 1834.

Huschke ueber die Stelle des Varro von den Liciniern, Heidelberg, 1835, s. 75.

Gans places Possession at the head of *jura in re*. To have a subject merely for a particular purpose is, he says, possession, to have it for all purposes, is property. The particular purpose may be altogether unlawful, the general purpose is nothing but the title to possession. The particular purpose, even when unlawful, is protected by Interdicts, because the purpose as something substantial in itself is to be protected (p. 211). Possession is incipient property, this commencement is protected by Interdicts, because the possibility exists of its ripening by means of Usucaption into property (p. 211—214). But the particular purpose which may be unlawful, is nothing more than the simple *Factum*, the general purpose is the Right, therefore this is only a repetition in different words of the relation of possession to property, as of a *factum* to a right; but this gives no answer to the question how the (perhaps wholly illegal) *factum* is entitled to legal protection. That the Intention in itself (even when unlawful) is entitled to protection, is laid down but not proved, for according to the universal nature of legal controversy, that intention only is protected which corresponds to a right, and an unlawful intention is resisted. The true exposition therefore can only lie in the incipient property, and this exposition would be satisfactory if Interdicts were only established to protect usucaption-possession, which alone can be termed an incipient property. But for the latter object, it is well known that the *Publiciana actio* was framed, Interdicts on the other hand protected possession even without title, and even unlawful possession, which certainly is not incipient property. In fact, therefore, nothing is hereby explained. More detailed observations on this view are to be found in Puchta, s. 294, Rudorff, s. 95.

Puchta objects to my description, that it only teaches what Possession *produces*, not what it *is*. But Possession, he says, *is* a right—not in the thing but—in the particular person, in the particular Will. The protection, therefore, which possession enjoys, is a personal protection, specially directed to the natural (not legal) subordination of a thing. A connection with the whole system of law is thus established, because five objects of all rights are admitted, Things, Acts, Third Persons, Persons depending onus, our own Person. I cannot consider the exposition here given of the protection of Possession as essentially different from my own. For I also attribute the protection to the inviolability of the person, and to the connection which exists between the person and the thing arising from the natural subordination of the latter. It is new and original, that a special class of rights should here be framed, which refer to the inviolability of the person. But this regards the plan of the system of Law as a whole, not the special foundation of possession. Further observations upon the Essay of Puchta, are to be found in Rudorff, p. 101, and Hasse, p. 184.

Rudorff does not disagree from my view, except in making the doctrine of self-protection the basis of the right of possession. Possessory interdicts, according to him, formed the first commencement of the prohibition of self-protection, which was afterwards embodied and made more stringent by the *Leges Juliæ*, and the imperial constitutions. The origin of interdicts, therefore, is to be found in the breach of the peace, in the disturbance of public order; to prevent such disturbance from accomplishing its object, and to nullify all the results flowing from it, it was necessary to maintain, or to restore the possession.—Undoubtedly, every act of violence presents itself in a double aspect as an object of legal cognizance, for it is both a violation of public order, and of the individual person. We may classify these two as relations of public and of private law; each of them may give rise to special legal institutes, but whatever may occur towards furthering the object of either, must always more or less avail towards the object of the other (*y*). Which now of these two is the main foundation of possessory Interdicts? According to Rudorff, it is the relation of public law, which is said to be proved more particularly by the connection found between possession and self-protection, as they are treated of in the law sources (p. 107). But this latter circumstance is sufficiently explained by the actual affinity which has been noticed between the two Institutes, and therefore is not sufficient to decide the question proposed. I would rather maintain that a reference to private law was the foundation of the right of possession, and for the following reasons. First, the juxtaposition of *vi, clam, precario,* appears to have belonged from the earliest times to the doctrine of Interdicts. These three facts may

---

(*y*) L. 27, § 4, *de pactis.* "....   *licam eausam contingit,*" &c.
interdicto unde vi, *quatenus pub-*

be well classed together in reference to the violation of the
person occasioned thereby; but the public peace is affected
only by the first, not by the two latter. Secondly, self-
protection assumes the existence of a lawful claim, which is
merely asserted in an unjustifiable manner; but with possessory Interdicts no such claim is needed—nay, the disturbance of possession, upon which the Interdict *retinendæ
possessionis* is founded, can scarcely ever be conceived as an
attempt to assert a right. Thirdly, if Interdicts are to be
considered merely as the commencement of the prohibition
of self-protection, how comes it that they were so early
framed in special appropriate forms, in times when no other
regulations against individual self-protection are to be met
with? The influence of the laws against self-protection upon
the right of possession (see *post*, §. 42), is, however, sufficiently explained by the above-mentioned affinity. See
other remarks upon Rudorff's Treatise in Hasse, p. 187.

Thaden endeavours, first, to prove that possession is an
actual right, and then, to assign the nature of this right. It
is a right, he says (p. 14), because theft can only be committed against a party actually entitled. But there is such
a thing as a *furtum possessionis*, and as this, in particular,
may be committed against a possessing pledge-creditor, who
has a true *possessio*, it is a clear proof that *possessio* itself,
and, consequently, Interdict-possession, is the right violated
by the theft. If it is asked further what the nature of this
right is? the answer is (p. 63)—it is a right in the thing,
introduced for the protection of a condition implicated in
the acquisition of property. For Usucaption-possession is
protected by the *publiciana actio :* but, besides Usucaption,
there are other modes of acquiring through Possession, to
which the above action does not apply. But as these acquisitions would otherwise be without any protection, possessory
Interdicts were invented for them. Now the modes of acquisition which contain the true clue to the explanation of the
right of Possession are as follows :—

1. The *longi temporis præscriptio*, particularly in provincial-

estates, which explains, *inter alia*, why Interdicts
chiefly applied to immoveables.

2. The *præscriptio longissimi temporis acquisitiva.*

3. Immemorial prescription.

4. The præscriptio longissimi temporis *extinctiva.*

Consequently, Interdict-possession is similarly constituted
to Usucaption-possession, and is only distinguishable in
point of quantity. I believe that I have given in the above
propositions the whole substance of the Essay.

The view here given presents an appearance of systematic
completeness which makes it incumbent on us to examine
carefully each element separately. But, at once, the ground
assumed as to the *furtum possessionis* appears to us wholly untenable; for if *possessio* were the juridical object of the theft,
the thief, thereupon, if it were again stolen from him, would
have the *actio furti,* for he undoubtedly has *possessio ;* but
it is clear he has no *actio furti* (z). On the other hand, that
action might be maintained by the following very different
persons, to whom *possessio* is altogether wanting, viz., by
the Fructuary and Usuary, both of whom have merely detention (a); even by the creditor, to whom an article is
pledged by simple contract, although he has not even detention, but only an *in rem actio,* to obtain the possession (b).
It is clear from this, that the true ground of the *furtum possessionis* is not a violated *possessio,* but rather a *jus in re,* in
which is contained a claim to some possession or other
(whether true *possessio* or mere detention, whether present
or future), and in which this advantage is rendered abortive
by the theft. As to the other grounds, they are not in fact
a whit better established than the one just refuted. Immemorial prescription has only been foisted into the Roman
law by the misconceptions of commentators. The thirty
years' limitation of suits was introduced so late, that it is
impossible to make it serve to explain Interdicts, which

(z) L. 76, § 1, *de furtis,* (47, 2), (a) L. 15, § 2, § 1 ; L. 46, § 3,
Comp. ; L. 12, § 1 ; L. 71, § 1, *de furtis.*
cod. (b) L. 66, *pr. de furtis.*

existed for centuries previously.   Nothing else remains then but the *longi temporis præscriptio,* in special reference to provincial lands.   The author maintains, that this prescription was not protected by the *actio publiciana,* because that suit only accompanies an actually running Usucaption. But this very reason is decidedly incorrect; for this action was employed, from very early times, in behalf of legal relations which were never capable of actual Usucaption, for instance, *usus fructus,* prædial easements, *ager vectigalis, superficies,* and, more especially, provincial lands (c).   To all these cases, therefore, and to the latter by name, the *publiciana actio* fully applied, and no necessity for the invention of interdicts can be suggested from this quarter.   And thus, in fact, the author has given no explanation at all of all that he professed to explain.

Hasse expounds Possession to be a right in the thing, but a relative right, that is a right, not availing against all the world, but only against the party who intends to seize the Possession by force, &c.   It would seem, however, that this right is not Possession itself; but the latter, as a mere condition of fact, is always accompanied by an anonymous right of this purport, and obtains protection by virtue of it. The Romans, he says, did not draw the distinction clearly between the two, and they designate them both by the term *possessio.*   Occasionally, however, the distinction peeps out even with them; namely, in L. 2, §. 2, 3, *de interdictis,* where the *causa proprietatis* and *possessionis* is to be explained by this distinction (p. 199-200).   The right in the thing, which only avails against wrongdoers, is very difficult to distinguish from an obligation of these parties arising out

---

(c) L. 11, § 1, *de publiciana;* L. 12, § 2, 3, *cod.*   " In vectigalibus *et in aliis prædiis, quæ usucapi non possunt,* publiciana competit, si forte bonâ fide mihi tradita sunt." The other prædia are simply provincial lands.   Comp. Cujacius, Obss. VII. 3 ; and in Paulum ad Edictum, Lib. 19.   Probably the passage here is even interpolated, and Paulus may have written, " In vectigalibus, stipendiariis, et tributariis prædiis."

of the actual possession which is assumed. I also cannot convince myself that the position, according to which Possession gives a claim to protection, is distinguishable, except in words, from the position, that this claim does not arise out of Possession, but out of a nameless unobserved right accompanying Possession. The exposition, however, of L. 2 *de Interdictis* appears to me altogether unsound, and contains undoubted error.

Rauh only touches upon the history of Possession, in so far as he objects to any attempted historical derivation of it, and he seeks to put in its place a derivation from a universal legal want. He explains Possession to be, a defence against self-protection (p. 46), and thus approaches the view of Rudorff. He adopts with this, Thibaut's last exposition of *civilis possessio*. He combines with it, however, startling errors of his own, which can in no way be justified by the above exposition. Thus, he holds that upon an ouster, the Interdict *de vi* is the first suit to come into operation; then the Int. *uti possidetis*, in which it is indifferent as to the party being at present in possession (p. 36). Interdicts must be *in rem scripta*, just like *actiones quod metus causa* (p. 50-52). The *dejectus* still continues juridical possession for a year, until he loses the Int. *de vi* by limitation (p. 49). The mistakes here are carried to the furthest by the intermixture of French practice.

Huschke lastly leads back the doctrine of Possession to the original circumstances of the Roman nation. The Romans or Ramnes, he says, represent the body; and, therefore, we find with them the Fact,—Possession, and its protection by the order of authority (Interdict). The Quirites or Tities represent the soul; therefore, with them we find, Right, Property, and protection of them by suits and tribunals. In the course of time Possession likened itself to property, without, however, being ever incorporated with it (p. 105). The Patricians subsequently usurped the place of the Ramnes, the Plebeians that of the Tities, in which two classes the ancient antithesis still continues. I will assume, quite independently of the confusion of this view, that it is all as well-founded and clear as, in point of fact, it is otherwise, and still nothing is accomplished by it towards the solution of the question before us. That was, the historical explanation of the cause why, in the earliest times, *possessio* was spoken of irrespective of property. But we find the same thing prevailing in a most distinct form at the time of the Classical Jurists, and in Justinian's Code ; this can only be explained by some practical demand, by an interest of the present time. Possessory Interdicts would undoubtedly not have been retained as a memorial of the ancient Ramnes, if the right of property had sufficed for practical purposes, for in those days Ramnes and Tities were altogether forgotten, and, indeed, even Patricians and Plebeians were never mentioned, except casually on occasion of some old historical legal institute. I should, therefore, not have mentioned Huschke's Essay in this place, or in connection with the others, at all, if he had not himself laid claim to the merit " of clearing up in some degree the confusion in which the science now stands, respecting the question whether Possession is a right or not, and what is the legal ground of Interdicts........." (p. 109). If, therefore, I have introduced the Essay in a wrong place, and demanded something from it, which, on account of any other excellencies contained in it, it was not capable of affording, the author himself must bear the blame.

SECTION VII.

CIVILIS AND NATURALIS POSSESSIO.

Hitherto I have deduced the juridical meaning of Possession from the system of Roman Law generally ; I now apply myself to an explanation of the terms used by the Roman jurists. The most difficult and important part of this inquiry relates to *possessio* simply, to *possessio civilis* and *possessio naturalis,* I will therefore commence with these terms (*a*).

In order to give a more pointed application to the proofs which must be deduced by interpretation, I will set out with a sketch of the results which those proofs necessarily establish. Originally, *possessio* denotes mere detention, that is, a non-juridical physical relation; and it is unnecessary to subjoin any qualification to the term to shew that a mere physical relation is intended, so long as no other notion is opposed to it, which makes a qualification necessary. But such detention under certain conditions acquires a legal character, as, through Usucaption, it gives rise to property: it is then called *possessio civilis,* and it now becomes necessary to distinguish every other species of Detention from it in terms; such detention is called *naturalis possessio,* i. e. that sort of *possessio* simply, which has not become a juridical relation like the *civilis.* But detention becomes a juridical relation in another way also, namely, because Interdicts are founded upon it; it is then termed *possessio* simply, and this is the meaning of the word when it is used without epithet, but nevertheless in a technical sense. All other detention in opposition to Interdict-possession is again called *naturalis possessio,* that is the physical relation in contradis-

(*a*) It has been recently asserted that it is useless to attempt to give an accurate definition of these notions, because the notions themselves and the designations of them had their origin in common life, and were subsequently adopted by lawyers, with all the consequent vagueness which was peculiar to them from such an origin; and that accordingly they stand in the same position as the expressions, *culpa lata,* and *levis,* &c. Zachariæ Besitz Verjaehrung, § 6, 7, 37. This observation has no foundation in fact. *Culpa lata,* and *levis,* denoted originally moral notions, and their foundation therefore is clearly traceable to a very different field from that of jurisprudence.—Quite otherwise with *Possessio civilis* and *naturalis,* for here the origin is altogether juridical, and here never existed any non juridical notion upon the subject; the expressions, therefore, could not have arisen in common life, and could not thereby have acquired the vague character ascribed to them.

tinction to the last mentioned juridical one, just in the same way as that term is used to express the like antithesis with reference to *civilis possessio.*

There are therefore two kinds of juridical Possession: *possessio civilis* or Usucaption-possession, and *possessio* or interdict possession (*b*), and all that has been said above (§. 5) on the juridical modifications which may occur as to the notion of Possession, relates to one of these two or to both together. The following relation exists between these two conditions; Interdict-possession is altogether included in that of Usucaption, but more requisites are demanded for the latter than for the former. Whoever therefore possesses *ad usucapionem* has a possession that will maintain interdicts(*c*), but not *vice versâ. Possessio naturalis,* as I remarked above, has two meanings, but both are negative and merely express a logical antithesis. I now proceed to the proofs of these propositions (*d*).

1. *Possessio civilis* and *possessio naturalis* as opposed to one another.

Civilis taken generally has two technical meanings. First of all it denotes the whole body of Private Law, as opposed to Criminal Law, and therefore in this sense it cannot come under discussion here, where we are exclusively within the province of Private Law. Secondly, it means in Private Law

(*b*) As to the former, this expression occurs in L. 16, de usurp. "*ad usucapionem* tantum possidet;*" see L. 1, § 15, *de poss.*; as to the second L. 9, de R. V. says, "*possessionem quæ locum habet interdicto uti possidetis vel utrubi.*"

(*c*) There is an apparent exception to this rule in the case of a pledge-holder, who is allowed to have Usucaption, but cannot maintain Interdicts. But even his usucaption has no *civilis possessio* for its foundation, but by a fiction he is treated as if he had it,

that is, an exception is made in his favour to the rule, sine possessione usucapio contingere non potest. (See *post*, ch. 26).

(*d*) The following are passages in which these leading terms are used pointedly: *Naturalis possessio,* L. 1, § 1; L. 3, § 3. 13; *de* poss. L. 2, § 2; *pro her*, L. § 9, *de vi*; *Possessio naturalis,* L. 38, § 10, *de usuris*; L. 38, § 7, de verb. obl.; *Possessio non solum civilis sed etiam naturalis,* L. 2, § 1, *pro her. Possessio quæ est naturalis,* L. 11, de a. r. dom.

itself all those rights which have sprung neither from the *jus gentium* nor the *jus prætorium*, but from a *lex*, from a *senatus consultum*, or from a customary law (*e*). There are many modifications, it is true, of this second meaning of *civilis* (*f*), still, it is in this comprehensive sense, that it is far most frequently used by Roman Jurists.

Thus, to cite merely a few instances, agnation is alone called *civilis agnatio* (*g*), although there are important consequences attached to every other agnation both in the *jus gentium*, and the prætorian law, and therefore they also most undoubtedly are juridical relations; the same remark applies to *civilis actio, civilis obligatio, &c.* When we apply the same signification of the word to *possessio civilis*, that sort of possession must be understood which the civil law recognizes, that is, on the existence of which it depends, whether a rule of the Civil Law is applicable or not. Now in the whole Civil Law, there is only *one* right to which Possession is a condition precedent, namely, Usucaption, consequently *civiliter possidere* means the same as *ad usucapionem possidere* (*h*).

(*e*) The German jurists, following the classical Roman lawyers, recognize the customs observed by the people as a source of law independent of the commands, expressed or implied, of the Legislature. English writers on the other hand, of the school of Hobbes and Bentham, consider all such customs as mere rules of morality which the governed observe spontaneously, and which only become laws when adopted as such by the Courts of Justice, *i. e.* by the Sovereign Power acting tacitly through its authorized tribunals. See Austin's Provinces of Jurisprudence defined, p. 26, ed. s. 99. [Transl.]

(*f*) For instance, in L. 2, § 5, 12, de Orig. Juris.

(*g*) L. 4, § 2, de gradibus.

(*h*) It does not clash with this remark that *possessio civilis* may also enure as the foundation of the *longi temporis præscriptio*, (§ 2), although the latter does not belong to the *Jus Civile*. For this took place merely by the simple transfer of the *possessio civilis*, which was originally moulded and designated in reference to Usucaption, to an institute which was wholly founded on the analogy of Usucaption as a supplement to it, and which therefore silently borrowed all its conditions except those directly op-

Now that Usucaption belongs to the Civil Law requires
no proof; Interdicts however, cannot be included therein,
as they wholly arose out of the Edict. But to leave no room
for cavil on this point, I will cite two passages from the
ancients which might give rise to the supposition that interdicts ought to be ascribed to the civil law. The first is from
Cicero (*i*); in order to prove that even a man, who had been
prevented by violence from entering his close, might as
dejectus maintain the *interdictum de vi*, Cicero uses the following example, "quæro si te hodie domum tuam redeuntem
coacti homines et armati, non modo limine tectoque ædium
tuarum, sed primo aditu vestibuloque prohibuerint, quid
acturus sis? Monet amicus meus te, L. Calpurnius, ut idem
dicas quod ipse antea dixit, injuriarum.   Quid? ad causam
possessionis? quia? ad restituendum eum quem oportet
restitui? *quid denique? ad jus civile?* aut ad (actoris)
notionem et ad animadversionem ages injuriarum?" Amid
all the difficulty of this passage (*j*), it is clear that Cicero
means to say; an action for the injury has nothing to do
with the restoration of the possession, or consequently with
the *jus civile;* and thus he appears to rank interdicts in the
jus civile.   But as the injury now in question, was, subsequently to the *Lex Cornelia*, a *crimen publicum* (*k*), it is
evident that the Civil Law is here opposed to Criminal Law,
and in this sense the whole Edict unquestionably belongs to
the *jus civile,* but there is nothing to shew that the other
meaning of *jus civile* was intended, and indeed the term

posed to the express object of the
longi temporis præscriptio, so that
no new technical terms were at
all required in the enactment.

(*i*) Pro Cæcina c. 12.

(*j*) This difficulty wholly disappears, if, according to Gara-
tonis' proposal, the word *actoris*
be struck out, and the punctua-
tion in the text adopted. Heise

proposes to read " *auctoris*," i. e.
for the punishment of the offender.

(*k*) " Lex Cornelia de injuriis
competit ei, qui injuriarum agere
volet ob eam rem, quod se pulsa-
tum, verberatum *domumve suam
vi introitam* esse dicat," L. 5, pr.
de injuriis. On this ground Cicero uses the words *notio* and
animadversio.

with this latter meaning had been shortly before used by Cicero himself (*l*). The second passage, through which one might be induced to place interdicts in the Civil Law, is in Petronius (*m*); "*jure civili* dimicandum ut, si nollet rem alienam domino reddere, *ad interdictum veniret*" (*n*). Some commentators (*o*) have explained the words "*ad interdictum venire*" to mean the jurisdiction of the Prætor generally, so that vindication also might be meant by it, but it would be difficult to cite any passage in proof of this. The simplest course is wholly to deny to Petronius any authority whatever on the meaning of a law term, which has been so clearly defined by writers both earlier and later than himself.

Possessio civilis, therefore, cannot be referred to Interdicts; nor can it to the other consequences of Possession, simply for this reason, that these consequences do not derive their validity as resulting from any species of juridical possession. Another special reason applies to *possessio civilis*, viz.; that the greater part of the above consequences do not belong to the Civil Law at all. Thus, delivery belongs to the Civil Law only in the case of a *res nec mancipi* (*p*), occupancy and the *actio publiciana*, which arose *inter alia* by the delivery of a *res mancipi*, do not occur at all, and the *fructuum perceptio* just as little, because it required "*possessio bonæ fidei*" of the principal matter. The non-necessity for evidence, which is the privilege of every defendant, has certainly never been included by any Roman lawyer under the *jus civile* any more than the right of self-defence (*q*).

What I have thus far proved by the general meaning of the term *civilis*, I will now establish by citations from the ancient jurists. One general remark is necessary as preliminary to the explanation of these passages. Assuming,

(*l*) Pro Cæcina, c. 12, " quod agas mecum ex *jure civili ac prætorio* non habes," *i. e.* you can neither maintain vindication, nor an interdict.

(*m*) Satyr. C. 13, (p. 48, ed. Burmann, 1709).

(*n*) As to this passage, see *post*, §. 41.

(*o*) Turnebus, for instance. (Adversa. lib. 19, cap. 6).

(*p*) Ulpiani fragm. tit. 19, s. 7.

(*q*) L. 3, de justitiâ et jure.

namely, that *possessio civilis* derives its name from the *jus civile*, the expressions *civiliter non possidere* and *jure civili non possidere* may have one of two meanings, according to whether the *civiliter* is referred to the effect or to the cause of the *non possidere*. For, firstly, it may mean that that possession which the civil law recognizes is wanting, and in this sense it expresses the simple negation of *civilis possessio* and is useful for our inquiry. Secondly, it may mean that all Possession generally is wanting, and although the reason for this is contained in the *jus civile*, still this signification does not concern us, as it does not relate to *possessio civilis*. Which of these two meanings is to be attributed in any given case may generally be predicated with certainty; where for instance it is evident from the context that Possession in fact exists, the first meaning is clearly intended, and if the contrary can be shewn (*r*), the expression is probably used in its second sense.

There are five cases in which *possessio civilis, civiliter possidere* and *non possidere* are mentioned. Two of them corroborate my views, the others do not enable any certain conclusion to be drawn in favor of this or of any other doctrine, it merely therefore requires to be shewn in respect of them, that they can be fully explained according to my interpretation, and consequently are not opposed to it.

(*r*) This very important distinction and its use in interpretation, by which my explanation of *possessio civilis* became first fully established, is to be found in Thibaut's appendix to his edition of Cuperus, and previously in his reviews of this work in the Alg. Lit. Zeitung, 1804, n. 41. Subsequently, Thibaut himself made this remark upon it. "With this addition we now consider the author's theory on *possessio civilis* to be incontrovertible." (Al. L. Z. 1806, § 530). A reviewer of Thibaut (Gott. Anz. 1804, p. 1431) remarks, happily, that a trace of this distinction, although without proof or application, is to be found in the Gloss on L. 24 *de poss.* "Dic ergo civiliter, *i. e.* de jure civili non possidet, neque civiliter, neque naturaliter." [Latterly, indeed, Thibaut has rejected this twofold meaning of *civiliter non possidere*, and, indeed, treats it as absurd, Archiv. xviii. 328, 329, without, however, refuting or mentioning his own previous views.] (Add. to 6 ed.)

1st. When an article is given in pledge the creditor is not considered to possess it civilly (s). "Sciendum est, adversus possessorem hac actione (ad exhibendum) agendum: non solum eum, qui civiliter sed et eum, qui naturaliter incumbat possessioni. *Denique creditorem, qui pignori rem accepit, ad exhibendum teneri placet.*" The two sentences are connected thus: the *actio ad exhibendum,* says the jurist, lies *not merely* against a civil possessor. He establishes this proposition by the case of a creditor, and to denote the transition from the rule to the example, he uses the word *denique* ('thus for instance') in which sense it occurs in many passages of the Digest (t). In the two extracts which follow the passage I am citing, the second of which must have been in juxtaposition with the passage itself in Ulpian's own work, many examples are added to the one above, so as to complete the subject (u). This connection is so close and natural, that it could never have been misunderstood, had not a false notion of *possessio civilis* been previously adopted. The Gloss remarks on the word *creditor* '*hic civiliter possidet,*' by which indeed a tacit reproach on the text may have been intended, so that it may not be altogether attributable to misconstruction. Frider (v) attempts to prove, even from this passage, that a creditor possesses civilly. Cuperus (w) does away with all

(s) L. 3, §. 15, ad exhibendum.

(t) "In omni feré jure, finitâ patris potestate, nullum ex pristino retinetur vestiquim; *denique* et patria dignitas quæsita per adoptionem, finitâ eâ, deponitur." L. 13, *de adopt.* "In quæstionibus læsæ majestatis etiam mulieres audiuntur: conjurationem *denique* Sergii Catilinæ Julia mulier detexit, et Marcum Julium Consulem indicium ejus instruxit." L. 8, *ad legem Jul. magist.* "Nemo enim in persequendo deteriorem causam, sed meliorem facit. *Denique* post litem contestatam heredi quoque prospiceretur, et heres tenetur ex omnibus causis." L. 87, *de R. J.* This meaning of *denique* may also be resolved into another which is sufficiently common. It often is used for *sané* or *certè*; Cæsar de B. G. lib. 2, c. 32; Seneca di Irâ, lib. 3, c. 18. A great number of parallel passages are to be found in Thon, p. 116. But see Thibaut, contrà Archiv. XVIII. 338.

(u) L. 4, 5, ad exhibendum.

(v) De materiâ possessionis, C. 4, § 13.

(w) De nat. poss. P. 1, c. 3, p. 35.

connection between the two sentences, as he arbitrarily
assumes that a different subject is commenced with the
word *denique*, without any reference to the preceding,
which would be however but mere repetition, since all possible cases are included under the *possessio civilis* and *naturalis* mentioned in the previous paragraph. He certainly
never would have had recourse to such a construction, which
makes the logic of the Roman Lawyers so contemptible, if
he could have discovered any other mode of reconciling his
notion of *possessio civilis* with the passage.

For it is clear that a creditor had no *possessio civilis* in
the pledge and, in order to shew what notion the Roman
Jurists intended to convey by the above terms, it is only
necessary to describe what the rights are which pertain to
a creditor's possession. The following passage contains a
very precise description of them (*x*), " qui pignori dedit, ad
usucapionem tantum possidet; *quod ad reliquas omnes
causas pertinet, qui accepit, possidet.*" Thus, the creditor
possesses in every juridical sense, except in respect of Usucaption, it follows that the *possessio civilis*, which is denied
him, can mean nothing else than the possession of Usucaption (*xx*).

2. The second case where mention is made of *possessio
civilis* relates to the prohibited donations between man and
wife. From such donations no *possessio civilis* accrues.
L. 26, *pr. de don. int. vir. et ux.* " licet illa (uxor) *jure civili
possidere non intelligatur*" (*y*). L. 1, §. 4, *de poss.* " Si vir,

---

(*x*) L. 16, de usurp. et usuc.

(*xx*) See, upon this passage,
Thon, p. 115, and Thibaut, p. 337.

(*y*) This is an instance of the
above noticed ambiguity of the
jure civili non possidere. For as
there is no doubt, as it will soon
appear, of the existence of a juridical possession in this case, nothing else can be meant by the
above expression than a negation

of a *possessio civilis.* Thibaut,
Abhand, s. 343, reads the passage
thus "even if we held (with some)
that a wife may not possess," thus
making Paulus refrain from expressing this opinion himself. He
is led into this strained construction by an assumption false in two
respects. 1st, That *jure civili
non possidere* necessarily means
to have no possession at all; 2nd,

uxori cedat possessione, donationis causâ, plerique putant
(and this opinion is here, as usual, tacitly approved of, for
Paulus himself adds an additional reason in support of it)
possidere eam; *quoniam res facti infirmari jure civili non
potest,*" thus the Civil Law does not recognize such possession. L. 1, §. 9, 10, *de vi.* " Dejicitur is, qui possidet,
sive civiliter sive naturaliter possidet : nam et naturalis
possessio ad hoc interdictum (de vi) pertinet. *Denique (z)
et si maritus uxori donavit, eaque dejecta sit, poterit interdicto uti; non tamen si colonus*" (a).

That the Roman lawyers were
divided in opinion as to possession
on donations between man and
wife. He draws this conclusion
from the *Julianus putat,* and *plerique putant,* which expressions
however are constantly used in
reference to the most incontrovertible propositions. It is not,
therefore, even necessary to cite
the reason in L. 1, § 4 *de poss.*
against actual opponents.

(z) The logical construction,
and even the expression is exactly
the same here, as in L. 3, § 15, ad
exhibendum; both passages throw
light on one another, and I may
refer wholly to the interpretation
which I have given above of the
latter passage.

(a) Thibaut (Abhand. s. 339)
puts forward a new explanation
of this passage, which, he says,
should be read thus, "if a husband makes a gift to his wife, and
she be turned out of possession,
he may bring an Interdict." But
according to the simple natural
construction, *poterit* must agree
with *ea* as the nearest subject,
not with *maritus,* which is more
remote. The natural construction
is therefore here exchanged for

a strained one, and no advantage
is gained by it, except the bringing forward a complicated difficult explanation of the passage,
instead of the simple juridical
meaning attributed above. According to my view, the conclusion of the sentence is easily filled
up thus, "non tamen si colonus
dejectus erit, poterit (colonus)
interdicto uti," *i. e.* attention is
called to the distinction which
exists as to the rights belonging
to an endowed wife, and to a
tenant, in reference to possession.
Thibaut has lately given (Archiv.
XVIII. 355) a more detailed exposition of the passage. The wife,
he says, has possession, but the
husband, nevertheless, may also
maintain the interdict, because he
may take up at will all injuries
done to his wife ; only, however,
in case where she herself, not
where her tenant, is turned out
of possession. For, if the wife's
maid receives a box on the ear,
it would not be suitable that the
husband should treat the maid
like his *carissima.* One is in
doubt how to commence any refutation of this exposition, in
which not one sound element is

Thus, in these three passages *possessio civilis* is denied; what then is the legal condition which is denoted by this expression? that juridical possession generally arises out of such donation, appears clearly from the second passage, and two other passages agree with this (*b*). The third passage

discoverable. *Inter alia,* how came Ulpian so singularly to lay down this proposition with reference to land given in gift, if the proposition applied generally to all land whatsoever of the wife? The mention indeed of a donation would be not only unnecessary, but confused and misleading, as the reader might be induced by it to suppose, erroneously, that the husband could maintain the interdict only because he continued to be the proprietor of the land, owing to the invalidity of the donation. See also Thon, p. 118. [Add. to 6 ed.]

(*b*) *L.* 1, § 2, *pro donato :* "*Possidere* autem uxorem rem à viro donatam   Julianus putat." *L.* 16, *de poss.* "Quod uxor viro aut vir uxori donavit, pro possessore *possidetur.*" Clearly as this proposition is expressed, it has, nevertheless, been constantly contradicted, in order thereby to defend some preconceived notion of *possessio civilis.* Cuperus (De Nat. Poss. p. 84) imagines that Paulus contradicts himself, in L. 1, § 4, *de poss.,* and L. 26, *pr. de don. inter vir et ux.* Fleck (De Poss. pp. 45, 118) goes still further, and affirms that in this passage every sort of possession is denied. In the absence of any arbitrary preconceived notion of *civilis possessio,* the only passage which can be cited against the

rule in the text is L. 46, *de don. inter vir et ux.* "Inter virum et uxorem nec possessionis ulla donatio est." But here it is clearly not the possession but the donation which is denied, it is accordingly merely laid down that the wife does not possess *pro donato,* and to this the passage already cited refers; L. 16, *de poss.* "quod uxor viro, aut vir uxori donavit, pro possessore possidetur," which is a passage from the same work of Ulpian as the L. 46, cited above. This rule therefore can have no operation on the existence of possession, for this reason, that it only refers to juridical succession (in donations), but the existence of possession is altogether independent of succession. (See above, §. 5). The main portion of this very simple exposition is old. (Duarenus in L. 1, § 4, *de poss.* p. 829; Valentia, Tract. ill. p. 52). Cuperus himself has made it still more clear, and mention of him shall be made hereafter in the fourth book on the *interdictum utrubi,* §. 41. If the heading of the passage in question did not so clearly require the above exposition, the above objection might be satisfactorily got rid of by another exposition even still more simple, if that were possible. The gift of a possession, which according to the passage cited has no effect, even mentions one of the consequences of such possession, namely, Interdicts. But Usucaption cannot arise from such possession. " Si inter virum et uxorem donatio facta sit, cessat usucapio" (c). Therefore, here again, by the *possessio civilis*, which is denied, nothing else can be intended but the possession of Usucaption.

3rd. The rule *nemo sibi causam possessionis mutare potest* applies not only to *possessio civilis* but to *naturalis* also (d). The rule itself, which till lately was very obscure, is made clear by Gaius (e), although, even since the publication of his work gross misconception of the rule has displayed itself. Now in the first instance we might be inclined to suppose the rule to mean that it was forbidden to alter the *causa*, even with the co-operation of another party. But the rule did not mean this, for if a *malâ fide possessor* purchased a thing from the party who had the ownership or the special custody of it, this would be a completely valid and effectual *causæ mutatio* (f). Conversely, if a tenant disclaims his landlord's title, he actually changes the *conductionis causa* into a *dejectionis causa*, and thereby acquires a true *possessio* (g). The above rule therefore did not stand in the way of such change, and no positive enactment was required on the subject, because the landlord was completely protected by the *Int. de vi,* and because such a disclaimer could never pave the way to Usucaption. The above rule, therefore, is only applicable to the few cases in which an *ex parte* arbitrary conversion into a valid efficient *causa* could have place, and

might refer to land in the provinces, in which sense many other passages connected with this doctrine use the expression *possessionis donatio,* L. 13, 15, c. de don. *inter vir et ux.* The meaning then would be, that not only the *dominium,* but also the natural ownership of land in the provinces cannot be transferred in this manner.

(c) L. 1, § 2, *pro donato.*

(d) What follows here has been completely recast in the 6th edition. The writers to be consulted on this rule are Merenda, XII. 28; Unterholtzner, Verjäh-rungs-lehre, p. 100; Thon, pp. 92, 114. Thibaut, p. 333, does not appear to have a clear conception of the rule itself.

(e) Gaius, Lib. 2, § 52—61.

(f) L. 33, § 1, *de usurp.*

(g) L. 12, L. 18, *pr. de vi.*

the operation of which upon Usucaption was prevented by
the above mentioned established rule of law. The following
cases are instances; first, so long as an heir did not take
possession of his inheritance, any one might enter and have
Usucaption of the estate *pro herede*, and neither *bona fides*
nor title were necessary for such Usucaption, and the latter
had the peculiarity of being completed in a year even with
respect to lands. The *causa* here, therefore, was of the kind
above described: for it was founded on selfish and even
dishonest intentions, and yet it formed a *justa usucapionis
causa*, by which it was distinguished from the case of disclaimer by a tenant. Gaius assigns as the reason of this
'*tam improba possessio et usucapio*,' that it was intended
thereby to compel the heir to enter upon the inheritance
with dispatch, which was desirable, both on account of the
sacra and of creditors generally. He adds that Hadrian had
altered this law, and allowed the heir to treat this Usucaption
even after its completion as a nullity, with the exception of
the *heres necessarius*, who was still forced to recognize it.
Now the above old rule of law operated upon this singular
enactment in the following manner. If any one had Usucaption *pro emptore*, or had physical possession as depositary,
and the owner died, the *usucapio pro herede* above described
might prove highly advantageous to such possessor; the
purchaser would then only need in the case of land, one
year's possession instead of two, which he would otherwise
require as purchaser, and the depositary, who hitherto had
been unable to have Usucaption at all, would now become
capable of it. Now, the above rule of law stood in the way
of possessors such as these; having once commenced to possess in a certain way they were not allowed at will and with
knowledge of their want of title to convert this possession into
a *possessio pro herede*. It appears clearly that this was the
true meaning of the rule from Gaius having used the same
expressions for the *usucapio pro herede*, as the ancient Jurists
employed when treating of the above rule. Gaius, for
instance, says of the *usucapio pro herede* "hæc autem species

possessionis et usucapionis etiam *lucrativa* vocatur, nam
sciens quisque rem alienam *lucrifacit.*" The two following
passages are the most express (*h*) upon the rule of law both
of them being from Julian, and therefore perhaps still older
than the above mentioned enactment of Hadrian, L. 33,
§ 1 D. *de usurp.* " Quod vulgo respondetur ipsum sibi causam
possessionis mutare non potest, totiens verum est, quotiens
quis *sciret se bonâ fide non possidere*, et *lucrifaciendi* causâ
inciperet possidere." L. 2.

§ 1 D. *de poss.* "Quod vulgo respondetur, causam possessionis neminem sibi mutare posse, sic accipiendum est, ut
possessio non solum civilis sed etiam naturalis intelligatur.
Et propterea responsum est, neque colonum, neque eum,
apud quem res depositur, aut cui commodata est, *lucrifaciendi causâ pro herede usucapere posse.*"

It appears to me quite clear also from this passage in what
sense it is that Julian in the last quotation uses the terms
civilis and *naturalis possessio.* He means to say that not
only he who had hitherto had Usucaption (*possessio civilis*)
is prohibited by the rule from converting his commenced
Usucaption into the more advantageous one *pro herede*, but
that he also who theretofore could not have Usucaption at all
(*possessio naturalis*) was hindered by the rule from creating
for himself by means of such a change, the Usucaption which
he otherwise could not have obtained (*i*). According to

(*h*) With the above passages,
the following, which are less express, may be compared; L. 3, §
19, 20; L. 19, § 1, D. *de poss.*;
L. 2, § 21, D. *pro don.*; L. 6, § 3,
D. *de precario.*

(*i*) Julian therefore clearly assumes that the rule was more
generally and easily received as
to *civilis possessio*, and that as to
naturalis, it was rather doubted.
Thibaut, p. 335, considers the
above necessary construction to
be irreconcilable with my ex-

planation of *civilis possessio*. But,
in point of fact, the *causa possessionis* spoken of in the rule approaches very near to a limitation
of the *justa causa* in Usucaption.
It is this, which the jurists warn
against, by remarking that the
rule does not merely refer to *emtionis* or *donationis causa*, but also
to *conductionis* and *depositi causa*
to *causæ*, therefore, which were
never looked on as such in respect
to Usucaption.

this explanation, the terminology, which was adopted above, is corroborated by this passage. The above rule indeed lost nearly all its significance after Hadrian's time, and wholly so in the Justinian code, therefore in most of the cases cited against me out of the Pandects, the rule itself could not have been applied. Secondly, the above rule might also find application in the case of *usureceptio*. For this also was grounded on *ex parte* proceedings, and was also without title, although it could not be always considered as unjustifiable. But whenever it was completely unjustifiable, namely, when the fiduciary debtor hired the subject from the creditor, then the above rule prevented Usucaption from operating (*j*).

4th. Two passages lay down the rule as to slaves, *civiliter non possident*.

" Peculium, quod servus civiliter quidem possidere non potest, sed naturaliter tenet, dominus creditur possidere" (*k*). " Hæc quoque stipulatio, *possidere mihi licere spondes?* utilis est: quam stipulationem servus an possit utiliter in suam personam concipere, videamus. Sed quamvis civili jure servus non possidet, tamen ad possessionem naturalem hoc referendum est: et ideo dubitari non oportet, quin et servus rite ita stipuletur. Planè si, *tenere sibi licere* stipulatus sit servus utilem esse stipulationem convenit; licet enim possidere civiliter non possint, tenere tamen eos nemo dubitat" (*l*).

In these passages the expression *civiliter non possidet*, is used to deny any sort of Possession generally, but only with reference to a rule of the *jus civile;* these passages therefore do not relate to *possessio civilis*. For on the one hand it is clear that a slave could not possess at all, and one does not see therefore, why, nevertheless, mention should be made of a deficient *possessio civilis,* on the other hand the expression itself *civiliter quidem possidere non potest*, is limited in these passages by terms which are always used, as shall be shewn subsequently, to express the antithesis to juridical Possession (*tenere naturaliter tenere*). The whole matter

---

(*j*) This excellent remark is derived from Thon, p. 109.

(*k*) L. 24, *de poss.*
(*l*) L. 38, § 7, 8, *de verb. oblig.*

is to be explained thus. Slavery itself, according to the Roman notions, proceeded from the *jus gentium;* but the acquisitions made by slaves for their masters, and the incapacity of the former to hold property, were part of the *jus civile,* as the Romans themselves were acquainted with other nations, who allowed separate property to their slaves (*m*). It might therefore be very properly said, *servus civiliter non possidet,* i. e. a slave is incapable of judicial possession, and the ground of this incapacity is in the *jus civile.*

(*m*) The Germans for instance; Taciti Germania, c. 25; other passages also make rather for than against this doctrine, 1st, D. L. 1, § 1, § 1, I. *de his qui sui;* "Igitur in potestate sunt servi dominorum, (Quæ quiden potestas juris gentium est, nam apud omnes peræque gentes animadvertere possumus, dominis in servos vitæ necisque potestatem fuisse), et quodcumque per servum adquiritur, id domino adquiritur." If the last word is to be read *adquiri,* the statement in the text is altogether erroneous; if *adquiritur* is the proper reading, my opinion is much more probable upon the whole construction than the one opposed to it. Haloander was the first to read *adquiri* in the Digest; in the Institutes it first appeared in Chevallon's edition in 12mo, (Paris, 1527); next in R. Stephanus, (Paris, 1528, 800), and J. Schoefer's (Mag. 1529, 12mo), and after all of these in Haloander, the latter of which is not mentioned in Gebauer's edition; *adquiritur* is the reading first of all, of the genuine Gaius (I. § 52), next, in all the known MSS. and oldest editions of the compila-

tions of Justinian; for instance, it is the reading of the Institutes in the three oldest manuscripts at Bamberg (Rosshirt Beytrage, U. 1, Ucid. 1820, s. 71), and in all the Paris manuscripts, 23 in number, of the Dig. Vetus; in 12 out of 13 Paris MSS., and in the 13th (a very modern one) the *adquiri* is evidently a clerical error, as in the Gloss on the same MS. adquiritur again appears. 2nd, L. 10, § 1, *de rer dom. adq.* at least does not impugn my position, for the words "ipse enim, qui in alterius potestate est, nihil suum habere potest," may just as well express a proposition of the Roman civil law, as of the *jus gentium.* The reviewer of Thibaut's edition of Cuperus (Gött. Anz. 1804, p. 1432) attributes the incapacity of slaves to hold property to the *jus gentium,* but the application of this rule to possession (the physical nature of which only obtained a juridical character through a peculiarity of Roman Law) to the *jus civile.* If it should be admitted that the above incapacity is *juris gentium,* (which I deny), this reconcilement is ingenious and satisfactory.

5th. The same rule *civiliter non possidet* (*n*), applies to the possessor of a thing composed of parts, so far as the question relates to the possession of the individual parts, for instance, to the wheel of a carriage.   Which of the two meanings of this expression is here intended cannot be very distinctly ascertained.   It may either be *possessio civilis* (*o*), which is denied, or any *possessio* at all, according indeed to the *jus civile* (*oo*).

So much on *possessio civilis*.   It scarcely need be repeated, that in all these passages *possessio naturalis* is used as the logical antithesis of *civilis*, as possessio, *quæ non est civilis*.   More shall be said upon this hereafter.

II. *Possessio* (as Interdict Possession), and *possessio naturalis* in opposition to one another.

I have here two things to prove—first, that *possessio* simply as a juridical relation is distinguished from *possessio naturalis*.   Secondly, that this distinction has no other object than to denote the juridical capacity or incapacity for Interdicts.

1st. *Possessio* simply as a juridical relation is opposed to the nonjuridical relation, which occurs under the following names; *esse in possessione, tenere, naturaliter possidere, corporaliter possidere* (*p*).

(*n*) L. 7, § 1, 2, *ad exhibendum.* " Sed si rotam meam vehiculo aptaveris, teneberis ad exhibendum. Et ita Pomponius scribit; *quamvis tunc civiliter non possideas.* Idem et si armario vel navi tabulam meam, vel ansam scypho junxeris," &c.

(*o*) Thibaut (Appendix to Cuperus, s. 162) denies this, because it would be absurd in treating of the *actio ad exhibendum* to introduce a remark that the defendant could not possess *ad usucapionem.* But this objection is easily met, for, in another passage, (L. 3, §

15, *ad exhib.*) Ulpian himself makes the very remark which Thebaid treats as absurd.

(*oo*) See *post*, ch. 24.

(*p*) In the Gloss it is termed *detentio asinina*, (Glossa in L. 29, *de poss.*) In another passage (L. 24, *de poss.*) this expression is explained, " tenere potest, *ut asinus sellam.*" Accursius, it is well known, constantly uses the "ass" as an illustration.   The later Italian Jurists use the term " tenuta," which expression also is to be found in Sarti in a charter of 1252, (De Claris Archygymn.

" Idem Pomponius bellissime tentat dicere, numquid qui conduxerit quidem prædiun precario autem rogavit, non ut *possideat* sed ut in *possessione esset ?* est autem longe diversum, *aliud est enim possidere longe aliud in possessione esse*" (*q*).

" Eum, cui ita non cavebitur, *in possessionem ejus rei* . . . . *ire,* et, cum justa causa esse videbitur, *etiam possidere* jubebo" (*r*).

" Qui in aliena potestate sunt, rem peculiarem *tenere* possunt, habere, *possidere* non possunt, quia possessio non tantum corporis, sed et juris est" (*s*).

" Neratius et Proclus et solo animo non posse nos *adquirere possessionem,* si non *antecedat naturalis possessio*" (*t*).

" Quod ex justâ causâ *corporaliter* a servo *tenetur* . . . . . dominus creditur *possidere*" (*u*). This same distinction, also lies at the bottom of the well known expressions in the *stipulatio aquiliana ;* quodve tu meum habes, *tenes, possides* (*v*).

By this logical opposition however, it is not intended to express that the above physical relation (detention) can never be included in juridical Possession, for, although juridical Possession sometimes occurs, in which detention has no place, still according to the rule (§. 5) they are inseparably connected; accordingly by *natural* Possession as opposed to juridical, *merely natural* Possession is to be understood, so that notwithstanding this logical antithesis,

---

Bon. prof. p. 78). " Corporatim possessionem et tenutam tradidisse." The expression *esse in potestate* is analogous to the term *esse in libertate,* the former denotes a logical opposition to *possession,* the latter to *libertas,* with merely this difference, that a peculiar and express provision protected the *esse in libertate.*

(*q*) L. 10, § 1, *de poss.*

(*r*) L. 7, *pr. de damno infecto.*

(*s*) L. 49, § 1, *de poss.* The concluding words have been already explained, (§ 5), and they lay down expressly the distinction between juridical and non-juridical possession.

(*t*) L. 3, § 3, *de poss.*

(*u*) L. 24, *de poss.*

(*v*) L. 18, § 1, *de acceptilat ;* § 2, I. *quibus modis toll. obl.*

natural Possession may be also contained in juridical Possession. And thus in many passages all the expressions, which elsewhere denote the nonjuridical relation, are in fact used with respect to juridical Possession, in order to denote the corporeal detention contained in it (*w*).

2nd. That the distinction in question was intended to denote nothing more than the juridical capacity or incapacity for Interdicts, may be as easily proved as the existence of the distinction itself. For that *possessio* in the juridical sense, is the ground of Interdicts follows directly from the name—*Possessory* Interdicts, and several passages expressly point out the indispensable necessity for Possession (*x*). At the same time the existence of Possession generally without any other juridical quality, is sufficient to ground Interdicts, even should the Possession have had a tortious commencement (*y*); therefore it is *possessio* simply, without any specific qualification, which forms the foundation of Interdicts.

On the other hand, it is clear that a tenant (*z*), a borrower,

---

(*w*) Thus, for instance, *corporalis possessio* (in L. 40, § 2, *de pign. act.*), *naturalis possessio* (in L. 38, § 10, *de usuris*, and in L. 3, § 13, *de poss.*) lastly, *in possessione esse* (in § 5, I. *de interdictis*, L. 11, § 13, *quod vi*, and L. 2, C. *de poss.*) Cuperus (de nat. poss. P. 1, C. 3,) gives three meanings to *possessio naturalis*. 1st, Simple detention. 2nd, Detention as a component part of juridical possession. 3rd, Possession which by a legal fiction is made equivalent to simple detention. But there is only *one* meaning in these different cases, that is, we do not ascertain and establish any of the above meanings from the passages where any one of them occur, but we are able to deduce them with certainty from the context, even if they had never been specially used. The whole of this view of Cuperus was already given in Donellus Comm. V. 7.

(*x*) " Interdictum autem hoc (de vi) nulli competit, nisi ei, qui tunc, cum dejiciretur, *possidebat*" (L. 1, § 2, 3, *de vi*)—" Creditores missos in possessionem rei servandæ causâ interdicto uti non posse; et merito, quia non possident, (L. 3, § 8, *uti poss.*) " si eam rem *cujus possessionem per interdictum uti possidetis retinere possim* . . . . . precario tibi concesserim; teneberis hoc interdicto." (L. 7, *de precario*) of § 4, 5, 6, I. *de interdictis*."

(*y*) §, 6 I. *de interd.*; L. 1, § 9, L. 2, *uti poss.*

(*z*) It sounds strange to the ear of an English lawyer to hear that a *missus in possessionem* and others, (of whom it is said *sunt in possessione, tenent sed non possident*), do not enjoy the right of possessory Interdicts (*a*).

It may therefore be laid down generally, whoever has *possessio* may have interdicts, whoever is only *in possessione* may not, and both branches of the proposition are co-extensive.

I have proved the above position word by word in order to make the demonstration stand out more clear; it will now be easy to explain a passage, which contains in itself the whole of what has been already demonstrated by the comparison of several different passages. The passage treats of vindication; this, of course, can only be brought against the possessor of the subject, the *judex*, therefore, has to inquire thereupon whether the defendant is in possession, and the only question is, who is to be looked upon in this action as possessor. This is decided in the following passage (*b*). " Officium autem judicis in hac actione in hoc erit, ut judex inspiciat, an reus possideat......Quidam tamen, ut Pegasus, *eam solam possessionem* putaverunt hanc actionem complecti, quæ locum habet in interdictis uti possidetis, vel utrubi.

a tenant had no *possession* in the Roman law. But in point of fact it is impossible to translate from one language into another a term denoting legal relations peculiar to the one country only. Thus the word tenant is used in the text to represent the Pachter of the author, which again represents the *colonus* of the Romans. Now each of these three terms connotes most various and unlike relations. How dissimilar, for instance, a Roman *colonus* was to an English tenant, may be seen by an extract from a Memoir by von Savigny himself, read before the Academy Royal at Berlin, in 1822, on the legal character of a *colonus*, and which Sharon Turner has translated in the Appendix to his Hist. Engl. vol. ii. p. 582. Still it is often convenient to use the nearest analogous term which the language presents, instead of giving a long circumlocution, or an uncouth Latin derivative, but I have been driven to the latter course in certain cases, such as *usucaption, usufructuary, usuary, bonitarious, quiritarian*, &c., and I trust the reader will pardon the neology.—[Transl.]

(*a*) L. 1, § 10, *de vi*; L. 3, § 8, *uti possidetis, &c.*

(*b*) L. 9, *de rei vind.*

Denique (c) ait, ab eo, apud quem deposita est, vel commodata, vel qui conduxerit, aut qui legatorum servandorum
causâ, vel dotis, ventrisve nomine in *possessione esset,* vel cui
damni infecti non cavebatur, quia hi omnes *non possident,*
vindicari non posse.   Puto autem, ab omnibus, *qui* tenent,
et habent restituendi facultatem, peti posse."

The word *possessio* had here first of all to be defined, it
must, therefore, be taken in the beginning of the passage as
generally as possible.   Pegasus considers that the proposition only applies to that sort of possession which enables
interdicts, and not to those cases, in which properly no possession at all exists; but Ulpian decides against him.   The
two jurists are of different opinions on the main question;
they give the same meaning to the word, and in this alone
they agree.   Both proceed from a general (natural) notion
of *possessio,* of which there are two kinds.   The one gives
rise to possessory Interdicts (d), the other consequently does
not.   Of a possessor of the second sort it is said soon after,
' *est in possessione,*' ' *tenet,*' ' *non possidet ;*' the other sort of
possession must necessarily, therefore, be *possessio* simply.
From this simple passage, therefore, a complete demonstration may be again adduced of the meaning which is to
be attributed to the notion of *Possessio,* as Interdict—possession.

(c) Here again, as in L. 3, §
15, *ad exhibendum,* and in L. 1, §
9, 10, *de vi, denique* marks the
transition from the rule to the
example.

(d) I say Possessory Interdicts
quite generally, although Ulpian
only mentions the interdictum *uti
possidetis,* and the interdictum
utrubi : for it is clear from
other passages that the remaining
interdicts required the same sort
of *possessio* as their condition, (L.
1, § 10, de vi), and that Ulpian

only mentions these two, because
they alone could occur in the
legal case referred to.   If, for
instance, the actual defendant
before the vindication suit had
brought those interdicts, his juridical *possessio* would have been
inquired into.   Does not the
question still turn, Ulpian means
to say, on the same sort of Possession also, although the Interdict should not happen to have
been brought before the vindication.

III. It has now been established, that there are two kinds of juridical possession, *possessio civilis* and *possessio*. What then is the relation which exists between these two juridical notions?

The right to Interdicts requires the existence of *possessio*, and nothing further; whoever has obtained possession, even by force, may bring Interdicts (*e*); and thus no other juridical quality is required than the existence of possession simply, to found the right to Interdicts.

On the other hand, Usucaption also requires the existence of *possessio* (*f*), but that alone is not sufficient; for the Possession must have commenced with *bona fides* and *justa causa*, and the thing possessed, moreover, must not be one of those which were specially excepted from Usucaption, such as *res furtiva, vi possessa*, &c. The relation, therefore, between these two notions is this, Usucaption-possession merely contains more conditions than Interdict-possession, and the latter is always included in the first. This relation could not be denoted in any other way than by terming the Possession for Interdicts *possessio* simply, and by adding to such *possessio* the epithet *civilis*, to designate the Possession of Usucaption: we thus find the same proof afforded by these names as had already been deduced from the juridical nature of the Institutes.

Upon the whole it follows that, in the two juridical meanings of Possession in the Roman Law, there is no division of *Juridical Possession* generally, but only *one* juridical *possessio* which, where it occurs alone, simply gives birth to Interdicts, but when accompanied with other qualifications, is followed by Usucaption also (*g*).

(*e*) § 6, I. *de interdictis*, L. 1, § 9, L. 2, *uti possidetis*.

(*f*) " Sine possessione usucapio contingere non potest," L. 25, *de usurp. et usuc.* Thus, for instance, Usucaption ceases to run directly the Possession is lost, L. 5, *Cod.*

(*g*) In the earlier Roman law a very similar relation existed between two other law notions, the *justum matrimonium* and the *matrimonium cum conventione in manum.* The first is always assumed in questions relating to the latter, consequently there is

The above view gives to the following passage, which many commentators have passed over as common-place, an important meaning, without at the same time in any way contradicting the twofold juridical nature of possession, on which the whole of my theory turns, " Et in summâ magis *unum genus est possidendi,* species infinitæ" (*h*). The *species infinitæ* refer to the numerous *causæ possidendi* of which we have before spoken, and to these, therefore, the *unum genus* is immediately opposed; but still the proposition is laid down universally, which would have been impossible, if there had been even in any one other respect several distinctly different and self-opposed juridical notions of Possession.

We have now obtained a general point of view as to all that is laid down in the Roman law respecting *possessio.* Such passages always have reference to both Usucaption and Interdicts, but in a somewhat different manner; the reference to Interdicts is direct, because as to them no other expression is required than *possessio* simply, but Usucaption is only indirectly referred to, because something is always needed in addition to *possessio,* to constitute *possessio civilis.*

This view of juridical *possessio* generally, according to which all juridical employments of the term *possessio* have invariably one and the same notion for their object, is the most important of all for general interpretation, and it presents the only measure for judging with any degree of certainty, as to the real value of any treatise on Possession. For it is clear, that exactly in the same proportion as the above general notion of juridical Possession forms the basis of any exposition, the meaning of *possessio* in the Roman law will be understood or mistaken (*i*).

no division of marriage generally at the bottom of the distinction, although there are two different kinds of juridical marriage.

(*h*) L. 3, § 21, *de poss.*

(*i*) And this is the main ground why the exposition of *civilis pos-*

sessio in Cuperus (and lately also in Thibaut) is so destructive to the whole theory of Possession. (See *post, addendum* to §. 10). For it completely unsettles the whole of what the Roman jurists have laid down with such remark-

IV. *Possessio naturalis* is used, as has been shewn above (num. I. II.), with two meanings. For, according to the original notion of Possession, every Possession is a physical relation, and therefore it is unnecessary to distinguish it as such by any predicate. But directly that Possession under certain conditions avails as a right, this juridical Possession becomes opposed to the non-juridical, where such conditions do not occur. Now we have discovered two sorts of juridical Possession, and at the same time two sorts of *possessio naturalis*, and these two meanings of *possessio naturalis*, shall now be contrasted with one another.

Both agree in this, that they are merely negative ideas, *i. e.* that nothing juridical is asserted by them, but merely something juridical is denied, and they are only distinguishable by the amount of what they respectively deny.

Possessio naturalis of the first sort, as opposed to *possessio civilis* (num. I.), means every detention which is not capable of Usucaption; no other juridical meaning, except such negation is implied by the term, and therefore this *possessio naturalis* comprises both the simple detention, which has nothing juridical about it, and the juridical *possessio*, which is merely not capable of Usucaption: in this sense *possessio naturalis* of a pledge is ascribed to a creditor (j), and so also a simple *possessio naturalis*, is said to arise upon a donation between man and wife. The passage which establishes the latter proposition has been cited above (num. I.), in proof of the notion of *possessio civilis*, but it is also expressly in point for *possessio naturalis* (k).

" Dejicitur is qui possidet, sive civiliter sive naturaliter possideat; nam et naturalis possessio ad hoc interdictum pertinet. Denique et si maritus uxori donavit, eaque dejecta sit, poterit interdicto uti; non tamen si colonus."

The meaning of the passage is, the Interdict lies on every (juridical) Possession, consequently not merely on *possessio*

able logic as to the existence or non-existence of *possessio*. (Add. to 6th ed.)

(j) L. 3, § 15, *ad exhibendum.* (See above, num. I.)

(k) L. 1, § 9, 10, *de vi.*

civilis, but on *possessio naturalis* also, though upon the latter only where it is (juridical) *possessio* (*l*). Thus, the possession of a wife like that of a tenant, is included under *possessio naturalis*, for both are alike incapable of Usucaption, but the wife alone may bring Interdicts, not the tenant, because her *naturalis possessio* only is to be considered as proper *possessio*.

Possessio naturalis of the second kind (num. II.), in opposition to *possessio*, denotes detention, which is incapable even of Interdicts, and therefore *a fortiori* of Usucaption also (num. III.) The distinction therefore is, that the negation is larger here than in the previous case ; whoever consequently possesses *naturaliter*, in this second meaning, has undoubtedly a *naturalis* possessio according to the first meaning, but a *possessio naturalis* of the first kind may be a true juridical *possessio*, and therefore directly opposed to the second *naturalis possessio*, as the instance cited of a donation between man and wife shews in the clearest manner.

Which *possessio naturalis* then is meant when the term occurs in our law sources? does it merely negative the right to Usucaption or that to Interdicts also? This is to be ascertained in each particular case only by finding out what the relative term is to which this expression is used in opposition. Thus a different meaning is to be ascribed to *possessio naturalis* when opposed to *possessio civilis*, or to *possessio* gene-

(*l*) It should be carefully remarked, that the first words (is *qui possidet*) contain the necessary limitation, and that without them the following words (*et naturalis possessio ad hoc interdictum pertinet*) would have been much too general, as it is undeniable that there are many cases in which *possessio naturalis* (that of slaves, for instance) would not allow of interdicts. In consequence of overlooking this limitation which occurred in the text itself, it was found necessary to introduce a qualification to the words *et naturalis possessio*, and accordingly the Gloss adds to them *et pro suo*, (more correctly *pro suo*, without the *et, i. e.* nam *et ea* naturalis possessio *quæ est pro suo*) which words are introduced into the text in several manuscripts and editions, and are even explained in the Gloss of Accursius as the common reading.

rally: if no counter idea is expressed, the term implied must be sought for from the context, in order to discover what the meaning intended is. The most important rule of interpretation, in reference to *possessio naturalis*, is never to lose sight of its negative nature, and therefore never to be drawn into the conclusion which almost all previous writers have adopted, because it appears so obvious, *naturaliter possidet ergo possidet*.

V. Let us now look back at the meanings under which the word *possessio* has occurred. Originally it denotes merely a condition of fact (*m*), and this meaning lies at the bottom of the term (*civilis, naturalis*). With this meaning the privileges of a defendant are ascribed to a *possessor* in vindication (*n*), although such privileges are by no means limited to juridical possession. The *furtum possessionis* is to be understood in the same sense also, inasmuch as the term applies even to such persons as have no juridical Possession (*o*).

(*m*) It is for this very reason, because neither the notion nor the word *possessio* contain any thing juridical in their *origin*, that its etymology is so unimportant, whereas that of pure juridical notions is generally so instructive. It is an old controversy whether Paulus (L. 1, *pr. de poss.*) derives the word '*a pedibus*,' or '*a sedibus*." The latter word occurs in the Florence manuscript, but is cited however, so early as the Gloss, merely as a various reading; most civilians give it the preference however, and justly, although Walther (Miscella. lib. 2, c. 19) defends the former very ably. Herman Cannegieter (Observations, lib. 4, c. 7) suggests a new reading, which in some sort combines the two others, but which is much worse than either;

he reads "*a pedis sedilus*." By reading "pedibus" the Gloss moreover is driven to hold that as to moveables there can only be an improper possession, because, though land is trodden on by feet moveables are not. (Glossa, in § 4, I. de Interdictis, and many other passages.) A French jurist thereupon proposes to make at all events an exception as to shoes. This opinion of the Gloss will be seen more clearly in the ninth section, *post*.

(*n*) § 4, I. *de Interdictis*; L. 9, *de rei vind*. See above, ch. 3, num. 4.

(*o*) For according to L. 15, § 2, and L. 59, *de furtis* it is a *furtum*, if the lender of an article purloins it from the borrower, supposing that the latter has a special right to the detention, of which he could

But, besides this, *possessio* used alone means juridical
Possession, and this is the *possessio* to which *possessio naturalis* is opposed (num. II).

If now in the law sources the question turns on *possessio*
simply, what sort of *possessio* is thereby to be understood?
Wherever no ground presents itself for restricting the notion,
it must be taken as generally as possible, and consequently
as the physical relation of detention; which rule of construction is proved by the example of the Roman Jurists
themselves (*p*). But there are two special grounds for such
restriction of the notion, and these require us in far the
greater number of cases where the word *possessio* occurs to
accept the narrower notion of juridical Possession.

For if, firstly, the *possessio* refers to Interdicts or Usucaption, as the consequences of *possessio*, none other than
juridical Possession can be conceived (§. 2).

So also, secondly, when the existence of possession is
predicated on juridical grounds, because it is only the juridical
notion of possession which admits of such predication (§. 5).
Thus in all passages, wherein it is discussed, doubted, or
contested, whether *possessio* is to be recognised or not, it is
always juridical Possession which is intended by this word.
An example, which has been already used for another purpose, may serve to explain this important rule of interpretation. It has been shewn above (num. I.), namely, that
although *possessio civilis* does not arise upon a gift between
man and wife, *possessio* simply does. Paulus lays down the
position thus, "si vir uxori cedat possessione, donationis
causâ *plerique putant possidere eam*" (*q*), (and he gives two
juridical reasons for this doctrine) and in another passage,

---

avail himself against the former.
It would not indeed be a *furtum
rei*, because it occurs with the
owner himself, still less a *furtum
usus*; it only, therefore, can be
looked on as a *furtum possessionis*; but, at the same time, as a
borrower has no juridical posses-

sion, it follows, that that is not a
condition for the *furtum possessionis*.

(*p*) Ulpian, for instance, thus
construes a stipulation, (L. 38, §
7, *de V. O.*), and Julian a rule
of law, (L. 2, § 1, pro herede).

(*q*) L. 1, § 4, *de poss.*

"*Possidere* autem uxorem rem a viro donatam, *Julianus putat*" (r).   As the question in these passages related to *opinions* respecting the existence of this Possession, and as juridical reasons are brought forward to establish its existence, it could not be the physical relation of detention, but only juridical Possession, which was meant here by *possidere.*

SECTION VIII.

POSSESSIO JUSTA, BONÆ FIDEI, ETC.

The Roman Law terms above defined are the only ones which have any direct operation upon the treatment of our subject; the following are only brought forward for the purpose of establishing by their aid a complete refutation of a greater portion of the most prevalent errors of interpretation. For this purpose, the most important are two other divisions of Possession which are to be found in Roman Jurists, possessio *justa, injusta,* and possessio *bonæ fidei,* and *malæ fidei.* Secondly, those cases also belong here, in which *possessio* simply denotes something quite different from Possession.

Justum particularly is used in two senses by Roman lawyers; sometimes it refers to jus (civile), and is then used just like *civile* or *legitimum,* as, for instance, *matrimonium justum, justa traditionis causa,* &c.   In other passages it has a much more indefinite meaning, and signifies merely justifiable :. thus in *absentiâ justâ, error justus,* &c. (a).   With Possession the word is used in its second meaning, and *justa possessio,* consequently, signifies that Possession to which one is entitled, whether it may juridically avail as Possession or not; for, first, the Possession which a creditor has in a pledge

(r) L. 1, § 2, *pro donato.*

(a) Instances of both meanings are given at length by Bris-

sonius, De Verb. Sign. v. *justus.* (p. 687, ed. Hal. 1743).

is called *justa possessio* (*b*), but as such Possession is not *civilis* (see §. 7, No. 1), it cannot be the first but the second meaning of *justum* which is intended. Again, a *justa pos-sessio* (*c*) arises even upon a *missio in possessionem*, and therefore, in a case where no question could ever arise as to juridical Possession (*d*).

This division, therefore, has reference to the general notion of physical possession (§. 7, No. 5); the notion even of *justa possessio* does not coincide with any juridical notion of Possession, and the whole division is consequently unimportant in a theory of juridical Possession (*e*). Here again therefore, as with *naturalis possessio* (see ante, §. 7), it is most important to avoid the conclusion, *juste possidet, ergo possidet*.

This division, however, is not only unimportant for our purpose, but is even incapable of being predicated of in general terms, and only admits of a definite meaning in particular cases (*f*). For, in addition to the above noticed indefinite meaning of the expression, there is also another more restricted meaning, which may even be considered as the most common of the two. In this second signification the division refers to the *vitia possessionis* (§. 2), and *justa possessio* then means such detention, whether it be juridical

---

(*b*) L. 13, § 1, *De publiciana;* L. 22, § 1, *De noxali act.*

(*c*) L. 7, § 8, *comm. div.*

(*d*) L. 3, § 23, *de poss.*

(*e*) "*In summâ possessionis* non multum interest, juste quis, an injuste possideat," L. 3, § 5, *de poss., i. e.* it is immaterial where the question relates simply to the existence of juridical Possession, where, therefore, Possession only is considered as the source of rights, and not as connected with any other matter which is not an essential part of the notion.

(*f*) Cuperus (De nat. poss. p. 2, c. 7), has thoroughly established the above position, although many of the different meanings of the division which he adduces are not essentially different, and some of his statements will have to be controverted hereafter. Most writers have confounded *possessio justa* with *civilis*. The most singular view is to be found in Madera, (Animad. cc. 2, 7, in T. 3, p. 488) : he explains *justum* by the *jus gentium*, (resting on L. 95, § 4, De solut.), and affirms that all possessio is *justa*, because it arose out of the *jus gentium.*

or not, as has commenced, neither forcibly, clandestinely, nor permissively (precario) (*g*). This distinction is certainly not very important as respects the nature of Possession generally, though highly so as to possessory Interdicts.

The expression *bonæ fidei possessio* is equally indefinite and equally unimportant for the theory of Possession simply. *Bona fides* refers to every possible ground of detention; whosoever conceives himself to have a lawful ground for the detention, which he is exercising, is called *bonæ fidei possessor*. Thus in Usucaption, every such person who through his *justa possessionis causa* believes himself to have actually acquired the property. So also in vindication, every defendant who considers his detention lawful whether he derives this right from his own property, or from a mere contract (a lease for instance) with the proprietor, in which latter case he does not at all lay claim to any juridical Possession. So also every defendant in a *hypothecaria actio*, who has had no notice of the pledge-right belonging to the plaintiff.

In the most important cases, *bona fides* has no effect except where a good title accompanies it, so that in all such cases, by *bonæ fidei possessio*, Possession with title may be understood, although this is not usually expressly stated. In these cases, therefore, *bona fides* is immediately connected with the *causa possessionis*, and therefore also with the rule expressed above: Nemo sibi causam possessionis mutare potest.

Different as the notions of *possessio* are, which have hitherto been brought forward, still the notion of *Possession* has been at the bottom of them all; there are other passages however remaining to be explained in which *possessio* means something quite different from Possession. Of these meanings, which have served from early times to perplex the theory of Possession, there are two in particular which must be mentioned, *Property*, and the *Relation of Defendant*.

To *hold property* is sometimes expressed by *possidere*, and

(*g*) See particularly, L. 1, § 9, L. 2, *uti possidetis*.

the *subject-matter of property* by Possessio (*h*).   It is easy to explain how such use of terms arose.   For as the distinction between Possession and Property turns upon a legal abstraction (§. 1), the distinction, naturally enough, was not generally taken either in the language of common life, or in the writings of unprofessional authors; accordingly, in the law sources the last mentioned meaning scarcely ever occurs except in wills, contracts, statements of cases, &c.   It is worthy of remark that in all such passages *possessio* and *possidere* are only used with reference to land (*i*); and that in this respect also the German term Besitzung (a Possession) is exactly analogous (*j*).

(*h*) " Interdum proprietatem quoque verbum possessionis significat; sicut in eo qui *possessiones suas legasset,* responsum est, L. 78, De V. S.——So also in many other passages of the Digest and Code, and just as frequently in Cicero, Quinctilian, &c. Upon this meaning also the definition of Cornelius Fonto (Gothofredi auct. ling. lat. p. m. 1331), *habere potest etiam fur et nequam; possidet* nemo, nisi qui rei. . . . . dominus est." Lastly, the same construction must be put upon the passage in the Edict, according to which *possessores* of land were not required to give security in civil process; (L. 15, qui satisf. cog.); *Possessor* there does not mean the possessor but the owner.

(*i*) Alciatus in L. 1, pr. de poss. no.24, (Opp. T. 1, p. 1195). This circumstance, probably, led to the opinion in the Gloss, that immoveable property only is capable of being possessed, (see *ante,* § 7). The exclusive reference of *possessio* in this sense to land

is so universal, that even *possessor* and *possidere* are frequently used absolutely in order to denote the possession of lands ; thus, L. 1, *De decret. ab ord. fac.; L.* 7, *De incend.* Cf. Roth. De re municipali. (Studtg. 1801), p. 43.

(*j*) It must not be confounded with this, that *bonitarian* property is also specially termed *possessio.* This arises from a purely historical source, which shall be explained fully hereafter (§ 13).

[It would seem that in English also *Possession,* and more particularly *Possessions,* as denoting the thing possessed, are only used of lands ; thus, in our translation of the Bible, "the house of Jacob shall possess their *possessions,"* Obad. 17; and in Matth. 19, 22, the young man "went away sorrowful, for he had great *possessions,"* and the Greek κτηματα has the same limited sense; but in neither of these two latter languages, possibly, is the limitation so definite as in German and Latin.] Transl.

Lastly, in addition to Possession and property, *possessio* also denotes *the relation of defendant*. For if property has to be recovered by vindication the suit can only be brought against the party who *possesses* the subject, the Possession, however, here meant is not to be taken in any juridical sense (§. 3, no. 4); but it followed naturally from this, that the plaintiff in every vindication suit should be called *petitor*, the defendant *possessor*, because the latter in fact possesses that which the plaintiff demands from him. Subsequently however, the procedure in vindication came to be used for other matters besides property, especially in questions touching the inheritance (*k*), for this reason the terms of the old action were retained, and the plaintiff and defendant continued to be called *petitor* and *possessor*. In most cases these names were appropriate, because even the *hereditatis petitio* was brought to recover subjects which the defendant was in possession of on some general ground (*pro herede* or *pro possessore*). But the terms were not limited to such cases only, and thus it happened that the defendant in an *hereditatis petitio* was still called *possessor*, even where no question was involved as to the possession of any subject. The defendant here was called *possessor juris*, because he refused to do something which the other party as heir conceived he was entitled to call upon him to do, because therefore, he made claim to a portion of the general inheritance; a defendant on the other hand was called *possessor corporis*, when he in fact possessed the subject-matter (*l*).

The following instances show who was a *juris possessor*:—

1st. He who, though he does not possess a portion of the inheritance in fact, still by possibility may possess it, because he has a claim thereto; in this case, it is the surrender of his claims which is sought from him (*m*).

(*k*) Cic. in Verrem. act 2, lib. 1, c. 45, " Si quis testamento se heredem esse arbitraretur, quod tum non extaret, lege ageret in hereditatem : aut pro præde *litis vindiciarum cum satis accepisset,* sponsionem faceret: ita de hereditate certaret."

(*l*) L. 9, L. 18, § 1, *De hered. petit.*

(*m*) L. 16, § 4, 7, L. 35, *De hered. petit.*

2. He, who possesses in the *peculium* of his slave the value of a hereditament (*n*) which the latter has sold:

3. He who has contracted any liability towards the inheritance, for instance, as a *negotiorum gestor* (*o*).

In like manner, vindication-procedure was used from the earliest times in suits respecting liberty (*liberale judicium*) (*p*), and here also the relation of the defendant with the privileges attached to it was denoted by the terms *libertatis, servitutis, possessio* (*q*).

Thus the relation of defendant is denoted by the term *possessor*, even where there is no subject-matter capable of being possessed; this proposition, however, is not universally true. It only admits of demonstration in the cases of *hereditatis petitio*, and *liberale judicium ;* with all probability, it may also be asserted of all actions in which the process of vindication might be used (*r*), but in all other actions it does not hold good at all (*s*).

(*n*) L. 34, § 1, *De hered. petit.*

(*o*) L. 10, *Si pars hered. petur.*

(*p*) The principal authority is in Livius, lib. 3, C. 44—8.

(*q*) Digest, lib. 40, tit. 12, Possessio *servitutis* must not be confounded with *possessio* servi.

(*r*) And even the suits as to servitude must be excepted, because in such actions the *possessor* might be plaintiff, § 2, T. de act.

(*s*) L. 62, *De judiciis,* lays it down indeed generally, *Inter litigantes* non aliter lis expediri potest, quam si alter *petitor,* alter *possessor* sit ; esse enim debet, qui onera *petitoris,* sustineat, et qui commodo *possessoris* fungatur." But *petere* and *petitor* refer only to actions in rem. (L. 28, de oblig. et act. L. 178, § 2, De V. S.), and with such limitation the passage entirely agrees with the rule in the text. Indeed it is probable that the Digest had in view the *hereditatis petitio* only, for the passage is taken from a work of Ulpian, (L. 39, ad. edictum), which treats nearly exclusively of inheritance. (L. 22, *qui* test. fac. poss. ; L. 1, 3, 5, *De bon poss. ;* L. 2, D. B. P. furioso ; L. 1, 3, De B. P. contra tab. ; L. De B. P. sec. tab. ; L. 6, *si tab. test. null.*) Besides, the question here is merely as to the use of the term in our law sources, Cicero uses the expression also in respect to controversies about tithes between the *publicanus* and land occupiers. In *Verrem,* lib. 3, C. 11, "cum in his, inquam, rebus omnibus publicanus *petitor,* ac pignerator, non ereptor, neque *possessor* soleat esse. . . . Utrum est æquius . . . . eum qui manu quæsi erit an eum qui digito licitus sit, *possidere.*"

When, therefore, any passage in the law sources containing an assertion relative to *possessio* is sought to be applied with precision to Possession, it must be first shewn that neither property nor the relation of defendant was intended; no general rule for interpretation can be laid down on the point, but a case will rarely occur in which this distinction will present any great difficulty.

SECTION IX.

MATERIAL (*a*) NOTION OF POSSESSION.

It has been now established, that all juridical Possession refers either to Interdicts or to Usucaption (§. 2), and that both of these are founded on one general notion of juridical Possession, which, in order to allow of Usucaption, only needs the addition of certain other conditions (§. 7).

The question may now be raised as to what constitutes juridical *possessio ?* what are the material elements of this notion? We commenced as from a starting point with the general notion of *detention*, i. e., the physical relation corresponding to property as the relation of law (§. 1), but this original notion of Possession becomes susceptible of juridical modifications, so soon as it is treated as the foundation of rights (§. 5). These modifications are for the greater part so special in their nature, that they can only be understood and discussed when the details of the theory of Possession are entered upon; but one of them is quite general, and must be mentioned here in order to give a complete view of the notion of Possession.

Every detainer, namely, in order to enure as Possession, must be voluntary, *i. e.*, to constitute a possessor, the will

(*a*) See note (*e*), *ante.* p. 3.

to detain as well as the detention itself must exist (b). This coincidence of the Will with detention (*animus possidendi*) must be now examined with minuteness. Detention has been above (p. 1,) defined as the physical condition corresponding to property as the legal condition. The *animus possidendi* consequently must consist in the intention of exercising ownership. But this definition is not sufficiently precise, because the party who detains may have this intention in one of two ways, viz., either for the purpose of exercising ownership for himself, or for another. If his intention be to exercise it for another, whose property he thus recognizes, no such *animus possidendi* can be said to exist, by which detention can be elevated into Possession. This proposition, which is expressed in terms in the Roman Law (c), may be very clearly deduced from the above given view of Interdicts (§. 2). There remains, therefore, only the first case in which the detaining party's intention has reference to property in himself (d), so that *animus possidendi* must be explained by animus *domini*, or animus *sibi*

(b) L. 3, § 1, *De poss.* "apicimur possessionem corpore et *animo : neque* per se animo aut *per se corpore.*"

(c) L. 18, pr. *De poss.* "nec idem est, *possidere* et *alieno nomine possidere.* Nam possidet, cujus nomine possidetur. Procurator alienæ possessioni præstat ministerium." This distinction is important with respect to Possession in several ways ; 1st, because the *animus sibi habendi*, i. e. the original notion of Possession is not applicable to him who has the detention; 2nd, because the same person either may or may not have a constructive possession (§ 25 to 27) ; 3rd, because the other party who has not the de-

tention is treated as possessor, (§ 28, 29).

(d) This division may be looked on as incomplete, since a third case may be conceived where a party detaining neither looks upon himself nor upon any particular individual as the owner, but intends to detain for a special purpose only, (to reap the profits, for instance). But this case is only distinguishable from the above in appearance. For whoever voluntarily exercises detention, without looking on any one in particular as the owner, undoubtedly has the *animus domini*, and in a legal point of view it is immaterial for what ulterior object he holds this property.

habendi (e), and he only is to be looked on as a valid possessor, who deals with the subject of which he has the detention as owner, that is, he must contemplate dealing with it practically, just as an owner is accustomed to do by virtue of his right; and, consequently, not as one recognizing anybody better entitled than himself (f). Nothing more, however, than this *animus domini* is comprised in the notion of Possession; undoubtedly, not a moral conviction of being owner (*opinio s. cogitatio* domini): accordingly, the notion of Possession is just as applicable to the case of a robber and thief as to the owner himself, and the two former are opposed, just in the same way as the latter is, to a tenant who has no possession, because he does not deal with the subject-matter as his own property (g).

(e) Theophilus, in § 4, I. *per quas pers. adq.*, et in § 2, I. *quibus mod. toll. obl.* These are the only passages which lay down this doctrine in terms, it does not occur in the Institutes or Digest, but it is everywhere implied.

(f) The expression *animus domini*, therefore, is only used here in order to denote the state of will required for possession, in comparison with what an owner feels he is allowed to do, and not by any means to indicate that the possessor has any precise notion in his mind of legal property, which, in the case of a thief, for instance, would be absurd. It appears, however, that several of the authors cited at the conclusion of this chapter have thus misconstrued the "intention of exercising property" required by me. Warnkönig, for instance, states my view thus, "To call the subject his own, that is, *ex jure quiritium suum*. He is bound

to go this length." Guyet to the same effect; Abhandl. p. 176.

(g) The above given definition of Possession is that of most civilians, more or less clearly expressed. Zachariæ (De poss. p. 5) objects to it, and substitutes the following, "Possessio nobis est : ea rei ad hominem ratio, e quâ appareat, esse alicui et animum rem sibi habendi, et reliquarum virium modum animo illi accommodatum." There is nothing new in this *animus*, as Zachariæ himself confesses (p. 6), although, indeed, there is in the second half of the definition (p. 10). What, then, is the measure of physical force correspondent to the *animus domini?* The *animus domini* consists in the disposal of a thing at will to the exclusion of all others, and therefore must include a *modus virium;* the latter therefore is nothing but detention in the sense in which it is understood by every one, and as

The application of this notion can only give rise to doubts in those cases where a party intends to exercise a right, the

I have expressly explained it above (p. 2). There is no new view therefore in this "*virium modus*," but solely in the *appareat*. Possession then, Zachariæ means to say, is that relation between a subject-matter and man, which intimates that the man has the *animus domini*, and that he is also able to put it into execution; according to this view, the *factum* in possession acquires an entirely symbolic character, as it is used for the purpose of making manifest or expressing something else (p. 11). I will pass over the fact that innumerable instances contradict this new element of Possession; for the element itself is left so indefinite that a direct denial of it would be extremely difficult if not impossible. But the reasoning on which Zachariæ founds his position refutes itself, for he wishes to shew that, according to his definition, cases hitherto inexplicable on the acquisition and loss of Possession may be elucidated. With respect to loss of Possession, it shall be shewn subsequently that Zachariæ has deduced nothing from his definition which does not also flow from mine. I will here, therefore, only mention the acquisition of Possession. Now the manifestation spoken of above may be viewed in two lights, either the thing manifested (the *virium modus*) exists, or it does not, and it is only a mistake of the party manifesting who thinks it does. In the latter case it is

clear no Possession is acquired: if, for instance, the key of a warehouse is given me outside the door in order to put me in possession of the goods contained within, but no goods are in fact within, I certainly cannot be said to have acquired Possession. The connection between my definition, therefore, and Zachariæ's is this; mine includes detention and *animus domini*, his definition however includes, besides these two, the above described manifestation, and therefore only an additional term to mine. Consequently, in all cases where, according to Zachariæ, Possession is acquired, it must be so according to my view also, but not vice versâ. Zachariæ therefore ought to be able to refute me by cases in which I affirm Possession, but in which he and the Roman law concur in denying it; yet, as all his cases are precisely applicable to my view, he contradicts himself. To give, as an example, one instance only which Zachariæ adduces in support of his doctrine, (p. 19); if, in the case mentioned in L. 18, § 2, *De poss.* a river be conceived to run between a tower and a field, so as to prevent ingress to the latter, undoubtedly, according to my view, no Possession is acquired, and so also according to Zachariæ's; for whoever is prevented by the river from exercising any dominion over the field, certainly cannot make any manifestation that he is able to do so.

relation of which to property is doubtful. Of this nature
are the following rights:

1. Bonitarian ownership (*h*). This right, in all cases
not peculiar to the old strict Civil Law, is treated exactly
like property, so that the immediate applicability of our
definition of Possession to it is quite clear. It is also wholly
immaterial whether the bare Quiritarian right (*nudum jus
Quiritium*) is in another person or not. In this respect, the
bonæ fidei possessio cannot be looked upon as a distinct legal
institute. For a bonâ fide possessor always claimed either
a Quiritarian or a natural property as a right already acquired; and as, therefore, he would conceive himself to
possess this right, and undoubtedly desired to exercise it,
this alone was sufficient to supply the *animus domini*, and
consequently, the Publician action was unnecessary, and
of no assistance in founding a true *possessio* in such a
case (*i*).

2. *Provincial lands*, in which, namely, according to an
old rule of the Roman Law, no Quiritarian property could
be required, *i. e.* as to which *commercium* in the strict sense
was wanting. One consequence to possessors, of the absence
of this Quiritarian ownership, was the impossibility of
acquiring any right to their Possession by the old Roman
forms, *i. e.*, by the *in jure cessio, mancipatio*, or *usucapio*.
But that, in every other respect, the possessors of these
lands were to be looked upon as owners, and that here also,
therefore, our notion of the *animus domini* is applicable is
quite clear, not only from the origin of this legal institute,

(*h*) In the two first editions I
included the in *bonis* and *bona fidei
possessio* under the common title
prætorian property. I was led to
this by observing that, in fact,
the two chief effects of both
these legal institutes are the same;
namely, Usucaption and the *publiciana actio*, (the latter however
not universally, but only in the

cases of derivative acquisition).
Still it is always necessary to
distinguish the two accurately.
The passage in which the dis-
tinction is drawn most broadly is
Ulpian, XIX. 20, 21.

(*i*) This view of the *bonæ fidei
possessio* was first given in the 4th
edition.

but also from many passages of the ancients (*j*). This relation, therefore, was very similar to Bonitarian property in Rome and Italy. Justinian, however, did away with all distinction between Quiritarian and Bonitarian property; and, as a consequence of this, allowed of a full unshackled property in land in the provinces (*k*), by which amalgamation, the connection of the earlier law institutes here contended for is confirmed.

3. Servitudes, *i. e.*, the rights introduced by the *jus civile*, which as detached portions of property (*jura, jura in re*) (*l*) are opposed to property itself as the totality of all real rights. It follows clearly from this antithesis, which is essential to the definition of servitudes, that whoever means merely to exercise a servitude cannot at the same time have the *animus domini*. And there is only one instance which affords any ground for doubting this proposition, namely, *ususfructus*. But the Roman Law does not recognize even the Fructuary as the owner, and, indeed, *proprietas* is the technical denomination of the right remaining after deduction of the *ususfructus*. In all easements, therefore, the animus domini is impossible.

4. The right of *superficies* is exactly like that of servitudes, and it is only on an historical ground that it is not included in them, namely, because this institute did not spring from

(*j*) Aggenus and Simplicius in Goesius, pp. 46—7, 76; Theophilus in § 40, I. *de div. rer.*

(*k*) Cod. *de usucap. transformanda.*

(*l*) That the Romans meant this and nothing else by *jus in re*, that *dominium* therefore is never included in it, but is expressly opposed to it, has been fully proved by Waechtler, De Jure in Re. Viteb. 1682 (also in Thomasii Diss. Lipsius, 1696, p. 235). Huber laid down the same doctrine even earlier, Animadvers. ad *jus in re.* Franck. 1675, 12 (also in the Digress. Lib. 4, C. 10, and in Feltmannorum Opp. Arnh. 1764, T. 2, p. 257); this latter writer however, with an extension which removes all precision from the notion; holding, namely, that the lender has the *jus in re.* Thibaut makes the same assertion; Versuche, B. 2, § 32. The only ground for this opinion is L. 2, § 22, *vi. bon. rapt.;* but the words '*vel quod aliud jus*' refer not only just as well, but much better, to *sive usumfructum.*

the *jus civile* but from an edict. It belongs, therefore, like easements to the *jura in re*, and Gaius expressly lays down that such is its relation, and that, therefore the *superficiarius* never can have the subject-matter *in bonis* (*m*). It follows from this, that the *animus domini*, and therefore Possession also, is impossible in the case of *superficies* (*n*).

5. *Ager vectigalis* and *emphyteusis.*

1st. *Ager vectigalis.* The first express notice of this occurs in the time of Trajan or Hadrian. Hyginus (*o*) gives this name to lands which were rented from the Roman people, from cities, from colleges of priests, and from the Vestal Virgins: the two first, he says, were generally given in lease for five or for a hundred years, the latter for one or five years. For reasons easy to be comprehended, the Digest mentions one only of these four cases, namely city lands, and even these under somewhat different terms: they are only called *vectigales* when let on hereditary lease; in other cases *non vectigales* (*p*). But the tenant universally and without any distinction between these two cases was allowed his real action (*q*).

2nd. *Emphyteusis.* The first trace of this term is in the Digest (*r*). The right itself is not defined, but it is expressly mentioned as a *jus prædii* and is classed with *ususfructus.*

(*m*) L. 2, *De superficiebus.* Superficiarias ædes appellamus quæ in conducto solo positæ sint, quarum proprietas et *civili et naturali jure* ejus est cujus est solum.

(*n*) The positive proof that the *superficiarius* was not possessor of the subject, shall be given hereafter (§ 23) when derivative Possession is treated of.

(*o*) In Goesius, p. 205—6. In another passage he says the rent was sometimes paid in money, sometimes in kind (usually one-fifth or one-seventh of the produce). Ib. p. 198. Pliny notices the subject generally, Epist. VII, 18.

(*p*) L. 1, *pr. si ager vect.*

(*q*) L. 1, § 1, L. 3, cod. It is very doubtful whether the other rights of *ager vectigalis* were also granted to the tenant for term of years. It would appear not to be so on a literal construction, as the words used throughout have reference to *ager vectigalis* only, yet as the real action was available in both cases, so also I think were the other rights, *i. e.* I think the narrower meaning of *ager vectigalis* was not the usual one, and the passage from Hyginus seems to afford a proof of this.

(*r*) L. 3, § 4, *De rebus eorum qui sub tect.*, cf. § 5, *eod.*

In the codes of Theodosius and Justinian the expression *prædia emphyteutica* very often occurs, but at first only amongst the patrimonial possessions of the *princeps* (s), and it is expressly distinguished from *ager vectigalis* (t).

A constitution of Zeno's (u) requires a special form of contract for the creation of an *emphyteusis,* which however does not concern the present inquiry. But it appears from the general terms of the constitution that emphyteusis was also in use with respect to private property, and also from the interpretation of the constitution given in the Institutes (v), that we must look upon it as an hereditary lease. No mention at all is made of the right to the subject-matter.

Justinian has defined this right; only incidentally it is true, but still with such clearness as to leave no room for doubt. He enacts that the (new) *emphyteusis* shall have all the rights which the (old) *ager vectigalis* possessed, *i. e.* that the same privileges should extend to hereditary leases (whether the landlord were a city or not) which had been previously confined to the leases (hereditary or temporary) of municipal lands (w).

If these expressions are compared with the above explained right of *ager vectigalis,* the question arises as to both of these legal relations now united into one, whether they are to be considered as a species of property (like land in the provinces) or as *jura in re* like *superficies :* I hold the second to be the true doctrine, for the Roman Jurists expressly ascribe

(s) Gothofred. Paratit. Cod. Theod. X. 3.

(t) L. 13, C. de prædiis et al. reb. minorum.

(u) L. 1, C. de jure emph.

(v) § 3, I. de locat.

(w) Inscriptio tit. 3, lib, 6, Dig. "Si ager vectigalis, id est emphyteuticarius, petatur." L. 15, § 1, qui satisdare cog. "Sed et qui vectigalem, *id est emphyteuticum* agrum possidet, possessor intelligitur," (evidently interpolations of Tribonian). I do not however mean to assert by this that Justinian was the author of this amalgamation of the two institutes, it is on the contrary, rather more probable that it already existed as customary law, for otherwise it is difficult to suppose that Justinian would have refrained from introducing his new measure with a grand flourish in a constitution of his own.

to the hereditary tenant a *jus in fundo* or *jus prædii* (*x*), and in the constitutions he is always distinguished from the *dominus* (that is the landlord) and opposed to him (*y*).

According to the notion of Possession previously set forth, no juridical Possession ought to be recognized in this case also, any more than in *superficies*. Nevertheless it is not so, and a true Possession cannot be denied (*z*); this apparent inconsistency must be explained fully infra (§. 13) (*a*).

6. Lastly. The right to a pledge must also be mentioned here, only because this right also gave rise to a real action. But, notwithstanding this action, the creditor can in no wise be looked upon as an owner, and on the contrary he necessarily recognizes the property to exist in another. It follows that he cannot have the *animus domini*, or consequently

(*x*) L. 71, § 5, 6, *de leg.* I ; L. 3, § 4, *de rebus eorum.*

(*y*) L. 1, 2, 3, C. *de jure emph.* L. 2, C. *de mancip. et col.* In another passage indeed (L. 12, C. *de fundis patr.*) the tenant appears to be termed *dominus*, but in fact this passage is speaking of a case in which a tenant in addition to his previous *jus in re* acquires true *dominium* also. Thibaut Abhandlungen, § 274, 281.

(*z*) L. 25, § 1, *de usuris* vide ch. 24, a. *post.*

(*a*) To avoid this inconsistency, the proper explanation of which I think I now perceive, I suggested in my second edition that an hereditary tenant might be looked upon as a Bonitarian owner. In support of this I remarked that the hereditary tenant possesses many important rights in preference to the usufructuary; but it by no means follows, from the different extent of rights in these two cases that they are dissimilar. The language of L. 1, pr. *de con-*

dict. trit. proves just as little ; "Quare *fundum* quoque per hanc actionem petimus, *etsi vectigalis sit.*" Exactly in the same sense, L. 12, § 1, *quib. modis pign.* uses the expressions *rem* persequi and vindicatio *rei* in reference to a pledge holder, though no one will deny that the right to a pledge is merely a *jus in re*. The employment of these terms in respect to the two latter rights appears to arise from one and the same ground, namely from the *corporis possessio* which is bound up with these kinds of *jus in re*. There is no such *possessio* in *ususfructus*, and therefore in respect of it, one never hears of a *rei* but always of a *juris* petitio, persecutio, vindicatio. Thibaut is the principal writer to consult as to the juridical nature of emphyteusis ; Abhandlungen, Num. XI., the substance of which however is to be found in his previous article in the Hallische Allgemeine Literatur, Zeitung, 1806, No. 144, § 530.

Possession, in the sense in which the notion of it has been hitherto developed.

According to the definition of Possession which has been above given, *he* is to be deemed a possessor whose purpose it is to exercise detention for himself, but not he who exercises it for another. In the latter case the party for whom the property is dealt with is rather to be looked upon as the possessor, though I can only allude to this point cursorily here. But Possession is treated as a right (§. 5), and therefore to such extent is capable of being transferred. For this reason the true original possessor may, even in the latter case, transfer the right of Possession to the party who is dealing with the property for him, and who, therefore, according to the previous definitions of Possession is not to be deemed a possessor. Thus, besides the *original* Possession, which depends on detention and *animus domini*, there is a *derivative* Possession also which is founded on the original Possession of another. The whole difference between this derivative Possession and the original Possession already defined, consists in the *animus possidendi*, for as respects detention they are both alike. The *animus possidendi*, namely, which in original Possession must be looked upon as *animus domini*, in derivative Possession is founded on the *jus possessionis* transferred from the previous possessor (*b*).

(*b*) It is worth remarking, that all that is peculiar in derivative possession turns merely on the *animus possidendi*, that is, merely on the state of consciousness of the person who wishes to assert Possession. It comes therefore to this, that such person must believe the possession to have been transferred to him by another possessor: whether the circumstances, giving rise to the original possession are good in law for that purpose is quite immaterial; for instance, the pledgee acquires a true *possessio* in an article improperly pledged by one to whom it did not belong. Consequently, no question arises here as to any *succession* in Possession (see *ante*, § 5). In all cases, on the other hand, where such succession actually takes place, (as, for instance, with the *accessio possessionis* in Usucaption), the mere state of knowledge in the possessor is not the sole thing regarded, but also the existence in fact of the juridical relation between him and the previous possessor.

Thus, for instance, the creditor has the juridical Possession of a pledge, although he has no intention of exercising ownership over it, because the debtor who had full Possession of the article, transferred to him the *jus possessionis* at the same time as the detention.

Derivative Possession, however, is by no means to be understood to arise in every case when the real possessor simply wishes it so to do, for, as it is in itself a departure from the original notion of Possession, it is only to be recognized in those cases where positive law has expressly made it valid (*c*); accordingly the notion of derivative Possession is to be looked upon as merely one of form, which only obtains reality from the fact, that certain cases occur which prove that its existence is recognized. In what cases however a derivative Possession is to be admitted, *i. e.* in what cases it must be admitted that the *jus possessionis* is transferred together with detention, shall be shown fully in the second Book, under the head Acquisition of Possession. It appears, therefore, that the most comprehensive description that can be given of the material notion of Possession is this; it is detention joined with the *animus possidendi*, which latter expression must be explained differently, according to whether original or derivative Possession is in question; in the former it denotes the *animus domini*, in the latter, the intention to enjoy that *jus possessionis* which formerly belonged to another (*d*). This division of Possession, however, is not to be understood to express different rights of Possession : the rights are exactly the same, the mode only of acquiring

(*c*) In contradiction to this it has been lately asserted by several writers that the right of Possession may be transferred at will to any tenant, &c. Thibaut, Archiv. B. 18, p. 322, and Pandekten, § 208, 8th ed ; see *post*, § 23. Add. to 6th ed.

(*d*) Thus explained, it is quite immaterial, so far as concerns the existence of Possession, whether we say *animus possidendi*, or *sibi possidendi*, or *sibi habendi*. Most writers have devoted far too much space to these expressions, as if they were capable of explaining the notions themselves.

G

them is different. It cannot be alleged, therefore, as an objection to this division, that the Roman lawyers have no names for it; the notions themselves are, without doubt, to be found in the Roman Law (e).

I am now able to give a table of the different meanings of *possessio*, which deserve notice in a theory of Possession, (§. 7), and at the same time to indicate the occasions when they will come into use subsequently.

(e) Zachariæ denies derivative Possession altogether, De poss. p. 6—9, and seeks to give a different explanation to the cases in which I affirm it to exist; he explains the possession of a pledge-holder namely, by a *juris quasi possessio*, a sequestrator's by a *ficta possessio*, without the existence of any *animus domini*, and lastly, *precaria possessio* by a true *animus domini*, just as in any other revocable property. The first and third of these are so evidently erroneous, that they do not deserve the pains of being refuted at any length. The first, because the Roman jurists say so frequently of a creditor, "*possidet, possessionem habet*," &c. (See especially L. 35, § 1, *de pign. act.*), and at the same time guardedly observe of a Usufructuary " in *possessione est, non possidet*." The third; for what has the *precario rogans* to distinguish him from a hirer, for instance, so as to confer on the former the *animus domini* which the latter decidedly is not capable of having? Certainly not juridical possession! Yet this is the very matter which should have been first proved. Thus, the explanation of the second case is the only one worth attention. Now, we will assume that Zachariæ has explained all three cases in this way, *i. e.* that he has denied in all of them derivative Possession, and has asserted a *ficta possessio* without any *animus*. But this non-necessity for *animus* cannot be admitted so absolutely, for the party who has no notice of the act of prehension, or a lunatic or infant, &c., would still not be capable in these cases to acquire Possession. Thus we come back again to the *animus possidendi*, distinguished however from the *animus domini*. But this is exactly what I term derivative Possession. For I asserted in my first edition, p. 216, and more distinctly in this one, that such Possession is a departure from the original pure notion of Possession, that it is a fiction of law consequently, and therefore only valid when express law has made it so.

Possessio (in the non juridical sense).	Possessio civilis.	Possession of a subject capable of Usucaption, (not stolen, &c.,) with *bona fides*, and *justa causa* (*f*).	Possessio (ad interdicta).	Possessio (in the non juridical sense).
	Possessio naturalis.	All *derivative* Possession, which always occurs in case of a pledge or *emphyteusis*, but only occasionally with a *depositum* and *precarium*. (See Book 2). All *original* Possession, with detention and *animus*, but without *bona fides*, or without *justa causa*, or of stolen property, &c. (See Book 2).		
		Detention by one not *sui juris*, or of a *res extra commercium*. (See post in the present chapter). ———— by a madman, or child. (Bk. 2). ———— of a thing possessed by another. (§ 11). ———— by one who is merely commissioned to hold Possession for another. (Bk. 2). ———— by a tenant, borrower, fructuary, &c. (Bk. 2). ———— by a *missus in possessionem*, except when this occurs under a decree. (Bk. 2). ———— occasionally in cases of *depositum* and *precarium*. (Bk. 2).	Possessio naturalis (esse in possessione, tenere, corporaliter possidere, non possidere).	

(*f*) All these qualifications also apply to the owner himself who does not stand in need of Usucaption: now is his possession also *civilis?* It is, in the sense that it embraces all the terms necessary to constitute *possessio civilis*; it is not, in so far as no case can be imagined in which it would be for the interest of the owner to have a *civilis* possessio. Thus he has a *juridical* possession, *i. e.* a Possession for Interdicts in every possible case, and therefore his Possession is in no way inferior to that of a Usu-

It follows, directly, from the notion of Possession which has now been completely developed, that there are certain subjects not capable of being possessed, and certain individuals not capable of possessing: I will just allude to these cases slightly, as they are neither of them of any great practical interest, nor do they throw any additional light on the nature of Possession (*g*).

Nothing can be a subject-matter of Possession which is not in *commercio*, and which we know not to be so; for then the *animus domini* is not merely illegal, as it is indeed with respect to the goods of another, which, notwithstanding notice, we may nevertheless possess, but also the rights to Usucaption and Interdicts, which in other cases, are attached to Possession independent of property, fall to the ground. Therefore, firstly, no one amongst the Romans could possess a freeman, if it were known that he was free (*h*), on the other hand such Possession was allowed if the freeman was understood to be a slave (*i*). By mancipation, consequently, the Possession was necessarily lost (*j*).

captor. Zasius (in L. 3, § *ex pluribus de poss. p. m.* 105) and many civilians in his wake denominate an owner's possession possessio *causalis*, (like *ususfructus causalis*), and the expression is apt enough, if care be taken not to include in it the *jus possessionis* which is different from any other : practically, there is no difference.

(*g*) These cases belong to this place, and not to the acquisition of possession, where they are generally treated of, for it is not at all the same thing, to be unable to *acquire* possession, or to *have* possession. A lunatic is merely incapable of acquiring, but a slave is incapable of possession, and therefore Possession is lost when the possessor loses his freedom, but not if he only loses his reason.

(*h*) Item quæro si vinxeris liberum hominem, *ita ut eum possideam :* an omnia quæ is possidebat, ego possideam per illum? Respondit, si vinxeris hominem liberum, *eum te possidere non puto.*" L. 23, § 2, *de poss.*

(*i*) S. 4, I. *per quas personas ;* L. 1, § 6, *de poss.* The *malæ fidei* possessio, therefore, here spoken of relates to the case where another person's slave is believed to be possessed, not where it is known that the party is a freeman.

(*j*) L. 30, § 4, L. 38, *pr. de poss.*

Secondly, all *res publicæ* and *communes* are incapable of being possessed; it is impossible to gain Possession of such property, and the Possession becomes extinguished if any property acquires such character. Thus the Possession of land ceases, if it is permanently overflowed by the sea or a river (*k*).

Thirdly, Possession is impossible, if the subject is set a part as *res sacra* or *religiosa*, and this case is expressly likened to the Possession of a freeman: here also the question turns upon whether the party, who had the detention, was aware of the legal character of the property, not on whether he intended to respect it or not (*l*).

As the above subjects cannot be possessed, chiefly because they are not matters of property, so also such individuals are incapable of possessing as are incapable of holding property: property however is not to be understood here in the strict sense of the Roman Civil Law, (*i. e.* as *justum* dominium), for undoubtedly, a party might enjoy the right of Possession, although he had not the *jus civitatis*. To this class therefore belong all such persons as are considered in the civil law not *sui juris*, such as children under paternal control, and slaves.

1. No one under paternal control (filius familias) can be a possessor (*m*).

This proposition is founded clearly on the more general rule that the son cannot hold property generally, and therefore it does not apply to the *castrense peculium*, or to

(*k*) "Labeo et Nerva responderunt, desinere me possidere eum locum, quem flumen aut mare occupaverunt," L. 3, § 17, *de poss.*, and L. 30, § 3, *cod.*

(*l*) "Locum religiosum aut sacrum non possumus possidere, et si *contemnamus* religionem, et pro privato eum teneamus, *sicut* *hominem liberum*," L. 30, § 1, *de poss.*

(*m*) L. 49, § 1, L. 30, § 3, *de poss.*; L. 93, *de Reg. Jur.* If the father is in confinement, the possession of the son becomes *in pendenti*, L. 44, § 7, *de usurp.* which is quite conformable to analogy; but it seems rather peculiar that a *pater familias*, who believes himself to be a *filius familias*, should nevertheless be capable of possessing, L. 44, § 4, *de usurp.*

the *quasi castrense* (*n*). But as what prevailed here as an exception, afterwards grew up into a rule with respect to the newer *peculia,* every son became capable of possessing, and, even when the father, as usual, had the usufruct in the *peculium adventitium,* still the son was the true possessor, and the father possessed like every other *fructuarius* (Book 2), in the name of the son (*o*). In the *peculium profectitium,* indeed, the son continued to have neither property nor Possession: but, as the same may be affirmed of every manager of another's property, no personal incapacity for Possession can be said to exist in a *filius familias.*

2. Slaves in the same way are incapable of juridical Possession (*p*), which is a necessary consequence of their having no rights whatever. It is remarkable however, that even freemen, when held as slaves, are incapable of possessing (*q*). Property, however, might not only be preserved, but acquired also (*r*) in that *status,* and thus a remarkable difference is exhibited between the acquisition of property and Possession (*s*). The ground of this distinction consists in this, in order to *hold* property nothing is required, but the mere existence of juridical qualifications which may inhere in the person of an owner, although the party is ignorant of it, but to *exercise* acts of ownership as

(*n*) " Filius familias .. *in castris adquisitum* usucapiet," L. 4, § 1, de *usurp.*

(*o*) Glossa in L. 49, § 1, *de poss.* where this point is accurately taken.

(*p*) L. 49, § 1, L. 30, § 3, *de poss.*; L. 24, *cod.*

(*q*) " . . . . cum possideatur, possidere non videtur."

(*r*) Ulpianus in Fragm. tit. 19, § 21, § 4, 1 *per quas personas ;* L. 19, L. 23, § 2 ; L. 54, § 4, *de adquir. rer. dom.*

(*s*) For this reason we must not always conclude that, in cases

" ubi per possessionem dominium quæritur," possession exists when property is acquired, and therefore even here the acquisition of property and the acquisition of possession are only exactly similar in the form of the acquiring act ; see above, § 3, No. 1. Wenk, De Traditione, p. 21, has overlooked this obvious distinction between the personal competency of the acquirer and the form of acquisition, and has charged me with an inconsistency which in fact does not exist.

a right requires a condition in which freedom of action is possible. A freeman therefore held in slavery, as respects Property, is not distinguishable from any other freeman, nor, as respects Possession, from any other slave.

Captives taken in war stand in the same condition as regular slaves (*t*), and so also those who have lost their liberty by virtue of a juridical sentence, (for instance, by a *damnatio in metallum*). In personal *status*, both of these latter resembled slaves, although they had no masters. But these relations have nothing to do with our subject.

[Addendum to 6th edition.]   The doctrines put forth in this chapter, as to *animus domini* being the prescribed condition for Possession, and also as to derivative Possession, have latterly been objected to on various grounds. In order to explain myself more briefly and clearly thereupon, I will premise with a few observations, which are not so much intended for the defence of my own views, as to state with precision the actual questions and the exact point, where the difficulties lie.

In reference to the purpose which forms the groundwork of detention, the four following classes of persons may first of all be distinguished from one another.

1. The actual and the presumptive owner, the thief, and the party who has obtained the detention of land by an ouster.

2. He who grounds his detention on a *jus in re.* For brevity-sake, I will always use the term fructuary to represent this class.

3. He who has the detention by a relation founded on a contract, but still on his own account. A hirer may serve as the representative of this class.

(*t*) L. 19, *ex quib. causis maj.*; L. 23, § 1, *de poss.*; L. 15, *pr. de usurp.* Accordingly, in such cases, neither postliminium, nor the fictio legis Corneliæ availed. It shall be shewn in the second Book to what extent juridical representation might introduce any alteration in these cases.

4. He who merely manages the Possession as agent for another. We will call this one proctor.

The case is clear with the first class. For with them an actual *animus domini* occurs, and however much the *necessity* of this for Possession may have been disputed latterly, no one.has ever doubted of its *sufficiency* to this end; and the sources also expressly recognize Possession in these cases.

No more difficulty is raised by the fourth case. According to the sources no Possession is to be recognized, and indeed there is no necessity for it, as the proctor has no object of his own to defend, and therefore he possesses, according to the true meaning of the phrase, *alieno nomine*, i. e., for another's benefit. There remain therefore only the cases of the second and third class, which agree in this that the party exercising detention is carrying out his own ends.

Now, as to the Fructuary (2nd class), no doubt occurs in the law sources. The owner has the exclusive Possession of the subject, and therefore the Fructuary is only to be looked upon as a manager. On the other hand the Fructuary has a special *quasi-possessio* equally protected by Interdicts. The Interdicts of both parties are related to one another, like their *in rem actiones.*

The Interdictory remedy of the Fructuary is founded on a practical necessity. For it may happen that the Fructuary is not in a condition to call in aid the protection of the owner by contract, either because the *ususfructus* may have arisen out of a *longa possessio,* or because possibly the property may have passed into other hands, either by alienation or Usucaption, but still these contingencies can not diminish the right of the Fructuary. The Fructuary would now be wholly without protection against acts of violence, if special Interdicts were not allowed him. But, by such allowance, the practical want was provided for, and yet the principle is preserved inviolate " *duo in solidum possidere non possunt.*" The above principle, however, must not be considered as a mere arbitrary rule, which with blind necessity opposed itself to the wants of daily life. It is rather an expression of the correct view, that by allowing a joint Possession to several persons *in solidum*, the relations of Possession would be inextricably confused, and the practical security, which is solely contemplated by the protection of Possession, would only be disturbed thereby.

Lastly, with respect to the hirer (3rd class), the language of the sources is again quite clear. The lessor has always *possessio* and Interdicts; the lessee undoubtedly has them not; but is only to be considered as the manager of another's Possession. The case in practice is only to be distinguished from the preceding case, by the absence of *quasi-possessio*. Less ground exists then for withholding Possession from the lessor, than with the Fructuary. In the case of the lessee there is an absence of any independent legal relation, to which a *quasi-possessio* could be logically annexed. But above all, no practical necessity occurs here for any more technical arrangement, as the lessee has always got an action on his contract, by which he can call in aid the protection of the owner. But if the lessor loses the property by alienation or Usucaption, all *right* of the lessee in reference to the subject demised immediately ceases, and therefore no occasion arises to protect the Possession for him : he from thenceforward only has an action on his contract for damages against the lessor, and this is sufficient for every actual interest he possesses.

If the cases above described, which are not the subject of any controversy, are considered according to their mutual connection, there will be found to exist in them as much logical consistency as there is an accurate perception of the wants in practice. The whole explains itself easily and simply by the assumption of *animus domini*, and if such cases only as the above had occurred, there scarcely could have arisen any question upon the whole subject. The adoption also of *quasi-possessio* does not make the above assumption a whit more doubtful. In *quasi-possessio* the *animus domini* may be conceived naturally as the will of the possessor to exercise this *ususfructus* as *belonging to himself,* and therefore without recognizing any one as better entitled in reference to the *ususfructus.*

But we have four several cases, which do not conform to the rule hitherto developed: Perpetual leases, and mortgages in all cases, *Precarium* and sequestration occasionally (*u*). *Possessio,* according to the above rule ought not to go with the detention, but with the property; and again the detention in the two first cases should be protected by a *quasi-possessio,* but not in the two latter. It is not so however in point of fact; for the *possession* in these cases is always united to the detention, and the owner has no protection of Possession at all. On this ground I have always treated these cases as anomalies, and have distinguished them under the common term—derivative Possession. The anomaly however does not consist merely in the existence of Possession where the *animus domini* is wanting, but also and much more in the absence of Possession in that party where *animus* actually exists; namely, in him who knows that he is the undoubted owner, and who might just as well here retain his *Possession* by means of an agent, as he clearly does in the case of a lease (*v*). I selected the expression *derivative* (abgeleiteten) Possession, in order to mark

---

(*u*) I say *four* cases, although this also is contested; but the nature and complexity of the question, and the difficulties are not substantially altered by one case more or less. One of my opponents, for instance, would ascribe *possession* to the Superficiary (Schroeter, p. 244); another will not allow that the *Emphyteuta* and the *Sequestrator* have the same Possession, (Bartels, pp. 200, 205); a third will not even admit the sequestrator into the province of substantive law, but thrusts

him without further question into the law of procedure (Sintenis, p. 250).

(*v*) Upon this point my opponents appear to me to be quite inconsistent. For even those who hold that the *animus domini* is not necessary for *possessio,* still admit that it is sufficient to ground it, whenever it occurs. But here the *animus domini* is found without *possessio,* and yet the treatment of these cases is denied to be anomalous!

more strongly the wide departure from the regular relation, and it consists in this, that the *possessio* must be taken away from him, who regularly would have it (by his own will), and be ascribed to another. I called this a *transfer of* Possession, an expression which might be easily misunderstood, as if I meant by it a juridical succession, but against which misconception however I gave express warning from the second edition of my work downwards (*w*).

Now how are these departures from the rule as to the relation of Possession to be explained? Very simply as respects the pledge-creditor and sequestrator by attending to the practical object of these two legal institutes, both of which required that Interdicts should be forbidden to the owner. It was therefore quite natural to sacrifice rigorous logical precision to practical necessity, and we find this explanation to be wholly satisfactory. Not so with *Emphyteusis* and *Precarium*. The wider extent of right in *Emphyteusis* compared to those of the Fructuary, throw no light upon the matter, for what has the more or the less to do with the question, as the adoption of a *quasi-possessio* here also would have fully satisfied all demands? Still less has any internal ground in the case of *precarium* been yet discovered for a satisfactory explanation. I have attempted to give an historical explanation of both these legal institutes, and I think it will be found not unsatisfactory on internal evidence. Those however who reject this evidence, must, as I conceive, admit the fact of these two anomalies, and merely disclaim any explanation of them.

After these general observations, I turn myself to the history of the battle which has been lately waged on this small field, with so much vivacity.

First of all, Rosshirt (*x*) protested against the term

(*w*) Second edition, p. 111, in not.—In spite of this express warning the above misconception appears to have been regarded by

some as a part of my view.

(*x*) Rosshirt zu der Lehre vom Besitz, Archiv., B. 8, No. 1, 1825, p. 9—11.

derivative Possession. He conceives that these four cases
must be looked upon as abnormal, for which no generaliza-
tion can be made, and that therefore no technical term
should be employed. I do not contend with him, for he is
not one of my opponents. And as to the objection which
he makes to a term, that I continue to think well chosen
and appropriate, I will not waste a single word.

Others disagree essentially with my view, as they object
to the anomalous character ascribed to the above four cases,
and rather seek to bring them all within the rule.

Schroeter (y) accomplishes this by pointing out that he
agrees with me in holding that *animus domini* is always
necessary for Possession, but maintains that this *animus*
can be established also in the above four cases, nay, even in
a fifth, that of the Superficiary. This is made out with *emphyteusis* and *superficies* by an imposing enumeration of the
rights of the occupant, in comparison with the limited rights
of enjoyment of the Fructuary (p. 237—244—255). But
I must again ask what the more or the less has to do with
the question, and where is the limit? Besides, on what
ground then is all right of Possession denied to the owner,
whom even Shroeter admits to have the *animus domini?*
Lastly, why is not the logical and practically sufficient
relation of *quasi-possessio* employed in this case, as well as
in ususfructus? In the same way he affirms of the pledge-
creditor, that he possesses exactly as if he were owner
(p. 255) (z). But if one keeps out of view the wholly uncertain and casual moment of alienation, there is scarcely
any one to be found, who bears less resemblance to an
owner than the pledge-creditor, he who can neither make use
of the subject, nor acquire any title in its profits! Lastly,
he affirms, as to *precarium*, that the owner *permits* the
animus domini; as to sequestration, that the owner gives a

(y) Schroeter ueber den abge-   (z) This portion of Schroeter's
leiteten Besitz, Zeitschrift von   Essay is vigorously combatted by
Linde, B. 2, 1829, pp. 233—269.   Sintenis, p. 421.

commission, to entertain this *animus* (p. 263—269). In truth, however, this means nothing more than that the owner has transferred his right of Possession to another, and it is undoubtedly a very strained construction that the *permission* or *commission* should be made to turn on the will, and not on facts, on which alone it can be established.

However all the other writers agree in holding that H. Schroeter's reference of the four cases to an existing *animus domini* is wholly unsuccessful, they deny, therefore, the identity of the *animus possidendi* with the *animus domini*, and endeavour to define the former notion in more comprehensive terms so as to embrace in them the four cases in question.

This is effected by Warnkœnig (a) after a negative fashion, for he affirms that every one has the *animus possidendi*, who does not mean to possess *alieno nomine*. But so much ambiguity is contained in these expressions that a satisfactory exposition is wholly impossible. For if *alieno nomine* is referred to the *end*, it applies only to the Proctor, as even the lessee is seeking his own ends. If it is referred to the absence of a special right in the subject, then the Fructuary must possess *suo nomine*, and consequently have *possessio*. Nothing then remains, but to exclude by the *alieno nomine* those persons who recognize the superior right of another, which is the case undoubtedly with the Fructuary. But then again the four well known cases remain without *possessio*. To guard himself from this objection, the author maintained that in pledging, *precarium*, and sequestration, the owner intends to *give up* and *transfer* the Possession (p. 175—7). But this is exactly my view, and has nothing to do with the particular will of the occupant. But as to *emphyteusis* he asserts that the occupant has a more extensive freedom of action than a mere *colonus* (p. 178). But the same may undoubtedly be said of the Fructuary also! Warnkœnig himself appears to feel the insufficiency of this explanation,

(a) Warnkœnig ueber die richtige Begriffsbestimmung des   *animus possidendi*, Archiv. B. 13, 1830, pp. 169—180.

as he admits that the non-possession of the Fructuary is more difficult to explain than that of the *Colonus* (p. 180).

Guyet says, the *animus possidendi* consists in the intention of exerting any legal relation over the subject, which relation however, we are not to limit to property (*b*). By this view we may establish without further difficulty *possessio* in the cases of pledging and *emphyteusis*. The possession of the thief is explained on the view formed of juridical Possession, and consequently on a legal relation (Abh. p. 151. If this is not a circle, what is?) The legal relation however must be immediate, on which account the Emphyteutary possesses, but not the *Colonus* (p. 373, 380). It may be thought then that the legal relation consists in the *jus in re*, but no, for the Fructuary also has as little of an immediate relation as the lessee (p. 373), and with both, the ground of their non-possession lies in their knowledge, that their relation to the subject is not a legal one (p. 374). But as in fact a legal relation of the strictest character exists in respect to these persons, that, which is denied to them, can evidently only be a legal relation in reference to Possession. The whole doctrine of the author therefore, consists in this; every one has, or dispenses with, the *animus possidendi*, who either wishes to have or wishes not to have, a legal relation to Possession, or in other words, the *animus possidendi* is nothing else but the *animus possidendi*. Upon this indeed there is no question. The author, it is true, does not seem to trust much to his own discovery, for he lays down in one place as to the Fructuary, that he also *might* well have *possessio*, and if he has it not, it is only on account of the fleeting nature of his right; for that in principle the distinction between him and the Emphyteutary is only founded on an express decision (p. 375).

(*b*) Guyet ueber den animus possidendi, Abhandl. Heidelberg, 1829, p. 133; and Noch einige   Bemerkungen ueber den animus possidendi, Zeitschrift von Linde, B. 4, 1831.

Bartels affirms (c), that all turns upon the animus *rem sibi* habendi. The intention of the Fructuary is not to have the *rem*, but only *jus in re*, and merely a partial dominion over the subject (p. 181—200). On the other hand, a pledge extends to the entirety of the subject (p. 198), (but only in a most restricted sense, namely, only so as to enable a sale in the case of a wholly uncertain contingency). Much space and labour are bestowed in shewing why the *animus possidendi* may exist in *Precarium*, namely, because the actual nature of the relation excludes the *alieno nomine* (p. 179—196). On the other hand the author escapes much of the difficulty of the subject by denying *possessio* to the emphyteutary and sequestrator altogether, on grounds which no one will probably admit as convincing.

Sintenis lastly, returns in fact, though without expressly saying so, to Rosshirt's theory (d). Originally and proximately, he says, *animus domini* is the chief matter. But besides this there are some cases of true *possessio* where no *animus domini* can be recognized, but only *sibi habendi*. In these cases an object will always be found in the special interest of the possessor (p. 248—251). But the author appears to consider, like Rosshirt, that these cases are special anomalies, for otherwise it cannot be seen, why the Fructuary and the lessee should not also be treated in the same manner, as undoubtedly an object founded on their own interest, is not absent with these parties. In fact, he explains the nature of pledge-Possession, correctly, by the peculiar object and requirements of this particular transaction, and consequently as an anomaly founded on practical grounds (p. 414—418). And thus the whole of his strictures amount finally to a decided protest against the term derivative Possession (p. 225—251), which may be safely left to itself.

Thus in all these modern treatises, much labour is wasted without any result, without indeed any important end in

(c) Bartel's Zweifel gegen die Theorie vom abgeleiteten Besitz, Zeitschrift von Linde, B. 6, 1833, pp. 178—214.

(d) Sintenis Beytraege zu der Lehre vom juristischen Besitz, Zeitschrift von Linde, B. 7, 1834, pp. 223—414.

view.   In the midst of this controversy, Thibaut has come forward in my defence (*e*).   He conceives that some, from a love of uniformity and system, have endeavoured to establish an *animus domini,* where it does not exist; others again have made the *animus tenendi* more extensive, in order to be able to comprehend derivative *possessio,* by which in the end every sort of *animus,* even that of the *colonus* and lessee is comprised.

SECTION X.

WRITERS ON POSSESSION.

The notion of Possession itself having been now defined in all its different bearings, the historical question still remains as to the definition of it given by the later Jurists.

Their definitions of Possession generally, which occur in great number, and as to which much controversy has arisen, are wholly unimportant (*a*), the contest turning entirely on expressions, not in the Roman Law, but in the definitions themselves.

The matter in dispute with these civilians, as amongst the Roman lawyers also, is as to the distinction between *naturalis* and *civilis* possessio, and I will here give the most remarkable of their different opinions on the point.   A special refutation of any of them will rarely be necessary, because for the most part opinions only are to be met with, unaccompanied by any expository reasoning, and for a general criticism of mere opinions, the views which I have put forth above (§. 7) are sufficient.

The oldest opinion to be found in the writings of the

(*e*) Archiv. B. 18, p. 327.

(*a*) Three of the earliest definitions, namely one of Bassian and two different ones of Azo occur in the Gloss (*in* L. 1, *pr. de.*

poss.), in Azo himself; Summa in Cod. tit. de poss., num. 1 et 19; and in Othrofred (in L. 1, de poss. p. 52).

author himself is in Placentin, and it is more logical and
sensible than that of most of his successors (*b*). There is,
he says, only one juridical Possession, although it may have
different effects attached to it, at one time allowing of
Usucaption (*plena*), at another not (*semiplena*): its presence
is always required for Interdicts. He defines his notion by
terms, some of which point at matters of fact (detention),
some at matters of law (*animus*); and according as the first
only, or the second, or both together, occur, he uses the
terms, *naturalis, civilis, naturalis simul et civilis:* but mere
naturalis possessio is, in a juridical sense, no *possessio* at all,
and is even opposed to it, because in the Roman Law,
Possession is not recognized in mere detention without *animus:* it is otherwise with *civilis* possessio, as in many cases
Possession may be preserved *solo animo.* This is undoubtedly a well-grounded view of the subject, and the terminology is only in so far objectionable that it makes the
distinction between possessio *naturalis* and *civilis* turn on
the juridical or non-juridical (see §§. 5 and 9) material
definitions of the notion, and not on the consequences of
Possession (see §. 7). The application of the notion in
particular cases is less successful than the exposition of the
notion itself. Azo, on the whole, puts forth the same

(*b*) Placentini Summa in Cod.
tit. de poss. p. 332—3, ed. Mogant.
1536, f. "Possessio distinguiter
ita, alia *civilis tantum* alia *civilis
et naturalis.* . . . . . alia *proprie et
plane*, ut ea quæ proficie ad usucapionem, alia *improprie et semi-
plene.* Hæc quoque profecto *naturalis possessio* in jure nostro non
recte dicitur *absolute possessio, sed
est oppositio in adjecto.* Fieri enim
potest ut quis possideat et civiliter *et naturaliter*, et civiliter *solummodo.* Ut autem quis possideat
tantum naturaliter, legibus subtili-

ter inspectis, et ad vivum consi-
deratis (ut reor) esse non potest.
Nam et fur et prædo et invasor
et *naturaliter* possidet et *civiliter.*
Nam et colono interversori datur
interdictum unde vi *quod profecto
ei non competeret nisi. . . . possideret. Civiliter solummodo* quis
possidet, puta saltus quos nullus
alius detinet . . . Quippe possessio
nonnisi una est, licet diversis modis *habeatur* bonæ fidei, malæ
fidei, juste, injuste, *naturaliter, civiliter.*"

H

views (c), except that he does not recognize any Possession which could be *civilis* and *naturalis* at the same time, but only uses the word *civilis* where the existence of Possession is based on a mere fiction (*ubi solo animo retinetur possessio*) (d). It is also more apparent in Azo, that *L.* 10, *C. de poss.* was the origin of this opinion, as the antithesis which is contained in the passage (e) is confounded with another one between *actual* and mere juridical (fictitious) Possession, and this latter again with *civilis* and *naturalis* possessio. This view appears to have been long the prevailing one (f). Even in the works of Alciatus and Duarenus (g) it forms the basis, although in both of them it is

---

(c) Summa in Cod. tit. de poss. num. 4 et 15, fol. 134—5, ed. 1537, fol.; and Lectura in Cod. in L. 10, C. de poss. p. 569, ed. 1577, fol.

(d) The same view is to be found in an unprinted Gloss of Rogerius in L. 3, § 5 de poss. (in a manuscript of the Digest. Nov. at Metz) "Sicuti ergo duo juste vel injuste naturaliter possidere non possunt in solidum, ita non potest esse ut corporaliter in totum unus juste alter injuste possideat. *Ex civili autem id est ficta possessione* et juste duos et injuste utrumque et unum juste et alterum injuste in solidum possidere continget, velut in re pignorata aut in emphyteusim inve feodum data si vel ambo bona vel uterque mala alter vero bonâ fide possideat R."

(e) "Nemo ambigit, possessionis *duplicem esse rationem:* aliam quæ *jure consistit*" (i. e. possessio *civilis* which is a mere fiction of law) "aliam quæ *corpore*" (possessio *naturalis* founded on natural de-

tention). The correct explanation of this passage will be found in § 12.

(f) A. Faber de error. pragm. IV. 9; Menoch De retinenda poss., remed. 3, num. 18 et 22 § 99. In Menoch this exposition is assumed as it were rather tacitly than explained and developed, and this is the case also probably with the majority of the old writers on Practice there cited.

(g) Alciatus in L. 115, De V. S. (Opp. T. 2, p. m. 987) et in L. 1, pr. de poss. Opp. Tom. 1, p. m. 1197). Duarenus in Disp. anniv. lib. 1, cap. 18 (p. 1315, ed. Opp. 1584, f.) "Civiliter vero (possidet) qui quamvis rei non insistet, civilis *juris interpretatione*, eam tenere *ne possidere intelligitur*." Cf. Comm. 1, in tit. de poss. cap. 1 et 4 (ibid. p. 816-7-8), et Comm. 2, in tit. de poss. ad L. 1, pr. ib. p. 820). The L. 10, C. de poss. is here expressly quoted, and also Theophilus (in § 5, de Interdictis) whose words could not have been the foundation of this opinion, because he was neither read nor

not accurately distinguished from the other theory. (See above.) Merillius, who also adopts this exposition, adds a query to it, which shall be discussed hereafter (h). If the fiction on which the existence of Possession founded itself was so gross, that mere *civilis* possessio was thought insufficient to include it, most writers, following Baldus, termed it *civilissima* (i).

The other view of the matter appears to be quite as ancient as the one just given, and it expresses more correctly the meaning of the Roman lawyers, as it makes the whole difference between *possessio civilis* and *naturalis* to consist in the juridical effect of Possession, explaining *civilis* possessio, therefore, as the sort of Possession favoured (in some respects) by Roman law, and consequently preferred to *naturalis* possessio. This doctrine is to be found in Bassian (Joannes), who was a contemporary of Placentin and Azo, and the instructor (*dominus*) of the latter.

All the later Jurists coincide, as to this doctrine, with the Glossers by whom it was first developed; but it has given origin to three different sects, who must be here carefully distinguished. The first of them, (and the views of this party approach nearest to the truth), understand by possessio *civilis* that Possession only which comprises within itself all possible effects arising out of Possession, the Possession, therefore, of an owner as well as that of Usucaption. Possessio *naturalis*, on the other hand, they term that Possession to which something is wanting, for instance, where Interdicts are available but not Usucaption. Both are distinguishable from mere detention (*tenere, esse in possessione,* &c.), which is not a juridical entity.—We may first of all notice favourably of this exposition, that it gives the notion

known when it first arose. (See Ferrettus on this passage in L. 10, de poss. Opp. T. 1, p. 611). The same exposition is to be found in Davy d'Argente's Notarum Juris select. Liber, Paris, 1615, 4to., fol. 7.

(h) Merillius Observ. lib. 2, c. 31, 32; see *post*, ch. 12.

(i) Tiraquellus in Tract. *Le mort saisit lè vif*, P. 1, Declar. 7, num. 3.

of possessio *civilis* correctly enough on the whole (*j*); but its second and higher merit consists in its simple view of juridical Possession (§. 7, No. 3), which, as opposed to mere detention is equally well conceived and expressed; on this account, the treatises in which this exposition is adopted are safer to rely upon than any other. The single fault (for faults of application are not in question here) consists in the improper meaning it ascribes to possessio *naturalis*. The principal authors in this class are as follow :—

Joannes Bassianus.

Odofredus in L. 3, §. 5, de *poss.* fol. 56, in L. 12, pr. ed. fol. 58, et in L. pr. uti possidetis, fol. 101.

Cujacius in Observ. Lib. 9, c. 33, 1569.

Georg. Obrecht de Possessione, ch. 3. 5, p. 524, Disp. Collect. Ursell. 1603–4.

Scipio Gentilis de Donat. inter vir. et uxor. cap. 30. Opp. T. 4, p. 297.

Valentia in Illustr. Jur. Tract. L. 1, Tract. 2, c. 3.

Ramos in tit. Dig. de Poss. P. 1, §. 18, 19, ap. Meermann. T. 7, p. 82 (*k*).

Betes in tit. Dig. de Poss. P. 1, c. 2, ap. Meermann. T. 7. 458.

(*j*) Only on the whole, however, for it is not altogether accurate. For instance, possessio civilis is constantly referred to *justa causa* alone in Usucaption, and the term consequently is used in cases where on other grounds such as *mala fides* Usucaption could not arise. Bartolus in L. 1, *de poss.* num. 8. This want of precision was the necessary consequence of omitting to deduce the meaning of *Possessio civilis* from the general use of the term.

(*k*) Although in the passage cited he adopts this view as his own, he nevertheless at § 21, 22, in some degree abandons it, where he lays down that the contradictions in the law sources and commentators are to be reconciled by conceiving a second sort of Possession besides this *possessio naturalis,* namely mere *detention,* and this undoubtedly is the right view. But he subsequently confuses and obscures this view by adding that there is a third sort also (different therefore from the second) namely *quatenus ei corpore insistitur* distinguishable from the *possessio quæ animo retinetur.* He then brings himself back to the view adopted by Placentin and Azo.

Pothier Pandectæ Inst. Lib. 41, Tit. 2, p. 121, and
Traité de la Possession, c. 1, art. 2, p. 8. 17.
We only gather Bassian's opinion from the incorrect and
meagre extracts in Accursius, where all sorts of doubtful
opinions are mixed up in the greatest confusion, although
he himself prefers Bassian's to the others; but the passages
in which the opinion occurs are sufficiently clear to give us
a very good idea of it (*l*). Possessio *civilis* is ascribed only
to the actual owner, and to him who has Usucaption; the
emphytenta, the *fructuarius*, the *vassal*, have *possessio naturalis*, and so also the *prædo*, who, without any title, is in
occupation of the Possession belonging to another; a tenant,
&c. has no Possession at all, but mere detention. Hence
we may understand the controversy which Bassian carried
on with Placentin and Azo (*m*), as to whether possessio
civilis and *naturalis* were different kinds of Possession, or
whether there was but one Possession only, the first being
asserted by Bassian, the latter by Placentin and Azo, who,
unlike their opponent, did not make the whole distinction
to rest upon different *rights of Possession*. The subsequent
history of Bassian's doctrine is remarkable. First of all,
Bartolus introduced an almost imperceptible modification
into it, but which led, in fact, to a most erroneous result (*n*).

(*l*) Glossa in L. 1, § 3, *de poss.*
"non ergo omnis detentatio est
possessio, sed triplex est: nam
alia *civilis* alia *naturalis in quarum utraque quærenda duo exigun-
tur*," (namely, *factum* and *animus*,
these therefore only avail as juridical Possession), "alia *detentatio; ut hic : qualem etiam habet
colonus*," Glossa in L. 3, § 5, *de
poss.* This passage contains all
the different applications of the
term, which are mentioned in the
work, and it is quoted expressly
as the opinion of Bassian.
(*m*) Glossa in L. 1, *de poss.* . . .

"non duæ sunt (possessiones)
sed *una* secundum Placentinum
et Azorem. At Johannes et alii
dicunt *duas* esse . . . quod est tu-
tius." Azo in lecturâ in L. 10, C.
de poss. "Et est hoc notandum,
quod quidam dicunt et *dominus
meus dixit* quandoque, quod *di-
versæ sunt possessiones* sc. civilis et
naturalis, *sed contra est.*" Odofred, in L. 1, *de poss.* f. 52, et in
L. 4, C. *de eod.* f. 105, 106.
(*n*) Bartolus in Digestum Novum, L. 1, pr. de poss. num. 7—
13. That he intends to lay down
something new appears, not only

He thought it probably unreasonable that a mere *prædo*
should have the same possessio (*naturalis*) as a vassal or
other party with good title, and therefore he assumed a
third true Possession also (different from mere detention),
and exclusive of *possessio civilis* and *naturalis*, which he
termed *corporalis*, and ascribed to the *prædo* only. He
then referred *possessio civilis* to ownership, on the *justa
adquisitionis causa* of which Possession is founded, *possessio naturalis* in the same manner to *jura in re*, and
distinguished from both the *possessio corporalis*, i. e., the
Possession to which all title is wanting. But as he makes
this division depend on the existence and quality of a right,
which lies at the bottom of all Possession, the appropriate
point of view for Possession itself is further removed in this
than in every other doctrine. Cujas, who, in his earlier
writings, laid down the more correct view of Bassian, in
clearer terms, perhaps, than any other writer, subsequently
adopted the exposition of Bartolus, but with an addition, which magnified the original error in it beyond all
bounds (*o*). He held, namely, what Bartolus had never
asserted, that possessio *corporalis* is not recognized in Roman
Law as a juridical relation, as the foundation of rights. But,

from the elaborate exposition of
his views, but also from the mode
in which he calls attention to
them. "Adverte ergo ad me.
Mihi videtur, quod antiqui et
moderni DD. multum deviarunt
a mente juris in hac materia."
(*o*) Cujacii Observatio, L. 27,
C. 7 (1585). Ejus Notæ Poste-
riores in Inst. § 4, *per quas personas* (1585). "Est *civilis* possessio, est *naturalis*, est *corporalis:*
civilis, naturalis, *justa* est: corporalis *injusta:* hanc pupillus sine
tutore amittit, non civilem, non
naturalem." Ej. Recitationes in
L. 1, *pr. de poss.* (1588), Opp. ed.
Neap. 1722, T. 8, p. 239, "Civilis

est, qua jure vel animo *domini*
possidetur....... Naturalis tantum ea est, quæ *alio jure* appre-
hensa est, *quam dominii*, veluti jure
pignoris, vel jure ususfructus.
Eam quæ *nullo jure* impudenter a
prædone *nullum jus, nullum titulum
adfingente* et prætextente sibi,
possidetur, *jus non novit, non
spectat.* Plerumque prædo omnis
et pervasor alienæ possessionis
sibi fingit titulum aliquem......
At si quis sit, qui nullum sibi
titulum adfingat, *ejus possessionem
non spectat.*" Ej. Scholi as. Comment. in Institutiones, § 4, *per
quas pers.* in Opp. T. 8, p. 960.

however, as it could not be denied that even the *prædo*
might have Interdicts, Cujas explains this by suggesting,
that an illegal Possession of that sort usually had some *pretended* lawful ground for Possession ; and that it was not the
Possession itself, but the pretended title which formed the
ground for Interdicts, without which pretext they would not
have been allowed.   It is scarcely possible to find any view
of Possession less conformable to the Roman Law than this.

The second sect makes the whole distinction much more
simple than the first party.   Possessio *civilis*, which is also
termed *possessio* simply, and which admits of Usucaption, is
by these writers opposed to nothing but possessio *naturalis*
(esse in possessione, *non possidere*), which consequently embraces all other cases, without distinguishing whether they
contain a true *possessio*, i. e., the right to Interdicts, or not.—
Thus, here also, possessio *civilis* is rightly explained, but it
is a most important error to confound *possessio ad interdicta* with mere detention, and for this reason, a correct
notion of juridical *possessio* (§. 7, No. 3.) is altogether
wanting in these writers.   The most important of these
writers are :—

Ferrettus in L. 1, pr. de poss. No. 11, 12. (Opp.
T. 1, p. 519, 520), et in L. 12 de poss. No. 31, 32.
(Ibid. p. 611).

Brissonius de Verb. Sign. v. *civilis*, No. 3, v. *possessio*, No. 3, 4, v. *justus*.

Muretus in Epistolis, Lib. 3, ep. 81. (Opp. ed. Ruhnkin.
vol. i. p. 643).

Galvanus de Usufructu, cap. 33, § 10. 12.

In this work, the deficiencies in the Roman Law-language,
which are assumed to exist in this Exposition, are filled up
by newly invented distinctions.

Vinnius in Select. Quæst. L. 2, c. 36.

This is the best exposition of the views of this party.

Domat, Lois Civiles, P. 1, L. 3, Tit. 7, préambule.

Westphal, Die Arten von Sachen, &c. Th. 2, c. 2,
§ 52—64.

Hofacker, in Princ. Jur. Rom. Rom. T. 2, § 759, 760. He explains that he has principally followed Galvanus. Malblanc, Princ. Jur. Rom. p. 1, § 192.

The third party still remains; these writers understood by possessio *civilis* all juridical Possession whatever, whether it gave rise to Usucaption or to Interdicts only; and to this juridical Possession they only oppose mere detention (possessio *naturalis, esse in possessione, non possidere*). The intrinsic error in this view consists in the wholly incorrect meaning ascribed to possessio *civilis,* from which it necessarily follows, that the simple idea of juridical Possession, on which, generally, every thing turns (*supra, §. 7*), and on the assumption of which the opinion itself is founded, is unavoidably lost sight of. For there is no point more clearly established by the Roman Jurists, than that in certain cases (such as donations between man and wife) no possessio *civilis* can be recognized; and, therefore, these cases must be altogether excluded from juridical Possession, whereby this doctrine becomes more faulty, as a rule of construction, than any other. At the same time, it is clear that of the three modifications of the notion here developed, according to which juridical consequences denote possessio *civilis,* none can pass so easily, as this latter, into the ancient exposition according to which possessio *civilis* denotes Possession by fiction of law (p. 98). For it only requires the addition of the following simple proposition, (which, however, is just as false as it is important in practice), where possessio *civilis* is impossible, the juridical fiction of Possession is also impossible ! For this reason, the two expositions are usually confounded by earlier writers (p. 99), and, indeed, with many of these authors it is often quite arbitrary as to which of the two sects they are to be assigned. The following are the chief authors of the party :—

> Martinus Gosia, whose views are contained in an anonymous manuscript Gloss to the title in the Code *de poss.* MS. Paris, 4517. " Duplex ratio possessionis est secundum M., alia pro suo, quæ civilis est,

alia pro non suo, quæ naturalis. Pro suo civilis juris est, quæ animo et corpore acquisitur, quandoque suo, quandoque alieno, ut in re peculiari et per quemlibet alienum. Retinetur autem quandoque animo solo, quandoque animo et corpore suo aut alieno. Quæcumque corpore retinetur alieno, pro non suo est quantum ad eum qui detinet, quæ dicitur naturalis et est facti ut colonaria."

Zasius in L. 3, § 5, de poss. Opp. ed. Frank. 1590, T. 3, p. 111.

Vaconius a Vacuna in Declarat. L. 2, declar. 68–71, fol. 63–68, ed. Rom. 1556, 4to. He compares possessio *civilis* to the imagination, and possessio *naturalis* to the senses, and works out this metaphor with great industry.

Corasius in *tit. de poss.* Opp. ed. Forster, Viteb. 1603, fol. T. 1, p. 921, 929.

Contius in Disput. Lib. 1, cap. 9.

Charondas in Verisim. Lib. 1, 4, 6, in Otto. B. 1, p. 699.

Friderus Mindanus, De Materiâ Possessionis, c. 1, No. 16, 20.

Turaminus de Subst. Poss. c. 8, Opp. p. 289, 299.

Oroz de Apicibus Juris Civ. L. 4, c. 2, § 8, 9.

Cuperus de Nat. Possessionis, P. 1, c. 3, 4, p. 24, 48.

Fleck in tit. Pand. de poss. p. 9, 15.

Thibaut, Über Besitz, § 11 (*p*).

It appears clearly from this review, that Cuper's opinion is anything but new, although he himself appears to consider it so; he has, undoubtedly, put forth a more complete and abler defence of it, than had ever been applied to this or any other single doctrine before his time, and by this *exhaustion* of *one* possible ground of error, he has earned for himself great credit. His excellent commentary on L. 10, C. *de*

(*p*) He has given up this doctrine in the Appendix to his addition of Cuperus. But in his Civil. Abhandlungen, pp. 339, 340, he appears to incline again to his former views.

Poss. is more valuable still, for it has completely cut away the ground for any other false doctrine. (See *supra*, p. 98). His elaborate arguments, as well as the unqualified approbation they have met with, make it necessary that I should add a few observations to the general contradiction to his theory, which is contained among the proofs of my own opinion. In order to express the opposition between possessio *civilis* and *naturalis*, Cuper lays down a line which is conclusive as to the result of his whole inquiry; he starts from the notion of possessio *naturalis* (i. e., from a negative idea), and states that it means *non-juridical* Possession, and then defines possessio *civilis* to be logically opposed to possessio *naturalis*, and, consequently, to be juridical Possession simply. It is thus very obvious how it was that the characteristic of possessio *civilis*, namely, its relation to *jus civile*, escaped him, and it is only remarkable, how a writer with such profound knowledge of Roman Law, should never once have recollected, in reference to this subject, the special meaning which *jus civile* bears in the Roman Law. It may be easily conceived, that he gives no direct proofs of his explanation of possessio *civilis;* he merely quotes, as if in allusion to a well-known matter, two other employments of the term (*cognatio* civiles, and *bonorum* appellatio civilis), both of which are sufficient of themselves to refute his theory. His exposition, being thus based on a false ground, was naturally incapable of being made to coincide with the Roman law, even in the clearest cases. Assuming, for instance, that possessio *civilis*, in point of fact, denotes juridical Possession, the meaning of that must be, that possessio *civilis* has juridical consequences, which the *naturalis* has not. Now, what are these consequences according to Cuper? not only Usucaption, but, amongst others, Interdicts also; but as express mention happens to be made in the Digest, of one Interdict which is valid without possessio *civilis* (*q*), it follows that only certain Interdicts belong to juridical Possession, and the definition must be expressed thus—

(*q*) L. 1, § 9, *de vi.*

Possession is called juridical (*civilis*), when it is followed either by Usucaption, or, at least, by the Interdicts *uti possidetis* and *utrubi;* non-juridical (*naturalis*) when it has not all those consequences, although it may have others, such as the Interdict *unde vi.* The unsoundness of this mechanical distinction between the different kinds of Interdicts will appear more clearly *post,* where Interdicts themselves are treated of; but as it is impossible to understand why the interdictum *de vi* should be less juridical than the other Interdicts, it is quite apparent, even here, what an arbitrary, illogical classification is ascribed to the Roman Jurists by this explanation; indeed, it would be difficult to understand how, notwithstanding this, Cuper could have ascribed such high praise to Roman Jurisprudence, if one did not recollect that such encomiums always form a part of every elaborate treatise on the Civil Law. Lastly, it has been already remarked, that the interpretation of several decisive passages in the Roman Law, must wholly fail according to this exposition (§. 7, No. 1), so that Cuper, whose talent for interpretation is by no means to be denied, felt himself driven to assert that Paulus must have contradicted himself (*r*), whereas, according to the whole of my exposition, it is impossible to imagine that any contradiction could have arisen, the terms he employed being so simple, and never having given rise to a single controversy between any of the different schools.

As therefore not one of all the above expositions has succeeded in securing general reception, many writers have conceived they should arrive at the truth best by adopting them all (*s*). In this way alone could it be insured that the

(*r*) Namely, in L. 1, § 4, *de poss.*, and L. 26, *pr. de don. inter vir et ux.*

(*s*) This is the case with the following writers amongst others, though certainly in very different ways : Fachinei Controvers. ; Merendæ Controvers. ; Thomasii

Notæ in Digestum. ; Oppenritter Summa Possessionis ; Glück's Commentar über die Pandekten ; Spangenburg vom Besitz. But, above all, with Zachariæ, Besitz, und Verjährung. A trace of this sort of exposition is to be found even in the Glossers on L. 38, §

reader would not altogether reject the view; and in order not to let it appear that contradictory opinions are quietly mixed up together, they are connected with one another by all sorts of names (*t*), and it is then tacitly assumed that such is the doctrine of the Roman Jurists also.

I have omitted to mention in this general review the only writer who has steered clear of the usual mistakes. I mean Donellus, in whom none of these errors of terminology are to be found, and therefore he cannot be reckoned properly as of either party. But as he only treats of Possession generally in the system of the whole Roman law, it did not consist with his plan to defend his use of terms, or to support his view controversially on distinct grounds, whereby alone it would have been possible to quote him as a clear authority and safe from all misunderstanding; and as moreover his clearly expressed view of Possession in relation to the whole system has never been made use of, it is the less surprising that no notice whatever should have been taken of the terminology he has employed.

[Add to 6th ed.] Since the appearance of my fifth edition, the last of the opinions here combatted (that of Cuperus) has been defended with great zeal, and the course of proceedings has been as follows. For many years past it had been rumoured that Professor Erb at Heidelberg had discovered an entirely new explanation of *civilis possessio*, by which mine was entirely refuted. Portions of this discovery came to light in several works, but still the whole of it was not to be gathered from any of them. Thibaut has mentioned it several times, but in his Work on the Pandects, (Lehrbuch der Pandekten) he still, in the seventh edition, adhered to my views. In his lectures however, he gave in to the new

7, de verb. oblig. (MSS. Paris, num. 4487, a.) "...... Civiliter possidere dicitur multis modis: dicitur enim possidere quis civiliter, id est, animo: dicitur possidere civiliter id est juste, dicitur etiam possidere civiliter, id est de jure civili, et hoc ad personas refertur ut hic....."

(*t*) For instance, the broadest, broader, narrower, narrowest, meaning *a forma* and *a modo*, &c., &c.

doctrine, and when these lectures were published, the more complete view of it was no longer withheld from the public. In the eighth edition of his Pandekten, the new doctrine filled the place of the earlier one, and finally was brought forward and maintained by him in a separate essay.

But in the mean time, whilst only fragments of the new discovery were made known, my exposition found a defender, whose learned and careful treatise won praise even from our common distinguished opponent.

The new exposition is as follows. *Civilis possessio* means no more than *possessio* simply, or juridical Possession, namely that relation to a subject, which gives a claim to Interdicts. The origin of the name *civilis* is to be found in the fact that Interdicts are also civil or positive institutes, and therefore belong to the *jus civile*. Nevertheless we must not suppose that all Interdicts absolutely require civil Possession; this is only true of *int. retinendæ possessionis:* for the Int. de vi is also available in the case of mere natural Possession. We must therefore resort to definitions, and hold that "*possessores* in the narrower sense are those occupants of a subject who may maintain ALL *remedia possessoria:* by which through the aid of an exception a door is left open to natural possessors," (p. 362).

My view with its foundation on passages from the sources is stated in the 7th section. Some portion of it is there placed in the notes, and other parts may be found in the more detailed essay of Thon. I can add nothing more here, for as to the correct exposition of the passages in question, the decision between me and my opponents must be left wholly to our readers. A few general remarks only may be here permitted to me.

First, it is not easily comprehensible to me, how this exposition of Erb's should pass for a new discovery, for it agrees in all essentials so completely with the view of Cuperus, that all which I have urged against the latter for the last thirty-three years in the present chapter, may be

used word for word in refutation of the new exposition
also.

Next, Thibaut does not term Interdict-Possession *civilis
possessio* merely casually, but on the ground that Interdicts
belong to civil or positive rights (p. 331). But is the Int.
de vi in any degree less positive and civil than the *Uti possidetis?* And yet the former is said to lie without *civilis
possessio.* Whoever can get over this glaring inconsistency
by the remark, that rules may have an exception, shall not
have me as an opponent.

The most important point however, here also as it was
with Cuperus, is not so much the incorrect use of terminology,
as the practical proposition inseparably bound up with it,
that the hirer or lessee may have the Int. *de vi.* To establish
this latter point a general principle is laid down (p. 361,
362) but which however, on the following much more conclusive grounds we can satisfactorily refute. The Int. *uti possidetis* (it is said) only relates to simple disturbances, which
generally affect the interest of the lessee only, without in-
juring the landlord, who therefore need not trouble himself
about the matter; on the other hand actual ouster is of so
much consequence, and puts the landlord also in so much
danger for his future vindication, that he will not fail to
protect both himself and his lessee by the Interdict. Therefore the Int. *uti possidetis* must be allowed to the lessee,
the Int. *de vi* he does not require, because this will not fail
to be employed by the landlord. But this general reasoning
avails nothing, when we have positive authorities on the
very point. In reference to this, I will bring together the
following passages:

    L. 9, *de rei vindicatione :*—apud quem deposita est, vel
      commodatæ, vel qui conduxerit—hi omnes *non possident.*

    L. 3, § 8, *uti poss.:* creditores missos—interdicto uti
      possidetis uti non posse, et merito, *quia non possident.*

    L. 6, § 2, *de prec :* colonus et inquilinus sunt in prædio :
      et tamen *non possident.*

L. 1, § 9, *de vi.* Dejicitur is *qui possidet.*

L. 1, § 23, *de vi :* Interdictum autem hoc nulli competit, nisi ei, qui tunc, cum dejiceretur, *possidebat :* nec alius deici visus est, quam *qui possidet.*

These five passages are from the same author, Ulpian. Now is it well conceivable that the same writer, who denies to the *creditor missus,* to the lessee, and to the renter, &c. *possessio,* and therefore also the Int. *uti possidetis,* that the same writer, I say, who expressly founds the Int. *de vi* on the condition of *possidere,* should nevertheless be willing to allow the Int. *de vi* to the above mentioned persons, *qui non possident?* Ulpian himself in another passage compares the Int. *retinendæ possessionis* with the Int. *de vi,* and states the only distinction to be that the former are to preserve a disturbed possession, the latter to reinstate one that has been lost (L. 1, § 4, *uti poss.*). It is scarcely possible to read these passages dispassionately, and conclude that Ulpian should have conceived to himself any other sort of *possessio* for the Int. *uti possidetis,* than that of the Int. *de vi.*

Thon (p. 140) has already pointed out the due weight belonging to L. 1, Cod. *si per vim.* Thibaut (p. 363), explains the *colonus* there as one to whom the landlord has granted a cottage and garden, and with it has given him at the same time, the charge of the whole estate. Whether such an interpretation can be admitted, I must again leave to the judgment of the reader.

At the period, when the here described new discovery was making its appearance here and there in uncertain forms, the same main idea, though with slight modifications, was brought forward in the following essay, *Wiederhold des Interdictum uti possidetis und die Novi operis Nunciatio, Hanau,* 1831. According to him, *civilis possessio* means Possession with *animus domini,* which is only conceivable on a *justa causa* (even though without *bona fides*). *Naturalis possessio* is Possession with *animus possidendi* without *justa causa,* and so without *animus domini ;* and here come in the pledge-creditor and *dejector.* Distinguishable from both is bare detention in another person's name, without *animus possidendi*, as in the case of a renter. *Civilis possessio* gives a title to all Interdicts, and the plaintiff must prove his *justa causa*. *Naturalis possessio* entitles to the Int. *de vi*, but not to *uti possidetis*, detention has no Interdicts at all (p. 5—14). Civil Possession exists in *precarium* and sequestration, but, as anomalous cases, the pledge-creditor has natural Possession, and the emphyteutory no Possession at all (p. 20—26). The ground of distinction between the conditions for the two chief Interdicts is said to be, that the Int. *uti possidetis* is intended only to serve as a means of fixing the positions in a suit of two claimants to property, and not at all to prevent violence (p. 85). It is impossible to calculate how wide a departure may be made from the truth, when an incorrect principle is assumed without careful examination as the foundation, and a fabric is thereupon erected, without stopping to examine critically, at each step of the proceeding, the results arrived at.

SECTION XI.

POSSESSIO PLURIUM IN SOLIDUM.

The examination of the notion of Possession appears now to be complete. The whole question turns upon two points, what is the juridical meaning of Possession in the Roman Law (§§. 2—8), and what are the material elements of the notion, *i. e.*, under what conditions is the existence of Possession to be recognized? (§. 9).

The whole of the following theory of Possession is inseparably connected with this notion, for whenever Possession is either acquired or lost, an application of this notion, or a modification of it, may be discovered. In these applications, however, in which the notion of Possession itself appears, a rule is to be found of such general extent as to influence every portion of the theory, and it cannot be explained in any other place than this.

The rule is this : *all possession is exclusive, plures eandem rem in solidum possidere non possunt.* The meaning as well as the correctness of the rule shall be here examined, and the inquiry will furnish an opportunity at the same time of making the results we have arrived at in terminology more clear by examples, than was possible by abstract propositions.

The question then is as to the possession of the *same* thing *in solidum.* Where any thing is possessed in *common* by several persons (the *compossessio* of modern Jurists), so that the possession of each mutually infringes upon that of the others, it is only in appearance that the same thing is the subject of their possession, for each possesses a part only, and not the remaining parts; and it makes no difference, juridically considered, that there is not a real but only an imaginary separation of these parts from one another. Each, therefore, possesses one part for himself, and the different parties stand to one another nearly in the same relation as the possessors of two adjoining houses. Accordingly, neither the word *compossessio,* nor the notion occur in the Roman Jurists, and the term merely expresses how far an individual is capable of possessing an undivided part of a thing, for that by itself connotes the possibility of other possessors of the remaining parts ; but the relation between these co-possessors has nothing peculiar about it.

The discussion of this point has become complicated, by the fact of different opinions having prevailed upon it amongst the Roman Jurists themselves. Some denied altogether the possibility of any such joint Possession; others would only admit, as an exception, that the *justa* possessio of one person was not excluded by the *injusta* possessio of others, &c. These various limitations of the second view of the case have no interest for us; it is instructive, however, to consider them as opposed to the first, and the question then assumes this form; is a *possessio* of the same thing by several persons possible? Should the question be answered in the affirmative, it would be then time to lay down the conditions of this possibility.

The question, as conceived in these general terms, makes *possessio* the object of it. But this word means two different kinds of Possession; first of all, the physical relation of detention; second, juridical Possession, *i. e.*, the groundwork of Usucaption and Interdicts (§. 7, No. 5), which then of the two meanings is intended in the above use of the term? The rule formerly laid down easily solves this difficulty. For as this question has been made a subject of inquiry by Roman Jurists, it could only have been the juridical notion which was under discussion, as physical detention could neither have been a subject for any juridical definition, nor require, from any legal effects flowing from it, that its existence should be defined juridically.

Possessio, therefore, is used above in its simple juridical sense, having reference to Usucaption and Interdicts (§. 7, No. 3), and by this preliminary statement of the question, the greater part of the erroneous answers which have been hitherto given to it are shown to be incorrect. Some, for instance, assert, that although it is true only one party may enjoy the *same* identical result of Possession, still it is conceivable, that there may be a Possession of several persons as to its different results: but there are, in fact, only two results of Possession, and they stand in such relation to one another, that it is always one and the same Possession which gives rise to both. Others have admitted *civilis* possessio on the one side, *naturalis* possessio on the other, and only exclude the *naturalis* possessio plurium in solidum; but this also is impossible, for the *naturalis possessio*, which may co-exist with *civilis possessio* in another, is either by itself a juridical Possession (and, therefore, here, where the question turns on *possessio* simply, is undistinguishable from *civilis possessio*), or it is mere detention, and therefore not a subject-matter for juridical inquiry.

If, then, it should be assumed that several persons may have the same Possession at the same time, it is clear that this is only possible by a fiction of law. For, according to the original idea of natural Possession (§. 1), the physical exclusive power over the subject was supposed; of this sort is the possession of a piece of gold which one holds in the hand, and which, it is clear, can only be conceived of one person at a time. But Possession avails as a right, and on this account is often assumed as a fiction when the original notion cannot find a place (§. 5): thus the possession of a house is looked upon as continuing, even when the inhabitant goes out, without having made it secure in any way.

In the same manner, the contemporaneous possession of several persons must be grounded on a similar fiction; for otherwise the original notion of Possession excludes its possibility, and, therefore, the question now under discussion must be put thus: is there any fiction of law by which more persons than one may be looked upon as contemporaneous possessors of the same thing?

The Roman Jurists, on this point, were divided into two parties. The one (Labeo and Paulus) denied altogether the possibility of such Possession; their opinion is not only approved of by the compilers of the Pandects, but may be acted on throughout in practice.

The second party (Trebatius, Sabinus, and Julian) recognized such Possession, still, however, in so far only as to allow of one person having *justa* possessio, and the others *injusta*; two *injustæ possessiones* could not exist any more than two justæ possessiones, one single case excepted, which stands in connection with one case of *injusta* possessio. The above distinction refers to the *vitia* possessionis (§. 2—8), and it is, therefore, only in the three following instances that the difference between these two doctrines is to be discovered; 1st. when possession of a thing is obtained *by force*, in which case the justa possessio of the former possessor must be held to co-exist subordinately to the injusta possessio. 2nd. In like manner, when a Possession which

I 2

another had previously enjoyed is occupied secretly. 3rd. When Possession is obtained by a *precarium.* In order that this last case may be understood, it is necessary to intercalate a few remarks on a subject which can only be fully developed when Interdicts are treated of. *Precarium* denotes the relation in which, without any legal formalities, the exercise of a right is permitted to another. The most frequent instance of this is the dealing with property, that is, physical Possession; because such Possession is the natural mode of dealing with property. But this *precaria possessio* may have place in two ways, either as simple detention, or as juridical Possession, is delivered over to another (*a*). In the former case no Possession passes at first, but it is subsequently acquired, when a refusal to return the article has been made; such possessio is, without doubt, *injusta,* and thereupon arises the *interdictum de precario* as an interdictum *recuperandæ* possessionis. In the second case Possession passes at once, but this *justa* possessio becomes *injusta* by refusal to make return, and thus the relation becomes similar to that in the former case. Therefore a *precarium* may found, first, an *injusta* possessio, and then exactly the same question arises as with possessio *violenta* and *clandestina;* secondly, a *justa* possessio, and this is the only case in which, according to many Jurists, two justæ possessiones can co-exist.

We will, therefore, proceed, first, to the rule generally, and then to the three cases of its application.

The decisive passage as to the rule itself is from Paulus (*b*).

" Plures eandem rem in solidum possidere non possunt, *contra naturam quippe est,* ut cum ego aliquid *teneam,* tu quoque id *tenere videaris.* Sabinus tamen scribet, eum, qui precario dederit, et *ipsum* possidere, et eum, *qui precario acceperit.* Idem Trebatius probabat, existimans, posse *alium*

(*a*) " . . . . Precario autem rogavit, *non ut possideret,* sed *ut in possessione esset,*" L. 10, § 1, de poss.

(*b*) L. 3, § 5, de poss. (Paulus, lib. 5, ad edictum).

juste alium injuste possidere: duos injuste, vel duos juste non posse (*c*): quem Labeo reprehendit quoniam in summâ possessionis non multum interest, juste quis an injuste possideat, *quod est verius:* non magis enim eadem possessio apud duos esse potest, quam ut tu *stare videaris* in eo loco in quo ego sto, vel in quo ego *sedeo*, tu *sedere videaris*."

This passage is divisible into the following propositions:—

1. Paulus's own opinion, which is here adopted by Justinian, is to be found at the commencement of the passage, and is repeated at the end; a joint Possession, says Paulus, by several persons is impossible, because all Possession is founded either on actual detention (tenere), or on detention by fiction of law (tenere videri); but no fiction can be assumed, where the thing imagined is in itself impossible, and as it is impossible that several persons should have actual detention of the same thing, no fiction of law can get over this impossibility.

2. Sabinus makes *precarium* an exception to this rule; in this case both parties are capable of having juridical Possession, without any distinction in fact, whether the possessio *precaria* be a *justa* or an *injusta* possessio.

3. Trebatius approves of this doctrine, but with the modification that it must be an *injusta* possessio precaria, in

(*c*) To this part of our passage may be referred L. 19, pr. de precario, (Julianus, lib. 49, Dig.) "Duo in solidum *precario habere* non magis possunt, quam duo in solidum *vi possidere*, aut *clam*, nam neque *justæ neque injustæ possessiones duæ concurrere possunt.*" It was evidently Julian's opinion on the other hand, that the possessio justa of one person might co-exist with the possessio injusta of another, but this position of his must have been omitted by the compilers. The question which Julian here intends to answer is this; is it possible to give a precaria possessio to several persons at the same time? But as precaria possessio immediately after it was given availed as *justa* possessio, it is very natural that Julian should treat *possessiones precarias*, to which this question referred as possessiones *justas* in opposition to *possessio violenta*, and *clandestina* as *possessionibus injustis*, although in certain cases *precaria possessio* might also be looked upon as *injusta*. Cuperus (De Nat. Poss. P. 2, C. 14) has denied this very simple explanation without substituting any other in its place.

order to allow of the Possession of the other party not being excluded; the proposition at the same time is extended to every case where a *justa* and *injusta* possessio concur, and excludes all other cases.

4. Both of these views had been already refuted by the proof which Paulus had adduced in support of his own doctrine; but Labeo (who thus agrees with Paulus) brings another special reason against Trebatius, on the ground that no distinction can be made between *justa* and *injusta* possessio, when the existence of Possession generally is in question. (See *ante*, p. 65).

The same proposition is laid down by Ulpian quite as generally as in the above passage from Paulus.

" Celsus filius ait, *duorum* quidem in *solidum* dominium, vel *possessionem esse non posse*" (*d*).

Celsus's opinion is here introduced by Ulpian, as in many other passages, only because it agrees with his own; this appears more clearly at the end of the passage, where Ulpian himself carries out the doctrine of Celsus to its legitimate consequences (*e*).

I will now mention the different cases, in which the rule itself is broken in upon:

1st. Whoever takes a thing by force undoubtedly obtains juridical Possession of it; but, according to the opinion of Trebatius, the previous possessor must also be looked upon as possessor. Now, thus much is clear that, even according to this doctrine, such continuing Possession can not be affirmed as to every respect; for as one set of Interdicts were available to recover back a lost Possession (*recuperandæ*

(*d*) This view has been expounded admirably by Cuperus, De Nat. Poss. P. 2, C. 18. The doctrine itself is an old one, see Gomez in L. Tauri XIV. No. 99, p. m. 289. Paulus therefore does not deny, what indeed could not be denied, that the rights of Possession might be allowed to several persons at the same time, but he lays down that such allowance is illogical, because it contradicts the nature of Possession. The *impossibility* of which he speaks must be so understood.

(*e*) L. 5, § 15, *Commodati*, Ulpianus, lib. 28, ad edictum.

possessionis), and others to retain Possession (*retinendæ possessionis*), it follows that, in reference to the Interdicts competent to the previous possessor, it was neither necessary nor even possible to assert such continuing Possession, and this view is not taken by a few Jurists only, but is to be found in all, and is clearly expressed even in the Edict. That which is sought to be recovered must have been previously lost, and that which is lost one cannot be said to have. Still the following passage must not be passed over, which seems to raise doubts even on this point (*f*). "Non alii autem, quam ei *qui possidet* (*g*), interdictum unde vi competere, argumentum præbet, quod apud Vivianum relatum est, si quis vi me dejicerit, meos non dejicerit, *non posse me hoc interdicto experiri: quia per eos retineo possessionem, qui dejecti non sunt*" (*h*). If we invert the order of this passage, which will not interfere with its logical construction, it stands thus: "Vivianus lays down, that he who is ejected from his land cannot, nevertheless, maintain an *interdictum de vi*, because his people, who had Possession at the same time as himself,

(*f*) L. 1, § 45, de vi.

(*g*) "Qui non possidet," according to the reading of Rehdigers' manuscript, and of the following editions of the Digestum Novum. Rom. 1476; Norimberg, 1483; Venet. 1485 ; Venet. 1494; Lugdun. 1509, 1513; Paris, 1514, 1535; and probably many others. That Accursius adopted the same reading clearly appears from his having cited L. 1, § 4, *uti poss.* as a parallel passage. Cras (Spec. ipr. Ciceronianæ, p. 15), and Fleck, (De interd. unde vi, p. 29), who follows him word for word, express themselves thus: Accursius particulam *non* inseruit: just as if Accursius wrote critical notes on the manuscript of Florence. Haloander adopts the Florentine reading, although Jauch (De Negat. Pand. p. 82), Cras and Fleck, loco. cit, assert the contrary. Jauch's mistake had been previously corrected by Markart (Interp. L. 2, C. 18). *Qui non possidet* is the reading also of a very good manuscript in the public library at Metz, of one in my own possession, of two at Vienna, and of sixteen at Paris; in three other manuscripts at Paris the *non* is inserted over the text; one however (No. 4482) reads, *qui possedit.* A Kœnigsberg manuscript also has the reading *non* possidet, Dirksen, Abhandlungen, I. 450.

(*h*) L. 60, T, 17, (Fabrot, Th. 7, P. 407).

were not also turned out; *for he exercises his former Pos-session through them.* This confirms (*argumentum præbet*) the general rule, that no one *who is out of Possession* can maintain the Interdict." The evident necessity afforded by the context for the reading non possidet, gives it such a de-cided preference, that neither the age of the Florence manu-script, nor the much more unimportant accordance of the Basilica can be urged against it. This reading, besides, removes all difficulties in the passage, without making it necessary to introduce any alteration into the text itself (*i*). The opinion, therefore, of Trebatius cannot have reference to the Interdicts of the previous possessor (*dejectus*), but only to those of the actual possessor (*dejiciens*); for if the latter wished to maintain the interdictum uti possidetis, against the former, he would undoubtedly be shut out by an exception (*j*); now, it would rather seem that Trebatius had this point of practice in view, and that he sought to explain it by ascribing a continuing Possession to the pre-vious possessor. With this explanation, which is made clearer, and more probable by a passage in Ulpian (*k*) the whole controversy is without any practical interest, but, nevertheless, the doctrine of Paulus does not lose its advan-tage of being more logical (*l*).

(*i*) Donellus (Comm. L. 15, C. 32, p. m. 801), gives a sound interpretation of the passage, and concludes from it that *non* must have existed in the text; his subsequent remark however is erroneous, "mendose legitur *in omnibus exemplaribus*, etiam Flo-rentinis, &c." Some read, qui *possedit*, i. e. whoever has pos-sessed, who possesses no longer, and a Paris manuscript agrees with this, (see the previous note) (*g*). This explanation however is very forced. It occurs first in Rutgers, (Var. Lect. lib. 6, cap. 20), to whom it was communicated

verbally by Bandius; Grotius approved of it, Flor. Spars, p. 185, ed. Amst. 1643, 12.

(*j*) L. 1, pr. uti possidetis, (that is by a plea in bar, shewing that as a possessor *per vim* the Interdict was not competent to him). Transl.

(*k*) L. 3, pr. uti possidetis.

(*l*) The same explanation may be given to the following passage, L. 17, pr. de poss. "Si quis vi de possessione dejectus sit, *pe-rinde haberi debet, ac si possideret:* cum interdicto de vi recuperandæ possessionis facultatem habeat." Still this passage may be better

But the position of Trebatius may have referred to Usucaption as well as to Interdicts, and then the meaning of it would be this: if a man loses Possession by violence, still Usucaption does not cease to run in his favour. But the contrary of this proposition is not only expressly laid down in the Digest (*m*); but it is also so opposed to the whole nature of Usucaption, that it is highly improbable any Jurist should ever have asserted it.

2nd. What has been said with respect to Possession by violence, may be repeated almost in terms as to clandestine Possession. At the same time, a particular rule as to land comes into play here, which can only be fully explained in Books 2 and 3. For the same reason, a passage in Ulpian (*n*) cannot be explained now, although it has given rise to much misunderstanding on the present point. Still it may be shown here that neither Ulpian, nor Labeo whom he cites, are applying the view of Trebatius in the case in question; for, first, neither of them had adopted this view (see *ante*, p. 118); and, secondly, Ulpian says at the end of the passage, that if the previous possessor is forcibly restrained from re-entering his close, the party in possession has a *violenta* possessio. But as this were not possible, if up to that moment the latter had a *clandestina* possessio (*o*); so, according to Ulpian's view, up to that moment he had not Possession at all, and, therefore, here also Ulpian does not admit of two possessors at the same time.

3rd. Both cases, namely, violent, and a secret Possession, are treated of together in the following passage (*p*). *Si duo possideant in solidum*, videamus, quid sit dicendum: quod

---

explained without any reference to the present question, either as relating to the *hereditatis petitio*, which lies against the dejectus as *possessor*, or to the bail to the action which he was not obliged to give. The heading of the title seems to make for the latter view compare L. 11, 12, qui satisd.

cog.

(*m*) L. 5, *de usurp. et usuc.*

(*n*) L. 6, § 1, *de poss.*

(*o*) Non enim ratio *obtinendæ* possessionis, sed origo *nanciscendæ* exquirenda est, L. 6, pr. de poss. Cuperus de nat. poss. P. 2, C. 20.

(*p*) L. 3, *pr. uti possidetis.*

qualiter procedat, tractemus. *Si quis proponeret possessionem justam et injustam:* ego possideo ex justâ causâ, tu
vi aut clam: si a me possides, superior sum interdicto: si
vero non a me neuter nostrum vinceretur (*q*): nam et tu
possides et ego." Ulpian is speaking of the interdictum uti
possidetis brought on the Possession which two persons have
in solidum. How is this possible? only where one possesses juste, the other injuste, for instance, *vi* or *clam.* The
doctrine of Trebatius is evidently referred to here, without,
however, being adopted, which, indeed, from other passages
would have been impossible (see *ante,* p. 118). Ulpian says,
si quis proponeret; he assumes, therefore, argumentatively
the opinion as a sound one, in order to shew how the interdictum uti possidetis was to be dealt with in conformity to it.
But he evidently only supposes the case, where an *injustus,*
not where a *justus* possessor, wishes to bring the Interdict; for
the latter, according to the express words of the Edict, and
therefore according to the words of all Jurists, had the interdictum de vi and not the interdictum uti possidetis. The
question then is, when an injustus possessor brings the Interdict
against a (previous) justus possessor, what is the course of
the suit? either, says Ulpian, the defendant has been turned
out of Possession by the plaintiff and then the plaintiff is
cast, so that here no distinction in practice arises upon the
controversy (' superior *sum* interdicto' according to the
opinion of all; of Trebatius, because the defendant was still
a possessor, and a better possessor than the other; of Paulus,
on the ground of the well known exception), or the defendant
has been turned out by a third party, who, in his turn, has
been ejected by the plaintiff, in which case the suit could
not be determined (*r*) (neuter vinceretur, that is, according

(*q*) So read Rom. 1476; Nor.
1483; Ven. 1485; Florent. cum
rel. "*vincetur.*" All the manuscripts which I am acquainted
with agree with the Florence
copy, (except that the Metz and
Leipsic MSS. read *vincet* instead

of *vincetur*), but the above interpretation may stand without this
reading.

(*r*) That this is the only possible sense of "neuter vinceretur,"
or "vincetur," that therefore the
Judge could not hinder either

to the doctrine of Trebatius; but otherwise according to Paulus and Ulpian, who would make the plaintiff succeed, because the defendant was neither in Possession himself, nor was any exception competent to him against the person of the plaintiff). Here a substantial difference between the two views occurs, and it serves to shew the preference due to that which I have taken; it is even probable, that Ulpian had no other view throughout this passage than to make the untenableness of the other doctrine apparent by the above consequence.

4th. With *precarium* there are two possible cases, either where there has been a delivery of mere detention, which by refusal is converted into *injusta* possessio; or, second, where juridical Possession has been given from the commencement (p. 116). No instance occurs of the first case, except in the general and disapproved opinion of Sabinus (p. 117); but there are several instances of the second, and with respect to it, the compilers of the Digest have been inconsistent enough to adopt the doctrine of Sabinus, which as a general proposition, and in all other instances they had rejected. The passage is taken from Pomponius (*s*), and it lays down expressly, that if a party delivers over the *possessio* itself to another, the latter undoubtedly acquires the Possession, but the former also continues his Possession, although this latter point had been doubted. Let us inquire again here as to the meaning of this continuing Possession. 1st. It cannot refer to the Interdicts of the first Possessor (the rogatus), because he undoubtedly had the interdictum recuperandæ possessionis (de precario); 2nd. Nor can it have any practical bearing on the Interdict of the other (the rogans), because this Interdict was excluded by a mere exception, without

party from using force against the other may be easily shewn, although it has been often questioned. For a sentence against the defendant is, as all concede, excluded by the phrase, and so also is an acquittal; for, firstly, every

acquittal with this interdict, which was a *remedium duplex*, operated as an adverse sentence; and, secondly, in the first case to which the second is opposed, this very acquittal is meant.

(*s*) L. 15, § 4, *de precario*.

any Possession in the defendant. 3rd. But as respects Usucaption, the position is important, for Pomponius affirms that Usucaption does not cease to run on account of this *precarium*. But exactly the same object is effected according to the other doctrine, and in a way which renders the fiction as impossible as it is unnecessary; for when the subject is given back, the intermediate Possession of the other party is added to that of the former possessor (*t*), and this *accessio* possessionis avails even when the party is forced to make restitution of the Possession (*u*), the *precaria possessio* thus becoming, through the refusal to deliver up, *injusta*. Now it is very natural that those Jurists who maintain an *accessio possessionis*, should affirm just the contrary of what Pomponius has laid down as a rule respecting the Possession of the *rogatus* (*v*), and it is less hazardous here, than in any other instance, to look upon the one passage in the Pandects as a repeal of the other, for the latter provides for all those cases which the former had been introduced to meet, though in a different manner.

The following are the results of this inquiry into the meaning of the Roman Jurists.

(*t*) " Si tamen *receperit* possessionem rupto precario, dicendum esse, *accedere* possessionem ejus temporis, quo precario *possidebatur*," L 13, § 7, de poss. Cuperus thinks it singular that the compiler of the Digest should have referred this passage to Usucaption, as it related originally to the *interdictum utrubi*. But as there is only *one possessio*, so also there is only *one accessio* possessionis. Every *accessio* of what sort soever presupposes nothing else than the relation of juridical succession between the previous and present possessor. For succession does not apply to Possession by itself, (§ 5), but only where something else is required

besides its mere existence, as for instance, continuance during a definite period of time as with the *interdictum utrubi* and Usucaption; but this accession is always the same in all the cases when it occurs.

(*u*) L. 13, § 9, de poss. " Si jussu judicis res mihi restituta sit, accessionem esse mihi dandam placuit." This rule applies to all cases universally where a juridical succession is established in fact, (as in a purchase) ; the restitution of Possession however must be compulsory. Giphanius in L. cit. Lectur. Altorph. p. 467.

(*v*) L. 15, § 4, *de precario*, (Pomponius, lib. 29, ad Sabinam).

1st. The rule plures eandem rem in solidum possidere non possunt has been recognized as a rule at every period.

2nd. The exceptions to it, upon which only any controversy has arisen, were of no great importance.

3rd. In Justinian's compilations the rule itself is recognized as a general rule (*w*).

4th. It may be for this reason, that in the latest Roman law-writers, no questions has been made to any exceptions, but even independently of this, no single exception to this rule can be affirmed.

From the foregoing two important rules may be deduced, which extend themselves over the whole theory of Possession.

I. Wherever, according to the express statement of the law sources, the previous Possession continues, it necessarily follows that no new Possession can have commenced.

II. Wherever the Roman Law recognizes a new Possession, the previous Possession must be held to have ceased.

The practical meaning of these propositions may be made clearer by the following examples:

1. Example of the first rule; it is expressly laid down that the Possession of a close, which has been occupied secretly by another, continues in the former possessor up to the time of his having notice that it is so occupied (Book 3). If now, such clandestine occupier is ejected forcibly by a third party, the latter, according to the general rule of acquisition (Book 2), would immediately become possessor; but, according to the above fundamental principle, he would not as yet have acquired the Possession.

2. Example of the second rule; it has been remarked above that, with respect to ager vectigalis and emphyteusis, a juridical Possession may be ascribed to the tenant. The

(*w*) "Si quis.... ea mente possessionem tradidit, ut postea ei restituatur, *desinit possidere*." L. 17, § 1, *de poss.* This passage and L. 13, de poss. are both from the same work, Ulpianus ad Edictum.

Roman Law does not speak of the landlord; but according to this rule, his previous Possession must necessarily cease at the commencement of the lease.

Neither of these rules belong in themselves to the juridical modifications of Possession, but they are deducible from its original meaning, and they may coalesce with another fiction, as is the case in the last given example. Opinions have been much more divided amongst modern Jurists than amongst the Romans upon the subject of the present chapter, simply because the former, unlike their predecessors (x), entertained wholly erroneous notions on the meaning of *possessio* generally, and of its different distinctions, which necessarily confused the whole question. The true doctrine, however, has been laid down by several (y); some have maintained a totally opposite view (z); but the greater number (a) have endeavoured by distinctions to recon-

(x) Even this however has not been uncontested; for Merillius, Observ. L. 2, c. 31, holds the whole controversy of the Romans to be mere logomachy, what some called possessio *civilis* and *naturalis*, others termed *possidere* and *in possessione* esse; see *ante*, p. 99.

(y) Cujacius in Observ. L. 9, c. 32, et L. 5, c. 22; Id. in L. 3, § 5, de poss., Opp. T. 5, p. 708, et T. 8, p. 257; Obrecht. de poss. cap. 8; Turaminus de substant. Poss. c. 1—3, Opp. p. 235—259; Merenda In Controv. L. 12, c. 13, 23, (the most correct of all); Valentia in Ill. Tract. lib. 1, Tr. 2, cap. 3; Ramos De Poss. Protermiss. c. 1, ap. Meerm. T. 7, p. 84; Retes De Poss. P. 1, c. 2, ib. p. 463.

(z) " Martinus cum suis Gosianis," Glossa in L. 3, pr. uti poss. Some also belong here who have made distinctions merely for the sake of not appearing to contra-

dict the law sources, as for instance Zasius in L. 3, § 5, de poss. Opp. T. 3, pp. 111—116; Conf. pp. 125, 132, 133, 155; and Oppenritter in Summa Poss. P. 2, C. 3.

(a) Azo in Lecturâ, tit. *uti poss.*, et in Summâ, tit. *de poss.*, n. 10—15, Glossa in L. 3, § 5, *de poss.* Odofredus in L. cit. fol. 55, 56; Alciatus in L. 1, pr. *de poss.* n. 64, 65.; Vaconius in Declar. 72, fol. 68; Duarenus in L. 3, § 5, de poss.; Opt. p. 853; Giphanius in L. 3, § 5, de poss.; Lect. Alt. p. 418; Galvanus de Usufructu, c. 34, in fin.; Cuperus de Nat. Poss. P. 2, c. 13—21. The whole description of the latter is well founded and correct, but he spoils it all in the end, because he wants a correct notion of *possessio*. This doctrine appears also to be implied in c. 9, X. *de Probab.*

cile the two extremes, admitting in some cases, and in others, rejecting the *possessio plurium*. Vaconius and Galvanus not only recognized the possibility of several persons being contemporaneous possessors of the same thing, but also of their having Usucaption at the same time: if the first Usucaption has terminated, the second may continue to run, and through completion of the second, the property is recovered which the first Usucaption may have acquired. A correct conclusion upon this doctrine was pronounced long ago in the Gloss (*b*).

The most extraordinary opinion of all is that of Westphal (*c*), who, after misunderstanding completely the Roman Jurists, explains himself on the matter thus: " Mere theoretical results are brought forward on this subject, which they (the Romans) imagined were deducible from the rules or nature of Possession, but which, if incorrectly deduced, afford no rule to us." He then puts this case to the Romans, " Suppose I turn a person out of Possession by force, and that I again am ejected in like manner by Caius, then both I and Caius are to be looked upon as Possessors! The Romans, probably, never had such a case in view."

The first rule for the acquisition and loss of Possession, which has been deduced from its *exclusive* character, has been usually contained in this maxim, *possessio* must be *vacua* in order to be acquired. For both in voluntary transfers and in forcible takings of Possession, the possessio must, at the actual moment of acquisition, be *vacua*: where that is not so, as, for instance, in the secret occupation of a piece of ground, the fundamental rule laid down above prevents any Possession being acquired, and therefore the application of this principle is very correctly denoted by the above maxim (*d*). Many writers have admitted this quali-

(*b*) Glossa in L. 3, § 5, de poss. (another opinion is here refuted by the following conclusion) "Ergo si omnes habeant bonam fidem omnes usucapiunt, quod est ab-

surdum."
(*c*) Ueber die Arten der Sachen, Besitz, &c. Th. 2, cap. 2, § 65.
(*d*) Obrecht de poss. cap. 8.

fication into their definition of Possession (e); but, although this may not be incorrect as to any practical conclusions, it engenders a false view, as if something express was thereby predicated of the notion itself, whereas the qualification is merely of a negative character. The Romans themselves use the expression in a similar sense it is true, but with a much more restricted meaning, namely, to denote, on occasion of the delivery of a piece of ground, that it is not possessed *animo* by any third party. The expression in this sense occurs in early law language (*f*); it is to be found frequently in the law sources (*g*), and the deeds of sale and delivery in the middle ages make constant use of it (*h*). It is to be found most frequently in deeds of Purchase, and in these, from the peculiar nature of the contract, it bears a somewhat more extensive meaning; for the vendor does not deliver a *vacua possessio* (according to the meaning of the deed of sale), if a third party has even a *missio in possessionem* (*i*), although the latter does not amount to a true Possession; and accordingly neither impedes the Possession of the vendor, nor the delivery and passing of the property.

Cuperus was the first who laid down these distinctions expressly (*j*), which were previously either altogether disregarded, or denoted by the term vacua possessio; but he makes a very partial use of them, as he does of his correct view generally of the whole subject.

(*e*) Obrecht de poss. cap. 2, § 13, "possessionem esse detentionem rei vacuæ," Cf. § 89.

(*f*) Cicero pro Tullio, c. 13. "Neque tamen hanc centuriam Populianam *vacuam tradidit.*" Auct. ad. Herennuim IV. 29. "Necesse est.... te aut *vacuum possedisse* .... vacuum cum ego

adessem, *possidere non potuisti.*" The expression occurs allusively merely in Cicero De Or. III. 31; Quinctiliani Declamat. XII. 4.

(*g*) Brissonius v. vacuus.

(*h*) Marini Papiri Diplomat. p. 331, not. 17.

(*i*) L. 2, § 1, De act. emti.

(*j*) De nat. poss. P. 2, C. 19.

SECTION XII.

I am now able to give a distinct view of the scope of the following Treatise. Possession, generally, is related to two juridical subject-matters, viz., Usucaption and Interdicts (§. 2); but Usucaption is not founded upon Possession alone, but upon that and other legal conditions which must co-exist from the commencement, whereas with respect to Interdicts, the mere existence of Possession is sufficient to give birth to them, directly any injury is sustained (§. 7, No. 3).

Thus, as the right to maintain Interdicts is the only exclusive right belonging to mere Possession, the law relating to Interdicts forms the subject of our inquiry. Consequently, no more mention will be made of Usucaption; although all that follows has an intimate connection with Usucaption, because exactly the same possession is required for Usucaption as for Interdicts. What the other conditions are which must be joined to Possession in order to admit of Usucaption, belongs to the theory of property. Still, on account of this close connection between Possession and Usucaption, the law sources which make mention of the latter are authorities in a theory of the former; and, accordingly, in the list of sources I made use of this remark.

The subject-matter of our inquiry forms, therefore, a portion of the law of obligations (§. 6), and two questions have to be answered in order to solve completely the problem which I have proposed. First, when is Possession to be held to exist, *i. e.*, when is the existence of the relation to be recognized, without which this *obligatio ex delicto* cannot arise? Secondly, what is required in addition to this

K

relation, in order that the *obligatio* may arise in fact (*a*) that is, what sort of disturbance must the Possession undergo to enable an *obligatio* to arise out of the disturbance? The first question, again, divides itself into two; how is Possession acquired? (Book 2). How is the Possession so acquired lost? (Book 3). The second question is answered by a description of the different Interdicts (Book 4) as these correspond to the different kinds of disturbances.

There still remains one relation of Possession which I have not yet mentioned, and which it is necessary to explain here, where I am giving a general view of each portion of my work. I have hitherto tacitly assumed that Possession can only exist with reference to corporeal things. In the Roman Law, indeed, this position but rarely occurs, and then only incidentally (*b*); nevertheless, it is so evidently at the bottom of the whole doctrine of the Roman Jurists, that no one can entertain any doubt about it, unless some false view be taken up previously to entering upon the subject. But now, also, a Possession referring to incorporeal things will have to be described, and the meaning of such Possession, both in the Roman Law itself and in our Jurists, must be inquired into here.

The right to Interdicts founds itself on any unlawful interference with the exercise of property; by violence, for instance. If, now, a forcible disturbance of the mere exercise of any other right can be conceived, it would be strictly logical to protect such rights by similar Interdicts. But this

(*a*) It is scarcely necessary to remark, that interdict-possession does not thereby at all become similar to usucaption-possession, in which case also something must be added to the mere existence of Possession. For the additional matters required in Usucaption are, in fact, modifications of Possession itself; on the other hand, with respect to Interdicts, the question merely relates to the particular kind of injury, and this clearly does not effect the nature of the Possession itself.

(*b*) L. 3, De poss. "Possidere autem possunt quæ sunt corporalia;" L. 4, § 27, De usurp. "quia nec possidere intelligitur jus incorporale."

is the case as to all the elements of property which are capable of existing as independent rights severed from property itself. *Ususfructus* is a right of this sort, as to which it is clear, on the first glance, that a violent disturbance may be as easily conceived as with respect to property itself; so also with respect to all other servitudes; and also with *superficies:* in short, with all rights generally, which, as several elements of property are opposed, under the names of *jura* or *jura in re* to *dominium*, as the totality of all real rights generally. It has been shewn above, with respect to these separate rights (p. 76), that no *animus domini*, and, consequently, no true Possession, can be ascribed to him who enjoys them. But as the enjoyment of them may be interfered with in exactly the same way as the enjoyment of property, it follows that Possession may have reference to other rights besides property, and this relation is, in fact, expressed in terms in the Roman Law. Thus, as true Possession consists in the exercise of property, so this *quasi* Possession consists in the exercise of a *jus in re;* and, as in true Possession, we possess the subject itself (*possessio corporis*) but not the property, we ought not properly to use the term Possession of a servitude (*possessio* JURIS). But as we have no other word to which we can couple the Possession in this case, as it is coupled with the subject in the case of property, nothing remains but to use the above improper expression: it must not, however, be forgotten, that it is, in fact, an improper expression, and that nothing else is meant by it than the exercise of a *jus in re*, which stands in the same relation to the actual *jus in re*, as true Possession does to property. The Roman Jurists saw all this very clearly, and it is only thus that their language, which appears so fluctuating on the point, is to be explained. In many passages, namely, *possessio* of this sort is altogether denied (*c*),

(*c*) *Neque ususfructus neque usus possidetur*, sed magis tenetur," L. 1, § 8; *Quod Legat.* add. L. 4, § 27; *De usurp.* L. 32, § 1; *De serv. præd. urb.*

K 2

in others, it is just as stoutly affirmed (*d*); in others, again,
the impropriety of the expression is denoted by *quasi possidere, quasi in possessione esse* (*e*).

With respect to this (so called) Possession of incorporeal
things, it is necessary to steer clear of two fallacies. First,
as there may be a question respecting a possessio *corporis*
or *juris* in the same person, these two must be carefully
distinguished; and, in consequence of their not having been
so, the notion of Possession has not been a little confused.
Thus, for instance, the *fructuarius* has in the subject itself,
i. e., in reference to property, no juridical Possession at all,
so that his *possessio* is simply *naturalis* (*f*), and the juridical Possession of the proprietor is as little interfered with
by him as by a mere tenant; but he has juridical Possession
of his *jus* ususfructus, and, therefore, he may undoubtedly
avail himself of possessory Interdicts. By improperly con-
necting this *possessio naturalis* with the right to Interdicts,
Bassian has been led into a double blunder (p. 101), as he
not only denotes Interdict-possession by *naturalis possessio*,
but also ascribes to the *fructuarius* juridical Possession in

(*d*) "*Jus* fundi *possedisse*," L.
7; De itin—"*jus possedit*;" L. 2,
comm. præd. "*possessionem* vel
corporis vel *juris*;" L. 2, § 2, *De
precar.* "nemo ambigit *possessionis* duplicem esse rationem :
aliam quæ *jure consistit*, aliam
quæ *corpore*, L. 10, c. de poss.
For, *consistere* jure, corpore,
means here that the object of
Possession may be either a *jus* or
corpus. Cuperus, P. 1, C. 4, has
thoroughly established this interpretation, and it may be looked
upon as the most successful portion of his Treatise.

(*e*) "Ususfructus nomine.....
quasi in possessione;" L. 3, § 17,
de vi, " ususfructus *quasi posses-

sio*;" L. 23, § 2, ex quibus causis
majores. " Longâ *quasi possessione* jusa quæ ducendæ nactus."
L. 10, pr. si servitus vindi. *Quasi-
possessio* never occurs as one
word, but *quasi* is used here ad-
verbially, as in *obligatio quasi ex
contractu*; so that no instance is
to be found in which it may not
be translated by gleichsam (as it
were). Compare Weber, Von
der Natürl. Verbindl. § 25, not.
1. (This remark might have been
made correctly up to the second
edition, but Gaius, Lib. 4, § 139,
shews that *quasipossessio* may be
used as a single expression).

(*f*) L. 12, pr. de poss.

the subject itself, which belongs, in fact, to the pledge-creditor; from which mistakes a third necessarily flows, in as much as two juridical *possessiones* (namely, one *civilis* and one *naturalis*) must be thereupon conceived to exist (p. 127). The second fallacy which we must avoid is this; mention will be made hereafter of a *possessio ususfructus*, and of a *possessio hereditatis* (bonorum) *i. e.*, of the *ususfructus*, or of the inheritance which arise out of the edict only, and not from the civil law (p. 137), just as we have already had a *juris possessio* in the *hereditatis petitio*, and a *libertatis* and *servitutis possessio* in the *liberale judicium*; but with these expressions, the *juris quasi possessio* now under discussion has no connection, as in these passages *possessio* itself no longer means Possession, but either a mere prætorian right, or the condition of defendant in a suit.

A great number of our Jurists have wholly misunderstood this part of the theory of Possession; for having overlooked the precise meaning of the Roman *jus* (in re), they explained the *juris quasi possessio* as the exercise of a right simply (*g*); now it is true, that enjoyment may be conceived as to every right, but not a forcible disturbance or Usucaption, and yet these are the only conditions under which the exercise of a right is looked upon as a juridical relation. From this empty abstraction, Hommel (*h*) arrives at a question which he himself gives up as unanswerable, why should not the physician, whom one ceases to employ, be protected in the possession of his right. Spangenberg (*i*) carries out this view so far, that he calls property the first available object of *quasi possessio :* but, as Possession also is considered as a right, one does not see why there should not be a *possessionis* quasi possessio; and this Possession of the second power would, in its turn, become the object of a new Possession, and so on, *ad infinitum.* Sibeth here, as everywhere else,

(*g*) It cannot be denied how-ever, that with most of them the canon law contributed to form this notion; as to which, see hereafter.

(*h*) Rhapsod. 489.

(*i*) Vom Besitz, § 102.

is quite original; he denies all *juris quasi possessio* (*j*), and falls foul of the Jurists who maintain it; the truth being that in this part, as in every other of his work, he does not know what he is writing about.

In addition, therefore, to the theory of Possession itself (Books 2—4), the theory of the application of its fundamental principles to *jura in re* must be added (Book 5).

But even then something more remains. The notion and the rights of Possession are defined in modern law in a very different manner to that in which they occur amongst the Romans. If, therefore, a theory of Possession lays claim to be of any use in practice, it must subjoin to the views of the Roman lawyers those modifications under which the above views obtain practical validity amongst us at the present day. But this portion of my inquiry (Book 6) will not be without value, even towards a thorough knowledge of the Roman Law itself; for there is no surer way to distinguish what is accidental from what is essential in any subject, than by adhering always to principles, and only varying in the conditions of applying them.

The remainder of this Treatise, therefore, will be occupied, first, in giving a complete statement of the Roman Law (Book 2—5); and, second, the modifications introduced into the law of the present day (Book 6). The Roman Law relates, first, to Possession itself (Book 2—4); secondly, to the application of its principles to *jura* in re (Book 2—3); and, lastly, to the precise form of the disturbance of Possession (Book 4).

(*j*) One of his best arguments runs thus, Vom Besitz, p. 80, "natural liberty casts every thing to the ground, for it is not only founded in reason but in the laws also." If natural freedom behaves herself thus, the sooner one deprives her of that natural liberty the better.

135

SECTION XIII.

HISTORICAL VIEW OF POSSESSION.

Lastly, the historical question has to be answered, how it happened that Possession, independent of any right to the thing possessed, obtained the protection of Interdicts. It might have been thought, for instance, that the law of property would have been all-sufficient, and that there would have been no occasion for Possession and its Interdicts, especially with a people like the Romans so much more disposed by nature, up to the utter extinction of the old national feeling by the civil wars, to legal procedure than to acts of violence. How then came the Romans, and that probably at a very early period, to adopt Possession as the ground of peculiar Interdicts (a)?

Were these Interdicts merely used to smooth the way to and facilitate litigated questions upon property, by settling beforehand which of the parties should be plaintiff, or defendant? But a special form already existed for this purpose with respect to property itself, the *manus consertæ* (b). Or were they intended to protect the Usucaption which had commenced, but was not yet completed? But then it would have been more consistent to require in them, as in the *publiciana actio*, exactly the same conditions as in Usucaption, instead of which, Possession without *bona fides* and without *justa causa*, was protected by Interdicts. Again, if Interdicts were introduced to protect Usucaption, they ought to have been co-extensive with it, and to have applied to chattels as well as to land. But the most important Interdicts of all, those *recuperandæ possessionis* were

(a) The relation between interdicts and vindication has been already slightly alluded to at the end of § 2, and will be discussed fully hereafter, § 37.

(b) I adopted this view formerly, see 2nd ed. p. 68.

applicable to land only (c), and thus they afforded to Usucaption a very imperfect protection.

Niebuhr has explained the origin of Possession in a very
satisfactory manner (d). Land, under the republic, was of
two kinds, *ager publicus* and *ager privatus*, in the latter of
which only could property be acquired. But Possession
and enjoyment of the *ager publicus* also, according to the
old constitution, were for the most part made over to individual Roman citizens, under the condition of being
reclaimable at will by the republic. Now we do not find
mention made of any legal form of conveyance of this Possession of the *ager publicus*, that is to say, any form of one
the most frequent and important transactions in ancient
Rome; although it is impossible to doubt, from the attach-
ment to regular and technical proceedings amongst the
Romans, that such a legal form must have existed, and
especially, that a protection of the tenant against arbitrary
violence must have been devised. Now, if we may assume
that Interdict-possession was in fact this legal form for the
ager publicus, we should have the solution of two problems;
for thus we see the original object and first cause of Possession; and, secondly, a legal form for the *ager publicus*.

If nothing more than this could be said, there would
remain merely an hypothesis, whose claim to reception
would depend upon its internal evidence. But, in support
of it, there occur also some most important historical
testimonials.

1st, Before all, it is observable that *possessio, possessor,*
and *possidere,* were used in several passages of widely distant times, as the peculiar technical terms denoting possession and enjoyment of the *ager publicus* (e). This identity

(c) This is always the case
with the *int. de vi*, the others are
treated of *post*, § 42, 43.

(d) Niebuhr Römische Ges-
chichte, vol. 2, pp. 161—170, 2nd
ed.

(e) Niebuhr has collected several passages, vol. 2, p. 101, 2nd
ed. I subjoin some others, Livius VII. 16. "Eodem anno C.
Licinius Solo .... est damnatus,
quod mille jugerum agri cum

of terminology between Possession and *ager publicus* cannot however be shewn more satisfactorily or simply, than by pointing out the original identity of the two subjects themselves, as above stated.

This identity also elucidates many other meanings of possessio, which, we shall now see, bear one simple and even essential relation to one another. For instance, *possessio* often means an inheritance, or an easement, which could not avail as rights according to strict civil law, but only according to the *jus gentium*, the latter in such cases being frequently imported into the prætor's edict. The following are examples of this:—

A. With respect to *damnum infectum*, the prætor says, in reference to the second *missio in possessionem*, which might thereby occur, *possidere jubebo (f)*. But this *possidere* means *bonitarium dominium* with the *conditio usucapiendi (g)*.

B. If *ususfructus* could not exist at civil law, but only by the prætor's edict, it was called *possessio* ususfructus, in opposition to *dominium* ususfructus, or to ususfructus qui jure consistit *(h)*.

C. Just so, the expression hereditatis or bonorum *possessio* is to be explained; for it nowise denotes the actual pos-

filio possideret, emancipandoque filium fraudem legi fecisset." So in all the other writers who mention the fact; Columella I. 3; Plinius Hist. Nat. XVIII. 3; Valer. Max. VIII. 6, 3. The latter however misrepresents the whole story in his usual careless way by transforming the evidently regular emancipation of the son into a wholly impossible emancipation of the land to the son, "dissimulantique criminis gratiâ dimidiam partem *filio eman-cipavit*." One of the most conclusive passages of all, and undoubtedly taken from some good old authority, is to be found in Orosius V. 18, (Ad. an. 661). "Namque eodem anno.... *loca publica* quæ in circuitu Capitolii pontificibus, auguribus, decemviris et flaminibus *in possessionem tra-dita erant* cogente inopiâ *vendita sunt*," i. e. they were reclaimed and converted into ager privatus.

(f) L. 7, pr. de damno inf.

(g) L. 15, § 16, 17, de damno inf.; L. 18, § 15, cod.; L. 3, § 23, de poss.

(h) L. 3, si ususf. petatur. (cf L. 1, pr., L. 4, L. 29. § 2, quibus mod. ususfr.; L. 29, de usu et usufr. leg.)

session of the deceased's property, but merely the special
nature of the prætorian law of inheritance (i). The prætorian heir, namely, is not *heres*, but, by a fiction, is treated
like an *heres* (k), so that the *bonorum possessio* bears the
same relation to *hereditas* as *dominium bonitarium* to
quiritarium.

But this meaning of possessio very naturally arose out of
the one given above, viz., the right to the *ager publicus*.
For all these cases agreed in this, namely, that without any
strict Roman property (*ex jure Quiritium*), something
similar in practice occurred, that is, an actual exclusive
claim of an individual to occupation and enjoyment, and
however different in other respects these rights might be to
one another, still this one universal resemblance might
easily give rise to their being denoted under the same
common term.

The right also to land in the provinces, without any doubt,
was called *possessio* from exactly the same analogy. The
same meaning of *possessio* was next transferred from the
right itself to the object of it. Thus, Javolenus lays down
in a very remarkable passage, that *ager* and *possessio* are
two different things in law; *ager* being a field held in Quiritarian property, but *possessio* a field either held in *bonitarium dominium*, (as, for instance, a *fundus Italicus*, which
had been merely delivered), or which, from its nature, is
incapable of being held in Quiritarian property (l). He
refers, by these latter words, specifically, no doubt, to land

(i) L. 3, § 1, de bon. poss.
(k) Ulpian XXVIII. 12.
(l) L. 115, *de verb. sign.* "Possessio et agro juris proprietate
distat: quidquid enim adprehen-
dimus, cujus proprietas ad nos
non pertinet, aut *nec potest pertinere,* hoc possessionem appellamus. Possessio ergo usus, ager
proprietas loci est." Alciat has
explained this passage cursorily,
but misunderstanding it in seve-

ral respects. De quinque pedum
præscript. num. 76—119, and in
L. 115, De V. S. Opp. T. 3, p.
350, T. 2, p. 987, his opponents
were even still more blind to
perceive its real meaning. Opusc.
de latinit. I. C. ad. Duker, pp. 64,
70, 85. Brissonius was the first
to give the right interpretation,
Select. Antiq. IV. 1, and most
writers have followed him.

in the provinces, but they are equally applicable to the old *ager publicus.*

Now it is undoubtedly a very strong proof of the correctness of the above historical view of the origin of Possession, that it brings several very peculiar meanings of the word *possessio* into the closest connection with one another (*m*).

2. On this view also, a very simple explanation is afforded of what otherwise appears so singular, viz., the application of *interdicta recuperandæ possessionis* to land only and not to moveables. This was a remnant of the original definition of Possession which applied only to *ager publicus.*

3. *Precarium* also, which in our law sources presents such an ambiguous character, may now be defined very clearly so as to explain its different peculiarities. It denotes, for instance, the relation of a client, who lived as a tenant on the *possessio* of his patron. The patron could eject the client at will, and the *interdictum de precario* was devised for the purpose of turning the latter out of possession, if he would not give up the land voluntarily (§. 44).

4. In the same manner an historical explanation is afforded of the illogical conclusion remarked upon above, that in the *ager vectigalis*, the tenant might have *possession* of it, although he had no more than a *jus in re* (p. 79). *Ager vectigalis*, namely, was moulded on the analogy of the old *ager publicus*, and whatever numerous and important distinctions might exist between the two (*n*), still nothing is more natural than that this analogy, without any other

---

(*m*) We might even go further, and deduce from this the meaning of Possessio as property simply, (see above, p. 68), if the above derivation were not so very natural, and it clearly appears how natural; when we observe, that in German Besitz and Besitzung have obtained the same meaning, although undoubtedly without any reference to the Roman *ager publicus.*

(*n*) [Added in the 4th edition.] I do not affirm by this, that no other explanation can be afforded of this circumstance. For undoubtedly it must also be taken into consideration, that for the most part other forms of process existed as to moveables having no reference at all to Possession (§ 41).

reason, should have given rise to several practical legal doctrines as to *ager vectigalis*. But as *possessio* had its origin with reference to *ager publicus*, one easily understands how it was allowed to continue with the *ager vectigalis*, as the latter form of *ager publicus*. This explanation undoubtedly coincides with that fondness for ancient forms which is so visible in the early Roman law.

5. The whole matter may be summed up thus. Originally, and from the earliest times downwards, there were two rights in land, *property* in the *ager privatus* with vindication, and *possessio* in the *ager publicus*, with a similar protection in the form we now see in the prætor's Interdicts. At a later period the prætor recognised this legal relation in terms in the edict, and thus gave rise to Interdicts as prætorian remedies, possibly with very little alteration of the law in principle. In the same way it was subsequently found convenient to apply the *possessio*, which had been originally devised for *ager publicus* only, to *ager privatus* also, although there was no very urgent necessity for it, and it probably never would have been applied in the first instance to the latter. Now this subsequent application of *possessio* to *ager privatus* is the only one which remains to us in the law sources, which scarcely take notice of *ager publicus*. Whether this extension of the original meaning was previous or subsequent to the adoption of Interdicts into the edict, and what the mode of introducing and treating the subject in the edict was, we are completely ignorant: the only historical knowledge we have is, that possessory Interdicts had been already introduced in the time of Cicero. Nevertheless, even in the edict we find certain traces of the original connection between *possessio* and *ager publicus*. One of these consists in the form of Interdicts, which was just the same for *possessio* as for locus publicus, flumen, &c.: a consequence of which is that these several subjects occur together in very close connection in the edict itself, as they do still in the Pandects. Another trace is perceptible in the form of the

Interdict *uti possidetis*. It runs thus, namely, in the Digest, uti *eas ædes* . . . . possidetis . . . . vim fieri veto (*o*). But at an earlier period the form was, "uti nunc possidetis *eum fundum* . . . . vim fieri veto" (*p*). This earlier form appears to have still in view the old connection with *ager publicus*, but as it gradually became obsolete and forgotten, *ædes* appears to have been inserted simply because *houses* at Rome were always fixed upon as the readiest and most familiar illustration.

(*o*) Niebuhr, Vol. 2, p. 166, 2nd ed.

(*p*) Festus *v. possessio*. He quotes at the commencement Gallus Ælius, from whom this form may have been taken. Lastly, Huschke has endeavoured with apparently good grounds to shew, that the Edict probably contained two different forms of this interdict, one for *fundus*, the other for *ædes*. (Ueber die Stelle des Varro, p. 110, s. 9).

BOOK II.

ACQUISITION OF POSSESSION.

SECTION XIV.

INTRODUCTION.

THE contents of this Book have been already indicated in the exposition of the material notion of Possession (§. 10). In every acquisition of Possession there is a physical act (*corpus* or *factum*), accompanied by an act of the will (*animus*) (*a*). The *factum* must be such as to place the person who desires to obtain Possession in a position which shall enable him, and him only, to deal with the subject at pleasure; that is, to exercise ownership over it. The act of the will must contemplate a dealing with the subject as one's own property: though if the Possession, by operation of law, is *derived* from the previous Possession of another, it is sufficient for the will to have in view this transference, so that in this way Possession may be acquired, although the property is recognized in another.

But Possession is considered a right, and every right, universally, is capable of being acquired, not only by one's own acts, but by the acts of one's slaves and children (*b*): and Possession, indeed, may be acquired for us by others, independently even of these juridical relations (*c*). But in

---

(*a*) "Adipiscimur possessionem corpore et animo, neque per se animo aut per se corpore." L. 3, § 1, *de poss.* Possessionem adquirimus et animo et corpore....

Paulus, V. 2, § 1; L. 8, *de poss.*; L. 153, de R. T.
(*b*) Pr. I. *per quas pers.*
(*c*) § 5, I. *per quas pers.*

all the cases in which Possession is acquired for us by others, the same rule of acquisition prevails as with our own acts, and it only need be stated here how this rule is to be applied.

This Book, therefore, will treat of the following matters:

　1st. The physical act, which is the first condition of all Possession.

　2nd. The will which must accompany that act, either in original, or in derivative, Possession.

　3rd. The application of these rules to acquisition through others.

It is only at the end of the Book, that it can be shewn distinctly how the acquisition of Possession distinguishes itself from the acquisition of all other rights.

SECTION XV.

PREHENSION.

Nothing seems simpler and easier to define, in any part of the theory of Possession, than the nature of the physical act (Prehension) which is required to gain Possession; and yet no point in the whole Roman Law has been so completely misunderstood as this. All commentators have supposed in such act an immediate bodily contact, and, consequently, but two kinds of it; a taking into the hand with respect to moveables, and a treading by the feet with respect to land. But as many cases occur in the Roman Law, in which Possession is acquired by physical acts undoubtedly, but still without any such actual contact, these acts have been looked upon as symbolical, by which, in virtue of a legal fiction, the true taking of Possession is represented (*actus adscititii, apprehensio ficta*). As this view of the subject is universal (*a*), it has never been considered necessary to establish its correctness; and as it is presented by all writers pretty much after the same fashion, it is sufficient, in tracing its history, to observe that it is to be found so far back as the Gloss (*b*), and that even Donellus is not guiltless of it (*c*).

Now it has been observed above (§. 5), that Possession undoubtedly is often admitted in Roman Law, without any actual prehension. There is no doubt, therefore, that a feigned Possession may be conceived, and the question accordingly may be expressed thus, is there, in fact, in these cases, any such fiction in the acquisition of Possession, by which symbolical acts are made to supply the place of actual prehension (*d*)? It need not be proved, that it is important for the theory to obtain a correct answer to this question; but there are also important practical conclusions which flow from it, although the immediate object of inquiry is merely as to the juridical *explanation* of particular cases, which are expressly recognised in the law sources themselves as modes of acquiring Possession; for if these cases are founded on a mere fiction of law, it follows that many limitations must be placed

(*a*) I say universal, because the exceptions are not only unimportant, but have had no influence. Some writers, from a misconception of natural law, have adopted the incorrect conclusion (leading, it must be observed, to wholly different consequences) that the point turns merely on the *manifestation of intention*. Amongst these latter are S. P. Gasser, Diss. de apprehensione possessionis, Hal. 1731, cc. 1 & 2; Beni. Pauw. Diss. de apprehensione possessionis, Trajecti, 1737, cc. 1 & 2. Traces of this doctrine are to be found still earlier, for instance, in Nookt, (Probabil. II. 6), who even makes the Roman jurists at loggerheads upon the principle of prehension.

(*b*) Azonis Summa in Cod. *tit. de poss.* num. 7, 8, fol. 134.

(*c*) Donelli Comment. Lib. 5, cap. 9.

(*d*) Thus *fictitious possession* is the genus, which includes as a species the possession founded on *fictitious prehension*. Several have laboured zealously, though without any object, in refuting this view: Alciatus, in L. 18, *de poss.* n. 3, 4, p. 1245; Duarenus, in L. 1, § 21, *de poss.* p. 840.

upon them, and such limitations, accordingly, have been affixed without hesitation by civilians, although never once mentioned in the sources themselves. Thus, every acquisition of this kind must be excluded where the transaction is illegal, and so undeserving of the benefit of a legal fiction (e); thus, also, when Possession is acquired through other persons, and not by one's own acts (f): indeed, this acquisition is limited merely to the conveyance of another person's Possession by delivery (g), or is considered simply as a consequence of property, which thus must always be acquired simultaneously, where Possession is capable of being acquired in this mode (h). Other consequences of the above doctrine, which relate more to details, will appear further on.

But the whole of this doctrine, taken generally, appears very improbable, when we consider the mode in which symbolical acts were employed in other instances in the Roman Law. Emancipation, manumission, vindication, all matters of this kind to which established forms were appropriate, are quite peculiar to Roman Law. All juridical transactions, on the other hand, which were in use with other people also, (such as sales, leases, &c.), had no established forms assigned to them. Now, Possession by itself is much less juridical in its character than the contracts last mentioned; indeed, originally it had nothing at all juridical in its nature. It acquires, indeed, a juridical character in two respects, one of which concerns Usucaption, which again is quite peculiar to Roman Law; but in this very case, whatever is wanting in Possession is supplied by its *continuance*, and, therefore, no ground exists, even in this

(e) Retes de Poss. P. 1, C. 2, § 8, p. 463; Gomez in Leges Tauri, L. 45, num. 20—31, 45—90.

(f) Zasius, in L. 1, § 21, de poss. p. 93, et in L. 18, cod. p. 150; Valentia in Ill. Jur. Tract. L. 1, Tr. 2, c. 14.

(g) Alciatus in L. 1, pr. de

poss. num. 56—61; Donellus in Comment. L. 5, c. 9; Obrecht de possessione, cap. 6. So much as is correct in this view will be given *post*, in § 19.

(h) Azo in Summâ, *tit. de poss.* num. 7, 8, fol. 134; Zasius, l. c. Wenck. Diss. de traditione, etc. pp. 6—8, p. 12, p. 43, seq.

L

relation to civil law, for having recourse to Roman forms at
the commencement of Possession. Accordingly, it would
be against all analogy to make symbolical acts a condition
precedent to the acquisition of Possession; but this reasoning receives additional corroboration from the wide application which would have to be made of these symbolical
acts. If the doctrine I am contending against only recognized symbolical acquisition in special exceptional cases
it might be conceived that, from the rare occurrence of
these cases, a slight inconsistency had crept into, and
maintained itself unperceived in, the treatment of the subject. But this is not so, for in the great majority of cases,
Possession is acquired in the mode which is termed symbolical. With land, for instance, symbolic taking of Possession
must nearly always occur, for to walk over every minute
portion of the estate would be almost impossible, yet the
part not walked over cannot be considered as physically
taken into Possession; indeed, even with moveables, it must
seldom occur that the whole article should be taken up by
the hand. It follows that, as, what they term, symbolic acquisition occurs in the majority of cases, it is impossible that the
above noticed inconsistency should have escaped the Roman
Jurists, and they must, from its constant recurrence, have
had their attention pointedly called to it.

If, now, the notion of fictitious Prehension be rejected
from the Roman Law, and all acquisition of Possession can
be based upon one and the same physical act, it is necessary
to define this physical act differently from what it has been
tacitly assumed to be by all law writers; for it is only
through such assumption, that it became necessary to adopt
a fictitious Prehension. The easiest way to arrive at the
correct notion will be to commence with the false one.

Whoever holds a piece of gold in his hand is the possessor
of it, of this there is no doubt; and from this, and similar
cases, the idea of *actual bodily contact* has been abstracted,
and thus is made the essential in every acquisition of Possession. But in the above case something else exists, which

is not necessarily connected with any bodily contact, viz., the physical power of dealing with the subject immediately, and of excluding any foreign agency over it. No one will deny that both of these co-exist in the above instance; and that the connection with bodily contact is merely accidental appears from this, that the power may be conceived to exist without the contact, and the contact, also in like manner, without the power. The *first*, because whoever at any moment is able to take up anything which lies before him, has just as much uncontrollable dominion over it, as if he had, in fact, taken it up. The *second*, because a man in chains has actual contact of the chains, yet it is easier to say that the chains have possession of him, than that he possesses the chains.

This *physical power*, therefore, is the *factum* which must exist in every acquisition of Possession: we may explain by it every single passage of the law sources in a uniform manner; bodily contact no longer forms an element in the notion, and no case remains which requires fictitious prehension to be assumed (*i*).

Historical evidence can be adduced in behalf of this view

(*i*) My reviewer in the Algemeine Literatur Zeitung, (1804, No. 42), objects to the whole of this view, and, in concurrence with previous jurists, adopts corporeal contact as the original ground of possession: this rule may subsequently have become relaxed in particular cases, but never to the extent of allowing my rule to be substituted for it. But this argument amounts to a *petitio principii*, for we can only ascertain the original foundation of possession by deduction from particular passages as has been performed in the text. The rule stated by me has always prevailed from the earliest times, not conceived, indeed, in such clear and general terms, but in particular limited instances; later jurists have merely stated the rule more plainly, excluding from it the accidental circumstances attending those cases, but not extending the rule itself in the slightest degree. It is only necessary to observe the mode in which the Romans dealt with a true *jus singulare*, (for instance, the keeping possession of land *solo animo*), in order to convince oneself that, *in this instance*, no *jus singulare* is in question.

in two ways, either from the general tenor, or from special passages, of the law sources. After which, it will be possible to define completely the notion of the physical act which is here only hinted at. For the general doctrine, a passage of Paulus is important, as it does not refer to any particular case, but lays down the rule without any limitation —"bodily contact is not at all necessary for acquiring Possession, it is sufficient to have the object on the spot before one's eyes" (*j*). On the other hand, not a single general passage speaks of the necessity of bodily contact. For if we refer the adipiscimur possessionem *corpore* (§. 14) to such contact we are immediately shewn our error, by observing that the same expression is applied to the loss of Possession (§. 32), in which, undoubtedly, no bodily contact can be imagined. *Corpus* means the external event, in opposition to the act *within* (*animus*).

(*j*) L. 1, § 21, *de poss.* "Non est enim corpore et tactu necesse apprehendere possessionem, sed etiam oculis et affectu." All the manuscripts read *actu*, which indeed is not improper, see (Wieling, Lect. 1, 19); but *tactu*, which can scarcely be called an emendation, gives the sense much more precisely, and is adopted in the Basilica. Faber Err. Pragm. 75, 2 ; Nordt Probab. II. 6 Wenck de Trad. p. 48.

SECTION XVI.

PREHENSION OF IMMOVEABLES.

I now pass on to an examination of the particular cases.

First, then, what must take place in order to acquire possession of immoveables (land)?

In order to acquire Possession it is only necessary to be *present on the land,* without the performance of any other act thereon: "Quædam mulier fundum (ita) non marito donavit per epistolam ..... Proponebatur, quod etiam *in eo agro qui donebatur, fuisset* cum epistola emitteretur; *quæ res sufficiebat ad traditam possessionem*" (*a*). Now, it is clear, that the above-mentioned notion of a bodily act may be applied in this case completely, for whoever finds himself upon the land may not only, at that moment, do with it as he pleases, but may exclude from it every one else. But these two powers do not refer to the portion of ground only on which the person happens to be standing, but to the whole of the land, and, therefore, it is not the mere act of treading with the feet which gives possession of the land, but presence upon the spot which enables him, not merely to walk over every individual portion of it, but to deal with it in any way he chooses at pleasure.

"Quod autem diximus, et corpore et animo adquirere nos debere possessionem, non utique ita accipiendum, ut qui fundum possidere velit, *omnes glebas circumambulet; sed sufficit quamlibet partem ejus fundi introire*" (*b*). For the same reason, further, it is not even necessary to *enter* upon the land; for, whoever comes sufficiently near to inspect the whole, has just as much power over it as if he had actually entered:

"..... ; *si vicinum mihi fundum* mercatum venditor *in meâ terrâ demonstret,* vacuamque se tradere pos-

---

(*a*) L. 77, *de rei vind.*　　　　(*b*) L. 3, § 1, *de poss.*

sessionem dicat: *non animus possidere cœpi, quam si pedem finibus intulissem*" (*c*).

All this stands in the closest connection with my notion as to a corporeal act; but modern jurists recognise here a fiction of law, by which the only true mode of acquisition, viz., that consisting in bodily contact, is supplied. Nevertheless, the Glossa has here struck out another path which is highly remarkable (*d*). The essential fact in the acquisition of Possession is not bodily contact, but perception by the senses; and, as there are five senses, Possession may be acquired by each of them, for instance, *by sight;* thus, Possession may be acquired by a view, even though the property be ten miles off, " per decem miliaria !" (*e*).

Bodily presence, therefore, is that which enables a dealing with the *thing* at will; but, suppose another person happens to be present at the same time, and that he also manifests his desire to possess the same subject? It is evident that his presence obstructs the possession of the former party, and there are only two ways of removing this obstruction, either by force, or by the voluntary act of the last comer.

In the latter mode, the voluntary act of one of two parties enables Possession to be given in every case of delivery. When a purchaser is brought upon the land by a vendor, both parties stand in exactly the same physical relation to it; and the intention of the vendor, up to this moment, has always been to be the possessor. But if he manifests his intention that the purchaser is to have the Possession, then, by his own free will, all the obstruction which his presence occasioned is removed. This is pointed at in the last cited passage by the words, "vacuamque se possessionem tradere dicat."

But the obstruction caused by the presence of another

(*c*) L. 18, § 2, *de poss.*

(*d*) Glossa in L. 18, § 2, *de poss.* Many moderns are of this opinion also, at least, in certain cases; Duarenus, for instance, in L. 3, pr. *de poss.* p. 843.

(*e*) Glossa in L. 1, § 1, *de poss.*

party may be removed by force, as well as by his own free
will : for it is clear, that the dominion of a possessor is just
as decided when he resists the intrusion of a stranger, as
when no intrusion has taken place. To this effect is the
following passage :

"Species inducendi in possessionem alicujus rei est,
prohibere ingredienti vim fieri; statim enim *cedere adver-
sarium, et vacuam possessionem relinquere possessionem*
jubet : quod multo plus est, quam restituere" (*f*).

The Basilica, the Gloss, and Cujas, refer this passage
to the prætor, who is carrying out a decree by putting a
party into possession (*g*), but neither the words, nor the
meaning of the passage afford any ground for this restricted
sense, and, therefore, with equal right, it is applicable to
every other case in which intrusion has been made and
repelled.

Personal presence, therefore, is the only *factum* by which
the possession of immoveables is acquired.   In order, however, to leave no room for doubt, I will just mention here
a limitation to this rule, which cannot be fully demonstrated before the third book. Possession of an immoveable
cannot be lost until the possessor has notice of the loss :
now, as a subject can only have one possessor at a time,
(§. 11), our rule is to be applied thus. The subject was
previously, either in the possession of another, or it was not
(*vacua possessio*).

In the latter case our rule is universally true. In the
former, however, the above-mentioned *factum* alone does
not convey the Possession, but notice to the previous
possessor must also appear.   In which case the acquisition takes place either against his will, (*dejectio*), or with
his will, (*traditio*), when he is either present, (*inducere in
possessionem*), or absent, (mittere in possessionem).

(*f*) L. 52, § 2, *de poss.*
(*g*) Basil. Lib. 50, tit. 1, (Ap. Miermann, tit. 5, p. 49); Glossa in L. 52, § 2, *de poss.*; Cujacius in L. 52, § 2, *de poss.*; Opp. T. 1, p. 315.

SECTION XVII.

PREHENSION OF MOVEABLES.

Secondly : in what manner is Possession of moveables acquired?

That this may be effected by a delivery from hand to hand there can be no doubt, and, therefore, it is not anywhere laid down in terms in the law sources. All that we have to deal with now, therefore, is, the cases in which Possession may be acquired without any manual acceptance.

First of all, here also, as with immoveables, personal presence is that which supplies the place, without any legal fiction, of an actual taking in the hand, and, therefore, it is quite immaterial whether the subject be actually handled, or whether it is capable, at any moment, of being so handled. This latter mode of Prehension is, indeed, the most usual, when the subject is of such a size, or weight, as not to be easily moved from its place. All this is proved by the following passages :—

1. D. 79. *de solutionibus.*

" Pecuniam, quam mihi debes, aut aliam rem, si *in conspectu meo ponere* te jubeam : efficitur, ut et tu statim libereris et mea esse incipiat : nam tum quod a nullo corporaliter ejus rei possessio detineretur, adquisita mihi, et quodam modo *manu longâ tradita* existimanda est." Here, again, the previous possessor is the only person who could prevent me from dealing with the thing at will, but it is expressly said of this very person, that by his conduct he recognises my Possession.

2. L. 1. §. 21. *De poss.*

" Si jusserim venditorem procuratori rem tradere, *cum ea in præsentiâ sit :* videri *mihi traditam* Priscus ait" (*i. e.,* to me personally, not merely to my attorney, through whom also, indeed, I might acquire Possession (*a*) : idemque esse

(*a*) Glossa interlin. (MS. Parisiarum, No. 4458 and 4455). On *mihi traditam,* " Y. (Irnerius) quasi expressim, præter illam adquisitionem quæ fit per Procuratorem."

si nummos debitorem jusserim alii dare, non est enim *corpore et tactu* necesse adprehendere possessionem, sed etiam *oculis et affectu* (*b*) : et *argumento esse* eas res, quæ propter magnitudinem ponderis moveri non possunt (*i. e.*, not easily moved, not by one man, for the things referred to are, notwithstanding, *mobiles*) ut columnas; nam pro traditis esse haberi, *si in re præsenti consenserint :* (et vina tradita videri, cum claves cellæ vinariæ emtori traditæ fuerint"—of which presently). This means, as the above mode of dealing is sufficient with things to which no other mode could easily be applied, so must it likewise be with respect to all other things (*argumento esse eas res,* &c).

3. L. 3, § 1, *de donat.*

" Species extra dotem a matre filiæ nomine viro traditas, *filiæ quæ præsens fuit donatas,* et ab eâ viro traditas videri respondit."

4. L. 51. *de poss.* (Javolenus, lib. 5, ex Posterioribus Labeonis).

" Quarundam rerum animo possessionem apisci nos ait Labeo; veluti si acervum lignorum emero, et eum venditor tollere me jusserit; simul atque custodiam posuissem, traditus mihi videtur. Idem juris esse vino vendito, cum universæ amphoræ vini simul essent. Sed videamus inquit, *ne hæc ipsa corporis traditio sit,* quia nihil interest, utrum mihi, an et cuilibet jusserim, custodia tradatur : in eo puto hanc quæstionem consistere, an *etiamsi corpore acervus aut amphoræ adprehensæ non sunt,* nihilominus traditæ videantur : nihil video interesse, utrum ipse acervum, an mandato meo aliquis custodiat : utrobique *animi* (*c*) *quodam genere possessio erit æstimanda.*" The meaning of this passage of Javolenus is as follows : " Labeo says, in many cases Possession is acquired incorporeally, for instance, in the purchase of a woodstack, by the mere taking the custody of it; and

---

(*b*) See *ante,* p. 148.

(*c*) Cujas reads, *corporis* in place of *animi,* (Recit. in L. 51, de poss.; Opp. T. 8, p. 314; also in Paratit. in Cod. Lib. 7, tit. 32). This emendation, however, is as unnecessary as it is bold.

so, also, in a purchase of wine. He adds, that this, perhaps, may well enure as a corporeal delivery, because it is
quite immaterial whether the purchaser takes charge in his
own person, or by another whom he appoints.   But I think
(Javolenus now says) (*d*) the acts of a deputy should not be
prayed in aid of the present question, for the question is,
whether the delivery in such case is complete without any
physical Prehension of the wood or the wine?   Now, undoubtedly it is complete, but for this reason it may be
affirmed, that the Possession in either case (whether with or
without a deputy) is, in a manner, acquired *incorporeally*" (*e*).

5. L. 14. § 1. De periculo et comm. rei vend.

"Videri autem trabes traditas, quas emtor signasset."
Sealing is not brought forward here as an act of Prehension,
but as a mode of dealing in practice from which the intention
of the parties could be deduced.   It is only in this way that
it can be explained why in another case, where exactly the
same physical act had place, a totally opposite conclusion is
drawn (*f*)

6. L. 1. C. *de donat.* (Severus et Antoninus).

"Emptionum mancipiorum instrumentis donatis et traditis,
et ipsorum mancipiorum donationem et traditionem factam
intelligis; et ideo potes adversas donatorem in rem actionem
exercere."

I interpret this passage thus.   Lucius, to whom the

(*d*) This is the usual, and, as
I now think, the correct division
of the passage.   In my two first
editions I conceived that Javolenus's own opinion commenced
with "*sed videamus.*"   This is
satisfactorily refuted by Wenck,
Diss. de traditione, p. 56, who
nevertheless completely misun-
derstands the whole passage,
which indeed was a necessary
consequence of his general theory.

(*e*) "*Animi quodam genere,*" i. e.
by *animus* only, in so far as the
term *corpore* is to be understood

wholly materially for corpore et
tactu, an interpretation which is
cautioned against in L. 1, § 21,
de poss.   But if *corpore* is taken,
as it should be, to denote the
external act simply, the acquisition in this case is, undoubtedly,
by *corpore* also ; so that the distinction in the above passage
does not, in any way, clash with
the general rules in L. 3, § 1, *de
poss.* (§ 14).

(*f*) L. 1, § *de peric. et comm.*
(see *post,* p. 159).

rescript is addressed, must have had some slaves given to him by a party who had previously purchased them, and who still had the title deeds. Lucius and the donor being in company together, the latter, in presence of the slaves, made known his intention to give them away, and at the same time handed over the deeds to Lucius. The slaves remained, however, with their old master, who subsequently repented of his generosity and withheld the delivery of them, alleging that the donation was a mere loose promise, and had not been completed. If this allegation were sustainable, Lucius, undoubtedly, could have no *actio in rem*, and, possibly, no action at all on account of the Lex Cincia, or because no stipulation had passed. All turned here on the intention of the parties to effect a donation immediately; if this intention were clear, nothing was wanting as to delivery, because the slaves were present. Lucius petitioned the Emperors, who replied, " the intention to make a valid gift at the time is clear from the delivery of the title-deeds, and therefore the delivery was complete; the property passed, and you may have a vindication against the donor." Thus explained, the passage contains an application of our proposition, that where the intention is clear, the mere presence of the subject-matter, without any other corporeal act, suffices for Prehension. Undoubtedly, in this explanation I am driven to assume that the slaves were present, which is not mentioned in the passage; but the passage is only a rescript in a particular case, the facts of which are not set out, and my assumption of what the fact was is probable and unforced (*g*),

(*g*) In the two first editions, I recognised, with Fulgentius, (Comp. Obrecht de poss. § 280), a *constitutum possessiorium*. But to suppose such an agreement, would be an assumption wholly foreign to the spirit of the text, and the slaves might just as well have remained behind accidentally in the house of their former master, *i. e.*, they may not have gone away at the time with Lucius. My present interpretation was the prevailing one with the Glossers. Glossa interlin. anon. MS. Paris, 4523, 4528, on the word *mancipiorum, præsentium in traditione, sicut dicitur de clavibus traditis coram horreo.* Gloss. of Pillius, MS. Paris, 4536. " *Sed*

and agrees remarkably with the *actio in rem* mentioned at the conclusion, from which, at least, it appears most clear that the donor had still possession of the slaves. Every other explanation of the passage requires equally a state of facts to be assumed, and, indeed, much more arbitrary and bolder facts than mine (*h*).

Of the rule, that Possession may be acquired by mere presence, without any other physical act, the following applications and more precise examples have still to be added :—

First,—If I allow a thing, which another person intends to deliver to me, to be given to a third party, the juridical Possession is actually in me, and passes from me to such third party (*i*). Herein is contained a simple application of our rule; for when the second party manifested his intention as .to the subject (before him), I become at once the uncontrolled owner of it, as much as if I had taken it into my hand; indeed, I exercise actual ownership over it by the dealing with it which I display in making a delivery to the

numquid est hoc intelligendum quando mancipia absunt; respondeo nequaquam, sed cum præsentialiter adsunt ut ff de rei vend. hæc si res. Pil." Accursius *v. instrumentis,* "*si præsentibus servis datis.*"

(*h*) Thus, Wenck, De Traditione, p. 30; who wishes to interpret the passage according to his view of a delivery without any possession, and who is here driven to the most arbitrary assumptions of fact, yet, nevertheless, introduces all kinds of mistakes also. Hufeland, Neue Darstellung, p. 124, in order to explain this passage, assumes a special law for the delivery of slaves, but no trace of any such law is anywhere to be found. The above passage, moreover, bears a remarkable

similarity to an edict of Antonine's, according to which, the form of donations between parents and children is to be construed liberally. L. 4, C. Theo. de don. Fragm. Vat. § 297, 314, (Comp. the Anm. von Bucholtz.) It might therefore be conceived, perhaps, that the passage in question had reference to the above special case, and that a hasty abridgement of it had been imported into Justinian's code, (added to the 6th ed.)

(*i*) "Species extra dotem a matre *filiæ nomine* viro traditas, *filiæ quæ præsens fuit, donatas, et ab ea viro traditas* videri respondi." L. 31, § 1, *de donat.,* cf. L 3, § 12, *de donat. inter vir et ux.;* L. 1, § 21, *de poss.* (p. 152).

third party. In this transaction, the simplicity of the external act which occurs may easily allow the principle of law, which completes the operation, to escape notice (*j*).

Secondly,—Presence is only capable of conferring Possession, in the cases where it is possible actually to handle the subject-matter at any moment. Thus, whoever is in pursuit of game, still has no Possession of it, although he get quite close to it; nay, though it be even wounded mortally, he may, in many cases, be unable actually to take it ("multa accidere possunt, ut eam non capiamus"); thus, even in such case Possession is not acquired, although some even of the Roman Jurists assert the contrary (*k*). Accordingly, game must be actually caught, or killed, to enable Possession of it to be acquired.

Thirdly,—When the goods are in a locked-up building, delivery, and, consequently, the acquisition of Possession, is admitted to take place by the delivery over of keys. It is very natural that keys, from the earliest times, should have been considered symbolical; and it was unnecessary to go much further, in order to lay down that any other article might have served just as well, and that keys were only mentioned by way of example in the Roman Law (*l*). Now it certainly cannot be denied, that keys might serve as well as any thing else for a mere symbol, and on occasions of the entrance of a sovereign, where the keys of the city are delivered to him, no other purpose can be well conceived. But there is another use for keys, however, which is even more common than the above, namely, to open locks; and that this is the use alluded to shall now be proved. For it has been shown above, that even as to moveables, mere presence,

(*j*) " .... Nam celeritate conjungendarum inter se actionum unam actionem occultari," L. 3, § 12, *de don. inter vir et ux.*

(*k*) L. 5, § 1, *de adqu. rer dom.* § 13, I. *de rer div.*; L. 55, *de adqu. rer dom.* decides another but similar case according to the

same principles. The decision lies in the words, "ut *si in meam potestatem pervenit*, meus factus sit."

(*l*) Schmaltz, Handbuch des Roemischen Privatrechts, § 199, Kœnisberg, 1801.

without any actual physical taking, enures as Prehension.
But this *factum* must be accompanied by *animus* also, in
order to enable Possession to be acquired, and this *animus*,
in the generality of cases, can only be ascertained by
inference, because it is seldom expressly made manifest.
Suppose a piece of ground is to be sold, the purchaser and
seller may be conceived to go frequently to the spot, without
the latter having the intention of giving, or the former of
taking, Possession.   So also with moveables, if the bargain
is completed, even though the goods are on the spot, still the
purchaser may not have the intention of taking Possession,
if the property is in a locked-up warehouse, of which he has
not the keys, because he might be prevented, at any future
moment, from dealing with the property.   For this reason,
Possession is only then deemed to be acquired when the
keys are handed over.

    1. L. 9, § 6. De adqu. rer. dom. (§ 45. I. de rer. div.)

    " Item si quis merces in *horreo repositas* vendiderit,
simul atque *claves horrei tradiderit* emptori, transfert proprietatem mercium ad emptorem."

    2. L. 1, § 21, de poss.

    " .... et vina tradita videri, *cum claves* (*m*) *cellæ
vinariæ emptori traditæ fuerint.*"

    Indeed, even if the purchaser has affixed his seal to the
goods, Possession is not acquired without delivery of the
key, although the act may undoubtedly avail as an act of
Prehension if the goods are not locked up.

    1. L. 1, § 2, de peric. et comm. rei vend.

    " *Si dolium signatum* sit ab emptore, Trebatius ait,

(*m*) Glossa interlin. MS. Paris,
num. 4458 and 4455, at the word
claves. " Y. (Irnerius) *quasi ad-
miniculum custodiæ,*" therefore,
not as symbol, but on the ground
of the natural dominion over the
subject which thereby arose,
(add. to 4th ed.) Quentzel also,
De litteris recognitionis, § 26,

Leidæ, 1754, grounds the effect
of keys upon the same principle,
(although he terms the delivery
of them symbolical), as by their
means the goods may be unlocked
and come at, and for this reason
he ascribes the same effect to the
delivery of a bill of lading. (Note
of Professor Falck).

traditum id videri; *Labeo contra. Quod et verum est;
magis enim ne summutetur signari solere, quam ut traditum
videatur.*"

2. L. 14, § 1. *eod.*

" Videri autem *trabes traditas,* quas emptor *signasset.*"
That is to say, it is just as usual to keep timber unlocked up,
as it is unusual with wine.

In all these instances, therefore, it is assumed, from the
probabilities in each case, that the parties *intended* delivery
when the keys were handed over; but the *animus possidendi,* by itself, can have no operation without Prehension,
it is always assumed, therefore, in those passages which
merely treat of the *animus,* whether the intention to deliver
may be surmised or not, that no necessary incident in the
Prehension is wanting, *i. e.,* that the delivery of the keys
takes place in the presence of the goods. And the compilers
took care, in the following passage, that no doubt should arise
on this point.

L. 74. *de contr. emt.*

" Clavibus traditis, *ita* mercium in horreis conditarum
possessio tradita videtur, *si claves apud horrea traditæ sint,*
(what follows now is especially serviceable to explain and
confirm my notion of Prehension,) quo facto confestim
emtor dominium et possessionem adipiscitur, *etsi non aperuerit horrea.*" That is to say, he who is separated from
the goods by a door locked up, has just as little possession
of them as if he were at a great distance, but if he has the
keys, he may at any moment take the goods in hand; and
whether he actually do this, or even unlock the door
or not, is quite immaterial, so far as the acquisition of
Possession is concerned (*n*).

(*n*) Wenck, de traditione, p.
50, explains this passage according to his erroneous assumption
that Possession may be acquired
through the property and for the
sake of the property, although
the otherwise essential requisites
of Possession are wanting.

SECTION XVIII.

As respects moveables, therefore, Possession may be acquired without any actual taking by the hand, provided only that the subject be on the spot (§. 17). But there is another mode, also, in which it may be acquired. Where, for instance, a man has got a thing in *his house*, he may acquire Possession of it from that fact only, without any additional act whatsoever.

L. 18, § *d. de poss.*

" Si venditorem, quod emerim, deponere *in mea domo* jusserim; possidere me certum est, *quamquam id nemo dum attigerit.*" It is not in any way implied here, that the bargain should be struck in the presence of the subject, nor that the purchaser should be at home when the delivery was made; accordingly, it is the simple act of delivery which transfers the Possession. The Roman Jurist expressly observes also, that the subject need not be given into the charge of any of the purchaser's servants in his name (" quanquam id nemo dum attigerit"), for otherwise it might be supposed that the Possession was founded on such circumstance.

L. 9, § 3. *de jur. dot.*

" .... quid enim interest, inferantur volente eo in domum ejus, an ei tradantur?"

The principle of this rule is easily discovered. Every one has the undoubted control over his own house, as over all other property, and, as arising out of this control, the custody of everything contained in the house. It clearly appears that this was the view of the Roman Jurists, because in a different, though similar, case, Possession is denied on the ground of such custody being wanting (*a*). From hence the requisites of the above sort of Possession, which are not mentioned in the passage itself, are easily deducible.

(*a*) L. 3, § 3, *de poss.*

For as the passage speaks merely of the actual *user* of the house in question, it follows:—

1st. Such acquisition requires neither property, nor juridical Possession, in the house. Whoever, therefore, hires a house or shop, may acquire Possession in the above mode, although he neither owns the building nor possesses it juridically; for even without the latter rights, he, undoubtedly, has the custody of all the things on the premises.

2nd. But for the same reason, on the other hand, such Possession is incapable of being acquired, if the party has not the actual user of the house, although both the property and Possession may reside in him. Thus the landlord of demised premises cannot acquire Possession in this manner, for the very same reason which enables his tenant so to do, although in this case the proprietor has in no way parted with his juridical Possession (*b*). This second proposition enables an explanation to be given of the following passage, which might otherwise throw a doubt upon the correctness of our rule (*c*). " Qui universas ædes possidet (possedit) *singulas res, quæ in ædificio sunt, non videtur possedisse*," i. e., the juridical Possession of the house does not necessarily give Possession, also, of all that is in the house, so as to conclude the second question by the former. Very properly, because we may have Possession of a house without living in it ourselves, for instance, when we purchase, and at the same time let it to the vendor (constitutum possessorium). But the apparent contradiction between this passage and our rule, may be removed in another way also. Namely,

(*b*) Both of these positions are elucidated and confirmed by the following passages; L. 5, § 2—5, *de injuriis*; L. 22, § 2, L. 23, § 3, *ad Leg. Jul. de adult.* Still the resemblance of these passages to the case in the text is not complete, because they are confined to the party's own *dwelling-house*, which is not the case here.

(*c*) L. 30, *pr. de poss.*
The Gloss and most modern jurists understand by the words, "res quæ in *ædificio* sunt," the bricks and timber of which the house is built. The meaning of the passage would then be very clear, but the interpretation is forced.

whoever acquires Possession of a house, as, for instance, by
turning out the party in possession, may, perhaps, know
nothing as to the different articles on the premises; he,
therefore, has no Possession of them, because he has no
animus possidendi.

From these more precise explanations of our rule, the
decision on another case, which has much resemblance with
the above, may be elucidated, I mean as to the Possession
of treasure trove. In the theory of property, the term
thesaurus comprehends every article of value which has been
concealed, and which, from the lapse of time, has lost an
owner (*d*): and this limitation of the notion is very proper
there, because it is only in such case that a question could
arise as to any special acquisition of property, and it is
therefore, only in that respect that the subject-matter finds
a place in the theory of property. But it is quite otherwise
with Possession, as to which, it is immaterial whether
the property be in another or not; in such case, all money
that has been buried is *thesaurus*, and it is the same thing
whether the owner can be discovered or not; for this reason,
the Roman Jurists apply the word *thesaurus* to both cases
indiscriminately, and this use of the term is so suitable, that
they never had occasion, in any one instance, to reject it.
Quite otherwise with the Gloss and the modern Jurists. In
the passages of the Roman Law treating of the Possession
of treasure, they distinguish between *thesaurus* in its wide,
and in its narrow, sense, a distinction which leads to nothing
but inextricable confusion of the simple rules of the Roman
Law. Lastly, it is self-evident, also, that there is no juridical distinction between treasure and any other moveable
buried in the ground; and that the Possession of the former
has only been treated of in the law sources, because it
happens to be the most important and most frequent of that
class of cases.

(*d*) Thesaurus est vetus quædam depositio pecuniæ *cujus non
exstat memoria, ut jam dominum*
non habeat: sic enim fit ejus, qui
invenerit, quod non alterius sit,"
L. 31, § 1, *de adquir. rer. dom.*

Now, where treasure, or any other moveable, is buried, does the possessor of the land, by that simple fact, acquire Possession of the subject, *i. e.*, does the act of burial constitute the *factum* upon which, if *animus* be superinduced, Possession actually grounds itself? There is a resemblance in this case to the one which has been treated of above (p. 160), namely, that a moveable becomes connected with an immoveable, without, nevertheless, being incorporated with it: in the first-mentioned case (where the article was deposited on the premises), the Possession was acquired by means of this connection, and the same result would appear to follow necessarily here also, provided only that the land is in our possession. But with regard to a house, the reason why Possession of moveables becomes acquired consists in the exclusive custody which alone is exerciseable there; it follows in the present case, therefore, that Possession of the treasure does not, by the above fact, accrue to the possessor of the soil (*e*). It is as necessary for him, therefore, as for any other person, in order to acquire such Possession, to *dig up*, or *take*, the treasure; and then, in the usual manner, Possession is acquired by actual handling, or by personal presence (§ 17). The above propositions are contained in the following passages of the Roman Law:—

1. L. 15, *ad exhibendum.*

" Thesaurus *meus* (*f*) in tuo fundo est, nec eum pateris

(*e*) How if the money is concealed in my house? If I know where it is, I possess it without the act of taking it from its place of concealment, *quia est sub nostrâ custodiâ:* if I do not know the spot, but merely that it is somewhere about the house, I am not in fact the possessor of it, because the discovery of it turns on mere chance. Thus undoubtedly, with respect to treasure also, there is a distinction between houses and land. Pfeiffer, without reason, denies this distinc-

tion, Recht der Kriegseroberung, p. 17, Cassel, 1823; and he also lays down, just as erroneously, that one may acquire possession of goods bought, not only by having them delivered at one's own house, but on the land of a third party, (add. to 6th ed.)

(*f*) Thus the *Thesaurus*, spoken of here, is not that which is meant where acquisition of property is in question (p. 162). The same remark applies to the following passage.

M 2

me effodere; cum eum *loco non moveris*, furti quidem aut
ad exhibendum, eo nomine agere recte non posse me, Labeo
ait: quia neque *possideres eum*, neque dolo feceris, quo
minus possideres," &c.

2. L. 44, *pr. de poss.*

" .... cum, si alius in meo condidisset (pecuniam)
non alias possiderem, quam si ipsius rei possessionem (g)
supra terram adeptus fuissem.

3. L. 3, § 3, *de poss.* (h).

Neratius et Proculus (et)
solo animo *non* (i) posse nos
adquirere possessionem, si
non antecedat naturalis possessio (j). *Ideoque* si thesaurum in fundo meo (k)
*positum sciam continuo me
possidere, simul atque possidendi affectum habuero; quia*

Neratius and Proculus lay
down that Possession can
not be acquired by a mere
act of the will, unless the
physical act in all Possession
—detention—has preceded
it. From this, they deduce
that the Possessor of land
may acquire the Possession

(g) *Possessio* here means Possession in its natural sense (§ 7),
and the *possessionem adipisci* is
used to denote the requisite for
the (juridical) *possidere* in the
same way as, in other passages,
naturalis possessio is used to express the same requisite, L. 3, §
3, 13, *de poss.*

(h) This passage has occupied
numerous commentators from the
earliest times. The best *scholiæ*
upon it are to be found in En-
gelb. De Man Diss. de Thesauro
ad L. 3, § 3, de poss. (Thes.
Diss. Belg. Vol. 1, Tom. 2, p.
305—386, contains this treatise,
mixed up with much rubbish),
and in Cuperus, p. 2, cap. 32—3.
I give my own view in a free
translation, and explain and support it by notes.

(i) See note (l), p. 165.

(j) That is, *posse* nos adquirere (solo animo) possessionem
si antecedat naturalis possessio.
This is clearly enough expressed
by the double negative, and thus
it is altogether unnecessary to
suppose that the positive portion
of the proposition has been
omitted by Paulus or his transcriber.

(k) This does not allude to
property in the *fundus*, but to
detention, and the expression
meus fundus is only used because
detention and property, in the
first instance and according to
the principle, go together. If
the land were demised, the question would turn upon the right,
not of the owner of the soil, but
of the tenant.

quod desit naturali posses-
sioni, id animus implet (l).

of treasure buried there by a
mere act of the will; because

(*l*) The meaning of the whole
passage is as follows : First,
a general rule, on which no
question arose, is extracted from
the writings of the first two
jurists ; then an application of
the rule, out of the same works,
is made to treasure; then, another
view on the same question is
mentioned and refuted ; lastly, a
third opinion is quoted upon the
same case, and is approved of.
Modern jurists have conceived
that the rule of Neratius stands
in (actual or apparent) contradiction with the application of
it : this error springs from two
causes. First, they clearly saw
that *naturalis possessio* here denotes the physical act in Possession, the *factum ;* but, as they
make this *factum* to consist in
bodily contact, they could not
understand how *naturalis possessio*
was to be recognized here ; but
this is readily apparent when the
factum is shown to mean the immediate power of dealing with
the subject, which was what
Neratius erroneously assumed.
Second, they translated " quod
desit naturali possessioni," by
" what was still deficient in *the*
naturalis *possessio ;*" but the *na-*
turalis possessio already existed,
and all that was wanted to be
added to it was the external act
to convert it into juridical possessio. The Gloss accordingly
says on the words, " si non antecedat naturalis possessio," et sup-
ple, *vel aliud quod pro eâ habea-*

tur." In later times, *naturalis*
possessio has been held to refer
to the land, and through the
latter it became indirect with
respect to the treasure also, and
even without the *naturalis pos-*
sessio of it, juridical Possession
might arise ; Paul de Castro, in
Dig. Nov. p. 1, fo. 56, Lugd.
1548 ; see further, Zasius, Cujacius, Chesius, and many others.
Some have erred still deeper,
by striking out the first *non*
(solo animo *non* posse) ; N. A.
Salis Sicilim. j. civ. Hannov.
1614, 8vo. p. 354 ; Nordt, Probabil. L. 2, c. 6, num. 4. Jensius
was the first to explain the passage correctly, though quite
briefly ; Strictur. p. 328, ed.
1739. Man gives the correct interpretation of "desit" at length,
l. c. p 351—53. He also explains naturalis possessio correctly, still he is of opinion that,
as a fiction of law is required,
the term has been improperly
used, and this doubt perplexes
him so much, that, after many
attempts to solve it, he finally
goes back to the commonly received doctrine, and refers naturalis possessio to the *fundus*, l. c.
pp. 351—9, 379. Cuperus's, p. 2,
C. 32, interpretation is throughout sound, but so brief that it is
impossible to see what defence
he would have made as to the
usual objections respecting *natu-*
ralis possessio. Wenck de Trad.
p. 12, gives this explanation of
the passage ; " in the first half,

Ceterum quod Brutus et Manilius putant, eum qui fundum longâ possessione cepit, etiam thesaurum cepisse, quamvis nesciat in fundo esse, non est verum; is enim qui nescit, non possidet thesaurum, quamvis fundum possideat; sed et si sciat, non capiet longâ possessione; quia scit alienum esse (m).

detention already existed, and, therefore, all that was wanting to detention, to convert it into juridical Possession, was the *animus possidendi*, which was thus supplied. On the other hand, the opinion of Brutus and Manilius, that the treasure is a part of the soil, and, therefore, is held along with it in

(from Neratius to implet), treasure without an owner is alluded to; in which case, the naturalis possessio, which was wanting in point of fact, was supplied by means of the property, and this view of Neratius is approved of by Paulus. But in the second half, (from Ceterum to quibus consentio), the question relates only to treasure lying in the property of another person." The first assumption (that Possession is acquired through the property) is not only incorrect, but the whole distinction between the two cases is arbitrarily imported into the passage.

(m) Throughout this passage *Thesaurus* means all buried money generally, without reference to its having an owner or not (p. 162). Therefore, *not merely* ownerless treasure, as is undeniably shewn by the words "quia scit alienum est." Just as little, however, does it mean merely such treasure as, though it might be in the land of another party, was, nevertheless, without an owner, which Cuperus asserted

on false grounds, (see *post*, § 33), and which most jurists have doubted, for the two following reasons: 1st, because the question turned upon usucaption of the treasure; but this was never needed as to things without an owner. Up to Justinian's time, indeed, every case of occupancy required Usucaption to supervene, in order to convert bonitarious property into justum dominium; and therefore, the whole of this doubt turns upon the usual errors as to the relation of "res nec mancipi," and Roman property, errors which were only first cleared up by Hugo: 2nd, on account of the words "quia scit *alienum* esse." Fruitless attempts have been made, partly by emendation, partly by commentary, to get over this objection. Bynkershoek, Obs. VII. 1; Cuperus, P. 2, c. 33; Man. l. c. pp. 343—5. My view is as follows: the possessor of the land must be taken to have not as yet discovered the treasure himself, and yet to know the fact; How could that happen? Only by his having obtained some

Quidam putant, Sabini sen-
tentiam veriorem esse, nec
alias eum, qui scit, possidere
nisi si loco motus sit: quia
non sit sub custodia nostra,
quibus consentio (*n*).

Usucaption, even if the Possessor knew nothing of the
treasure, this opinion (they
say) is undoubtedly incorrect,
even according to their own
assumption, for the trea-

knowledge of the burial of the
treasure; but he would then
know at the same time that it
belonged to another; L. 31, § 1,
de adq. rer. dom. "depositio....
cujus *memoria non exstat.*" The
question therefore here must
relate to treasure belonging to
another person, not that the
whole passage treats of such treasure only, but because *knowledge*
as to the treasure cannot well be
conceived of in any other way.

(*n*) The Gloss and nearly all
the interpreters find this conclusion very remarkable, as asportation of the subject in other
cases is not needed to acquire
possession, and as to certain subjects (such as land) it is impossible. For this reason the majority refer the whole passage
merely to treasure which still
belongs to another party, (see the
preceding note), and therefore
asportation becomes necessary
here, just as in L. 15, ad exhib.,
and L. 44, pr. de poss., as a special act to exclude the previous
possessor, which explanation is
itself founded on entirely false
principles. Odofred (fo. 55)
comes to just the opposite conclusion, as he refers the passage
to strict treasure trove, *i. e.* to
treasure having no owner, and,
accordingly, he requires an actual

handling for all ownerless property, "quia possunt intervenire
multi casus, quibus nostra non
fiunt...... præterea non est ibi
aliquis, qui velit in me transferre
possessionem." Bynkershoek, Obs.
VII. 1, reads loco *notus* in place
of loco motus, and thus by aid of
an emendation, and of a strained
interpretation, he arrives at a
result which is wholly false. In
this case however, as in all others,
the *immediate presence* of the subject is what constitutes prehension; but as it can scarcely be
conceived that any one should
dig up treasure without taking
it out of the ground and carrying
it off, the *loco motio* might, by
inadvertence, be referred to as
the act of prehension, and this
the rather, as the *only* object was
to contradict the doctrine of Neratius, who grounded Possession
on a mere act of the *will*. This
correct explanation of the words
nisi si loco motus sit, is to be
found only amongst the very
oldest Glossers. Glossa interlin.
MS. Paris, 4458, a. G. (Guerne-
rius) "vel pro moto habeatur
veluti si coram positum Thesaurum oculis et affectione videatur apprehendisse, sicut in aliis
rebus ut, l. c. I. 1." Glossa,
interlin. Paris, 4455; "Vel pro
moto habeatur veluti si præsens

sure, in fact, is not a part of
the soil, and, consequently,
is not possessed along with it
by the possessor of the soil,
and the latter must have special notice of its being there;
but even if he has, and therefore has the Possession of the
treasure, according to the first
doctrine, he could not have
Usucaption of it, because at
the same time that he had
notice of the treasure, he
would know also that it belonged to some one else, and
therefore he would be *in malâ
fide.* Some think, with Sabinus, the Possessor of the
land could not acquire Possession of the treasure by a
mere act of the will, but that
he must dig it up, for it is
only by so doing that he
obtains the custody. This
is the correct doctrine.

Thesaurus oculis et affectu ap-
prehendatur quod in possessione
necessarium est," M. (Martinus).
The result is, that the three passages cited in the text exactly
correspond; it is wholly immaterial whether the buried treasure mentioned in them has an
owner or not, or whether it has
been previously in another person's possession or not.

SECTION XIX.

PREHENSION DEFINED MORE STRICTLY.

I have now shewn, by interpretation, what I had previously assumed, that it is the immediate power of dealing with a subject (§ 5), and not actual contact which constitutes Prehension. This view does away with all fictitious Prehension, because all those cases in which a fiction upon arbitrary assumptions has been imagined to exist may be comprised within the notion of actual Prehension.

But, having proved the truth of this notion, I must now explain it more fully; and the readiest mode to do so, will be by bringing together some passages which have been already elucidated.

When a man wounds a wild animal (*fera naturæ*) mortally, and follows it up close, he does not nevertheless obtain Possession of it until he actually catches or kills it; for it is possible, in many ways, that it may altogether escape him (§ 17), and, therefore, he has not been able, at any one period of time, to deal with it at will, which is the indispensable requisite in the acquisition of Possession. Just so, and for the same reason, the owner of a field does not obtain Possession of treasure trove until it is actually dug up (§ 168); because, here also, it might easily happen that some other person may discover the treasure; and, therefore, it never would be, at any one moment, in the Possession of the owner of the soil.

On the other hand, Possession of a thing may be acquired simply by the fact of its having been delivered at one's own residence, even though we are absent from the house at the time (§ 18); yet still in this case, also, it is not impossible, but that some one else might immediately enter the house with strong hand, so as to prevent us from having the article in question in our power, at any one moment. In like

manner, Possession of land may be delivered from a neighbouring tower (§ 17), although it might happen there, also,
that, at the very moment when the new possessor was about
to enter upon his purchase, another party should step in with
a claim to the Possession, and forcibly prevent his entry.

What, then, is the principle which allows of Possession
being acquired in these cases, yet not in the first? Evidently this, that the possibility of being prevented from
exercising control over the subject, before it comes actually
to hand, is very great in the first instance, but so slight in
all the others, that it never enters into the contemplation of
the possessor. Every one will acknowledge that a wounded
hare may easily get away from him, or that he may search
in vain for hidden treasure so long that some one else
may forestal him; but that the sanctity of his house should
be interfered with by force, or that in the short space of
time necessary to enter an adjoining field, a new possessor should spring up, who was not previously to be
seen, are circumstances so improbable, that no one would
take their possibility into consideration. Therefore it is
that in the latter cases, though not in the first, the consciousness of physical power arises, and it is this which constitutes
the notion of the act by which Possession is to be acquired.
That is to say, the power to deal with the subject at pleasure must be capable of being conceived by the party who
wishes to acquire Possession, as a *power exerciseable on the
spot.*

We have thus discovered a new element for the material
notion of Possession (§ 9), by the aid of which we may at
once most easily take cognizance either of the gain or loss
of Possession. Every case of Possession, namely, is founded
on the state of consciousness of unlimited physical power (*a*).

(*a*) If the above proposition is
read thus, "whoever means to
exercise a physical control over
a subject possesses it," nothing is
easier than to refute it, and in
this shape it has been in fact
refuted by Zachariä, De Poss, p.27.
But I conceived that I had guarded
myself so completely against
such a misconception, that I do

To *create* this feeling, the desire (*animus*) to have the subject as one's own must exist (*b*); and at the same time, the physical requisites of power, which are capable of giving rise to this consciousness (*corpus*). Possession becomes *continuous* by the continuance of those conditions (corpore et animo) by which it was originally acquired: but it is very evident, that the same immediate physical power is not necessary to continue the Possession, as was required to give rise to it; and continuing Possession depends rather on the constant power which exists of *reproducing* the original relation at will. For this reason, we do not lose Possession by mere absence from the subject, which we have once appropriated to ourselves, although the physical relation in which we now stand to it, would not have sufficed in the first instance to obtain Possession (*c*): which is a distinction between the physical conditions of acquiring and continuing Possession, that could not thoroughly be explained without reference to the state of consciousness of the possessor (*d*).

not know how to add anything which can make my expression more precise. For I expressly stated, that facts must exist sufficient to give rise to the above feeling of consciousness, so that the consciousness is merely alluded to in reference to these facts ; partly for the sake of explaining how those facts operate, and partly to define the notion of the said facts more precisely. But in what relates to the continuance of Possession I have just as clearly stated, that *that* depends on the ability to reproduce similar facts to those by which the Possession was acquired, (1st ed. §§ 29 & 32), which ability indeed does not cease by removal from the subject and forgetfulness of its possession, although it does by actual loss and *animus non possidendi*.

(*b*) For the question cannot arise here on a *derivative* Possession as a mere modification of the original notion (§ 9).

(*c*) This distinction between the continuance and the acquisition of Possession is apparent in the language of the law itself; thus, under the same state of facts, the *custodia* is denied in one passage, (L. 3, § 3, *de poss.*), and recognized in another (L. 44, *pr. de poss.*); but the first passage alludes to acquisition, and the second to continuance of Possession.

(*d*) Zachariä considers it no slight advantage of his notion of Possession, that it makes the acquisition and continuance of Possession depend on the same conditions, De Poss. p. 27. But this uniformity does not flow from his notion, but from the following

The above may, perhaps, also serve to clear up the disputed question as to the nature of Prehension. For it has been already remarked (§ 16), that the generality of writers consider the Prehension, which does not consist in an actual taking by the hand, as merely fictitious and symbolical, and many of them, accordingly, only allow of it in cases of delivery, or, indeed, only when a case of property is in question. Others have adopted, it is true, the correct notion of Prehension, but they are inclined to draw a distinction between a delivery, and a forcible ex-parte seizure (e). In point of fact, such distinction does exist, though it is referable, not to the principle itself, but to the application of it. If it is asked, for instance, what the conditions are, under which the fact of personal presence enables the consciousness of physical power to arise, it is clear that these depend, especially in reference to inter- ference by a third party, very much on the special circumstances of the case. In the simplest form, however, this consciousness is felt on the occasion of a delivery, where the previous possessor having attained, by habit, a higher degree of security as to his control over the subject, the benefit of this security at once passes to the new possessor. Thus, the same outward act will often avail to give Possession in a case of delivery, which would be insufficient in a case of ex-parte occupancy. In examining this question, the immediate practical point of the dispute almost disappears, as in most cases the question whether Possession has been acquired or not receives nearly the same answer from both contending parties. The disputed question still remains, as to the legal principle and its foundation, and, indeed, as to

proposition, "initio possessionis probato, tamdiu ejus retentio præsumitur, donec probetur contrarium, i. e. finis," p. 16. But this sentence is completely foisted in, and follows so little from his general notion, that it rather contradicts it. For, according to his notion, the words, "Signa e

quibus constet alicui inesse animum, etc." should have reference to the existence of Possession ; but, in the above proposition, they stand out as mere medium of proof which may be supplied by a (foisted in) presumption.

(e) Thus, for instance, Hufe- land, Neue Darstellung, p. 88.

many practical consequences of this principle, since my opponents treat several cases of acquisition by delivery, which appear to me to be actual acquisitions, as merely symbolical, and, therefore quite contrary to the nature of Possession, would make them dependent on mere juridical conditions (§ 16). Furthest removed of all from the correct view of Possession, are those who would merely give rise to it as a consequence of property (*ibid*). They not only confuse all the relation to fact which is comprised in the notion, but they have not even the letter of the law for them in any one instance; for many of the passages, from which I have deduced above (§§ 16, 17, 18) the general notion of Prehension, speaking, it is true, only of delivery, nevertheless, never require that the delivering party should be the owner or even the bonâ-fide possessor, and, therefore, they are not at all more applicable to cases of a delivery of property, than to other cases where no right in the subject is acquired by delivery.

This being the general principle of Prehension, as it has been thus abstracted from the different cases determined by the Roman Jurists, all other cases which have not been expressly discussed in the Roman Law, may be decided in conformity with it. Suppose, for instance, a question arose as to the Possession of an estate, which contained several farms, spread over a wide district; would it be sufficient here, also, to make an entry at one spot only, so as to become possessor of the whole? The Roman Law does not mention this case, for the fundi, of which the Roman Jurists speak, are evidently patches of ground of limited extent, which might be surveyed at one glance. According to our fundamental principle, Possession would not be acquired by the above act, but only by such acts as would enable the moral conviction of physical power to arise as to *every portion* of the estate; thus the estate, which, juridically considered, is looked upon as an entirety (universitas), is, in such acts as have no juridical form, regarded as made up of different parts. But this would be quite other-

wise, if, according to the usual doctrine, we allowed Possession of land to be acquired by symbolical acts; the effect
of such symbolical acts would extend to the whole estate,
because, juridically, it is one and entire, and, therefore,
its physical position and extent could make no difference.

----◆----

SECTION XX.

ACQUISITION BY A PREVIOUS ACT OF PREHENSION.

A full explanation has now been given of the external
act which, with co-existent *animus*, gives rise to Possession.

It only now remains to explain the case where the
physical relation has occurred before the Possession can be
considered as acquired.

That the *animus* in this case also, as the second condition
in all acquisitions, must supervene, is quite clear; but as
respects Prehension, with which alone we are now engaged,
no new act is at all necessary. To this extent Possession
is acquired by *animus* only (*a*), because at the moment of
acquisition nothing but a mere declaration of intention
usually occurs.

At the same time it is clear that for the acquisition of Possession the same remote physical relation would be sufficient
in this case, as would have been sufficient to preserve a Possession already acquired (p. 171), it being assumed that in the
former case also a previous act of Prehension had occurred.

The most important case under this head relates to what
is called *traditio brevi manu*. Two very different matters
are meant by this expression; one, the delivery of property

(*a*) L. 3, § 3, *de poss.* "Ne-   sionem, si non antecedat naturalis
ratius et Proculus (et) solo animo   possessio," (p. 165), note (*l*).
non posse nos adquirere posses-

when the Possession has been already given over (b), which is a case of no interest here, as it works no change of Possession; the other, delivery of Possession, where the party had previously had mere detention, in which case Possession is acquired in the mode already described. The following passages have reference to the latter class.

1. L. 9, § 5, *de adqu. rer. dom.* (§ 44, I. *de rer. divis.*)

"Interdum etiam sine traditione nuda voluntas domini sufficit ad rem transferendam: veluti si rem quam *commodavi,*

(b) L. 21, § 1, *de adqu. rer. dom.* " Si rem meam *possideas, et eam velim tuam esse;* fiet tua, quamvis possessio apud me non fuerit," cf. L. 46, *de rei vind.* It is quite unnecessary that this transaction should take place in presence of the subject, for L. 47, *de rei vind.* evidently refers to what is termed a fictitious possessor, *i. e.* to a defendant who was not actually in possession, (cum *possessionem ejus possessor nactus sit*), and thus *res absens* means the subject which was not in his possession. The following passages also do not apply here, L. 11, *pr.,* L. 15, *de reb. cred.,* L. 34, *pr. mandati;* for whoever owes money upon a *mandatum,* has both the property and the Possession of the specific pieces of money; and if this *obligatio* is converted into a mutuum.... not the least change is worked either in the property or the Possession; the question therefore, whether such conversion is permissible (a question on which the above passages are in open contradiction with one another) does not belong at all to the theory either of

Possession or property. My reviewer in the Juristischen Archiv. B. 4, S. 411, objects to this, on the ground, that a mandatory to collect money does not in any way become owner and possessor of the money, "it being assumed that the money collected remains with him *in specie.*" But on this very assumption the direct contrary may be laid down; 1st, because in these passages it is the law of obligation only that is treated of, in which it is natural and usual to leave out of view altogether, whether the mandatory has kept in his possession the identical pieces of coin; 2nd, because, in the passage cited L. 34, *pr.,* a *depositum* is expressly opposed to *mandatum* on this very point; "nec huic simile esse, quod si pecuniam apud te depositam convenerit, ut creditam habeas, credita fiat: *quia tunc nummi, qui mei erant, tui fiunt.*" And quite rightly, for the keeping of the money *in specie,* which is a matter of chance with the mandatory, was the express duty of the depository.

aut *locavi* tibi, aut apud te *deposui* (*c*) vendidero tibi; licet enim ex eâ causâ tibi non tradiderim, eo tamen, quod patior eam ex causâ emtionis apud te esse, *tuam efficio.*"

2. L. 62, *pr. de evictionibus.*

" Si rem quæ *apud te* esset (*d*) vendidissem tibi, quia pro traditâ habetur, evictionis nomine me obligari placet."

3. L. 9, § 9, *de rebus creditis.*

Deposui apud te decem, postea permisi tibi uti: Nerva, Proculus, *etiam antequam moveantur* (*e*), condicere, quasi mutua tibi hæc posse aiunt: et est verum ut et Marcello videtur; *animo enim cæpit possidere.*

In these passages the immediate question is as to the delivery of property, but by an act of which it is said *per possessionem* dominium quæritur—they are therefore fully in point as to Possession also, (§ 3), *i. e.* they not only shew that in these cases the Possession itself passes along with the property, but also that in like manner the Possession may pass without the property; for instance, where a vendor does not happen to be the proprietor, or where a bailee obtains a true *possessio* by the virtue of a pledge, or by *precarium,* or *emphyteusis.*

Under this mode of acquiring Possession there is also to be included *conditional gifts.* With these, in the first instance, no Possession passes; but, directly the condition is performed, the Possession, which up to that moment had been exercised in the name of another, immediately accrues.

L. 38, § 1, *de poss.*

.... existimandum est, *possessiones sub conditione*

(*c*) No juridical Possession is conveyed by these acts, see *post,* § 26.

(*d*) L. 63, *de V. S.* " *Penes te* amplius est, quam *apud te,* nam *apud te* est quod qualiterqualiter a te teneatur, *penes te* est, quod quodammodo *possidetur.*"

(*e*) Therefore without any fresh act of prehension. In the next passage, L. 10, *de reb. cred.* the exact contrary is asserted in another case, but that is, because there the condition was, the actual employment of the money, without which, according to the intention of the parties, no question of *mutuum* could arise.

tradi posse, sicut res sub conditione traduntur (*f*) neque aliter accipientis fiunt, quam conditio exstiterit.

A limitation, however, which runs through the whole of this mode of acquiring Possession, must now be noticed, although it can only be thoroughly developed hereafter.

Whoever, namely, allows his Possession of a moveable to be exercised by another, does not lose his Possession by a mere act of will in that party, but only by an actual *furtum,* and thus a *contrectatio* must intervene; (Book 3.) The bailee, therefore, can obtain such Possession only by *contrectatio,* for otherwise there would be two Possessions of the same thing at once, (§ 12) and this constitutes a real exception to our rule.

———◆———

SECTION XXI.

ANIMUS POSSIDENDI.

The nature of the corporeal act by which Possession is acquired has been now fully defined; but such act must be accompanied by a definite act of the mind (*animus*), in order to enable Possession actually to arise, and this latter point must now be discussed.

Now this act of the mind consists originally in the fact of the possessor dealing with the subject as his *own property* (*animus domini*); this notion is sufficiently clear in itself, and it is only necessary to caution against confounding this *animus domini* with the moral *conviction* of the party being the owner [*opinio domini*], (§ 10). But the right of

(*f*) That is, as in the case of property, (and so indirectly with Possession also), conditional deliveries occur, so is it also with Possession only, without any reference to property. Comp. L. 2, § 5, *de donat.*; L. 38, pr. *de damno inf.*

N

Possession may, in certain cases, be alienated apart from the property, and in the *derivative* Possession which thereupon arises, there is no longer any *animus domini* which can be added to the act of Prehension, so as to give rise to Possession, but a mere *animus possidendi,* i. e., the intention can only be to acquire the Possession in this manner, and in reference to the legal right so transferred.

This notion, also, does not require to be further elucidated; on the other hand, it is very important that the cases should be known in which the Roman law recognizes a derivative Possession, and in which, consequently, an exception to the rule of animus *domini* is made. This inquiry, therefore, belongs properly here.

But there are cases in which, without reference to this distinction, and yet in respect of the deficient *animus,* no Possession can be acquired. Whoever, for instance, generally is incapable of exercising a will, cannot acquire Possession: and in the same way Possession never can arise as to a subject which cannot be conceived of as capable of appropriation.

We have here, therefore, three questions respecting the *animus possidendi.*

1. What persons are incapable of acquiring Possession because they are incapable of exerting a will? (§ 22).

2. What are the subjects in which no Possession can be acquired, because no *animus possidendi* can exist as to them? (§ 23).

3. In what cases is derivative Possession allowable? *i. e.* when is it allowable without an animus *domini?* (§ 4—6).

SECTION XXII.

First, then, what persons are incapable of acquiring Possession, because they are incapable of exercising an act of will (a)?

Among these, the first to be enumerated are, *juridical persons*, i. e., those who by a fiction of law are considered as subjects to which rights may be ascribed. Thus an inheritance (*hereditas jacens*) may have and even acquire all other rights, such as property for instance, but not Possession. Prehension, even after a manner, may be conceived of, when, for instance, the subject-matter is locked up in a house belonging to the inheritance; but an *animus possidendi* being altogether inconceivable in this case, it is impossible for an inheritance to acquire the right of Possession.

L. 1, § 1, *si is, qui testamento liber.*

"...... possessionem hereditas non habet quæ (*i. e.* quippe quæ) est facti et animi."

For the same reason corporations also are incapable of acquiring Possession.

The same incapacity, which exists generally as to juridical entities, may apply also to individuals in respect of particular idiosyncracies. Thus lunatics are unable to acquire Possession on account of their incapability of an *animus possidendi*. Therefore there can be no question here, or with lunatics generally, as to an *auctoritas curatoris*, by which the lunatic himself might be enabled to acquire Possession.

L. 1, § 3, *de poss.*

(a) All these persons, namely, (corporations, lunatics, children), are incapable of acquiring Posses- sion by themselves only; to what extent they may do so through agents is treated of *post*, § 2.

Furiosus, et pupillus sine tutoris auctoritate, *non potest incipere possidere; quia affectionem tenendi non habent,* licet maxime corpore suo rem contingant: sicuti si quis dormienti aliquis in manu ponat. *Sed pupillus* tutore auctore incipiet possidere.

L. 18, § 1, *de poss.*

Infancy also, like lunacy, prevents the acquisition of Possession; but here it is necessary to define the period at which the incapacity ceases. Now it is clear that the incapacity is removed by puberty in this as in other similar cases; there are only two cases, therefore, remaining to be mentioned, namely, impuberty in its strict sense, and childhood.

As to the capability of wards (pupilli) (*b*), who are no longer children, the rule is, that Possession is always acquirable under the authority of the guardian, but without it only in the case when the ward is sufficiently advanced in growth to make the acquisition in person, and to have an express intention to that effect:

L. 1, § 3, *de poss.*

" .... *pupillus tutore auctore incipiet possidere.* Ofilius quidem et Nerva filius, etiam sine tutoris auctoritate possidere incipere posse pupillum aiunt: eam enim rem facti, non juris esse; *quæ sententia recipi potest, si ejus ætatis sint, ut intellectum capiant.*"

L. 26, C. *de donat.*

" Si quis in emancipatum minorem, prius quam fari possit, *aut habere rei quæ sibi donatur adfectum,* fundum crediderit conferendum .... per .... servum transigi placuit (*c*).

(*b*) The *ætas pupillaris* with the Romans ended at 14 years. Theophilus I. 111, 19, § 10, makes three stages of this period; 1st, *infantiam*, id est, necdum fandi potentem ætatem ; 2nd, *proximam infantiæ*, quæ jam fandi potestatem consecuta est, et 3rd, *proximam pubertati*, quæ proxime pubertati accedit. See Vicat's Vocab. Utr. Jur. ad voc. *pupillaris*. [Trans.]

(*c*) By these very distinct passages others may be explained, which mention in general terms the validity of such acquisition

The question as to children is more difficult. That a child cannot by itself acquire Possession follows from this, that even wards did not possess this right without limitation; that the guardian may acquire Possession in the name of the child is just as clear, but is beside the point. But the question is, can a child obtain Possession by his own act, if the auctoritas of his guardian is subsequently added? It would seem that this ought to be answered in the negative on two grounds; first, because in all other cases an auctoritas of the guardian is recognized by the law (d), only with respect to wards, strictly so called, and not as to children; second, because the acquisition of Possession is not a juridical transaction, and, therefore, the will of the possessor must be looked at, without any power of supplying it by a fiction at law. But as the guardian himself is able to acquire Possession in the name of the child, although the child expresses no acquiescence, it follows that the second ground cannot be alleged against the validity of the *auctoritas:* and again as, according to the analogy of another case of Prehension (e), the whole transaction may be looked upon as if the guardian himself acquired the Possession in the name of the child, the first reason also falls to the ground, being founded merely on the juridical nature of *auctoritas.* The Roman Jurists themselves originally differed on this question : subsequently, the validity of the *auctoritas* was looked upon as admitted, and the ground of this validity was expressly put on the analogy to acquisition

without stating the conditions on which such validity is founded : L. 1, § 11, de poss.; L. 32, § 2, cod.; L. 9, pr. de auct. et const. tut. I think, according to L. 26, Cod. de don. especially, that the capability of the ward must be expressly defined in each individual case; so that § 10, I. de inut. stip., which treats of every *infantia major* without distinction

as capable, ought to be referred to stipulations only.

(d) § 10, I. de inutil. stip.; L. 1, § 2, de admin. tutor.; L. 5, de R. I.

(e) L. 1, § 21, de poss. " Si jusserim venditorem procuratori rem tradere, cum ea in præsentia sit: videri mihi traditam Priscus ait."

through the guardian, the explanation of which was thus made clear:

L. 32, § 2, de poss.

" Infans possidere recte potest, si tutore auctore cæpit; nam judicium infantis suppletur auctoritate tutoris; *utili·* *tatis enim causâ hoc receptum est, nam alioquin nullus con-* *sensus infantis est* (*f*) *accipienti* (*g*) *possessionem.*"

The tutor *auctoritatem interponens* is evidently opposed to the tutor *accipiens* possessionem, and the validity of the first transaction is demonstrated by the (uncontested) validity of the second. The meaning of the passage, therefore, is this: "The validity of the *auctoritas* is admitted as a departure from the general rule *utilitatis causâ ;* and if it be objected that the possessor himself has no *animus possi-* *dendi,* exactly the same may be said where, it is not the

(*f*) Thus read, *Cod. Rehd. ;* two MSS. at Paris, (num. 4456 & 4485), a MS. at Munich, (No. 21), the Louvaine MS. and Ed. Ven. 1494, with two other editions of it by Tortis, 1499 & 1502. Five Paris MSS. (Nos. 4479, 4480, 4486, 4486 a.); a MS. at Notre Dame, a MS. penes me, and edd. Ven. 1485, 1491, Lugd. 1508, 1509, read *consensus infanti est* (or *est infanti,* which is the same thing). *Flor.* "*. . . . sensuse* sit infantis :" the mistake was corrected in the MS. itself, *sensus est* being inserted ; nevertheless, Gebauer has printed *sensus sit,* which neither occurs in the text nor gives any meaning. Edd. Rom. 1476, Nor. 1483, Lugdun. 1513, Lugdun. 1519, Haloander, Paris, 1514, 1536, "sensus infantis est ;" upon which Gebauer observes, " Hal. trajicit voces, *sen-* *sus infantis est,* ut nunc existimo,

auctoritate alicujus codicis suffultus," *i. e.* Gothofred had here by accident omitted to notice the various readings of the old editions. The other MSS. read either *sensus infantis est, sensus infanti est,* or *sensus est infanti.*

(*g*) ACCIPIENTI according to Cod. Rehd. : *three* Paris MSS. Nos. 4458, 4479, 4487 ; the Munich MS. No. 21, and ed. Ven. 1485. Still, in Rehdigers' MS. the word *accipitientis* is inserted in a different hand, instead of *accipienti.* The other editions and MSS. read with the Florence MS. *accipiendi;* the Louvaine MS. *acquirendi.* From this review it appears that the complete reading which I propound as the correct one, is only to be found in the Munich MS. No. 21, but that all the parts of it are to be found in the several old MS. and editions.

child who acquires Possession *auctore tutore*, but the guardian himself does so, in the name of the child, for here, also, the child has not an *animus possidendi* (*h*). But as, nevertheless, in this latter case Possession is considered to be acquired, it is consistent to allow of it in the other case also." This interpretation proceeds on the reading given in the text. According to the usual reading ("nam alioquin nullus *sensus* infantis est *accipiendi* possessionem"), several authors interpret it in this way (*i*), "for *otherwise*, i. e., without the guardian's authority, the child could have no *animus possidendi* (sensus s. intellectus accipiendi possessionem)." But this interpretation is inadmissible; first, because the child could have no *sensus*, even in the case where the guardian interposed his authority, and, therefore, the *alioquin* would be unmeaning; and, secondly, also, because the passage is not occupied with shewing the necessity of the *auctoritas*, but in explaining on what ground Possession could be gained through the *auctoritas*, according to the opinion then generally received. Nevertheless, the first given interpretation is not inconsistent with the common reading also, although the sense is far more vague and indistinct. It may be easily shewn how the original reading was transformed into the present one. The reference of the *accipienti* to *tutore* being somewhat obscure, the copyists sought to make it agree with *infans*, first, by inserting infanti instead of infantis(*j*); second, by changing accipienti into accipientis (*k*) or accipiendi (*l*), which last change was then followed by another of *consensus* into *sensus*.

Another passage, also, is in point here (*m*), which has become very celebrated through the various interpretations

---

(*h*) *Nam alioquin* (for *nam et alioquin*, " in another case also ;" this case itself is immediately afterwards pointed out by the word *accipienti*), "*nullus consensus infantis est accipienti* (sc. tutori) *possessionem.*"

(*i*) Glossa in h. l. ; Cujacius

in h. l., Opp. T. 8, p. 297; Giphanius in h. l. Lectur. Altorphi, p. 394.

(*j*) Ed. Ven. 1485 ; Ven. 1491; Lugd. 1508, 1509.

(*k*) Cod. Rehd.

(*l*) Cod. Flor. rel.

(*m*) L. 3, C. de poss.

it has received, and the use that has been made of it in
practice.   In interpreting it, attention must be paid to the
fact that the emperor, at the end of the passage, assigns a
reason for his decision, and says, this reason has already
been given by Papinian in a *responsum*.   Wherever the
reason of the last decision is to be found, the rule itself must
also occur, it was natural, therefore, to search in the first
place for the passage quoted in Papinian's *Responsa*.
But this passage is no other than the *L.* 32 *de poss.*, which
has been interpreted above.   In the Florence Manuscript,
indeed, the citation is Paulus, lib. 15 ad Sabinum (*n*), but
Alciat adds from other manuscripts this citation, Papinianus,
lib. 11, Responsorum (*o*), and, assuming the correctness of
his evidence (*p*), this reading is evidently more probable than
the former.   For L. 30 *de poss.* is also cited from Paulus,
lib. 15 ad Sabinum; and, on the other hand, there is not a
single passage in the whole 41st book from Papinian's
Responsa.   Therefore, it cannot be explained how a copyist
should have inserted the citation of Alciat in the passage of
the Florence manuscript.   On the other hand, the mistake
is easily conceivable, for it often occurs in the Digest, that

(*n*) The edition of Senneton,
Lugd. 1550, f. reads Pauli, li. 12.
So also the Ed. Juntina of 1594,
4to, has in the text Paulus, lib.
12, and inserts the Florence reading merely in the margin.   A
Paris MS. No. 4487, has the citation *Pomp.*; the other MSS. and
ed. which I am acquainted with
agree with the Florence copy.

(*o*) Alciatus in L. 1, § 3, *de
poss.*; Opp. T. 1, p. 1208; "Sua-
detur et auctoritate Papiniani,
quem adducit, qui infra expresse
loquitur cum tutor intervenit:
dict. L. *quamvis* (32) in fin. ad-
scribitur, enim aliquibus in codi-
cibus ea lex *Papiniano lib. Res-
pons.* 11." In another passage

Alciat describes his old MS. to be
without a Gloss and with Rubricks
(Dispunct. lib. 1, proem.)

(*p*) For Cujacius affirms all
such statements of Alciat to be
false; Comm. in L. 133, *de verb.
obl.* Opp. T. 1, p. 1249.   But,
allowing for the exaggeration, all
that remains as a fact is, that
Alciat has cited some of the Florence readings incorrectly, and
upon this subject Augustin
(Emend. III. in Otto IV. p. 1504)
has explained the error so satisfactorily, that we are not justified in
attributing in any case, as for
instance in the present, a wilful
untruth.

one extract merely runs into the other, and thus the copyist might look upon L. 30 and L. 32 as *one* extract, into which the short L. 31 was merely intercalated (*q*).

From this connection between the above passage (L. 3, Cod. *de poss.*) and L. 32 *de poss.*, it follows that the meaning of the former can be nothing but this; a child may acquire Possession of a subject, if the guardian supplies the deficient *animus* of the child by his *auctoritas*. This rule is applied in the above rescript to a particular case, and which must he taken to be as follows: something had been given to a child, the donor had delivered the Possession to the child itself, and the guardian had interposed his *auctoritas*. A doubt thereupon arose whether Possession could be acquired in a case like this. The doubt was founded on the fact, that in this case the Prehension and the *animus* had not co-existed in the same person; for the guardian had the *animus possidendi* for the child, but the corporeal act, which amounted to Prehension, was the act of the child; it was, therefore, questioned whether, under these circumstances, the Possession was not prevented from arising. This question was submitted to the emperor, who answered in the rescript which is contained in the following passage:—

Donatarum rerum a qua-cunque personâ infanti vacua possessio tradita (*r*) corpore quæritur. Quamvis enim sint auctorum sententiæ dis-

Where a subject is given to a child, possession may, undoubtedly, be acquired in such case by the corporeal act of the child. For although

(*q*) [Add. to the 4th ed.] It ought not to be concealed how-ever, that Bluhme's discovery of the order of the extracts in the Digest does not tell for the read-ing here adopted. Zeitschrift fuer geschichtl. Rechtswiss. IV. 418.

(*r*) From this word it clearly follows, that *animus* could not be

held to exist in the child itself, in contradiction to the rule, but merely that its corporeal act should avail as a valid act of prehension. But as *animus* was required in all Possession, it was to be supplied here independ-ently of the child, and thus must consist in the *auctoritas* of the guardian.

sentientes (*s*); tamen consultius videtur *interim* (*t*), licet animi plenus non fuisset affectus (*u*), possessionem per traditionem esse quæsitam : alioquin sicuti consultissimi viri Papiani responso continetur (*v*), nec quidem *per tutorem* (*w*) possessio infanti poterit acquiri" (*x*).

the earlier authorities were of a different opinion, it is, nevertheless, more expedient to look upon the Possession as acquired in the meantime by this delivery, although the child itself, whose physical act intervened for the purpose, was not then capable of exercising any *animus*. The ground of this conclusion, which Papinian had previously assigned in a *responsum*, consists in this, that otherwise it would be inconsistent to allow of Possession being acquired by the corporeal act of the guardian himself.

Of the different interpretations of this passage, the more important may be divided into three classes.

Even the earliest Glossers appear to have here referred to the *auctoritas* of the guardian, upon which the whole turns. Alciat gave additional weight to this construction by his various readings (p. 184), and that no writer adopted the

(*s*) *L.* 32, § 2, *de poss.* "utilititatis enim causa hoc *receptum est.*" Previously, therefore, the contrary must have been laid down by the authorities.

(*t*) Namely, until the child arrives at puberty, for then Possession would commence in the usual way.

(*u*) This *affectus minus plenus* is not looked upon here to avail by a fiction as *affectus plenus*, but is juridically considered to amount to no *animus* at all, and this circumstance is merely said to present no obstacle in the case.

(*v*) *L.* 1, 32, § 2, *de poss.*

(*w*) This opposition of *per tutorem* to *auctore tutore* relates to the acquisition of possession through the corporeal act of the guardian in the name of the child, *L.* 1, § 20, *de poss.*

(*x*) Papinian supports the validity of the acquisition *per tutorem* on the validity of the *auctoritas* in these words, nam alioquin nullus consensus infantis est *accipienti possessionem*, p. 182.

same view, may be owing to the ill use which Alciat made of it. But even without the combination thus made passages, Donellus has established the same interpretation out of the four corners of the passage itself, in such a satisfactory manner, that it would seem to leave no room open for further controversy (*y*).

According to the second doctrine, this passage establishes something altogether peculiar; a child, namely, even alone, and, without his guardian, is capable of acquiring Possession (*z*). Some interpret the position quite generally, as applicable to every case of delivery whatsoever (*a*): others limit it to gifts, because such only are spoken of (*b*): others, again, confine it merely to such objects, the Possession of which would peculiarly interest children, *e. g.*, toys (*c*).

(*y*) Glossa interlin. *L.* 3, *C. de poss.* (MS. Paris, no. 4517), probably by Irnerius at the word *corpore*, " *sed auctoritate tutoris*," at *alioquin* Y. (Irnerius), "utrumque enim fit magis favore benignitatis, quam stricta ratione juris, remoto itaque altero consequenter et alterum removetur." Glossa in *L.* 3, *C. de poss.* " Vel dic secundum Joannem quod hic fuit tradita cum auctoritate tutoris. Et quod dicit; *alioquin*, id est, *si diceres non acquiri cum auctoritate tutoris per infantem eadem ratione nec per ipsum tutorem.*" Cf. Azonem in h. l. Lectura, p. 568; Odofred. in h. l. fol. 104; Alciatus in *L.* 1, § 3, *de poss.; Opp.* T. 1, p. 1208; Cujacius in *L.* 1, § 3, *de poss.; Opp.* T. 5, p. 695; T. 8, p. 241, and in *L.* 3, *C. de poss.; Opp.* T. 9, p. 1014; Obrecht *de Poss.* C. 10, § 365—374. Donellus in Comm. j. civ. L. 5, C. 11, p. 191, Ed. Hann. 1612; Giphanius in L. 26, *C. de donat.; Lectura Altorph.*

p. 196.

(*z*) Glossa in *L.* 3, *C. de poss.;* Azo in h. l. Lectura, p. 567; Duarenus in *L.* 1, § 3, *de poss.* Opp. p. 827; Giphanius in *L.* 3, *C. de poss.;* Explanat. Cod. P. 2, p. 243; (compare the previous note); Cuperus de poss. P. 2, C. 24.

(*a*) Azo, l. c.; Cuperus, l. c.

(*b*) Duarenus, l. c.; Giphanius, l. c. Duarenus requires besides that the subject-matter of the gift should be a moveable.

(*c*) Azo in l. c. "Alii distinguunt, aut dedit eis res, quarum voluit infans retinere possessionem, ut denarios, castaneas, et similia ludicra; aut quarum noluit retinere possessionem, ut castrum, vel talia. In primis bene habet affectum, et acquirit possessionem, in aliis non. *Et in eis intellexerunt veteres*," that is the earlier Glossers. Therefore it is wholly incorrect to call Dinus (ob. circ. 1298) the originator of this doctrine.

Even according to this interpretation, the latter words of
the passage might be looked upon as consistent with the
decision (d), but then the ground for it which the emperor,
following Papinian, assigns, would be so illogical, that
it bestows on the first opinion an undoubted prepon-
derance (e).

Lastly, a third view takes a middle course between the
two first-mentioned (f). According to this, the child alone
may acquire Possession, but only in the meantime (interim),
i. e., until that which was deficient should be supplied by
the authority of the guardian. According to this explanation, also, the passage contains something new ; first, because Possession would still be acquired in the interim,
contrary to the general principle (g); second, because it is
quite unusual that the auctoritas should be supplied subsequently. Besides, the connection between the reason at the
conclusion, and the rest of the passage, is just as faulty in
this as in the previous interpretation.

[Add. to the 6th ed.] The two passages which have been
commented on in this chapter have lately received a most
elaborate discussion in an article of Puchta's, in the Rhein.
Museum, B. 5, p. 33—64, in which the earlier opinions are
again brought forward and defended, but with more logic
and acuteness than has ever yet been applied to them. The
writer interprets the reading adopted by him as the correct
one in L. 32—sensus est accipiendi—thus: " for otherwise,

(d) Glossa in L. 3, C. de poss,
" id est, si non quæritur infanti,
quia non habet affectum ; nec
tutor ei quæret eadem ratione.
Utroque ergo modo ei quæritur
favore benignitatis magis, quam
stricti juris ratione, Irnerius.
Sunt ergo hic duo, quorum altero
remoto, et alterum removetur."
To the same effect, Duarenus and
Cuperus.

(e) Donellus, l. c.

(f) Beyma in Var. Tit. Jur.
pp. 325, 414: Retes de poss. P.
1, C. 4, (Meerm. VII. p. 469).

(g) Still, according to Retes,
this possession in the interim
would only amount to detention.
But then the whole matter would
have been so clear by itself, that
an Imperial Rescript with juridical reasons assigned would never
have been needed.

indeed (apart from the *utilitas*), the intention directed to the acquiring of Possession would be wanting in the child." He applies the passage in the Code to a child acting without a guardian, and the *animus*, which would be insufficient by itself in such a child, is awakened and completed by the expressed will of the *tradens*, in the same way as, in another case, the *auctoritas* of the guardian (which was also against the strict rule) had effect. By his excellent mode of treating the subject, the writer has brought the point completely to an issue, and thus the reader may now see each interpretation in its best form, and exercise his choice between the two with the amplest means for decision.

SECTION XXIII.

POSSESSION OF A PART OF A SUBJECT.

If the *animus possidendi* must be conceived of as able to exist, so also the nature of the object to be possessed must be such as to allow its being contemplated as a distinct subject-matter (p. 178). Under what conditions, then, is it possible to acquire Possession in an *individual part of an entirety?*

This acquisition may be contemplated in two ways: either the individual part alone may be possessed, or it may be possessed with and by means of the whole. The three following rules apply to the first case, the fourth rule to the latter.

1st. If the part is so constituted that it forms a distinct whole by itself, *i. e.*, if the notion of the entirety to which this part belongs is a mere arbitrary assumption, there is no doubt of the power to acquire Possession in such part only. This presumes that there are *actual* portions, in fact, of one whole; but this presumption only arises in the case of land

in aid of a separate Possession (*a*) : in land, consequently, it being altogether arbitrary how farthe limits of
any entirety are to be considered to extend, Possession may
be acquired in any individual portion of the land of definite
extent, although the previous Possession may have treated
it as part of a larger whole.   But it turns entirely on the
extent of the portion which may be thus acquired, being
defined, *i. e.*, Possession of the subject can only be acquired
so far as the new possessor contemplates it as a definite
object of Possession.

2nd. If the entirety is divisible into merely imaginary,
not actual, parts, Possession in like manner of each individual portion is allowable, it being understood, that in this
case, also, the limits of each part must be fully defined.
Now in this case, the definition of the parts is simply
arithmetical, and, consequently, the relation of the part to
the whole is all that requires to be known in order to be able
to acquire possession of the part; that is, the whole is looked
upon as unity, and the part as a fraction, and we need only
know the numerators and denominators of this fraction in
order to acquire Possession.   Whoever, for instance, succeeds
as heir to a third part of an estate, acquires thereby the
third part of the property in every individual subject belonging to the deceased.   If he sells and delivers a single
acre belonging to the inheritance, the purchaser acquires
the Possession of a third of this acre, because it is this third
part which he looked upon as the object of his new Possession.   The first and second rule are to be found together
in the following passages :—

1. *L.* 26, *de poss.* (Pomponius, lib. 26 ad Q. Mucium.)
" *Locus certus ex fundo* et possideri, et per longam possessionem capi potest; et *certa pars pro indiviso*, quæ intro-
ducitur vel emptione, vel ex donatione, vel qualibet alia ex
causa.   *Incerta autem pars,* nec tradi, nec (usu) capi

(*a*) *L.* 8, *de rei vind.* " ....   cum habet; *nunquam enim pro-*
quæ distinctio neque in re mobili   *viso possideri potest.*"
neque in hereditatis petitione lo-

potest (b); veluti si ita tibi tradam, *Quidquid mei juris in eo fundo est* (c): nam qui ignorat (d), nec tradere, nec accipere id quod incertum est, potest."

2. *L.* 32, § 2, *de usurp.* (Pomponius, lib. 32, ad Sabinum).

" *Incertam partem possidere nemo potest.* Ideo si plures sint in fundo, qui ignorent quotam quisque partem possideat; neminem eorum mera subtilitate possidere Labeo scribit" (e).

3. *L.* 3, § 2, *de poss.*

(b) That is, no Possession can be obtained therein.

(c) This example, as well as the rule itself, applies equally to both of the above cases. Thus Possession is impossible on the same grounds, whether the question be as to a *locus* incertus ex fundo, or an incerta *pars pro indiviso.*

(d) Viz. quanta pars sit.

(e) What is it which is here disapproved of tacitly as mere subtlety? Not the rule, for Pomponius lays it down in this and the previous passage as undoubtedly correct, and it also follows expressly from the notion of Possession. It is therefore only this application of the rule which is objected to, which application must be taken to be as follows: Two persons occupy a piece of ground at the same time, to which each makes a claim as a vacant possession. Neither of them is willing at the moment to contest the possession with the other, because there is a third party whose interference they both dread; they therefore recognize each other as con-possessors. Now, strictly speaking, it

is only by a juridical act that an ideal division can be formed ("introduciter ex emptione," &c. *L.* 26, *de poss.*); consequently, there is no possessor in this case, and therefore a third party may occupy the Possession with force. But all these consequences turn upon a mere subtlety, and it is evidently much more natural to look upon each of the two as the possessor of *one-half,* although no express authority on this point can be adduced. It is still simpler however, and more intelligible to conceive the following to be the case alluded to in the passage. Gaius dies possessed of a field. Seius and Titius know they are his sole legatees, but do not know in what proportions they are to take, as they have not yet seen the will. In this uncertainty they take possession. On subtle principles neither of them would be a possessor; in fact, however, both of them jointly must have as much right in the land, as any individual would have by an act of prehension of the whole; they would thus have a joint right to Interdicts. (Add. to 6th ed.)

" Incertam partem rei nemo possidere potest; veluti si hac mente sit, ut quidquid Titius possidet, tu quoque velis possidere."

3rd. Except in these two cases, it is impossible to acquire Possession of an individual part of a subject. In most cases, this impossibility is also a physical impossibility, and, therefore, does not require any express definition; for instance, it is clear, that no one can acquire possession of a brick in a wall, or a wheel of a carriage, so long as the connection of these parts with the whole exists. But irrespective of this physical impossibility, such Possession is also impossible on juridical grounds; thus, for instance, a building cannot be possessed without the soil on which it stands, the reason of which evidently is that the building, as a part of a whole, is looked upon as inseparable from the soil. This proposition, namely, that house and soil juridically go together, that they are only portions of one and the same entirety, and, therefore, are not distinct independent subject-matters, is to be found expressly laid down in many passages (f). It flows directly from this proposition, that there cannot be different proprietors in the soil and the building, or in the different stories of the same house (g). It also follows, that no single part of such subject-matters, but only the whole, can be given in pledge (h). But it also follows, from the same principle, that a like impossibility exists as to Possession; therefore a house, and the soil on which it stands, cannot have different possessors, just as with respect to a statue, one person cannot possess the head and an arm, and some one else the remaining parts, at the same time; and direct proofs of the application of this rule to Possession are producible (i).

(f) L. 49, pr. de rei vind.; L. 20, § 2, de S. P. U.; L. 98, § 8, de solut.; L. 21, de pign. ait.; L. 23, pr. de usurp.; L. 44, § 1, de O. et A.

(g) L. 50, ad L. Aquil.; L. 2, de superfic.; L. 98, § 8, de solut.;

L. 17, Comm. præd.

(h) L. 21, de pign. ait.

(i) L. 44, § 1, de O. et A. " Sic et in tradendo si quis dixerit se solum sine superficie tradere, nihil proficit quo minus et superficies, transeat, quæ natura

4th. Whoever acquires the Possession of an entirety, possesses the entirety only, and not each individual part by itself. The three first rules applied to the Possession of the part, which was capable of being acquired severed from the entirety; here the question is as to a part which is possessed as a portion, and by means, of the entirety, but, nevertheless, as a distinct subject: it is this Possession whose possibility is denied. This rule, it is true, is principally important with reference to Usucaption, at the same time, however, it may come into operation as to Interdicts also, at least as to the old form of the *interdict-utrubi*, when it is applicable exactly as in Usucaption (*j*).

The first instance in which this rule is applied is as follows: whoever has the Possession of a carriage, does not also acquire Possession in the wheels as distinct subjects; and so also with other subject-matters composed of different parts (*k*). If, for instance, a carriage is stolen, property in it could not be acquired by Usucaption; but suppose one of its wheels

solo cohæret." (But delivery depends immediately on Possession, and only indirectly on property.) *L.* 15, § 12, *de damno infecto*. ".... si ex superficie, inquit, damnum timeatur, non habebit res exitum ; nec profuturum in possessionem ejus rei mitti, quam quis possidere non possit." *L.* 25, 26, *de usurp.* " Sine possessione usucapio contingere non potest." " Nunquam superficies sine solo capi longo tempore potest." For I consider the second of these two passages as a simple consequence of the first. See, however, Zeitschrift fuer geschichtliche Rechtswissenschaft IV. 415.

(*j*) Numerous objections may be urged in opposition to the cases which Thibaut has brought forward, Anhang zu Cuperus, p. 163. For the appurtenant quality of a moveable, which may be connected with an immoveable, might also subsist with the possession of the moveable by itself. Besides which, in the *int. quod vi*, Possession is not in question; in the *int. de vi* the *dejectio* from a moveable is immediately connected with the *dejectio* from the soil itself, and in the *int. uti possidetis*, the interference with the possession of a portion (even when the latter is possessed by itself) may still always be looked upon as an interference with the possession of the entirety.

(*k*) The special law as to buildings shall be noticed particularly hereafter.

had not been stolen, this also would not be subject to Usucaption, because the wheel in itself had not been possessed,
but only the carriage. Just so, conversely, a stolen wheel
is subject to Usucaption with the rest of the carriage, if the
latter has not been stolen. Again, if the entirety, which I
possessed, is taken to pieces, a new Possession begins to run
as to the different pieces (because up to that moment I had
not had Possession of them), and this proposition again is best
elucidated by Usucaption. For, if in such case Usucaption
as to the whole is complete, the property in every part is
acquired, and this property, naturally enough, does not cease
on the division into parts (*l*); but if the division takes place
before the Usucaption is complete, a fresh Usucaption must
begin to run for each divided portion, but the *justa causa*
for the entirety extends itself to such portion also (*m*), and
so also does the prehension of the entirety, so that thus
Possession of the divided portion is acquired by the mere
division, without any new act by the possessor (*n*).

Both of these propositions, even independent of their
special historical proofs, must be assumed here to be correct,
simply for this reason, that the only limitation of Possession
which is discussed in this section, turns upon the deficient
animus possidendi ; and thus prehension, or even the *justa
causa possessionis,* is not in question.

Second instance. Whoever buys a piece of land, possesses the land as a whole, and not the individual portions

(*l*) Unterholzner contests this
proposition, Verjährung, p. 95;
without which, however practically, Usucaption could not exist.
If, for instance, I have acquired
a moveable by Usucaption, any
one, according to this, might de-
feat my already acquired property by a mere arbitrary act of
breaking the subject to pieces;
and just so, if I had gained land by
Usucaption, the property in the
trees might be made to cease by
the simple act of cutting them
down.

(*m*) *L.* 11, § 6, *de public. in
rem act.* The expressions in this
passage relating to dismantled
buildings are applicable to every
entirety when taken to pieces.

(*n*) See the application of these
principles to the *fructuum perceptio* in the next chapter.

of it by themselves (o). This case, however, distinguishes itself from the preceding in this, that the notion of one entirety is an arbitrary assumption, and, consequently, an actual division into parts is impossible. Therefore this rule is limited in its application to the *justa causa*, with respect to which only it occurs in the Law Sources (p).

Third instance. Whoever has Usucaption in land, acquires simultaneously, according to the erroneous view of certain Jurists, Possession of treasure buried in the land (q). But the error of this doctrine does not consist in affirming that Usucaption runs as to the part concurrently with the entirety, but in treating the treasure as a portion of the land; therefore, in this instance, an erroneous application is made of the rule.

Fourth instance. Whoever possesses a house does not also possess the individual bricks and beams of which it is composed. If he did so, he would gain a title sooner to the bricks, &c. as moveables than to the house; but this, according to our rule, is impossible (r). It follows, also, as a clear consequence to our rule, and in perfect analogy with the

(o) *L.* 2, § 6, *pro emtore:* "Cum Stichum emissem, Dama per ignorantiam mihi pro eo traditus est. Priscus ait, usu me eum non capturum; quia id, quod emptum non sit, pro emtore usucapi non potest. Sed si fundus emtus sit, et ampliores fines possessi sint, totum longo tempore capi: *quoniam universitas ejus possideatur, non singulæ partes.*"

(p) Suppose, therefore, that I have bought a piece of ground, part of which belongs to the vendor, but not the remainder, I may undoubtedly have Usucaption as to this latter part, *to this extent,* therefore, I possess it as a separate portion. (Add. to 6th ed.)

(q) *L.* 3, § 3, *de poss.* See *ante,* p. 164.

(r) *L.* 2, 3, *pr. de usurp.* "Eum, qui ædes mercatus est, non puto aliud, quam ipsas ædes, possidere; nam si singulas res possidere intelligetur, ipsas ædes non possidebit; separatis enim corporibus, ex quibus ædes constant, universitas ædium intelligi non poterit; accidit (accedit) eo, quod si quis singulas res possidere dixerit, necesse erit, (ut) dicat (in) possessione superficiei temporibus de mobilibus statutis locum esse, solum se capturum esse ampliori (tempore): quod absurdum, et minime juri civili conveniens est, ut una res diversis temporibus capiatur: ut puta

other cases, that if a house is pulled down before the Usucaption is complete, the Usucaption to the bricks, &c., as
moveables, must commence *de novo* (*s*). But a special case
exists on this point, namely, where a house has been gained
by Usucaption, the latter does not extend to the building
materials as parts of the entirety, and if they should be severed,
Usucaption as to them must commence anew, although the
house itself may have been long acquired. This, however,
is only true where the house and the materials belong to
different owners; if there is but one owner the general rule
prevails, so that the former owner, after such Usucaption,
can maintain vindication neither as to the house nor to the
severed materials (*t*). The ground of this exception is as
follows: if any subject is conjoined with another, as a part
forming one whole, the owner may demand its separation
by an *actio ad exhibendum*, and then he may have his vindication for the separated portion just as for any other article.
Not so with building materials; here the owner cannot
obtain a separation (*u*), and it naturally followed from this,

cum ædes ex duabus rebus constant, ex solo et superficie, et universitas earum possessione temporis immobilium rerum dominium mutet." So read : Cod.
Rehd., Edd. Rom. 1476, Nor.
1483, Ven. 1485, Ven. 1494,
Lugdun. 1509, 1513 ; Hal. Paris,
1514, 1536. So also, *seven* of the
best MSS. at Paris, the Metz and
Leipsic MSS., and one *penes me*.
The Florence reading is wholly
insensible: "Possessionem temporis immobilium rerum omnium
mutet." cf. *L.* 8, *quod vi*.

(*s*) *L.* 23, § 2, *de usurp.* "Si
autem demolita domus est, *ex integro res mobiles possidendæ sunt,
ut tempore, quod in usucapione
rerum mobilium constitutum est,
usucapiantur: *et non potest recte*

*uti eo tempore, quo in ædificio fue-
runt,*" rel.

(*t*) *L.* 23, § 7, *de rei vind.*
"Item si quis ex alienis cæmentis
in solo suo ædificaverit, domum
quidem vindicare poterit, cæmenta
autem resoluta prior dominus vin-
dicabit, *etiamsi post tempus usucapionis dissolutum sit ædificium postquam a bonæ fidei emptore possessum
sit: nec enim singula cæmenta usuca-
piuntur, si domus per temporis spa-
tium nostra fiat.*" *Cf.* L. 59, in f.
eod. *L.* 7, § 11, *de adquir. rer.
dom.*

(*u*) § 29, 1. *de rer div.*; Dig.
lib. 47, tit. 3. That this constitutes the ground for the exception
is clearly shewn by *L.* 23, § 6, 7,
de rei vind.

that the Usucaption, which the owner could not interrupt by vindication, was not permitted to run.

In the application of this rule, there is also a distinction between the gain and loss of Possession. For if the possession of a subject has once commenced, it is not lost by the fact of its being subsequently converted with other subjects into a new whole (*v*), and it is necessary to call particular attention to this proposition, because it has been supposed that the passage of the Roman law, which contains it (*w*), presents a contradiction to our rule (*x*). But in this case, as

---

(*v*) It must be understood, however, that on such junction the part does not assume a different form (specificatio) : for then the existence of the previous subject-matter, and consequently the possession of it would cease. *L.* 30, § 4, *de poss.* " .... desinimus possidere ...... si, quod possidebam in aliam speciem translatum est." *L.* 30, § 1, *de usurp.* " .. cum utrumque maneat integrum."

(*w*) *L.* 30, § 1, *de usurp.* "Labeo libris epistolarum ait, si is cui ad tegulorum (tegularum) vel columnarum usucapionem *decem dies superessent*, in ædificium eas, conjecisset, *nihilominus eum usucapturum, si ædificium possedisset.* Quid ergo in his quæ non quidem implicantur rebus soli, sed mobilia *permanent*, ut in annulo gemmâ? In quo verum est, et aurum et gemmam, (*i. e.* each as a separate article), possideri, et usucapi, *cum utrumque maneat integrum.*" It follows necessarily from the word *maneat*, that the articles were first of all possessed singly previous to their being united into one entirety.

(*x*) Westphal, Arten der Sa-

chen, § 46, p. 548, was the first, so far as I know, to draw attention to this distinction between the gain and the loss of possession. He is followed by Winkler Diss. De interrupt. usuc. ac præscr. Lips. 1793, p. 37 ; (on the other hand, Unterholtzner opposes it, Verjaehrungslehre, § 50). Cuperus, p. 29, asserts that there are irreconcileable differences between the Roman jurists. So also, Fleck, De adq. Poss. p. 31, &c. Man has laid down correctly the special law as to building materials, Ad L. 3, § 3, de poss. § 15, p. 339 ; but he confounds this exception with the general rule, which has been here clearly distinguished. Unterholtzner, Verjaehrung, p. 97, altogether denies the continuance of possession, where things previously possessed are bound up into a new whole. He endeavours to get rid of the quoted passage, *L.* 30, § 1, *de poss.*, by reading in the first half, *nihilo magis*, instead of *nihilominus*, (wholly arbitrarily, and quite contrary to the following words, *si ædificium possedisset*, which evidently form a limitation in acquisition, an exception must be made where building materials are in question; it is true, a case on this point is brought forward, in which the commenced Usucaption was not put an end to, but the Jurist says expressly as to this, that a period of ten days only was wanting to complete the Usucaption, consequently, so short a period (*y*), that a *usur-*

to the proposition). He subsequently gave up this opinion, and now takes the *decem dies* literally only, and as a special case not to be accounted for, Verjährungslehre, § 49. As to the second half of the sentence he asserts, p. 94, that the setting of the stone in the ring is not to be looked upon as a junction, but merely as a sort of enclosure in a case, (abandoned by him afterwards, Verjaehrungslchre, § 50). This doctrine, however, is completely opposed by *L.* 6, *ad exhib.*; *L.* 23, § 2, 5, *de rei vind.* If this *L.* 30, § 1, *de usurp.* were alone in question, no doubt would remain, but certainly *L.* 7, § 1, *ad exhib.* (see *ante*, § 7), raises considerable difficulty. For this passage *may* mean that the very act of joining the wheel to the carriage may put a stop to the usucaption possession of the wheel, or even to all possession whatever of it, (§ 7). But we must recollect that upon this point the Roman lawyers held different opinions, (for my attempt to reconcile them in the two first editions of this work, pp. 213, 254, is untenable).

It *may*, however, also be taken that the wheel in this case had been stolen, and therefore was not in *civilis possessio.* Lastly, the *quamvis may* also mean "even

if also" (on some ground not expressed) "the civilis possessio should be wanting," in the same way, in another passage, Thibaut interprets *licet* (see *ante*, § 7). From the above ambiguity in the passage, it would seem that the express language of *L.* 30, § 1, *de usurp.* must be preferred. There is less difficulty with *L.* 1, § 2, *de tigno juncto,* for even when the possessor of a house has a true *possessio* in the bricks, he still could not be compelled to restore these bricks, and thus with respect to the *results of vindication,* (which alone are referred to), he was not to be looked upon as *possessor.*

(*y*) The *decem dies* thus merely mean, any short period of time: just as the *decem dies* in *L.* 50, *de minor.* and the *paucissimi dies* in *L.* 16, *de fundo dotali.* (I have here left my views in the 3rd edition to stand unaltered. Subsequently Professor Falck has communicated to me the following interpretation of the *first* half of *L.* 30, § 1, *de usurp.,* which I now concur in).

"The *tegulæ et columnæ* are not to be taken here as part and parcel of the house, but as moveables simply placed in the building; (meaning, of course, that the pillars were not actual supports to

patio (*z*) by vindication could scarcely have been possible in the interim.

SECTION XXIV.

POSSESSION IN PARTS OF A SUBJECT—*Continued.*

What is called the *fructuum perceptio* of a *bonæ fidei possessor* is only to be explained by the rules in the preceding chapter, and it deserves mention here, on account of its manifold connection with Possession, though it cannot be made intelligible in any other way than by contrasting it with the other cases in which perception of the profits is permissible (*a*).

the building, but merely ornamental) ; this bare act of connection would not interrupt the commenced Usucaption, and the *decem dies* merely denote any short period sufficient to complete the time for Usucaption, which the provision of law applicable to the case required." *L.* 23, § 1, *de usurp.* speaks also for this interpretation, for there likewise *columnæ* (circumstanced, namely, like the above) might be vindicated, and give a cause of action for eviction against the vendor, (otherwise with *tabulæ*, *L.* 36, de evict.) It is true that *L.* 1, *de tigno juncto*, says the contrary as to *tegulæ*, but only with a *quidam aiunt*, and as to such particular cases there might easily arise some question. The rules laid down in the text are untouched

by this new interpretation. This new interpretation, which I adopted first in my fourth edition has been objected to by Thibaut, Archiv. fuer die civilistische Praxis, B. VII. p. 79. But possibly his objections may be removed by the further development of that interpretation, which I now present.

(*z*) [Usurpatio is an interruption of Usucaption, see Dig. lib. 41, 3, l. 2, 5, and somewhat resembles our keeping alive a title by continual claim.—Transl.]

(*a*) As this subject is only of an indirect interest for us, it is evident that I need not carry it out in all its details. For the same reason, the numerous modern writers who have treated of it are not mentioned. (Add. to 6th ed.)

I. The true owner acquires the property in the profits at the moment of their *arising* by *accession,* which is only an application to property of the rule " fructus rei frugiferæ pars est." It is only by *severance* of the profits from the principal subject that he becomes owner of the profits as of an individual self-existing object, but this circumstance is wholly immaterial in respect to property, and, therefore, with good reason is unnoticed in the Law Sources. For the most part, this severance of the profits bears exactly the same character as the actual division of any entirety (for instance, the cutting up of a carcass, or the pulling down of a house), which also, so far as property is concerned, is of no importance. Consequently therefore, the property in the profits is either quiritarian or bonitarian, as the property in the principal is quiritarian or bonitarian, so that in the former case Usucaption would never be necessary for severed profits although it would in the latter.

II. The tenant, fructuary, and, generally, every person who derives his right to the profits from the owner, acquires then by *perceptio,* i. e., by a taking of Possession (*b*). For on a demise, &c., there exists, in relation to the profits, 1st. The *justa causa dominii quærendi ;* 2nd. The permission to take Possession; and, consequently, the act of Prehension is a true *traditio,* by which the property in the profits passes from the owner of the principal to the tenant, &c. (See No. I.) Now if the landlord was the quiritarian owner of the principal, and so, consequently, of the profits, the tenant would acquire, by perception of the profits, either a quiritarian or a bonitarian property in them; quiritarian, namely, when the profits were *res nec mancipi,* (such as all profits of the soil); but bonitarian, if they were *res mancipi* (such as a horse) (*c*).

III. The *bonæ fidei possessor* naturally enough enjoys

(*b*) *L.* 13, *quibus modis ususfr.* *L.* 25, § 1, *de usuris.*

(*c*) This follows from the quiritarian property in a *res nec man-* cipi being transferable by simple delivery, but not so in a *res man-cipi.* Ulpian, tit. 19, § 3, 7.

exactly the same *accession* as the actual owner (No. I.), for the rule which points out the ground of such accession is quite general. Whoever, therefore, has the *bonæ fidei possessio* of land, acquires in like manner the profits as they respectively accrue. No question, however, arises as to *this* acquisition; for so long as the profits are unsevered from the principal, there can be no doubt as to the right of the *bonæ fidei possessor* to the profits, any more than with the true owner, because the profits themselves are comprised in the principal: by the *severance*, however, an entirely new right arises, and the previous one ceases. This new right is to be explained thus: the foundation of *bonæ fidei possessio* is juridical Possession. But where an entire subject-matter is broken up into its component parts, a new Possession commences as to those parts, because previously (as independent entireties) they had not been in Possession. As to such parts, therefore (in the present instance, the profits of the soil), a new *bonæ fidei possessio* must also commence. But according to the rules of Possession on the division of an entirety into parts, both prehension and *justa usucapionis causa* are transferred from the entirety to the several parts; thus in the present case, also, a new *bonæ fidei possessio* in the profits arises on their mere severance, and neither a new act of pre-hension (properly fructuum *perceptio*), nor a new *justa causa* are here necessary (*d*). The *bonæ fidei possessor*, therefore, is

(*d*) L. 48, *pr. de A. R. D.* L. 25, § 1, *de usuris.* L. 13, *quibus modis ususfr.* To treat this position as something altogether anomalous, as a reward of *bona fides,* without any other connection with the legal system, is altogether opposed to the spirit of the classical Roman law. It is here explained on grounds, which have been already shewn to be satisfactory. On the other hand, however, it is not to be concealed that in fact the *bonæ fidei possessor* has some special claim as to the profits *pro culturâ et cura* (§ 35, l. *de div. rer.*) But this special circumstance does not at all relate to the acquisition of *property* in the profits, but to the law of obligations. For if the possessor disposed of or consumed the profits, so as to benefit himself thereby, in strict law he would have to account for the gains, and might be compelled thereto, not by vindication of the principal, but by a special action (condictio) distinguishable from the fructuary and the tenant in this, that the former acquires his new right by mere separation, whether it happens by accident, or by the act of another, but the latter only by their own perception (p. 200). On the other hand, the distinction between the true proprietor and the *bonæ fidei possessor* may be laid down thus: the former has a true property in the profits, both before and after severance, and the *same* property at both periods; the latter has the *possessio* of the profits before and after severance, but a *new* Possession from the moment of severance, though not on a new ground, as the ground of the former possession is transferred to the new one. This peculiarity of *bonæ fidei possessio*, which, on the first glance, appears a mere subtlety, has the most important practical consequences.

(A.) On account of the connection between *bonæ fidei* Possession and Usucaption. For upon severance there arises with a new *bonæ fidei possessio* a new Usucaption also, and an invariable one indeed of three years, because all profits are moveables. Before the severance, the profits were implicated in the usucaption of the principal, and, therefore in land the Usucaption was from ten to twenty years (*e*).

for the value of the consumed profits. He was discharged however from this liability, and was allowed to retain the gains he had made, and this is all which is meant by the expressions, *ejus fiunt fructus*, fructus consumptos *suos facit;* which terms have been incorrectly applied to the acquisition of *property*. That they have nothing whatever to do here with property appears most clearly from the fact of their relating entirely to consumed profits, for of course, after consumption, all property must have ceased; and also because this special right also exists as to so called *fructus civiles* (for instance, rent), although in such case, there could be no question as to *property* being acquirable in this manner. This view, in short, may be supported by as many proofs as any other point in the Roman law on which any special discussion is required.

(*e*) In this respect also the bonitarian property of the old law (No. 1) was in complete accordance with the *bonæ fidei possessio.* Thus, whoever had land *in bonis* required two years for Usucaption, but if he had timber, he would prescribe as to this in one year.

(B.) On account of the special exceptions in favor of *bonæ fidei possessio* and of Usucaption, especially as to *res furtiva* and *vi possessa*. So long as the profits existed as a portion of the principal, those exceptions necessarily extended themselves to the former; but the new *bonæ fidei possessio,* which arises upon severance, is altogether independent of them. Thus, if in *res furtiva* the profits arose whilst in possession of the thief, they would still continue *res furtiva,* not because the principal was so, but because the profits themselves were comprised in the *furtum.* If, on the other hand, the profits had previously accrued with the *bonæ fidei possessor,* this ground was inapplicable, and in such case it is undoubted that Usucaption had place as to the profits (*f*). So also (and still clearer) with the *res vi possessa.* For in this case, there is no instance where the denial of Usucaption would extend to the (severed) profits, because this denial is limited to immoveables, and all profits are moveables. This example very far removed therefore from contradicting the rule itself (*g*): on the other hand, it leads to a closer exposition of it than could previously be made.. For the acquisition of profits by severance, which has been here explained, avails not only to the party (as I had assumed cursorily,) who actually has Usucaption-Possession of the principal, but to him also who only combines within himself the *positive conditions* of it, (*possessio* (*h*), bona

(*f*) L. 48, § 5, *de furtis.* L. 33, *pr. de usurp. etc.* The controversy amongst the Roman lawyers on the *partus ancillæ* turns on wholly special grounds.

(*g*) Zachariæ uses it for this purpose. De Poss. p. 30. A second objection of the same writer has evidently still less in it;

namely, the *fructuum perceptio* is an *adquisitio naturalis,* but the *bonæ fidei possessio* is a positive enactment, introduced even later than Usucaption.

(*h*) At what moment is the *bona fides* necessary?—On the prehension of the principal, or on the acquisition of the profits?

fides justa causa), and the principal in that case may or may not admit of usucaption (*i*).

IV. The tenant of *ager vectigalis,* and so also the *emphyteutor,* acquires generally, as tenant, the true property in the profits by delivery (No. II.), but this delivery does not consist, as with the previous tenant, in a new act of prehension, but in the act of severance, as in the case of the *bonæ fidei possessor,* because he has juridical possession of the principal. This delivery at the same time passed all Roman property, because all profits of the soil were *res nec mancipi.* Consequently, his right to the profits was still more beneficial than that of the *bonæ fidei possessor.* But the *period of time* at which this acquisition arose was the same for both (*j*), and is founded on the same grounds as to both, namely, the rules of Possession above explained (§. 23). As moreover, no other explanation of this period of time can be given, except from the above rules, this circumstance affords conversely a direct proof of the juridical Possession of the *ager vectigalis.*

Just in the same position, however, is the mortgagee of land, who by mutual contract is allowed to perceive the profits. He also derives his right to these profits, like a tenant, it is true, from the proprietor; but he has also at the same time the *possession* of the soil, like the *emphyteutor* (§. 26), and thus the property in the profits must be ascribed to him before severance, although direct proofs for this assertion are not producible.

The Roman lawyers are not united on this point: see *L.* 48, § 1, *de A. R. D. L.* 23, § 1, *cod. L.* 11, § 3, 4, *de publiciana; L.* 25, § 2, *de usuris.* This question has no reference to the present inquiry.

(*i*) *L.* 48, *pr. de A. R. D.,* and so also § 1 of the same passage, ".... is qui non potest capere propter rei vitium, fructus suos facit."

(*j*) *L.* 25, § 1, *de usuris.*

205

SECTION XXV.

DERIVATIVE POSSESSION.

We have still, in connection with the *animus possidendi*, to inquire into the nature of derivative Possession. (p 178). The peculiarity of this Possession is, that the previous possessor transfers his *jus possessionis* without the property; consequently, the act of prehension does not differ from other cases, and in like manner a distinct act of will must accompany it, but this will must merely have in view the acquiring of a *jus possessionis*. The intention to deal with the thing as one's own property (*animus domini*) is therefore impossible, because the property is expressly recognized in another.

It becomes necessary now to give a complete description of the cases of derivative Possession, *i. e.*, all the juridical transactions must be analysed, in which detention is transferred without property, and in each case it must be ascertained whether or not the *jus possessionis* passes, at the same time with the detention. Now these juridical transactions are divisible generally into three classes, in the first of which derivative Possession never arises (§. 25), in the second it always arises (§. 26), and in the third occasionally only (§. 27). As to all generally, the observation which has been already made (p. 178), applies, that all derivative Possession is an exception to the general rule, consequently the rule is, that in juridical transactions of this kind *no* juridical possession arises, and in every case in which, nevertheless possession is to be considered as having passed, the existence of this possession must be expressly proved and explained.

First class: Cases in which juridical possession is never transferred simultaneously with the custody. All these cases coincide in this, that the previous possessor does not lose by such transfer his *jus possessionis*, the receiver, therefore, does not acquire such possession, but merely as an agent exercises the possession of another.

The first of these cases, and the one least open to doubt is, where detention is transferred for the purpose of enabling the party to manage our Possession, and either this Possession alone, or the whole of our property generally (*procurator* in the strict sense) (*a*).

Next comes the case of *commodatum* (*b*). Whoever transfers the use of his property to another in this form, no more loses his possession in it than the borrower acquires it (*c*).

Thirdly, exactly the same relation arises out of contracts of demise (*d*), for, in the nature of this contract also, no ground exists for considering the possession as alienated (*e*). For, as respects Usucaption, this contract can have no operation upon it whatever; but on the score of interdicts also it is wholly unnecessary to ascribe Possession to the tenant. For the contract itself protects the tenant against wrongful acts on the part of the owner, and if the possession is dis-

(*a*) " Quod servus, *vel procurator*, vel colonus tenent, *dominus creditur possidere*." *L.* 1, § 22, *de vi.*; *cf. L.* 9, *de poss.*

(*b*) *Commodatum* denotes strictly a *gratuitous* loan, see Inst. III. 14, § 2.—[Transl.]

(*c*) " Rei commodatæ et possessionem et proprietatem retinemus." *L.* 8, *commodati*; *cf. L.* 3, § 20, *de poss.*

(*d*) It seems strange to the ear of an English reader, especially a legal ear, that possession should be denied to a lessee. But in truth the Latin *colonus*, the German *Pachter*, and the English *farmer*, represent wholly different characters, which are unknown except in their respective countries, and hence it is impossible to find an equivalent term in other languages for no-

tions altogether foreign to them. An excellent account of the Roman "*colonus*" has been given by von Savigny himself, an abstract of which may be found in Sharon Turner's Hist. of England, vol. 2, App. p. 582.—[Transl.]

(*e*) " .... . Et colonus et inquilinus sunt in prædio, et tamen non possident." *L.* 6, § 2, *de precario*, " Et per colonos *et inquilinos* aut servos nostros possidemus." *L.* 25, § 1, *de poss.* Some writers have been led astray by two passages, in which interdicts are ascribed to the tenant (*L.* 12, 18, *de vi*). But it is there assumed that the tenant has turned the owner forcibly out of possession: the possession of the tenant, therefore, springs from this *dejectio*, and not from the tenancy.

turbed by a third party, the interdicts of the owner are sufficient; as, even in this case, the tenant may demand, by virtue of the contract, that the owner should bear him harmless, or make over to him his interdicts (f).

The following cases have been improperly considered as exceptions to the rule that the tenant only possesses in the name of the owner; 1st, Where the tenant is, at the same time, owner of the subject which previously had been in another person's possession, it is true that the previous possession then ceases (g). But the reason of this merely is, that in such case, no contract of demise is recognized; this is, therefore, no exception to the rule, but a clear example of it. 2nd, Where the transfer of possession is expressly made. But such an agreement so completely contradicts the essence of a demise, that the latter is looked upon as put an end to, if, by a subsequent transaction, the possession is transferred (h). Many authors have denied this position, from a misunderstanding of the *possessionis locatio* which has been above explained (§. 5); it does not denote a case of letting, by which the Possession would be acquired, but a case where the landlord had only got the mere possession. This is the only distinction between this case and the usual one where the landlord has both possession and property; it has this in common with the other cases, that the tenant only manages the possession which belongs actually to the landlord (i).

A fourth case, in which detention is transferred without

(f) Compare § 9, *ante*.

(g) On this position, as well as upon the exception of *locatio possessionis*, compare § 5. An instance of this exception occurs in § 26.

(h) *L.* 10, *de poss.* (see *post*, § 27). With many, this is merely a consequence of the still more important general rule, according to which the right of possession generally is capable of being transferred at the mere will of that party, who, according to the general rule, should be considered as merely the manager of another person's possession. Comp. § 9, *ante*. (Add. to 6th ed.)

(i) L. 37, de pig. act. (See *post*, § 26).

Possession, relates to a form of Roman procedure—the *missio in possessionem*. This permission of the Prætor to take possession was required for two different purposes : 1st, to transfer property, (*i. e.* bonitarian with *conditio usucapiendi*) (*j*). Possession, indeed, might be acquired in this mode, but it would not be a derivative, but an original possession, because the new possessor possessed *pro suo*, i. e. for the purpose of dealing with the subject as his own. 2nd, For the purpose of giving security previous to a conveyance, to allow the profits to be enjoyed, &c., &c. In these cases, simple detention without possession was acquired. The reason was this, the *missus in possessionem* could not have Usucaption, which is what distinguishes this *missio* from the other kind; neither was possession necessary for the sake of interdicts, because the party already had an appropriate interdict different from the possessory one, and even more advantageous to him (*k*). It is, therefore, easily comprehensible why, in every *missio* of this sort, the *missus* should have no Possession, but merely detention in the name of the previous possessor (*l*).

(*j*) To this case belongs the *missio ex secundo decreto damni infecto* causâ (*L.* 2, *pr. de damn. infect.*) ; it is also expressly remarked that, in this case, juridical possession arose, which was never the case on a *premium decretum*. (*L.* 3, § 23, *de poss.; add. L.* 15, § 16, 17 ; *L.* 18, § 15, *de damno infecto*). In like manner, and with the same effect on the right to the different subject matters, all *bonorum possessio* was given, although, perhaps, the word *missio* never occurs in the B. P. *edictalis.*

(*k*) *Digest, lib.* 43, *tit.* 4.

(*l*) *L.* 3, § 23, *et L.* 10, § 1, *de poss.; L.* 3, § 3, *uti poss.* Thibaut, über Besitz, p. 13, contends for an exception in favour

of *fraudulenta absentia, L.* 7, § 1, *quibus ex causis in poss.*, but the *bona possidere* in this passage has no more reference to juridical possession than has any other *missio* of creditors, (*L.* 3, § 8, *uti poss.*), and even the expression "bona possidere" is used in other cases of this kind, when, undoubtedly, no juridical possession exists. *L.* 12, *quibus ex caus. in poss.* The rule itself appears to be contradicted by *L.* 30, § 2, *de poss.* "Item cum Prætor idcirco in possessionem rei (ire) jussit, quod damni infecti non promittebatur ; *possessionem invitum dominium amittere Labeo ait.*" But it is clear that this is not laid down in contradiction to the foregoing passages, because the last passage

The fifth and last case of this class relates to the detention which is founded on a *jus in re*. Whoever, in this case, transfers the subject to another, simply because the latter has a right to the *ususfructus, usus,* or otherwise in the same, does not thereby lose his possession, and the fructuary exercises, in the same way as a mere tenant, this possession of the property. The reason is easily assigned. On the ground of usucaption no alteration of Possession is required, since, through a *jus in re* no alteration of the property could arise. On the ground of interdicts just as little also ; for the *jus in re* is protected against the inroads of a third party by its own interdicts (§. 12), and this protection is not weakened by the fact that the owner may also maintain an interdict on his own Possession against the intruder; but even the possible collision of the owner himself with the fructuary, does not make it necessary to deny possession to the owner. Both may maintain interdicts ; but these interdicts are related to each other like the *rei vindicatio* and the *confessoria actio,* i. e. like the rule and the exception, consequently no collision could occur by means of this relation which were not easily soluble (§. 9, add. to 6th ed.) These positions must now be proved.

As to *ususfructus,* it is most easy to demonstrate that the fructuary has no possession at all.

L. 6, §. 2, *de precario* (*m*).

and *L.* 3, § 23, are from the same author, viz. Paulus ; and therefore the opinion of Labeo must have been quoted here, as that of Q. Martius was in *L.* 3, *cit.,* and the "ineptissimum est" applied to the latter must be understood as to the former also. As the doctrine of Paulus it can only stand good for the *secundum decretum.*

(*m*) Comp. *L.* 1, § 8, *de poss.*; L. 10, § 5, *de adqu. rer. dom.* § 4, I.

per quas pers. ; L. 5, § 1, *ad exhib.* On the other hand, Cicero says, Pro Cæcina, C. 32, p. m. 308. " Cæsenniam *possedisse propter ususfructum non negas.*" It is not necessary to assert as to this that formerly a different rule must have prevailed, or that Cicero, by mistake, or for the benefit of his client, laid down here an erroneous proposition. For it cannot be denied that the Fructuary had some sort of possession,

P

" .... et fructuarius, inquit, et colonus et inquilinus sunt in prædio, et tamen *non possident.*"

L. 12, *pr. de poss.*

"Naturaliter videtur possidere (*n*) is qui usumfructum (*o*) habet."

Just in the same way it is expressly pointed out in another passage, on the relation of *ususfructus* to property, that the exercise of property, (*i. e.* Possession), and the exercise of *ususfructus* must be looked upon as wholly independent of each other, so that the one is not impeded by the other.

L. 52, *pr. de poss.*

" Permisceri causas possessionis, et ususfructus non oportet: quemadmodum nec possessio, et proprietas misceri debent; *neque impediri* (*p*) *possessionem, si alius fruatur; neque alterius fructum amputari* (*q*), *si alter possidere.*"

This exceedingly simple relation of Possession to *ususfructus* has, up to this time, been recognised by very few (*r*).

viz. the *juris quasi possessio* with the right to interdicts; and in Cicero's case, the existence of interdicts was all that was in question. It is only the *possessio* proper, *i. e. possessio ipsius rei* which the Fructuary does not enjoy, and Cicero does not affirm that he had that. The consequences, indeed, which he deduces from the above position are to be ascribed to the license of an advocate.

(*n*) That is, *jus possessionis habere non videtur.* The meaning of this passage is only to be ascertained clearly by its connection with the other passages, because the expression *naturalis possessio* is ambiguous, (§ 7). Glossa interlin. ad v. *naturaliter.* (MS. Par. 4458 a.)—"id est corporaliter tantum M.," *i. e.* Martinus.

(*o*) Rom. 1476 : "*usum.*"

(*p*) *Neque* is the reading of

seven Paris MSS., one at Metz, of the Leipsic, and my own; also Cod. Rehd., Edd. Rom. 1476; Nor.1483; Ven.1485; Ven.1494; Lugd. 1509, 1513; Hal. Paris, 1514, 1536. The Basilica also confirm this reading. (Meerm. VII. 49). Flor. "namque."

(*q*) *Amputari* is the reading of the MSS. and editions cited in the last note. It is clear that the *ususfructus* is lost by *non usus;* therefore, in this passage the mere *possessio* of another does not point to this, because the exercise of *ususfructus* and of property are independent of one another. Florentin. "*computari.*"

(*r*) Placentini Summa in Cod. L. 8, T. 4, p. 373, et L. 8, T. 5, p. 376. Alciatus in L. 1, *pr. de poss.* n. 42, 43, p. 1200. Retes de Poss. P. 1, C. 4, § 11—13. (Meerman. T. 7, pp. 472—3).

Most writers ascribe to the fructuary juridical Possession of
the subject along with the *juris quasi possessio* (*s*), partly on
account of their misunderstanding *naturalis possessio,* partly
because there was no appropriate interdict in this case, as in
other servitudes, but the *interdictum de vi* and *uti possidetis*
itself. But what the name was of the interdict which was
granted, is evidently a very different matter from the right
generally to maintain an interdict; that the fructuary should
have the same interdicts as belonged to Possession proper,
is undoubtedly somewhat singular, and arose from the extension of those interdicts beyond their original scope (*t*);
but at the same time this circumstance is wholly accidental,
the right of the fructuary to interdicts generally, is altogether
erroneously considered as an exception to the rule, and
neither this right, nor the above accidental circumstance,
make it in any way necessary to ascribe to him any possession of the subject itself.

What is thus laid down as to *ususfructus* applies *à fortiori*
to *usus,* and to the other easements in which detention of the
subject occurs, as in all these cases a still smaller right is
severed from the property than in *ususfructus.* This, also,
may perhaps constitute the ground why no mention at all is
made in the Law Sources of Possession in these different
relations (*u*).

The above doctrine, however, refers not only to servitudes
but to every *jus in re* generally, and, consequently, to *superficies* also. For as to the latter, a special interdict was
framed (*v*), not, therefore, the interdictum *uti possidetis,*

(*s*) Joannes Bassianus (see
ante), Glossa in L. 23, § 2, *quib.
ex c. maj.,* in L. 3, § 9; L. 9,
de vi; in L. 4, *uti poss.,* in
L. 6, § 2, *de prec.* Bertholus in
L. 1, *pr. de uti poss.,* Nos. 9,
12. Cujacius in Obs. IX. 33,
XVIII. 24, not. prior. in § 24, I.
per quas pers.; Comm. in L. 12,
pr. de poss.; App. T. 8, p. 271;
Comm. in Cod. L. 7, T. 32; Opt.

T. 9, p. 1007; Galvanus de Usufructu, C. 34. Accursius and
Cujacius have, so to speak, mixed
up all the views together; Galvanus discovered other means to
confuse the subject completely.

(*t*) Donelli Comm. J. C. L. 15,
C. 32, p. 801; C. 33, p. 803.

(*u*) See *post.*

(*v*) Digest. Lib. 43, Tit. 18.

which, nevertheless, was applicable in every case of juridical possession. In proof of this, the following passage is in point, which, treating of *superficies*, expressly describes the above developed relation between property and every *jus in re*, as that of a rule to its exception.

L. 3, §. 7, *uti possidetis.*

" Sed si supra ædes, quas possides, cœnaculum sit, in quo alius quasi dominus moretur, interdicto uti possidetis me uti posse, Labeo ait, non eum qui in cœnaculo moraretur; semper enim superficiem solo cedere. Plane si cœnaculum ex publico aditum habeat, ait Labeo, videri non ab eo ædes possideri qui κρυπτας possideret, sed ab eo cujus ædes supra κρυπτας essent; verum est in eo, qui aditum ex publico habuit. Ceterum superficiarii *proprio interdicto* et actionibus a Prætore utentur; dominus autem soli, tam adversus alium, quam adversus superficiarium *potior erit interdicto uti possidetis ; sed Prætor superficiarum tuebitur secundum legem locationis* et ita Pomponius quoque probat."

This passage has been constantly misunderstood, from not perceiving that it does not speak throughout of the same case. It consists, in fact, of two independent paragraphs, as an entirely new subject is commenced with *Ceterum.* In the first paragraph the case is this. I possess a house, the upper story of which is inhabited by another person, not, indeed, as a lodger or a fructuary, but as a *quasi dominus*, in the same way that I inhabit below, so that each of us singly, *i. e.* if no question arose between the two, might be considered without question as a true possessor. What then would be the case as to possession and interdicts? It might be thought that each should have interdicts for his own story; this view, which would solve the difficulty in the simplest way, is not contradicted by the Jurist, but is tacitly passed over as out of the question, the reason of which evidently is, that there could not be, in any mode whatever, different possessors of the different stories (p. 192). Nothing, therefore, was left than to ascertain which of the two was *possessor of the house*, and to ascribe interdicts to

him only. Now the Jurist says, according to the rule the
inhabitant of the ground floor is the true possessor of the
house, and the other must give way to him, because the
residence of the former is connected with the soil, on which
the building rests. Still this is not universally true, for if
the chief use of the house belongs to the inhabitant of the
upper story, and the other party only occupies a cellar or
basement (κρυπτη), the former party is to be looked upon
as the true possessor of the house, and he is protected by
interdicts, and the latter must give way. In this first case,
therefore, it is assumed that each party is inhabiting *quasi
dominus;* now comes the second case. A wholly different
relation arises where the inhabitant above does not live in
the house as a *quasi dominus,* but by virtue of a *superficies.*
The difficulties in the former case do not arise here, but
every thing is governed by the common relation between
possessio and *quasi possessio.* For the owner alone is possessor of the whole house, and he has the *int. uti possidetis*
against all the world, even including the superficiary, but the
latter also as plaintiff might maintain the special interdict *de
superficiebus* against every one, including the owner, and if
sued as defendant, he would use the latter interdict as an
exception, by which he could protect himself against the
int. uti possidetis of the owner. Thus the whole of this
explanation turns upon the proper division of the paragraphs,
which is clearly enough marked by the word *ceterum,* and
it has only escaped notice generally from the fact of the first
half of the passage also containing the word *superficies;* but
it is evident that the word is used there (just as in the foregoing §. 5) not to denote any legal relation, but only in the
physical sense, to point out the opposition between the
house and the land. If the above division and explanation
are adopted, it is quite clear, from the contrast between these
two cases, that in the case of *superficies,* the Jurist ascribes
to the landowner alone the *corporis possessio* of the whole
and all its parts, and to the superficiary, on the other hand

the *juris quasi possessio* of those parts, to which his contract extends (*secundum legem locationis*) (*w*).

Placentin (*x*) is, perhaps, the only author who recognised this complete similarity of Possession in every *jus in re*, i. e. in *ususfructus*, *superficies*, &c. &c. Most writers have satisfied themselves with inquiring into the relations of Possession, first with reference to *ususfructus;* and, secondly, to *superficies*, because it happened by accident that the Law Sources mention Possession as to these two cases only (*y*).

(*w*) Du Roi, Spec. Observ. de jure in, &c. Heidelb., 1812, p. 62, maintains that *superficies* is not a *jus in re*, but a sort of bonitarian property or *dominium utile*. He avails himself of exactly the same arguments by which I attempted, in the second edition, to establish a bonitarian property in the emphyteutor, namely, that he enjoyed practically nearly all the benefits of property. He goes however too far in this when he uses these words, from L. 73, 75, de R. V. " Superficiario...... Præter causa cognitâ in rem actionem pollicetur," to found the conclusion that a superficiary may maintain a *rei vindicatio*, because these passages occur under the title *de rei vind.* He is also driven, p. 65, to adopt an *æquitas*, which is not only opposed to *jus civile*, but also to *jus naturale*, and which certainly is in complete contradiction to the notion of *æquitas*. I conceive that we cannot ascribe to *superficies* any more than to *emphyteusis*, any other legal character than that of a *jus in re*, by the relation of which

to property every thing is satisfactorily explained. It is true, indeed, that these more recent *jura in re* are brought very close to property, much closer than it was thought either possible or expedient according to the old strict notion of property. Upon this ancient simple view of property, which would not even admit of a mortgage in its modern sense, the theory of servitudes was formed, by which the narrow limits of the permitted servitudes are to be explained, which are usually looked upon by modern jurists as idle subtleties of the old law.

(*x*) Summa in Cod. L. 4, T. 4, p. 373; L. 8, T. 5, p. 376.

(*y*) It has been again contended by several recent writers with much pains, that the superficiary possesses the *corporis possessio*, in which case the conclusion, somewhat overlooked by these writers, inevitably follows, that the ground landlord has not got such possession. Schroeter in Linde's Zeitschrift, Band 2, pp. 244—55. Bercholtz's Versuche, p. 83, (add. to 6th ed.)

SECTION XXVI.

DERIVATIVE POSSESSION.—*Continued.*

Second class; detention, which is never delivered without the possession. (p. 205).

There are two cases in this class.

1st. The Possession of the Emphyteutory (*a*). For as in general this Possession is undoubted, and yet is without the *animus domini*, it can only be considered as derivative Possession. It is, however, on historical grounds only (*b*), and not on the nature and conditions of this law-relation, that it is to be considered as a case of derivative Possession, and not a mere *juris quasi possessio*.

2nd. The possession of a pledge-holder, *i. e.* the possession founded on a *contractus pignoris.* For it is only on such contract that the possession arises, and not on every case of mere pledging: namely, not on a simple prætorian pledge (*c*), such as arose out of every *missio in possessionem* (*d*), for the *missio* in most cases had no possession as its consequence ; just as little also on the *pignus in causa judicati captum*, which is regulated by the analogy

---

(*a*) *Emphyteusis* was the property given in waste lands on the condition of cultivating them and paying a certain rent. See Vicat. Vocab. Utr. Jur. ad voc.— [Transl.]

(*b*) See *ante*, § 13, and § 24. Schroeter explains the possession of the Emphyteutory differently ; Linde's Zeitschrift, B. 2, pp. 237—243, (add. to 6th ed.)

(*c*) If the defendant does not appear upon a vindication, and thereupon, a *missio* is given to the plaintiff, the possession would appear according to L. 8, in f. c. *de*

præscrip. 30, *l.* 40, *ann.* to be given to the latter. Vulgarus ascribed it to him only at the end of a year ; Martinus immediately, under condition however that it might be recoverable from him within the first year ; Odofredus, in L. 3, in f. *de poss.* fo. 57. But the above passages apply just as well to detention only, and the nature of the prætorian pledge makes this the necessary construction.

(*d*) L. 26, *pr. de pign. act.* L. 12, *pro emtore.*

of the prætorian pledge (*e*); lastly, not on a mere contract, where the thing is hypothecated without any delivery (*f*).

The possession of the pledge-holder is to be explained thus. For a long period, the Romans had only two ways of securing the performance of an *obligatio* by means of the property of the debtor. Originally it was customary to transfer to the creditor the property in a subject by mancipation, with a promise, however, by the creditor, at the moment of mancipation, to deliver the property back (*pactum de emancipando, fiducia*). This form, however, was not only cumbersome, but also was restricted to certain species of things (*res nec mancipi*) (*g*); therefore, it became usual, merely to hand over the subject to the creditor, without any other right arising out of such delivery, than that accruing to the debtor of demanding the re-delivery at some future time (*actio pigneratitia*). That in such case, no *animus domini*, and, consequently, no original Possession, is to be recognised, has been already laid down above. If any possession, therefore, is to be found in this case, it must be a derivative one, and it is that on which the question now turns. In the first instance, therefore, the creditor merely obtains by this delivery the natural security which the custody of the thing affords, as a means of obtaining payment out of it hereafter; if he loses the actual possession his

(*e*) Odofredus, l. c.

(*f*) L. 33, § 5, *de usurp.* In this case therefore a *juris quasi possessio* may very well be conceived, although it is not any-where mentioned. In like manner we have no reason for asserting that the creditor in such case, who obtains detention by the *actio hypothecaria* obtains with it juridical possession. It might be thought he required the *possessio* to enable him to sell and deliver; but he makes the delivery always in the name of another, like a

mandatory, who also requires no possession in himself in order to transfer the property, (add. to 6th ed.) This *pactum hypothecæ*, however, is not to be confounded with another transaction which on first glance appears the same, viz. *pignus* mixed up with *constitutum possessorium.* Of this more hereafter.

(*g*) (Add. to 4th ed.) The *in jure cessio* might however be also used for that purpose. (Gaius II. 59), and it was applicable to subjects of either description.

security is gone. Then comes the question as to possessory Interdicts, and it is easily demonstrable, from the nature of this contract, to which of the two parties these interdicts belong; not to the debtor, for then it would be open to him to re-obtain the physical possession of the subject in an improper manner (*h*); but undoubtedly to the creditor, for it was the essence of the contract that he should have the detention, and interdicts merely avail to protect or to recover this (*i*). A slight alteration occurred, when subsequently a real action (*actio quasi Serviana*) was given to the pledge-holder to recover his lost possession. Interdicts were now less indispensable to him, but he still retained them, for the owner also obtained interdicts, although from the earliest times he had his vindication : it is a gross error, therefore, to make this real action, or the consequences of it, the foundation of the creditor's *possessio*, and to view it as arising out of the action, and assumed merely for the purposes of the action, whereas, on the contrary, it might have altogether ceased when the real action was given. According to this view, the relation would be as follows; the creditor has juridical Possession, but not also the right of Usucaption (*civilis possessio*), because neither *justa causa* nor *bona fides* were present; the debtor had not the right of Interdicts, and, therefore, generally, no juridical Possession, Usucaption itself would thus cease for him, which he had enjoyed up to that moment (§ 7). But this last consequence not only does not follow immediately from the

(*h*) It might be objected, that the same would hold good with a hirer, also with a borrower, &c. But the case of a pledge delivered is distinguishable from contracts such as those, by having for its express object the giving a security to the creditor against his debtor; it turns therefore, unlike the above contracts, on a distrust of the debtor, and it would therefore be wholly inconsistent with it to allow interdicts to the latter. Thibaut has explained this relation very correctly, and in more precise language than mine; Archiv. B. 18, p. 324, (add. to 6th ed.)

(*i*) We are not therefore called upon, with Unterholtzner, Verjährung. (p. 160), to look upon this Possession in pledge-law as a remnant of the ancient *fiducia*.

nature of the contract of pledge, but is even directly opposed
to the interest of the pledge-holder. For if a third party
had the Roman property in a subject over which the debtor
had previously had Usucaption, if such Usucaption were
complete, the former would be excluded from his vindication; but if the Usucaption were interrupted, the owner
would not lose his right of vindication against the creditor,
any more than against any other possessor. This conflicting
interest of the creditor, in reference to Interdicts and Usucaption, introduced into the contract of pledge, an exception
to the rules of Possession which is to be found in no other
transaction. The whole case may be summed up thus; the
creditor has *possessio*, i. e. the right of Interdicts, but not
civilis possessio, i. e. not the right of Usucaption; the debtor
has not the right of Interdicts; indeed, speaking generally,
he has *no possession* at all, but, nevertheless, his commenced
Usucaption continues to run as if he still retained Possession.
It is not so immaterial as it might appear at first sight,
whether the proposition be expressed in the above terms,
which are authorized by a passage in the Roman law (*j*),
or whether it be said that the debtor actually has Possession,
and, consequently, the Possession is divided between him and
the creditor. For, firstly, according to our definition, the whole
exception relates to the rule, *sine possessione usucapio contingere non potest*, not to the other rule, *plures eandem rem in
solidum possidere non possunt*, by which view the universality
of the latter rule is secured against all attack.   Secondly, it is
shewn by this definition on which side alone the exception
to the rule holds good; it is the right of the debtor which
causes a departure from the rule, the right of the creditor is
wholly comprised in the rule as to derivative Possession, and
on this ground the possession of the pledge-holder might be
used with ample justice to corroborate the general notions of
civilis and *naturalis possessio*, which would be altogether
illogical in the opposite case.

(*j*) *L.* 36, *de poss.*

I must now cite my authorities for these statements as to the Possession of a pledge.

1st. The creditor has the juridical Possession, but not the right of Usucaption.

L. 16, *de usurp.* (*k*).

" .... Qui pignori dedit ad usucapionem tantum possidet; *quod ad reliquas omnes causas pertinet, qui accepit, possidet.*"

2nd. It is a consequence of the above proposition, that the creditor may let the thing out on hire like any other possessor (*l*); and this even to the debtor, although the latter is at the same time owner of it; the letting, however, would then amount to a *possessionis locatio* (p. 207), and the debtor would have the management of another person's possession of his own property.

L. 37, *de pign. act.* (*m*).

" Si pignus mihi traditum locassem domino, per locationem retineo possessionem: quia, antequam conduceret debitor, non fuerit ejus possessio: cum et animus mihi retinendi sit, et conducenti non sit animus possessionem apiscendi."

3rd. The debtor has properly no possession at all, but there is feigned in him a *possessio ad usucapiendum,* i. e., so far as relates to Usucaption he is treated as if he had possession, although he has it not in point of fact.

(*k*) Comp. *L.* 40, *pr. de poss.;* L. 15, § 2, *qui satisd. coq.;* L. 35, § 1, *de pign. act.;* L. 3, § 15, *ad exhibendum.* The L. 7, § 2, *C. de præscript.* 300, 40 *ann.* can not be urged effectively in opposition to this; for the "possessing in another's name," is an expression of ambiguous meaning, the *debitor* also is in fact treated as if he had had *possessio,* (*ad usucapionem*); and lastly, if even the contrary be true, the old law must in fact have been altered in that constitution, because Justinian was not defining the right of possession, but merely the term of prescription of the *actio hypothecaria.*

(*l*) L. 23, *pr. de pignoribus.*

(*m*) Comp. L. 37, *de poss.* It appears clearly, from both passages, that the *possessionis locatio* (L. 28, *de poss.*) was not such a *locatio* as gave the lessee a juridical possession. (See *ante,* § 5, 23.)

L. 36, *de poss.*

" Qui pignoris causâ fundum creditori tradit, *intelligitur possidere.* Sed et si eundem precario rogaverit, æque per diutinam possessionem capiet, ... cum plus juris in possessione habeat, qui precario rogaverit, quam *qui omnino non possidet*" (*n*).

L. 16, *de usurp.*

" Qui pignori dedit, *ad usucapionem tantum possidet.*"

L. 1, § 15, *de poss.*

". . . . . . ad unam enim tantum causam *videri* eum a debitore possideri ; *ad usucapionem* . . . . ."

4th. This feigned possession of the debtor is founded entirely on the legal nature of the contract of pledge; when therefore such contract cannot be looked upon as valid, the above Possession has no place ; this is the case (inter alia) where the creditor is also owner of the pledged article.

L. 29, *de pign. act* (*o*).

" Si rem alienam bonâ fide emeris, et mihi pignoris de-deris, ... deinde me dominus heredem instituerit; *desinit pignus esse* . . . . . . *idcirco usucapio tua interpella-bitur.*"

Modern Jurists entertain widely different opinions on the possession of a pledge, the greater part of which do not belong to this place, as they relate to the notions of *civilis* and *naturalis possessio.*

Placentin (*p*) strives with great pains to deny all posses-sion to the creditor. Donellus has been misunderstood, not altogether without his own fault, to support the same doctrine, but he only denies the possession of a creditor where he is treating of the original notion of Possession

(*n*) These words, with the commencement of the passage and in connection with the following citations, give this result, *debitor omnino non possidet, sed ad unam causam (usucapionis) intelligitur possidere.*

(*o*) Comp. L. 33, § 5, *de usurp.*

With this is connected the diffi-cult L. 16, *de obl. et act.*, upon which should be consulted Che-sius, In Juris. Rom. et Att. T. 2, p. 872.

(*p*) Summa in Cod. *tit. de poss.* in fin. (p. m. 333).

with *animus domini* (*q*); he afterwards speaks of the delivery of mere Possession, and then makes correct mention
of the pledge-holder (*r*). His error, therefore, consists in
this, that the distinction between original and derivative
Possession, with its application to the present case, is rather
tacitly assumed by him than expressly laid down. Duarenus, and still better has Valentia well defined the
relations of debtor and creditor (*s*). Westphal's opinion
is expressed in these terms (*t*): "That the mortgagor has
only got a Possession for Usucaption is a gross error of
the Jurists. . . . . . . We see how little the statements of the
old law writers are to be depended upon"(*u*).

————

SECTION XXVII.

DERIVATIVE POSSESSION.— *Continued.*

Third class: Detention, which is delivered sometimes
with, sometimes without Possession. Two cases belong to
this class, *Depositum* and *Precarium.*

First, as to *depositum*, there is no doubt as to the rule.
According to the rule, therefore, the Possession here is as
little alienated as in a case of hiring, &c.

L. 3, § 20, *de poss.* (*a*).

" Sed si is, qui apud me *deposuit*, vel commodavit, eam

(*q*) Comm. Jur. liv. L. 5, C. 6,
(p. m. 183).

(*r*) Comm. Jur. liv. L. 5, C.
13, (p. m. 193).

(*s*) Duarenus in L. 1, § 15, *de
poss.* Opp. p. m. 834—5. Valentia in Ill. Jur. Tract. L. 1,
Tr. 2, C. 11.

(*t*) Arten der Sachen, &c. §
151.

(*u*) Latterly another explanation of the possession of a pledge-
holder has been attempted by
Schroeter, in Linde's Zeitschrift,
B. 2, pp. 255, 263. Sintenis has
written an express article to refute it, *eod.* B. 7, pp. 414—35.
(Add. to 6th ed.)

(*a*) Comp. L. 23, § 4, *de usurp.*
L. 9, § 9, *de reb. cred.*

rem vendiderit mihi, vel donaverit, non videbor causam possessionis mihi mutare, *qui ne possidebam quidem.*"

The exception to this rule occurs in a very special case. When the property of a thing is vindicated, but the thing itself is deposited with a third party (*sequester*), the parties might agree expressly that such third party should have the Possession, and by this Possession all the previous Usucaption was interrupted; and this is the only case in which a *Depositum* would work a change of Possession (*b*).

L. 39, *de poss.*

"Interesse puto, qua mente apud sequestrum deponitur res; nam si omittendæ possessionis causa, *et hoc aperte fuerit approbatum;* ad usucapionem possessio ejus partibus non procederet; at si custodiæ causa deponatur, ad usucapionem eam possessionem victori procedere (*c*) constat."

L. 17, § 1, *depositi.*

"Rei depositæ proprietas apud deponentem manet, sed et possessio, *nisi apud sequestrem deposita est* (*d*); *nam tum demum sequester possidet*; id enim agitur ea depositione, ut neutrius possessione id tempus procedat."

With the *precarium* the relation is just the converse; in this case either Possession or mere detention is delivered over; but the first is the rule, and the second must be the

(*b*) Schroeter, Bartels and Sintenis, entertain different opinions as to the *sequester;* Zeitschrift Von Linde, B. 2, p. 266 ; B. 6, p. 205 ; B. 7, p. 249. (Add. to 6th ed.)

(*c*) For in this case, *i. e.* when the contrary is not expressly declared, the *sequester* merely exercises the possession of another.

(*d*) "Deposita (possessio) est," not "deposita (res) est." The meaning therefore is not, "*Depositum* gives no possession, except in the case of a *sequestratio*," but "*Depositum* gives no possession

except when a *sequester* is concerned, and then only when the possession is expressly made over to him (deposita possessio"). For that the *sequester* does not always, but only in excepted cases, become possessor, is not only clear from the terms of the first passage, but also from these words in the present, "nam *tum demum* sequester possidet." Duarenus, De sacris eccles. minis. III. 10 Opp. p. m. 1567, was the first to give this explanation, but he expounds *deposita est* unnecessarily by *omissa*.

result of an express agreement (e). The reason why the delivery of Possession is to be looked upon here as the rule, consists in this, that it works no injury to the owner (*rogatus*) (*f*). For his Usucaption-possession is continued by *accessio possessionis* (*g*), and he has an appropriate interdict *recuperandæ* possessionis to recover back the alienated Possession.

1st. By the rule, Possession itself is transferred in cases of *Precarium*;

L. 4, § 1, *de prec.* (*h*).

" Meminisse autem nos oportet, eum qui precario habet, *etiam possidere.*"

2nd. That detention only should pass, express agreement is required;

L. 10, pr. § 1, *de poss.* (*i*).

" Si quis ante conduxit, postea precario rogavit, videbitur discessisse a conductione . . . . Idem Pomponius bellissime tentat dicere, numquid qui conduxerit quidem prædium, precario autem rogavit, non *ut possideret, sed ut in possessione esset?* (*j*) . . . . quod si factum est, utrumque procedit." Indeed, even in this last case, the Possession is lost, if the *rogans* is also owner of the subject; but this loss is founded, as in the case of hiring, on the mere fact that, under such circumstances, no *precarium* exists. For this reason, the proposition itself meets with an exception, when the owner with notice, consequently with reference merely to the possession of another, enters into the precarium (*k*);

(*e*) Duarenus in L. 10, *de poss.* Opp. p. m. 869. Schroeter and Bartels have widely different opinions upon *Precarium*, Linde's Zeitschrift, B. 2, p. 263; B. 6, p. 179. (Add. to 6th ed.)

(*f*) This point is still more clear according to the rejected opinion of the older jurists, who ascribed possession to the *rogatus*

as well as to the *rogans*. (See § 12).

(*g*) L. 13, § 7, *de poss.*

(*h*) Comp. L. 22, *pr. eod.*

(*i*) Comp. L. 6, § 2, *de prec.*

(*j*) In the first case the immediate question was as to *precario rogare.*

(*k*) See *ante*, § 5.

which *precarium solius possessionis* is not to be confounded with the transfer of juridical Possession by *precarium*, since both the possession and the mere detention may be transferred by that *precarium* as well as by any other. A very important case occurs connected with the contract of pledge. When the debtor asks for the pledge *precario*, this *rogatio* is valid, because it evidently has reference to the juridical Possession of the creditor (*l*): the Usucaption-possession of the debtor naturally continues (*m*); the possession of the creditor continues at the same time, when the *precarium* had merely detention for its object, and this latter must be presumed in accordance with the intention of the whole contract of pledge (*n*).

SECTION XXVIII.

ACQUISITION THROUGH AN AGENT.

The only remaining case to be inquired into on the acquisition of Possession is the acquisition by means of another party, and this question, according to the above given explanation of the terms describing the notion of possession (p. 170), must be expressed, (certain expressions excepted), thus; How is it possible to acquire through the acts of another party the consciousness of physical dominion over a subject?

This whole mode of acquisition, but especially one case of it (that termed *constitutum possessorium*), is usually con-

(*l*) L. 6, § 4, *de prec.*
(*m*) L. 36, *de poss.*; L. 29, *de pign. act.*; L. 33, § 6, *de usurp.* (All three passages are from the *Digesta* of Julien). L. 16, de obl. et act. from the same work of Julian will be discussed hereafter with the so-called *constitutum possessorium.*
(*n*) L. 33, § 6, *de usurp.*

sidered as fictitious prehension, which view, in this case, as in every other, induces important practical consequences (§ 15). Now it is not to be denied, that this acquisition has something quite peculiar in it; but it has been omitted to inquire in what this peculiarity consists. It turns principally on these three points; what is the party required to do through whom the Possession is to be acquired (the agent)? what must the (new) possessor himself do? what relation must exist between the two? The first and second points contain in substance nothing which in any way diverges from the general rule as to all acquisition; quite differently with the third, however, and therefore some juridical considerations are connected with this latter point, which do not relate to the two first at all. This distinction will appear more clear by two examples. According to the common opinion (a), acquisition of this kind is not allowable by illegal acts, for instance by force, because such illegal act would not warrant a fiction; but in fact, there is nothing whatever juridical in the act of prehension in such case, any more than in any other. On the other hand, the relation between the agent and the possessor is altogether juridical; for this reason the legal invalidity of such relation is sufficient to prevent the acquisition of Possession. Therefore, the above erroneous view proceeds from a similar mistake to that of Labeo (b), and our Jurists would have done well to avail themselves of the conclusion of Javolenus.

The first point, therefore, which must be inquired into is, as to the sort of act to be performed by the agent. Now it is evident at once that he must not do less, than if he were purporting to acquire possession for himself; that is, there must be an act of prehension accompanied with *animus possidendi*, and on this ground, whoever is incapable generally of exercising an act of will, is incapable of undertaking such an agency (c). But the *animus*

(a) Duarenus in L. 1, § 13, *de poss.* Opp. p. m. 833.

(b) L. 51, *de poss.* (*Ante*, § 17).

(c) L. 1, § 9, 10, *de poss.*

Q

possidendi has this peculiarity, that if the principal is to be the possessor in fact, the agent must not have the intention of acquiring for himself, but for his principal: if the agent intends to make himself, or a third party, possessor, that result necessarily follows from his conduct, provided only that no special conditions (such as slavery), stand in the way, in which case no possession at all is acquired (*d*).

This rule is not open to doubt, but an exception must be made to it in the case of delivery. For in such case the intention of the *tradens* is conclusive, and the acquisition of Possession proceeds according to the intention, even where the agent fraudulently intends to make the acquisition for himself, or for a third party (*e*). It is evident that this

---

(*d*) L. 1, § 19, 20, *de poss.* ".... . cum autem suo nomine nacti fuerint possessionem, non cum ea mente, ut operam duntaxat suam *accommodarent nobis: non possumus adquirere.*" This reading (of *ten* Paris MSS., of those at Metz, and at Lyons, of the Edd. Rom. 1476; Nor. 1483; Ven. 1485; Lugd. 1509, 1513; Paris, 1514) is evidently better than the Florentine...... "nobis non *possunt* adquirere," as the agent never even *intended it*, and his *ability* to acquire for us was not in question. Haloander reads "nobis accommodarent; non possunt adquirere;" just as if the agent himself would not become the possessor, which is altogether incorrect.

(*e*) Ulpian says this most expressly in L. 13, *de donationibus*, which is the most unambiguous of all the passages on the subject. The following passages, however, appear to contradict it: 1st. Ju-

lianus, L. 37, § 6, *de adqu. rer. dom.* But in this passage, "nihil agetur" must refer to "ex mente procuratoris;" just as it is said in the above cited L. 13, "nihil agit *in sua persona sed mihi adquirit*," (Wenck, De Traditione, p. 64), so that the *nihil agetur* may be rendered by *id non agetur.* 2nd. Ulpian himself, in L. 44, § 1, *de furtis.* But the whole of this passage relates to a *falsus* procurator, who afterwards, for shortness, is called *procurator* simply: no agency at all therefore was in question, and the *non ejus nomine accepit* means that he received without any orders. 3rd. L. 59, *de adqu. rer. dom.*; L. 2, C. *de his qui a non dom.* But in these cases the terms of the order were, that the *procurator* should purchase in his own name, and thus even acquire the property which was afterwards to be transferred to the mandans. Many other attempts have been made to re-holds good only as respects the immediate operation of the delivery, so that a fraudulent agent immediately afterwards may acquire the possession for himself, in which case the rule as to loss of Possession through an agent comes into operation (§ 35).

Secondly, it is required that the possessor himself should have the intention of acquiring this possession, consequently the acquisition is wholly excluded, when the party, for whom the possession was intended to be acquired, knows nothing of it (*ignoranti possessio non adquiritur*). This proposition however, is easily misunderstood, because the expression used may bear a double meaning. For, first, *ignorantis* possessio may signify the possession of him who knows nothing of the whole transaction, and consequently who could not have intended to make the acquisition ; this is the case contemplated by the rule, such *ignorantis possessio* is impossible, but there are three exceptions to this impossibility, by which Possession generally and Usucaption are not prevented by such *ignorantia;* viz., the cases of *peculium,* of acquisition by guardians, and of corporations (*f*). Secondly however, he also may be called *ignorans,* who desires to acquire possession of a thing, and has given a party a commission to receive it for him, but who has not yet had notice of the performance of that commission, *i. e.* of the actual prehension ; the above rule does not refer to this sort of *ignorantia,* which enables Possession generally to arise, but not Usucaption. Who-

concile this contradiction, comp. Glossa in L. 37, § *de adqu. rer. dom.* Duarenus in L. 1, § 20, *de poss.;* Opp. p. m. 838—9; Beyma in Var. Dig. tit. p. 330; Valentia in Ill. Jur. Tract. L. 1, Tr. 2, C. 13, p. m. 66, et in Epistolar. Exerc. 9, *ib.* p. 159 ; Retes apud Meermann. T. 7, pp. 475—6, et p. 406.

(*f*) The rule is in Paulus, in

Rec. Sent. L. 5, tit. 2, § 1. "Possessionem adquirimus et animo, et corpore ; *animo utique nostro ; corpore vel nostro vel alieno.*" Comp. L. 3, § 12, *de poss.* The exceptions are mentioned later in this section, p. 229—235. Paulus himself shews very satisfactorily the connection between the rule and the exception as to *peculium,* L. 1, § 5, L. 3, § 12, *de poss.*

ever, therefore, gives such commission commences to possess directly the commission is performed, but Usucaption
only dates from the time of the possessor having notice of
the performance. It will be more convenient to bring forward the proofs of all these positions on discussing the third
point.

Thirdly, a juridical relation is required between the
possessor and his representative, to enable Possession to
arise in this manner. We may lay down that the rule
requires either an *order* or a *commission* to precede the
acquisition, according as the question arises upon a relation
of juridical authority (a father's over his children, or a
master's over his slaves), or upon a free relation.

I. Juridical authority of the possessor over the agent (*g*).
That the right of Possession should be acquired in this
case has nothing singular in it, as rights of all kinds are
capable of being acquired through slaves and through
children in their father's power. Possession may be
acquired through a slave by his owner, by the *bonæ fidei
possessor*, and by the *fructuarius*. The owner, to be
capable of such acquisition, must have the possession of his
slave at the time; if some one else, or no one at all,
possesses the slave, the owner, as such, cannot acquire
Possession through him, so that ocasionally no acquisition
of property, or even of Possession is made (*h*). It is a direct
consequence of this that the owner cannot acquire pos-

(*g*) Cuperus has discussed this
case thoroughly ; De Nat. Poss.
p. 52, pp. 100—106.

(*h*) L. 21, pr., L. 54, § 4, *de
adq. rer. dom.* L. 1, § 6, *de poss.*
With a runaway slave, the *possessio servi* and *adquisitio per
servum* continues so long as he
does not come into the possession
of another, or as he does not consider himself free. L. 1, § 14;
L. 50, § 1, *de poss.* (These two
excepted cases are referred to by

the words " quem non possidet,"
in L. 54, § 4, *de adqu. rer. dom.*,
and the *possessio* of L. 15, *de
public. in rem. act.* is evidently
natural detention). By the *libertatis possessio* the *servi possessio*
is necessarily excluded, but not
otherwise by the mere *liberale
judicium :* for in that case the
adquisitio per servum, like the
possessio servi, itself is in suspense. L. 3, § 10, *de poss.* L.
25, § *de. lib. caus.*

session through a slave whom he has given in pledge (*i*). The *bonæ fidei possessor*, as such, acquires possession like every thing else through the slave, only in so far as this acquisition is founded on the labour of the slave, or on the property of the possessor (*j*); *bonæ fidei possessor* denotes however him only, who believes himself to be owner, consequently a pledge holder acquires nothing through the pledged slave (*k*), although he possesses the slave, and possesses him legally, and thus in a certain sense *bona fides* cannot be denied him. The *fructuarius* acquires through the slave, under the same limitations as the *bonæ fidei possessor* (*l*). These cases, therefore, present another instance of the usual relation of property to every *jus in re;* for by that rule the owner acquires through his slave, because he has at the same time juridical possession of him, but in the above two excepted cases, it is not the owner, but the fructuary for whom the slave acquires possession like every thing else.

As a master acquires through his slave all rights generally, and consequently Possession also, so likewise does a father through his children. This acquisition however is founded upon the right of paternal authority only, not, as with slaves, upon the possession of the child itself, because the latter is not conceivable: therefore no *usus fructus* has place here, nor any analogous relation to *bonæ fidei possessio.* Whoever, therefore, in error believes that he has a son under his control cannot make any acquisition through him (*m*).

A special rule was introduced as to both these cases of juridical authority, when the acquisition of Possession was founded on a *peculium.* In such case Possession was acquired

(*i*) L. 1, § 15, *de poss.*

(*j*) Gaius, Lib. 2, § 94; L. 1, § 6, *de poss.* L. 21, pr. *de adqu. rer. dom.*

(*k*) L. 1, § 15, *de poss.*

(*l*) L. 1, § 8, L. 49, pr. *de poss.* [Add. to 4th ed.] This acquisition however was contested, be-

cause the slave himself was not possessed by the fructuary, Gaius, Lib. 2, § 94; who however does not clear up the question. The passages cited from the Digest evidently refer to this controversy.

(*m*) L. 50, *pr. de poss.*

although the master or father knew nothing of the acquisition (*n*), and even Usucaption might commence together with the Possession (*o*). As therefore in the case of a *peculium,* no question arises as to the will of the possessor himself, those persons also are capable of acquiring Possession in this manner, who have no will at all (*p*). Indeed this Possession is possible even in the name of a prisoner (*q*), although in such case not only the *animus possidendi,* but also the personalty of the possessor is wanting.

In the earlier law there were two other kinds of authority besides the master's and father's, called *manus* and *mancipium.* But whether Possession might be acquired through these latter also was much contested, because these kinds of authority were not accompanied by any *possessio* of the dependent person (*r*). It is remarkable that this doubt should only have been started as to these conditions, and as to slaves, in respect to *ususfructus,* although there was just as much ground for it as to sons under paternal authority.

II. The relation between the possessor and the agent may be a free relation. For it is a rule, that except in the two relations of juridical authority mentioned above, no right can be acquired through foreign agency, but this rule only applied (at least in the time of the classical jurists) to *civil* not to natural acquisitions, and Possession belongs to

---

(*n*) L. 1, § 5, *de poss.* L. 4, *de poss.* L. 44, § 1; L. 24, L. 3, § 12, *de poss.*

(*o*) L. 1, § 5, *de poss.* L. 31, § 3, § 47, *de usurp.*

(*p*) For instance, children, lunatics, inheritances. L. 1, § 5, *de poss.;* L. 29, *de captivis;* L. 16, *de obl. et act.*

(*q*) The point was disputed among the earlier Roman jurists. The above is laid down as the decided rule in the Digest, without distinction whether the possession commenced previous

to, or during, the imprisonment; consequently, this rule applies equally to acquisition and loss. Now the prisoner, when he dies, is either a prisoner or a free man: in the first case the lex Cornelia applied, in the second the *postliminium.* L. 29, L. 22, § 3, *de captivis;* L. 23, § 3, *ex quib. caus. maj.;* L. 44, § 7, *de usurp.;* L. 12, § 2, *de capt.;* L. 15, pr. *de usurp.*

(*r*) Gaius, Lib. 2, § 90. (Mention was first made of these relations in the 4th ed.)

the latter class. Possession therefore may be acquired without any juridical authority over the agent, and property in like manner, if it were acquired by means of the Possession, *i. e.*, by delivery or occupancy (*s*).

What then is the foundation of this relation ? a *commission* to acquire the Possession; for the rule cannot be laid down more definitely. For this commission did not require any of the conditions which in other cases were necessary to constitute a juridical transaction, and to make it valid in the civil law; thus for instance even a slave might undertake it, supposing, that he were not *possessed* by any one as a slave (*t*), for then he would not be master of any of his actions, and therefore could not by the acts in question transfer to another the dominion over any subject: in the same manner a pupil may be an agent (*u*), although except in this instance he cannot enter into any juridical transaction. But all those grounds which render juridical transactions invalid, because the *will* of the agent himself has not been exercised, as for instance, mistake on an essential point, make also this acquisition of Possession invalid (*v*). But so, conversely, a juridical transaction is not alone sufficient for this mode of acquisition, if the commission mentioned above is not expressly contained in it; thus for instance, the landlord

(*s*) L. 1, C. *per quas pers.* § 5, I. eod. Paulus, V. 2, § 2. L. 53, *de adqu. rer. dom.* L. 20, § 2, *eod.* L. 8, C. *de poss.*

(*t*) L. 31, § 2, *de usurp.* L. 34, § 2, *de poss.* In this way even the owner himself, whose slave is in the possession of freedom, may without all doubt acquire Possession through such slave, (p. 228); it follows also, that the *bonæ fidei possessor* may acquire through the slave, if the matter did not arise *ex operis servi*, or *e re possessoria* (p. 229), because the validity of this ac-

quisition is undoubted where the slave had no possessor at all; finally, the cases of the *malæ fidei possessor*, and the pledge-holder who could not acquire through the slaves in their possession, appear to be quite special exceptions, L. 1, § 6, 15, *de poss.*

(*u*) L. 32, *pr. de poss.* What is said here as to the continuance of possession, in opposition to an *obligatio*, necessarily holds good from the commencement also.

(*v*) Thus, for instance, where the tenant or pledge-holder is also owner of the subject (p. 207—220).

has juridical Possession of the subject of demise (p. 206), but if he die, although the *jus obligationis* passes to his heir by mere entry upon the inheritance, the Possession does not: in order to acquire this, something else must be done by which the tenant becomes the representative of this Possession for his new landlord (*w*).

The above rule that Possession may be acquired for us even by free persons was probably introduced pretty early by judicial decision.

1. L. 51, *de poss.*

" .... ait Labeo .... si acervum lignorum emero, et eum venditor me tollere jusserit; *simul atque custodiam posuissem traditus mihi videtur*" (*x*).

2. L. 41, *de usurp.* (Neratius L. 7, membr.).

" .... quamvis per procuratorem possessionem apisci nos, jam fere conveniat."

3. L. 13, *pr. de adqu. rer. dom.* (Neratius Lib. 6, reg.)

" Si procurator rem mihi emerit ex mandato meo, eique sit tradita meo nomine: dominium mihi, id est proprietas adquiretur, etiam ignoranti."

4. L. 1, C. *de poss.* (Impp. Sev. et Antonin.)

"Per liberam personam ignoranti quoque acquiri Possessionem, et postquam scientia intervenerit, usucapionis conditionem inchoari posse, *tam ratione utilitatis quam juris pridem* (*y*) *receptum est.*"

(*w*) L. 30, § 5, *de poss.* "Quod per colonum possideo, heres meus, *nisi ipse nactus possessionem,* non poterit possidere." Merenda in Jur. Cont. L. 2, c. 32. Cicero indeed appears to assert the contrary: Pro Cæcinâ, C. 32; but how little he himself rests on the correctness of this statement appears from the next sentence, where he finds the following words necessary, " Deinde ipsa Cæcina," etc.

(*x*) The passage itself has been explained above (§ 17); here it is cited merely for the result of Labeo's opinion. By itself, a slave might also be comprised under the word *custodia;* but Javolenus, who in the succeeding portion of the passage evidently has the same case before his eyes, expressly uses the word *mandato.*

(*y*) Glossa in h. L. " alias *pridem,* et alias *prudentiâ.*" The first reading is much more probable, for *ratione juris* is more dis-

It is clear from these passages that at the time of the last quoted Rescript the rule had been long recognized (*pridem*), that it prevailed also in the time of Neratius, and even of Labeo: many authors, however, contend that it was introduced by this passage of the Code, induced thereto by Ulpian and the Institutes (*z*); but it is very natural that Ulpian should quote a rescript of the reigning emperor, although the contents of it had been long before recognized without any express law, and the Institutes which possibly follow Ulpian, do not at all lay down that Severus had newly introduced this rule, but merely that he had referred to it in his constitution (*a*).

I am now enabled to explain some limitations of the rule which I could only hint at above. When this relation of agency is well established, Possession is acquired immediately upon the prehension of the agent, even when the possessor has no notice of the performance of the commission, and in this case it may be said "*ignoranti adquiritur possessio.*"

tinctly opposed to *ratione utilitatis* than *jurisprudentia* would be ; for *ratio juris* consists in L. 53, *de adqu. rer. dom.* (quod *naturaliter* adquiritur sicuti est possessio rel.) Besides, it is easier to conceive how the word *jurisprudentia* arose out of an abbreviation which must have been used so frequently by every civil law transcriber, easier than to suppose the word *pridem*, as a false reading had crept into the text. *Pridem* moreover is the reading of the Gottingen MS., in which indeed a correction appears to have been made, but without leaving any trace of the previous reading. Lastly, *pridem* is the reading of seven Paris MSS., of one in my own possession, of a very old one at Fulda, one at Munich, (No. 22), one at Vienna, (No. 16), and of an old copy in the Bamberg library (D. I. a.)

(*z*) L. 11, § 6, *de pign. act.* ".... Constitutum est ab *Imperatore nostro*, posse per liberam personam possessionem adquiri." § 5, I. per quas pers. ".... Per liberam personam veluti per procuratorem placet non solum scientibus, sed et ignorantibus nobis adquiri possessionem, *secundum Divi Severi constitutionem.*"

(*a*) (Add. to 4th ed.) If the whole of § 95, in the second book of Gaius, had been preserved, all doubt hereupon would possibly have disappeared ; in its present state the passage affords us no assistance.

But Usucaption only commences when the possessor learns
that the Possession has been acquired (*b*). It has been
affirmed by some that at all events this last position contains
something new which Severus must have added to the old
rule, but this opinion is almost more untenable than that
which ascribes the whole rule to that emperor. But the
above given sense of an *ignorantis possessio* can only be
admitted when it is possible for it to exist; accordingly the
possessor must always know and intend that the Possession
should be acquired for him, in most cases, indeed a case of
agency cannot otherwise be well conceived. For this reason
a *negotiorum gestor* may also obtain Possession, but not before
ratihabitio (*c*): and the same may be affirmed of a *procurator universorum bonorum,* because this special acquisition
was not expressly within the scope of his authority:

    1. Paulus in rec. sent. L. 5, T. 2, § 2.

"Per liberas personas quæ in potestate nostra non sunt,
adquiri nobis nihil potest. Sed per procuratorem adquiri
nobis *possessionem* posse, utilitatis causâ receptum est (*d*).
Absente autem domino comparata non aliter ei, quam si
rata sit, quæritur" (*e*).

    2. L. 42, § 1, *de poss.*

"Procurator, si quidem *mandante domino rem emerit* (*f*),

(*b*) L. 1, C. *de poss.* § 5, I.
per quas pers. L. 49, § 2, *de
poss.*; L. 47, *de usurp.* The
exception in L. 41, *de usurp.*
does not so much refer to this
rule as to the Lex Atinia. (L. 4,
§ 6, *de usurp.*)

(*c*) L. 24, *de neg. gestis.*
The recognition which is necessary in strict juridical transactions of course does not apply to
Possession.

(*d*) That is, "but an exception
has been made to that rule in
behalf of possession."

(*e*) The term *procurator* being

ambiguous, Paulus expressly calls
to mind that only an express
agent for this Possession is spoken
of, not a *procurator bonorum,* who
has been appointed during the
absence of his master, and who,
during such absence, may have
acquired some Possession or other.

(*f*) That is, "when he had a
commission to make this purchase," (for usually such commission extends alike to the contract and to the acquisition of
possession and property). The
antithesis, therefore, is the same
as in the previous passage.

protinus illi adquirit possessionem; quod si *suâ sponte emerit,* non: nisi ratam habuerit emptionem."

In the teeth of these very express passages many Jurists have considered an *ignorantis possessio* through this kind of *procurator* possible: and because Severus must have intended to lay down something new, the above must be looked upon as the effect of his constitution, and as a rider to the older law, although in fact the position cannot be laid down either as to the old or as to the modern law.

In this acquisition through free persons there are however two exceptions to that rule which require the will of the possessor to intervene at the commencement of Possession (comp. p. 177).

1. Juridical persons, although incapable of immediate consciousness, may nevertheless acquire Possession through the agency of free persons.

This is undoubtedly so as to *municipia (g)*; and as in another passage the acquisition of Possession by other corporations is assimilated to that of cities *(h),* we may affirm the same of these other corporations.

2. Persons under guardianship, who also, juridically, have no will, may nevertheless acquire Possession through the acts of their tutors and curators (and thus by the agency of free persons) *(i).*

This acquisition of a guardian in the name of his ward has been previously made use of above to explain two passages, in which the simple *auctoritas tutoris* was made the foundation of the acquisition of Possession (p. 182—186). Many civilians have misunderstood those passages to mean that the *adquisitio per tutorem* was there altogether denied *(j).*

(g) L. 1, § 22, L. 2, *de poss.*
(h) L. § 3, *ad exhibendum.*
(i) L. 13, § 1, *de adqu. rer. dom.;* L. 1, § 20, *de poss.;* L. 11, § 6, *de pign. act.* The L. 26, C. *de don.* is evidently merely a supplement to this rule; for in the case stated in this passage, where

the guardian of a ward has an obstacle in his way, the slave occasionally is permitted to complete the acquisition, L. 2, C. Th. de don.
(j) Especially the concluding words of L. 3, C. *de poss.* (p. 186).

although both those passages, and others also (*k*), show that such denial cannot be made with any probability.

Lastly, it is self-evident, that the relation of agency by which possession is to be acquired may extend itself through several parties. Thus if A. commission B. to acquire Possession for him, it is the same thing whether B. executes the commission in person or through C.; in both cases A. becomes the possessor (add. to 6th ed.).

———◆———

SECTION XXIX.

CONSTITUTUM POSSESSORIUM.

The rule that a simple commission without juridical authority is sufficient to establish the acquisition of Possession through the acts of another,—is to be traced in still another application of it which needs explanation, and as to which our Jurists have been wider to seek than as to the rule itself. Whoever is in a condition, generally, to acquire Possession for another by his own acts, is not the less competent to do so, because up to that moment, he, the agent, may have had juridical Possession of the subject. At the same time, it is clear that in such case, although the rule need not be differently expressed than in the other instances, the application of it must be so to a certain extent. For as the act of prehension has then already taken place, it need not be repeated, and the whole transaction may therefore be looked upon as the converse of a *brevi manu traditio;* for as in that mode of delivery, he who previously had detention without the Possession, by mere *animus possidendi* acquires the Possession without any new act (p. 174); so, in like manner, in the present case, by a

(*k*) See the last note but one.

mere act of the will, Possession is converted into detention, and the right of Possession itself, (which alone is in question here), is immediately transferred to another person. Modern Jurists designate this mode of transferring Possession *constitutum posessorium*. The term was not known to the Romans, but the transaction was very familiar to them, and even if it were not specially mentioned in the Roman law, it would not be less clear.

The position itself, which I have here laid down, is expressed in terms equally general, and, as the mere logical application of well-known principles, in the following passage:

L. 18, *pr. de poss.*

" Quod meo nomine possideo, possum alieno nomine possidere; nec enim muto mihi causam Possessionis, sed desino possidere, et alium possessorem ministerio meo facio: nec idem est, possidere, et alieno nomine possidere. Nam possidet, cujus nomine possidetur. Procurator alienæ possessioni præstat ministerium."

Thus, this acquisition of Possession is permitted by means of a mere agreement, without any corporeal act as to the subject itself: nevertheless, a very celebrated passage expressly opposes simple agreement to delivery; by the latter, property is capable of being transferred, not by the former (*a*). This circumstance leads us to a closer examination of the so called *constitutum* itself. For the contract which states the transfer of the property, a purchase, for instance, is very different from a *constitutum :* the latter contains a declaration that the previous possessor intends to be the agent for the Possession of another, which declaration is neither contained in a mere contract of purchase, nor is generally to be implied, it must therefore be expressly declared, or necessarily follow from the other circumstances of the case. If there is any express decla-

---

(*a*) L. 20, C. de pactis :   dominia rerum, *non nudis pactis*
Traditionibus et usucapionibus   transferuntur."

ration in the case, that the previous possessor is only for the future to manage the Possession of another, all doubt disappears, but this state of facts is very rare.   Except in that case a *constitutum* is not to be presumed, except in so far as it must be presumed to result from other parts of the *res gesta* (*b*).

Firstly, *constitutum* by the rule is not to be presumed. An instance of this position has been already given; if A. B. buys wine in cask, and seals the casks, he does not thereby become possessor and proprietor of the wine (*c*).   Now it is clear that he does not even have the natural detention of this property, so long as it lies in the vendor's cellar; but it is just as clear that the vendor, by a mere *constitutum*, may transfer the Possession to him, and it is only because a *constitutum* is not to be presumed, that in that case the transfer of Possession is denied without further separation. —The following passage contains a second example of the position.

L. 48, *de poss.*

" Prædia cum servis donavit, eorumque se tradidisse possessionem, litteris declaravit : si vel unus ex servis, qui simul cum prædiis donatus est, ad eum, qui donum accepit, pervenit, mox in prædia remissus est : per servum prædiorum possessionem quæsitam ceterorumque servorum constabit."—The *donor* must have said in a letter, " That he thereby made a gift of the estate and the slaves." What is the effect of this piece of evidence?   That he, the *donor*, is from thenceforward to be considered *procurator alienæ possessionis ?*   No, for a *constitutum* is not to be presumed; therefore it is only a permission to the donee to take

(*b*) But when the conditions of a *constitutum* are present, it is immaterial whether the previous possessor has the detention himself, or whether a third person is managing it for him.   Thus, if the possessor of a house has let it, still he can deliver the posses-

sion to me by a *constitutum*, just as well as if he lived in the house himself, since by § 28, the agency may be carried on through different hands, Compare § 35, *post.* (Add. to 6th ed.)

(*c*) L. 1, § 2, *de peric. et comm. rei vind.* (§ 17).

Possession at any time (*missio in possessionem*), this act, by the consent of the donor, is made equivalent to a delivery, but the new Possession only takes its commencement from *such act.*

Secondly; a *constitutum* is nevertheless presumed, when its existence necessarily follows from the other circumstances in the case. This position will appear clear and certain from the following instances:

1st. Whoever gives a thing as a gift, and at the same time hires it, may not say any thing in terms as to the Possession; but his intention is, that a contract of hiring should immediately ensue between himself and the donee, it is, therefore, a necessary consequence that the donee should be possessor, and he himself the occupant of another's possession, conse-- quently, the Possession passes here by a *constitutum* (*d*).

2nd. The same thing happens with *ususfructus*; whoever, therefore, gives away or sells an article, and retains the *ususfructus* for himself, does, by a *constitutum*, in fact transfer the possession and the property, and only proceeds to enjoy, like any other fructuary, the Possession of another (*e*).

3rd. If a thing is pledged, but at the same time the use of it is permitted to the pledger *precario*, the possession of the thing is thereupon acquired by the creditor through a mere

(*d*) L. 77, *de rei vind.*

(*e*) L. 28, L. 35, § 5, C. *de donat.* (To this rule, which as a general principle, no Roman jurist ever threw a doubt upon, Theodosius 2nd introduced an exception with respect to donations, as to which generally many special limitations occur ; two years later however he repealed his provision ; L. 8, 9, C. Th. de donat.) A point of this kind occurred in a part of the Hanau Succession case. Cramer, Opusc.

T. 1, p. 641, demonstrated the most usual errors of practitioners in mathematical forms, but the answer which followed, on the side of Darmstadt, is one of the best essays which has ever appeared on Possession ; Kortholt de possessione ea lege, ne contra trad. dum vivit exerc., tradita. Giessæ, 1738. As to the application of this rule in the middle ages, see Savigny Gesch. des Roemische Rechts, B. 2, p. 153.

constitutum (*f*). This transaction has much resemblance to a simple *pactum hypothecæ;* whether the one or the other be intended, can only be expressly decided in each particular case, but when it is made out that it is not a *pactum* joined to a *precario,* but a *contractus pignoris,* the transfer thereupon of Possession by *constitutum* is an immediate consequence (p. 224), and does not require any express evidence of it.

4th. In a *societas universorum bonorum* delivery of all the individual goods is looked upon as made, directly that the contract is completed (*g*) ; and this can only be conceived by means of a *constitutum.* The reason is probably this; on account of the complexity of the circumstances an actual delivery would be very difficult, and was therefore unusual, consequently that sort of transaction on the other hand was usual, and to be presumed, by which alone actual delivery could be supplied, but such transaction was nothing else but *constitutum.*

Modern jurists, from the earliest times, have been very far from adopting this simple view of the Roman law, according to which a particular name for this operation was never once found necessary. The *constitutum* has always appeared to them a strange phenomenon, as one of the most remarkable fictions in the acquisition of Possession, and therefore many have gone so far as to attribute the application of *constitutum* to an invention of practitioners, and therefore look upon it only as an exception in the theory, and allow of it merely in those cases where the Roman law has casually mentioned it to explain how its rule applied (*h*).

(*f*) L. 15, § 2, *qui satisdare cog.* " Creditor, qui pignus accepit, possessor non est, tametsi possessionem habeat, aut sibi traditam, aut *precario debitori concessam.*"

(*g*) L. 1, § 1, L. 2, *pro sorio.*

(*h*) Azo even (Summa in cod. tit. de poss. n. 7, 8) says of *Constitutum* through *ususfructus,* " et est hoc unum mirabile mundi." The best essay on the subject is by G. Mascovo De Const. Poss. Harderov. 1733, and in Opusc. ed. Puettman, p. 101 ; but he also adopts the common view as his

SECTION XXX.

RESULTS OF THIS BOOK.

The acquisition of Possession has been now completely described, and it is clear, from this description, that in such acquisition, there occur conditions which distinguish it from the acquisition of every other right. For all mere juridical grounds, which in other cases give rise to, or prevent, the acquisition of a right, have no such operation with respect to Possession.

First, then; mere juridical events, which do not comprise an act of prehension, give no Possession. For instance, the acquisition of an inheritance : all rights generally, in so far as they belong to the property, and are not merely personal, pass thereby immediately to the heir, but not Possession, because the entry upon the inheritance does not contain any act of prehension of the individual subjects of the inheritance (a). Even with the *suus heres* there is no

ground-work, and is led away by the peculiarity attending a donation into a complete confusion as to the relation between rule and exception. Some writers have denied a *constitutum* altogether, the fact nevertheless they admit in certain particular cases, but explain it somewhat differently; Giphanius De Donat. L. 10, *de donat.*; Lect. Altorph. p. 120, 121; Schuch De Const. Poss. in L. L. Rom. non fundato, Erf. 1732 :— Tiraquellus is wholly useless; De

Jure Const. poss. Opp. T. 4, p. 135, ed. 1574.

(a) L. 23, *pr. de poss.* "Cum heredes instituti sumus, adita hereditate, omnia quidem jura ad nos transeunt; possessio tamen nisi naturaliter comprehensa ad nos non pertinet." L. 1, § 15, *si is qui test. lib.* " . . . . Nec heredis est possessio, antequam possideat: quia hereditas in eum id tantum transfundit, quod est hereditatis ; non autem fuit possessio hereditatis.

R

exception to this rule (*b*). Many modern codes have laid down the contrary as to heirs very inconsistently (*c*), which may possibly have arisen from a misunderstood passage of the Roman law itself (*d*). The same thing occurs with mancipation, as with the acquisition of inheritance; the mancipation without doubt might be so framed as to make the acquisition of Possession follow immediately; indeed, this would necessarily be so with moveables; but not with land (*e*); consequently as to the latter the property passed without Possession, for prehension did not occur, and a *constitutum* by which it might be supplied is not to be presumed.

Secondly : if the conditions of acquisition occur, the Possession is not excluded on juridical grounds of invalidity. Taken generally, this position has always been admitted, but it has been limited by the exceptions which are made in all cases of fictitious prehension (§ 15); but these exceptions are groundless, because there is no such thing as fictitious prehension.

According to this rule, Possession may be even acquired through a criminal act, namely, by personal violence, and this position enters into so many well known cases, that it is not at all shaken by the following passage (*f*).

(*b*) Giphanius, Lect. Altorph. p. 480. The position however has been much contested.

(*c*) This is the meaning of the rule: "Le mort saisit le vif." Tiraquellus in tract. *le mort*, &c. Opp. T. 4. The same thing occurs in the Spanish majorats. Leges Tauri, No. 45; Gomez in Ll. Tauri, p. 232, ed. Lugd. 1744—6. Comp. c. a. Braun, De Poss. ipso jure in heredem transeunte, Erlang. 1744.

(*d*) L, 30, *pr. ex quib. caus. maj.* "....Possessio defuncti quasi juncta, descendit ad heredem." Cujacius in L. 23, *pr. de poss.* Opp. T. 8, p. 287. This passage relates merely to the fiction in Usucaption.

(*e*) Ulpianus in fragm. tit. 19, § 6. "Res mobiles *non nisi præsentes* mancipæri possunt...... immobiles autem etiam plures simul, et quæ *diversis locis sunt,* mancipari possunt."

(*f*) L. 22, *de poss.* (Javolenus, lib. 13, *ex Cassio*). Cuperus, P. 2, C. 23, refers the passage, by a most strained construction,

" Non *videtur possessionem adeptus* is, qui ita nactus est,
ut eam retinere non possit."

The *non videtur* can only be true, even according to the
words, in a particular sense, for that, which we cannot
retain, we must at the moment actually *have*. What is
referred to is not very difficult to discover (*g*) ; a *res furtiva* or
vi possessa is not capable of Usucaption, and this incapacity
only ceases when the owner recovers possession of it. But
this latter Possession must be so constituted as to be *capable*
of continuing, *i. e.*, it must not be open to attack on the
ground of its origin (*h*). But if a *fundus vi possessus* is
again recovered by the owner by force, or if the owner
gets back the *res furtiva* into his possession by a valid
precarium (*i*), the incapacity for Usucaption is not removed,
because the possession of the owner in both cases may be
attacked by Interdicts.

What is true of forcible acquisition applies *a fortiori* to
those transactions which are legal in form, but only invalid
on juridical grounds. Thus in donations between man and
wife no right is transferred; but Possession passes (§ 7).
So also upon a delivery made by a lunatic, or a ward, no
property can be acquired, although the Possession may
be (*j*). On these juridical grounds *succession* is always to be

to the *interdictum quod legatorum*,
because Javolenus speaks twice,
in the same book, of Interdicts;
L. 5, *de tab. exhib.*; L. 198, *de
Reg. Jur.*; but *furtum* is also
twice spoken of in two not very
distant passages, lib. 15, ex Cassio; L. 71, 73, *de furtis.*

(*g*) The Gloss on this passage
in fact discovered it.

(*h*) L. 4, § 12, 26, *de usurp.*;
L. 13, § 2, *de V. S.*

(*i*) See above, p. 222, Cujacius,
Obs. XXIV. 12, seems much put
to it for a good instance as to

moveables; in the case which he
cites there is no *res furtiva* at all.
According to all principle, the
case belongs to this head also,
where the owner shall have succeeded in obtaining by force a
chattel that had been stolen from
him, because it might be again
recovered from him by the *Int.
utrubi*. (Add. to 6th ed.)

(*j*) The grounds which might
raise a doubt as to this position
belong to the following book, for
they relate to the question, whether a lunatic or ward would lose

R 2

looked upon as invalid; but succession has no reference at all to the existence of possession (§ 5), and consequently the latter is not excluded, because the former cannot take place.

possession in such case? That the other party *acquires* it, according to the assumption above, no one will deny.

BOOK III.

LOSS OF POSSESSION.

———◆———

SECTION XXXI.

IN the second Book the commencement of Possession has been discussed; in this, we have to treat of its termination. The termination of Possession is evidently the same question as the continuance of it, because a possession can only continue up to the time of its being lost. If modern Jurists had availed themselves of this simple observation, which had been already made in very early days (a), we should have been spared, not only a whole chapter in their theories, but also several contradictions, in which occasionally we have the direct contrary laid down as to the *loss* of Possession, to what had been affirmed as to its *continuance*.

We have now to seek for the rule which regulates the continuance, and, at the same time, the loss of Possession. We shall endeavour, first, to deduce this rule from the notion of Possession; this notion has already obtained from our inquiry into the acquisition of Possession, a precisely

(a) Azo in Summa Cod. *tit. de poss.* "Cum enim intitulatur de amittenda possessione, ergo de retinenda, vel quousque retineatur : tamdiu enim retinetur, quamdiu non amittitur." Glossa in rubric. Dig. *tit. de poss.*, not., " quod hic dicit *amittenda* sed Cod. eod. dicit *retinenda*, quod in idem recidit, quia contrariorum eadem est disciplina." On this occasion the Commentators subsequent to Accursius, Alciat himself not excluded, usually enter into a learned discussion, whether the rule "contrariorum eadem est disciplina" is universally true; for instance, in canon law, or feudal law, &c.

defined and real character, and even its relation to the continuance of Possession has been already cursorily pointed out (*ante*, p. 172-3).

For, as Possession has been seen to consist in physical power, associated with consciousness, it follows that in every case of acquisition two things are necessary, a corporeal relation, and *animus*. The same must also concur for continuance; and this, therefore, must depend upon the same association as the acquisition of Possession; should such association cease, *i. e.*, should either the corporeal act alone, or the *animus* alone, or both together terminate, the continuance of Possession also ceases. For all the distinction which can be discovered between the conditions of acquisition and continuance, refers only to their extent, not to their essence, *i. e.*, a point is always discoverable at which all distinction wholly disappears. This point, for instance, in the corporeal relation, occurs where there is an utter impossibility of dealing with the subject; it occurs with respect to *animus*, where there is an express determination not to be possessor; for it is clear that in both these cases, Possession could be no more initiated than continued, and therefore the conditions of acquisition and continuance fully coincide in this case.

What is here stated may be expressed in the following propositions—·

1. To enable the Possession to continue, there must be a corporeal relation and *animus*.

2. If either one or the other, or both together, cease, the Possession is lost.

3. This rule stands in immediate logical connection with the rule which defines the acquisition of Possession.

We will now search for historical proofs of this rule, and possibly we shall see in them that the point of view from which it has been hitherto contemplated, will afford us good service.

247

SECTION XXXII.

LOSS OF POSSESSION. — *Continued.*

The rule which has been laid down in the foregoing
Section, is so expressly recognized both in several applications of it (*a*), as well as in certain exceptions to it, that a
complete historical proof of it might be deduced from these
only. But besides these examples the rule itself occurs in
a passage which has not generally been brought to bear on
the subject.

L. 44, § 2, *de poss.*

" .... ejus quidem, quod corpore nostro teneremus (*b*),
possessionem amitti *vel* animo, *vel* etiam corpore."

But even here this circumstance is only casually alluded to;
on the other hand there is a passage to be found in which, with
express reference to this case, a general rule is put forward,
and this rule appears to be entirely opposed to the one above
laid down, as it declares that neither a corporeal act alone,
nor *animus* alone, is sufficient to work the loss of Possession.

L. 153, de R. I. (*c*).

" Fere, quibuscumque modis obligamur, hisdem (iisdem)
in contrarium actis liberamur; cum quibus modis adquirimus,
hisdem in contrarium actis amittimus. *Ut igitur* (*d*) *nulla
possessio adquiri nisi animo et corpore potest, ita nulla amittitur, nisi in qua utrumque in contrarium actum* " (*e*).

(*a*) I will merely notice the
most express ; L. 3, § 13, L. 29,
de poss. (Loss by mere *factum*).
L. 3, § 6, L. 17, § 1, *de poss.*
(Loss by mere *animus*).

(*b*) This case states the rule,
and at the same time the modifications of the opposite case are
here laid down.

(*c*) I mention this as the only

passage, because L. 8, *de poss.* is
evidently merely a portion of the
same ; the very unimportant va-
riances shall be mentioned presently.

(*d*) L. 8, *de poss.*, which only
begins here, says " quemadmodum," instead of " *ut igitur*."

(*e*) L. 8, *de poss.* " *actum est.*"

We cannot suppose that there was any difference here amongst the ancient Jurists, partly from the nature of the case, and partly also because the passage is from Paulus, whose writings contain the most decided examples of the true rule (*f*).

By far the greater number of interpreters endeavour to get over this difficulty by referring the whole passage to a special excepted case, namely, land still continues to be possessed, although another usurp the occupation, so long as the previous possessor has no notice of it. They therefore make this distinction; either the Possession is lost *solo animo*, and then the loss presents no difficulty, and consequently the rule of Paulus is untrue; or it is lost *solo corpore*, and then the rule is correct, but only with respect to land (*g*). But the Jurist so evidently intends to lay down a general rule, that this exposition cannot be defended on any of the hypothetical cases which have been brought in aid of it (*h*).

The whole difficulty evidently lies in the word '*utrumque*;' that *both together* (*corpus* and *animus*) must cease in order to work the loss of Possession, is what seems to contra-

(*f*) L. 3, § 6, 13, *de poss.*

(*g*) Bulgari et Placentini ad titt. ff. de R. T. Comm. Colon. 1587–8, p. 113. Azo in Summa Cod. *tit. de poss.* num. 15; Glossa in L. 3, § 6, et in L. 8, *de poss.* Odopedus in L. 3, *cit.* fol. 56; Cujacius in notis ad § 5, *de interdictis*, et in paratit. in Cod. *tit. de poss.*; (also Opp. T. 4, p. 625; T. 5, p. 710; T. 8, pp. 258, 269, 877; T. 9, p. 1015). Giphanius in Lect. Altorph. pp. 420, 421, 422; Merenda in Contr. L. 12, C. 24; Cuperus, De Poss. p. 2, c. 36. We must not be led astray by Cuperus and others beginning by objections to this exposition, for it always comes to the same thing

at the end, with merely some difference of expression. Romuleus, p. 18, who himself subscribed to this opinion, mentions a remarkable emendation of certain jurists not named by him; these read, in L. 8, *de poss.*, "*non quemadmodum*," for "*quemadmodum*."

(*h*) Cujacius lays much stress on the word "*fere*," ("c'est à dire, le plus souvent, ou presque le plus souvent.") Opp. T. 4, p. 625, which however is not used in reference to Possession, and if it were, would not make any great difference. Giphanius and Cuperus rely chiefly on the blending of the title.

dict the other examples. First then let us establish the meaning of *uterque* (*i*).

Uterque is used generally to denote the common relationship of a predicate to several subjects (or conversely). Of this there may be three cases:

1st. An express assertion of a conjunctive relation, so that in any given case the one subject cannot exist without the other. This is the usual meaning of *uterque*.

2nd. An express assertion of a disjunctive relation, so that in any given case the one subject cannot be joined with the other, and thus the predicate may apply to the one only, or to the other only, but never to both together. This is the usual meaning of *alteruter*.

3rd. An indefinite assertion, so that the common relation only is denoted, leaving it altogether undecided whether such relation is conjunctive or disjunctive, whether it be that this is not known, or merely not noticed and expressed. Both *uterque* and *alteruter* are used in this sense, so that occasionally the two expressions are synonymous, and indeed in certain cases the false notion is sometimes induced, as if *uterque* were used to denote the disjunctive relation as opposed to the conjunctive, and *alteruter* to denote the conjunctive as opposed to the disjunctive.

(*i*) I know of only one exposition which strikes out a somewhat similar path, by altering the text and reading *utrumcumque*, Friessen de genuina poss. indole, Jenæ, 1725, § 14 : but even this emendation is much less forcible than the ordinary exposition. The happiest emendation would be " utcunque," and then the meaning would be " possession is not lost, unless in *some way or other* there is something done *in contrarium*," namely, *in contrarium* to those conditions of acquisition which had been just mentioned. This would remove all difficulty (§ 31). This emendation is also to be found in Suse, Gurlitt, Animadv. ad auct. Vet. Spec. 3, p. 18, ed. 1806. It has been objected, on the other hand, that *actum est*, without any express subject could not be employed in this manner ; but Paulus himself so uses it in L. 5, *de her. vel act. vend.* At the same time it must be confessed that every emendation has this special ground against it, that the passage occurs with one uniform reading in all the MSS. on two several occasions in the Digest.

Uterque is thus used synonymously (in the above sense) to *alteruter*, in the following amongst other passages (*j*):

Varro De Re Rustica, I. 2, § 14.

" Quocirca principes, qui *utrique* rei præponunter, vocabulis quoque sunt diversi, quod unus vocatur vilicus, alter magister pecoris."

Cicero de officiis III. 15.

" *Uterque,* si ad eloquendum venerit, non plus quam semel eloquetur."

Paulus in L. 10, § 13, *de gradibus.*

"Frater quoque per *utrumque* parentem accipitur, id est, *aut* per matrem tantum, *aut* per patrem, *aut per utrumque.*" The first *utrumque* is here indefinite, the second definite as expressing a conjunctive relation.

Celsus in L. 16, *de leg.* 2.

" Si Titio aut Sejo, utri heres vellet, legatum relictum est; heres alteri dando, ab utroque liberatur; si neutri *dat, uterque* perinde petere potest atque si ipsi soli legatum foret, nam ut stipulando duo rei constitui possunt (*k*), ita et testamenti potest id fieri."

Justinian in L. 8, § 5, C. *de bon. quæ liberis.* (*l*).

(*j*) This meaning of *uterque* occurs even in the Gloss in L. 8, § 5, C. *de bon. quæ lib.*; again, in the appendix to Brisson, p. 1372, ed. Heinec. but one passage which is cited there, L. 2, *pr. de eo quod certo loco* proves nothing, and the L. 16, *de leg.* 2, wholly fails. Azones Brocardica, Basil. 1567, 8vo. p. 199. " *Utrumque* id est *alterum.* C. de bon. quæ lib. C. ult. § ipse; ff. de contr. emt. l. sed Celsus, § si fundum, ff. de pact. l. rescriptum, § si pactum, ff. de pignor. l. si grege, § 2." Azones Glossa, in L. 8, § 5, Cod. de Con. quæ lib.; (MS Paris, No. 4519, and also in the Fulda MS. of the Code); on the word *utraque* "disjunctive id est ex hac vel ex illa, non conjunctim; sic ff. de pactis rescriptum, § si pacto ff. de lib. et posth. Si ita, et ita ponitur unicuique disjunctive S. comm. divid. penult. Az."

(*k*) From this comparison to the usual case of co-defendants, it is quite clear that the actual demand of the one shuts out the right of the other, and that it is quite immaterial which of the two sues, consequently, that the two cannot bring their action jointly.

(*l*) The sense is so clear in this passage, that Haloander has inserted *alterutrâ* in the text; but this does not prove that he had found this reading in any manuscript, the Gloss endeavours

"Ipsum autem filium ...... alere patri necesse est ...... et ab ipsis liberis parentes, si inopia ex *utraque* parte vertitur." *Unusquisque* is used in the same sense in a constitution of Alexander Severus, L. 3, C. *de comm. div.*

"......... cum autem regionibus dividi commode aliquis ager inter socios non potest, vel ex pluribus singuli: æstimatione justa factâ, unicuique sociorum adjudicantur."

Lastly, *alteruter* also is used conversely in the same sense in a passage of Ulpian.

L. 1, § 3, *uti possidetis.*

"......... aut convenit inter litigatores, uter possessor sit, uter petitor, aut non convenit. Si convenit, absolutum est ...... Sed si inter ipsos contendatur, uter possideat, quia *alteruter* se magis possidere affirmat, &c." (If there is a controversy between the two as to the possession, it is clear that each (*uterque*) must affirm *se magis possidere*).

Now, in the passage in question the train of thought is this. With contracts the rule is that the rescinding must be performed in the same way as the making, and cannot be effected either without any act at all, or even by an act of a different kind (for instance, by a *pactum* instead of an *acceptilatio*). Just so is it with Possession. For as Possession is acquired by a distinct act (and indeed by a twofold act, corporeal and mental), so it is only lost conversely by the same, and this is true of both the grounds of acquisition, *i. e.*, of the corporeal act and of the mental. Thus the emphasis evidently does not lie upon *utrumque* but upon *in contrarium actum est;* it was meant to be laid down, that the loss could not occur either without some

to justify the special meaning which *utraque* bears here without mentioning any various reading, and the later editors have admitted *alterutrâ* into the text evidently following Haloander, and without noticing it as a various reading. Russard, for instance, expressly says that all his MSS. have *utraque*. Nine Paris MSS. also, which I have consulted, read *utraque* (some with the interlinear Gloss, *i.e. ex alterâ*, which strengthens the evidence of our reading); so also two MSS. at Vienna, two *penes me*, and the one at Fulda.

new facts (*m*), or by facts of another kind, but only by such facts as gave rise to the acquisition, and that this necessary uniformity did not apply merely to the corporeal, or merely to the mental act, but to both in common. It might undoubtedly have been asked further, whether this common relation was conjunctive or disjunctive; but no question arose there on such point, which therefore is left wholly undecided, accordingly *uterque* is used in the *third* meaning above explained, and our passage expresses nothing on the point (*n*).

The correctness of this exposition might, however, be contested on another ground, on account of the internal arrangement of the passage. The loss is evidently compared with acquisition (*o*); now for acquisition, both a physical act and *animus* are necessary, so also, it would appear, for loss. But, even leaving out of view that Paulus is not addressing himself to *this* question, this resemblance is only in point of

(*m*) This constitutes the positive and important portion of this rule; a caution is thus afforded against the possible error of supposing Possession might be lost by the mere absence of the possessor from the subject, or through mere ignorance (§ 31, 32). [Add. to 6th ed.]

(*n*) I therefore now consider the view in my first and second editions to be incorrect, according to which *uterque* was made to stand for *alteruter*, and thus to express that only *one of the two* was required, not both together. If the word were ever used with this precise meaning, it would still be an inconceivable piece of negligence in Paulus, if he wished to express the disjunctive relation to select the very term which, in the generality of cases, is expressly used to denote the conjunctive in opposition to the disjunctive. The essential part of my present exposition is to be found in Thibaut, A. L. Z. Ergänzungsblätter, 1806, B. 2, S. 534. The same also (though from another point of view) is to be found in Hugo, Gott. Anz. 1804, pp.295,1807,p.1909; for undoubtedly it is not so much a peculiar meaning of the word *uterque* that is asserted, as a widely branched logical relation to which the term is applicable, and in so far we may well say that the same case may occur in all languages.

(*o*) " .... *Quibus modis adquirimus, iisdem in contrarium actis amittimus. Ut igitur* nulla possessio adquiri.... potest; *ita* nulla amittitur....," p. 247.

fact an apparent one; "corpus and *animus* together are required for Possession" means only that "Possession is founded on the *conjunction* of *corpus* and *animus*," and therefore the acquisition can only be compared to loss, when the loss results from this *conjunction* ceasing. But this conjunction not only ceases when both the elements of it fail, but also when either one of them ceases to exist.

It has therefore now been proved by interpretation also, that the continuance of Possession, as well as its acquisition, depends upon *corpus* and *animus* together, or (which is the same thing) that Possession can only be lost either by *corpus* or by *animus*. I will now bring forward some applications of this rule, partly for the purpose of explaining it, partly to develop it more completely.

But as the continuance of Possession, like its acquisition, may be effected by the agency of another; the details of this inquiry will have to embrace the following points:

I. The corporeal relation, as the first condition of the continuance of Possession (§ 33).

II. *Animus*, as the second condition of the same (§ 34).

III. Modifications of these rules by the continuance of possession through an agent (§ 35).

SECTION XXXIII.

LOSS BY EXTERNAL EVENTS.

The first condition for the continuance of Possession is a physical relation to the thing possessed which enables us to deal with it. This power however need not be, as in the acquisition of Possession, a present immediate power(p. 171), but it is sufficient if the relation of immediate dominion over the thing can be *reproduced* at will (*a*), and the Possession is only then lost, when the power to deal with it at will is altogether gone. This rule shall now be applied both to moveable and immoveables. But several examples of it are so clear in themselves, that they do not require further elucidation. To such cases belong the death of the possessor, or his becoming a slave (*b*), or the annihilation of the thing possessed, and this either physically or juridically (*c*). There are other examples again which must be examined and explained more minutely.

The possession of a moveable becomes lost, when another person makes himself master of it, either secretly or by force (*d*); and here the exclusion of our own dominion over the subject is very decided. Whether the other party actually acquires the possession is altogether immaterial; where, for instance, the slave of another, without the order of his master, purloins the article, neither the slave (§ 9) nor the master (*e*) acquires this Possession; we however lose it, because the physical power of disposing of the subject is never the less withdrawn from us, although no one else may have the right of Possession. It is otherwise indeed when the slave of the possessor himself steals the subject (*f*),

(*a*) L. 3, § 13, *de poss.* "Nerva filius, res mobiles, excepto homine, quatenus sub custodia nostra sint, hactenus possideri : idem *quatenus, si velimus, naturalem possessionem nancisci possimus.*" That Nerva only applies the rule to moveables, and even then excepts slaves, does not at all derogate from its validity as a rule. For the exceptions as to slaves and land are expressly recognized in the Roman law : for as to slaves, a *servus fugitivus* is possessed ; as to land, its possession is not lost until the possessor has notice of the loss.

(*b*) L. 30, § 3, *de poss.*

(*c*) Where the thing becomes *extra commercium*, or is specified, L. 30, § 3, 4, *de poss.*

(*d*) L. 15, *de poss.* "Rem quæ nobis *subrepta* est, perinde intelligimur desinere possidere, atque eam, quæ *vi nobis erepta est. . . . .*"

(*e*) For otherwise, the ground of possession would lie either in the will of the master, or in *peculiaris causa,* but both are wanting here, comp. L. 24, *de poss.*

(*f*) L. 15, *de poss.* See *post,* § 35.

but there the continuance of Possession proceeds on the ground that the thief himself is in our possession and, therefore, through him, the stolen article also. But our power may also be excluded without the interference of any other party, namely, when the spot where the subject is kept is either unapproachable by us (*g*) or unknown (*h*). In the latter case, however, a qualification is necessary. Whoever conceals a thing in his house, or buries money in his grounds, does not lose the possession by not being able immediately to find it (*i*); for the special provision employed for its preservation (*custodia*) (*j*), secures to him the finding for the future. Therefore, the possessor must *either* know the precise spot where his property is, *or* he must have it in a special *custodia; custodia* however is not an indispensable condition for continuance (*k*), for he who leaves a subject

---

(*g*) L. 13, *pr. de poss.* "...Cum lapides in Tiberim demersi essent naufragio et post tempus extracti .... dominium me retinere puto, *possessionem non puto.*" It is evident that a mere temporary obstruction, such as the overflowing of a field in our possession, or the falling in of a bridge which leads to it, &c., &c., does not destroy the Possession.

(*h*) L. 25, *pr. de poss.* "Si id, quod possidemus, ita perdiderimus, ut ignoremus; ubi sit: desinimus possidere." Comp. L. 3, § 13, *de poss.*

(*i*) L. 3, § 13, *de poss.* "... Desinere a nobis possideri.... *Dissimiliter atque si sub custodia mea sit, nec invéniatur: quia præsentia ejus sit, et tantum cessat interim diligens inquisitio.*" L. 44, *pr. de poss.* "Peregre profectu-rus, pecuniam in terra custodiæ causa condiderat: cum reversus locum thesauri immemoria non

repeteret.... Dixi quoniam *custodiæ causa* pecunia condita proponeretur, jus possessionis ei, qui condidisset, *non videri peremptum:* nec infirmitatem memoriæ damnum adferre possessionis, quam alius non invasit."

(*j*) For this is the general meaning of *custodia*, and the distinction as to acquisition and loss is merely one of degree.

(*k*) On the other hand, L. 47, *de poss.* cannot be cited in opposition; "...... rerum mobilium neglecta atque omissa custodia, quamvis eas nemo alius invaserit, veteris possessionis damnum adferre *consuevit*, idque Nerva filius retulit." The *consuevit* does not imply a general rule, but only the usual consequence of an *omissa custodia*, which certainly cannot be controverted. Papinian, besides, quotes the younger Nerva, whose opinion shall be immediately discussed.

behind him in a forest, and afterwards recollects exactly where it is, in no way loses his Possession. Upon this point the following passage requires explanation:

L. 3, §. 13, *de poss.*

"Nerva filius (*l*), res mobiles ...... quatenus sub custodia nostra sint, hactenus possideri. Idem (*m*) quatenus si velimus naturalem possessionem nancisci possimus." That is, Nerva says, the continuance of Possession may be founded on *custodia;* the same (Nerva) says, it may also be founded on the mere power of the possessor to obtain the natural detention, whenever he chooses. For, you cannot say of a man who has got a thing in his house, but cannot find it; *si velit*, naturalem possessionem nancisci potest: nor of one, who recollects where he has left a thing lying in the forest, sub *custodia* ejus est. These two sentences therefore do not mutually explain each other (on which ground the Florence reading is objectionable), but they describe two different modes of the continuance of Possession: and the examples, which follow in the passage, show very clearly, that Possession is not to be considered as lost in either of the cases here mentioned.

With respect to the possession of animals these rules are to be applied thus:

1st. Tame animals are possessed like all other moveables, *i. e.* the possession of them ceases when they cannot be found (*n*). 2nd. Wild animals are only possessed so long as some special disposition (*custodia*) exists, which enables us

---

(*l*) Scil. *ait.*

(*m*) Scil. "ait, hactenus possideri." "*Idem*" is the reading of three Paris MSS. (Nos. 4454, 4458, 4458 a), and of Ed. Rom. 1476; the Florence MS. has "*id est;*" most MSS. and editions have a mere abbreviation (*i.*); "*item*" would also give the correct meaning.

(*n*) L. 3, § 13, *de poss.* "....

Pecus simul atque aberraverit.... desinere a nobis possideri." Exactly the same principles applied to the possession of slaves, only the *animus revertendi* made some difference, L. 47, *de poss.*, Possession in a runaway slave was feigned, L. 15, § 1, *de usurp.*; L. 13, pr., L. 15, *de poss.*; see *ante*, p. 228; and was suspended merely by *liberale judicium*, (p. 228).

actually to get them into our power (*o*). It is not every *custodia*, therefore, which is sufficient; whoever, for instance, keeps wild animals in a park, or fish in a lake, has undoubtedly done something to secure them, but it does not depend on his mere will, but on a variety of accidents, whether he can actually catch them when he wishes, consequently, possession is not here retained: quite otherwise with fish kept in a stew, or animals in a yard, because then they may be caught at any moment (*p*). 3rd. Wild beasts, tamed artificially, are likened to domesticated animals, so long as they retain the habit of returning to the spot where their pos-

(*o*) L. 3, § 2, L. *5, pr. de adqu. rer. dom.* (§ 12, I. de rer. inst.) " Quidquid autem eorum ceperimus, eo usque nostrum esse intelligitur, donec nostra custodia coercetur, cum vero evaserit custodiam nostram, et in naturalem libertatem se receperit ; nostrum esse desinit, et rursus occupantis fit. Naturalem autem libertatem recipere intelligitur, cum vel oculos nostros effugerit, vel ita sit in conspectu nostro, ut difficilis sit ejus persecutio." For this is the only case in which the loss of Possession is immediately followed by the loss of property, so that the one term may be used for the other.

(*p*) L. 3, § 14, 15, *de poss.* " Item feras bestias, quas *vivariis* incluserimus, et pisces, quos in piscinas conjecerimus, a nobis possideri. Sed eos pisces, qui in *stagno* sint, aut feras, quæ in *silvis circumseptis* vagantur, a nobis non possideri. .... Aves autem possidemus, quas *inclusas* habemus," etc. It is clear that it is intended to draw a distinction between large and small inclosures, and so the Gloss understood the passage. A *silva circumsepta* may be very large, and one may hunt in it in vain for any particular animal enclosed therein ; therefore, we have no possession of such animal, although, in point of fact, it is confined in the chase. It is not, therefore, necessary to read with Hoffman, Obss. VIII. 7, "silvis *non* circumseptis;" or with Fleck, De Poss. p. 82, to look upon these words as meaning an enclosure not sufficient to prevent the game from escaping; or, lastly, to say with Sammet, Opuscula, p. 162, "sylva circumsepta est, quæ fines habet arcifiniios." The reading adopted by many " evaganter" is altogether impermissible, as all the change that would be effected by it is excluded by the " *in silvis.*" This passage, with its various interpretations, has been treated very elaborately, though not very well, by Nettelbladt, Diss. De vero sensu, L. 3, § 24, *de poss.*, Hal. 1774.

S

sessor keeps them (*donec animum*, i. e., *consuetudinem, rever-tendi habent*) (*q*).

The rule for the loss of Possession of immoveables is exactly the same. Here also Possession is lost whenever the power of dealing with the subject ceases; it is continued, so long as this power lasts, except that the notion of this power must be somewhat differently expressed in degree as to continuance, than as to acquisition.

Consequently, the Possession of land is lost by every act which disables the previous possessor from dealing with it. Such act may consist, *first*, in the possessor being made a slave, or incarcerated on the land (*r*); *secondly*, (and this is by far the most frequent case) in the possessor being prevented from coming on the land (*s*). Whether the person who offers the obstruction, intends to possess for himself, or merely to put an end to the other's Possession; for instance, to interrupt a commenced Usucaption, is altogether immaterial (*t*). It is a more difficult question, whether the Possession is lost when the possessor is not actually ejected, but quits the land previously through fear. Some passages lay down expressly, that in such case the Possession is lost:·

L. 33. §. 2, *de usurp.*

" Si dominus fundi homines armatos venientes *extimuerit*, atque ita profugerit, quamvis nemo eorum fundum ingressus fuerit, vi dejectus fuerit " (*u*).

(*q*) L. 4, L. 5, § 4, 5, *de adqu. rer. dom.* (§ 14, 15, I. *de rer. div.*) L. 3, § 15, 16, *de poss.*

(*r*) L. 1, § 47, *de vi.* " Quid dicturi essemus, tractat, si aliquo possidente ego quoque ingressus sum in possessionem, et non dejiciam possessorem, sed vinctum opus facere cogam? quatenus res inquit, esset? Ego verius puto, *cum quoque dejectum videri, qui illic vinctus esset.*" Paulus, V. 6, § 6.

" Vi dejectus videtur et qui in prædio vi retinetur."

(*s*) The technical expression is *dejectio.* See *post*, § 42.

(*t*) L. 4, § 22, *de usurp.*

(*u*) *Extimuerit* is a conjecture of Cujacius, in L. 9, pr. *qu. metus,* and L. 33, § 2, *de usurp;* Opp. T. 1, p. 962, 1133; which the various reading of Russard " *extimaverit*" makes very probable, because then only the *a* would have

L. 9, pr. *quod metus.*

" .... non videre vi dejectus, qui dejici non expectavi, sed profugi. *Aliter atque si posteaquam ingressi sunt* (*v*) *tunc discessi.*"

Cicero, Pro Cæcina, cap. 16.

" .... usitatum, cum ad vim faciundam veniretur, si quos, armatos, quamvis procul, conspexissent .... optime sponsionem facere possent, *ni adversus edictum prætoris vis facta esset.*"

L. 3, §. 6, *de vi.*

" Si quis autem visis armatis, *qui alibi tendebant* .... profugerit, *non videtur dejectus.*"

Other passages, again, seem to point out the Possession as continuing:

L. 9, pr. *quod metus:*

" Denique tractat (Pomponius), si fundum meum dereliquero *audito quod quis cum armis veniret,* an huic edicto locus sit ? et refert, Labeonem existimare, Edicto locum non esse, *et unde vi interdictum cessare : quoniam non videre* vi dejectus, qui dejici non expectavi, sed profugi."

L. 1, §. 29, *de vi.*

" Idem Labeo ait, eum qui metu turbæ pertonitus fugerit, (vi) videri dejectum. Sed Pomponius ait, vim sine corporali vi locum non habere. Ergo (*w*) etiam eum qui fugatus est supervenientibus quibusdam, *si illi vi occupaverunt possessionem,* videri vi dejectum."

to be struck out. The common reading "*existimaverit*" gives a false meaning, and at the same time a false construction (*venientes existimaverit,* instead of *venire existimaverit.*)

(*v*) This does not mean actual entry, any more than in the other passages, but presence on the spot, which is denoted by "*ingressi sunt.*"

(*w*) *Ergo* is the reading of three Paris MSS. (4458 a, 4486,

4486 a,) and of Cod Rehd., Edd. Rom. 1476, Nor. 1483, Ven. 1485, 1494, Lugd. 1509, 1513, Paris, 1514, 1536. Florent. "ego," and so also many other copies. Glossa, " al. *ergo,* al. ego." If *ego* is the reading, Ulpian is attempting to reconcile Labeo and Pomponius : but there is no difference between the two, as the previous passage shows, and Pomponius only intends here to correct the indistinct expression of Labeo.

L. 3, §. 7, *de vi.*

Paulus, V. 6, §. 4.

This contradiction has been frequently attempted to be reconciled by referring the first class of passages to a present violence, the second class to an anticipated violence (*x*). But, however correct this distinction may be in itself, it is nevertheless incorrect to refer it to the continuance of Possession, because it is only true as to *dejectio;* for, in fact, the latter passages do not speak at all of the actual continuance of Possession, but only deny a *dejectio;* there would be no ground, therefore, in such cases for an *Int. de vi,* (and just as little for an *actio quod metus causa*), this is the whole meaning of these passages, but still the Possession is lost in each case, if not *corpore,* at all events *animo* (*y*). But in all these cases, it is immaterial in what mode the possessor's presence on the land is prevented; *i. e.,* it is the same thing whether the possessor is turned out in fact, or prevented from coming in (*z*).

On the other hand, the possession of land continues so long as the power of dealing with it at will is not put an end to, and the constant corporal presence of the possessor, which, in the generality of cases, is altogether out of the question, is not required for this purpose (*a*). It is important

(*x*) Cujacius (see *ante,* p. 258, n.) and Cras., Spec. Jur. jur. C. p. 22—25. I maintained the same opinion in my second edition.

(*y*) Hufeland, Neue Darstellung, p. 157, *et sqq.*

(*z*) L. 1, § 24, *de vi.* "... si quis de agro suo, vel de domo processisset nemine suorum relicto, mox revertens, *prohibitus sit ingredi vel ipsum prædium, vel si quis eum in medio itinere detinuerit et ipse possederit"* (i. e., the *detinere* must have effected its purpose) "vi dejectus videtur." Comp. L. 3, § 8, *de vi.* Paulus, V. 6, § 6.

(*a*) L. 3, § 11, *de poss.* "Saltus hibernos æstivosque animo possidemus, quamvis certis temporibus eos relinquamus." L. 1, §. 25, *de vi.* "Quod vulgo dicitur, æstivorum hibernorumque saltuum nos possessiones animo retinere : id *exempli causa* didici Proculum dicere, nam ex omnibus prædiis, ex quibus non hac mente recedemus (recedimus), ut omississe (amittere) possessionem vellemus, idem est." The *saltus hiberni æstivique* are extensive grazing-grounds used by cattle either in winter only (such as the Maremma), or in summer only, (such as

to consider this proposition in the point of view in which it is brought forward, *i. e.*, as the simple consequence of the general rule as to continuance, not by any means as an exception to the rule.   It is only in this view that a certain *extension* of the proposition can be fully understood, in which, in point of fact, there is an exception to the rule previously laid down as to the loss of Possession of immoveables.

For, that Possession does not cease, by the mere absence of the possessor from the thing possessed, must be looked upon as a consequence of the general principle; for this reason, namely, that by such absence, although the power of dealing with the thing at will becomes a more remote relation, it is not at all put an end to by it.   Should any thing else supervene, in addition to absence, which causes this power to cease in point of fact, then, to make the rule apply strictly, the loss of Possession ought to be affirmed universally.   But here a remarkable limitation of the rule occurs.   For if, during our absence, the land which we possessed is occupied by another, who is in a condition to resist our re-entry by force, from that moment the physical power to deal with the land at will, is just as much taken away from us, as if a thief had stolen a moveable from our house; nevertheless, in the former case, the previous Possession continues up to the time of the possessor receiving notice of the occupation.

Before I establish the above proposition itself, I will just call attention to certain consequences of it, which if the rule is true, must be necessarily true also: 1st. He who occupies land in the absence of the possessor does not at the moment acquire any juridical Possession (p. 125) (*b*).   2nd. If the

the Apennines), and which therefore, from their nature, are unused for half the year. L. 67, *de leg.* 3 ; Varro De Re Rust. Lib. 2, C. 1, T. 1, p. 220, Script. Rei. Rust. ed. Schneider.

(*b*) It may be therefore said, that the old technical phrase, possessionem *vacuam* tradere, (p. 127) is connected with this proposition. At the same time this phrase might also be used in reference

possession of land becomes lost by the *acts* of another (*c*), this can only take place through *animus* (*d*), not that the possessor must give up the right of Possession voluntarily, but a distinct fresh act of consciousness must always have place, when the Possession is lost, but this could not be maintained according to the strict rule for loss, which prevails absolutely as to moveables. This remark will be made use of in the following section. 3rd. Clandestine Possession of land cannot arise, if the other party himself possesses the land at the same moment. For *clandestina possessio* means such Possession as is commenced with an intentional concealment of the act of prehension from the present possessor (*e*). If then land should be occupied in this manner, according to the proposition, whose corollaries we are now considering, the whole proceeding may be thus characterized; by the occupation itself no Possession is acquired, consequently, also, no *clandestina possessio*. If the previous possessor is informed of the occupancy, he *either* enters upon his Possession forcibly, in which case he cannot be said to have ever lost it, and the other party was never a true possessor (*f*), or, on the other hand, he is forcibly driven away (*g*), and then, from that moment, the other party

to the positive modifications of Possession which are here spoken of, namely, to exclude the mere apparent possession which might occur in the absence of the possessor, although nothing else had taken place which prevented the possessor from dealing with the subject.

(*c*) For if, indeed, the Possession is lost by a mere act of God, for instance, by a river changing its course, the knowledge of the possessor is not at all required.

(*d*) Every Possession, namely, with the exception of the continuance through an agent, which special case will be discussed in

the 33rd section.

(*e*) See *post*, § 43.

(*f*) Just as in the case of L. 17, *de vi.* " Qui possessionem vi ereptam vi in ipso congressu recuperat, *in pristinam causam reverti potius quam vi possidere* intelligendus est....." Thus the Possession here was not actually lost at any moment.

(*g*) It is therefore here also quite immaterial whether the forcible act is actually accomplished, or whether the collision is avoided through fear, (p. 258), but the fear must be well grounded, *i. e.* there must be an occupation in fact to which it had reference.

acquires the Possession, but this Possession is not *clandestina*, but *violenta:* or, lastly, neither of these cases occurs, *i. e.*, the previous possessor simply omits, and not through fear, to claim his former Possession, in which case there is no *vitiosa possessio*, because the new Possession commences by the will of the previous possessor himself, which will, however, as it only has reference to the Possession, may very well consist with the intention of recovering the lost property in another mode, for instance, by a vindication. Thus, in this latter case, the Possession is lost, not *corpore* but *animo*.

Hitherto we have only developed the consequences of the above proposition; the proposition itself must be now established, for it is only upon its foundation that these consequences arise. At the same time, it is necessary, for reasons which can only be assigned hereafter, to shew, that this proposition was not merely recognized generally by the Roman Jurists, but also the particular period at which it was adopted must be pointed out.

I. Papinian, Paulus, and Ulpian treat the proposition as an undoubted rule.

L. 46, *de poss.* (Papin., lib. 23. qu.)

" Quamvis saltus proposito possidendi fuerit alius ingressus, tamdiu priorem possidere dictum est, *quamdiu possessionem ab alio occupatum ignoraret.*"

L. 3, §. 7, 8, *de poss.* (Paul. lib. 54, ad edict.),

" Si animo solo possideas, *licet alius in fundo sit, adhuc tamen possides.* Si quis nuntiet, domum a latronibus occupatam, et dominus *timore conterritus, noluerit accessere, amisisse eum possessionem placet.*"

L. 6, §. 1, *de poss.* (Ulpian., lib. 70, ad ed.) (*h*).

L. 7, *de poss.* (Paulus, lib. 51, ad ed.) (*i*).

II. Celsus, Neratius, and Pomponius also allude to this proposition, but in such manner as if, probably, it had not quite the same extent in their day, nor were looked upon by all jurists as an absolute rule (*j*).

(*h*) See *post*, No. III.
(*i*) See *post*, No. III.
(*j*) For we have nothing at all of Neratius, but a very general citation from him by Paulus; the above statement therefore applies only to the two other jurists.

L. 18, §. 3, 4, *de poss.* (Celsus, lib. 23, Dig.).

" Si dum in alia parte fundi sum, alius quis clam animo possessoris intraverit; non desiisse illico possidere existimandus sum, *facile expulsurus finibus, simul atque sciero.* Rursus si cum magna vi ingressus est exercitus, *eam tantummodo partem, quam intraverit obtinet*" (*k*).

L. 25, §. 2, *de poss.* (Pomp., lib. 23. ad Q. Mucium).

" Quod autem solo animo possidemus, quæritur utrumne usque eo possidemus, donec alius corpore ingressus sit, ut potior sit illius corporalis possessio?   An vero, QUOD QUASI MAGIS PROBATUR, usque eo possideamus, donec revertentes non (*l*) aliquis repellat: aut nos ita animo desinamus possidere, quod *suspicemur repelli nos posse ab eo, qui ingressus sit in possessionem?   et* (*id*) VIDETUR UTILIUS ESSE."

III. Labeo lays down an exactly contrary rule, for which reason a modification of his decision is given by Ulpian in complete accordance with the above proposition:

L. 6, §. 1, *de poss.* (Ulp., lib. 70, ad ed.).

L. 7, *de poss.* (Paul., lib. 54, ad ed.) (*m*).

" Qui ad nundinas profectus, neminem reliquerit, et dum ille a nundinis redit, aliquis occupaverit possessionem, *videri eum clam possidere, Labeo scribit* (*n*).   *Retinet ergo posses-*

(*k*) Thus, it is only where it is *probable* that I shall succeed in ejecting the intruder (a limitation not mentioned by Papinian and the others) that the Possession is preserved for me by the above fiction; otherwise not: nevertheless, the following special point occurs at all events, viz. the new Possession only extends to that portion of the land which is actually entered upon.   The circumstance of the previous possessor being on the land is evidently only mentioned to describe the possibility of ejecting the other party more immediately and pointedly.

(*l*) " *Donec non,*"—so long as

(we are), not—"donec nos," until we: the first is the Florence reading and Haloander's also; the second in several of the MSS. of Gebauer, and besides in Ed. Rom. 1476, &c.   Both give the same sense, on account of the double meaning of *donec,* and the transposition which Brenkmann proposes is wholly needless.

(*m*) Both these passages must be taken together, because the result given above (p. 262) appears most clearly when they are thus brought in connection.

(*n*) Here, then, Labeo asserts something which contradicts the proposition in question. (P. 262).

sionem is qui ad nundinnæ abiit (o). Unde (p) si revertentem dominum non admiserit, vi magis intelligitur (q) possidere, non clam (r). Et si nolit in fundum reverti, quod vim majorem vereatur, amississe possessionem videbitur (s): et ita Neratius quoque scribit " (t).

It now becomes easy to give a brief and connected review of the contents of this section. To enable Possession to continue, there must always be a possibility of *reproducing* the immediate condition which has been described as the foundation of acquisition, and, therefore, through this condition, the feeling of physical dominion over the thing possessed; with the ceasing of this possibility Possession also ceases. But this proposition undergoes an exception with

(o) Here begins Ulpian's correction; the *ergo* does not contradict the connection between the two passages; for Labeo's opinion is not objected to as erroneous, but is shewn to be modified by another later rule. It is as much as to say, "in every case, when formerly *clandestina possessio* was recognized, this new rule now prevails," and with this meaning the *ergo* is well applicable.

(p) " *Unde*," according to the reading of Edd. Ven. 1485, 1491, 1494; Lugd. 1508, 1509, 1513, 1519; Paris, 1514, 1536. Florent. and all the Paris MSS. " *verum*,"— but a conclusion is much rather intended to be denoted by the word than an opposition.

(q) "Intellegiter" in five Paris MSS. (Nos. 4477 a, 4477 b, 4480, 4482, and the one in the St. Victor library); so also Edd. Rom. 1476, Nor. 1483, Ven. 1485, Ven. 1491, 1494, Lugd. 1508, 1509, 1513, 1519; Paris, 1514, 1536.

On the other hand, Florent. "intellegi." By this reading the sense is confused; the last sentence would then belong to Labeo's opinion, *retinet ergo*, &c. is a mere parenthesis of Ulpian, and the *verum*, (instead of *unde*), which is now inadmissible, would then be necessary. But then it would be altogether impossible to bring the opinion of Labeo himself, and the correction of it subjoined by Ulpian into any tolerable harmony, especially when we call to mind the very simple rule which is expressly laid down *in princip.* of the same passage; " non ratio obtinendæ possessionis, sed origo nanciscendæ exquirenda est."

(r) Therefore, up to this time the party had no Possession, from now he has rather a *violenta* than a *clandestina possessio*.

(s) By these words the rule of Ulpian is only expressed more distinctly. (P. 263, No. 2).

(t) See *ante*, p. 263, n.

respect to land; here the physical impossibility is not sufficient to terminate the Possession, until it is brought to the
notice of the possessor.

———◆———

SECTION XXXIV.

LOSS BY ANIMUS.

The second condition for the continuance of Possession
is the *will* of the possessor (*animus*), and the same relation
exists in this case as with the physical condition, which has
been already pointed out as the first condition.

Thus, to the continuance of Possession, it is only necessary for the *animus*, just as for the corporeal relation, that
the power to *reproduce* the original volition should always
be at hand: it is neither necessary, nor indeed possible,
that the consciousness of Possession should exist at every
moment. It follows, therefore, that Possession is not lost
by the possessor not calling to mind the subject-matter, or
consequently, his Possession for any period long or short;
indeed, the same may be affirmed if the possessor fall into
a condition in which no exertion of will is possible: for
instance, if he become a lunatic. For, as in this case, the
impossibility to exercise any distinct volition as to the
Possession, is merely personal and accidental, so, in relation to the thing possessed, there is no essential difference, whether this Possession should have been forgotten
for a longer period, or whether the possessor himself should
have become lunatic. It is only another expression of the
same view, to say, that to effect the loss of Possession by
animus, a new and contrary mental act (animus in contrarium actus) is required. (§ 32).

Therefore, Possession is lost by mere *animus*, whenever

the possessor at any moment *intends* to give it up (*a*) ; for, at that moment, the reproduction of the original intention is rendered impossible by the contrary determination of the will, and it is upon this impossibility, as upon the physical impossibility, that the loss of Possession arises. Therefore, there must be a new act of prehension, if the previous possessor should again determine to take possession, because the previous volition had from that moment ceased to exist.

But, as in this case the loss of Possession is not founded on a mere negation of will, but on a new act of will opposed to the former, (the *animus possidendi*), it is clear that whoever is incapable of exercising a will cannot lose in this way, any more than he could acquire, Possession (*b*). Therefore, a lunatic cannot lose Possession thus (*c*) : the same remark applies also to a ward, and, in all cases, so that the limitation, which was stated above, (§ 22) as to acquisition by him does not at all apply here (*d*). This inca-

---

(*a*) L. 3, § 6, *de poss.* ".... si in fundo sis, et tamen nolis eum possidere; *protinus amittes possessionem.*" L. 17, § 1, *de poss.* ".... possessio autem recedit, *ut quisque constituit nolle possidere.*" Comp. L. 30, § 4 ; L. 34, pr. *de poss.*

(*b*) The modifications of this proposition in the case of an agent belong to the following chapter.

(*c*) Glossa in L. 11, § 3, *de poss.* " Licet enim desinat habere animum possidendi, non tamen habet animum non possidendi." L. 27, *de poss.* (See *post*).

(*d*) L. 29, *de poss.* " Possessionem pupillum sine tutoris auctoritatis amittere posse constat ; *non ut animo,* sed ut corpore desinat possidere : quod est enim facti, potest amittere. Alia causa est,

si forte animo possessionem velit amittere : *hoc enim non potest.*" It is just as clearly expressed here, that a ward may lose Possession by an outward act, as (which mainly concerns us here) that he cannot do so by *animus :* the first position also coincides completely with the general principle, and the only doubt thereon arises on the following passage ; L. 11, *de adqu. rer. dom.*, " Pupillus .... alienare ...... nullam rem potest, et *ne quidem possessionem quæ est naturalis.*" But *alienare* possessionem signifies so to lose Possession as to give rise to a juridical succession; but this is not possible, because the *animus* of the previous possessor must intervene. Supposing, then, that a ward sells and delivers a chattel, the purchaser undoubtedly acquires Possession, but he does

pacity must even be affirmed of another case of loss, which is very similar to the former, but not to be confounded with it. Possession of land, namely, only becomes lost by another person's occupying it, when notice of this reaches the previous possessor (p. 262). This act of consciousness is, nevertheless, very different from the determination not to possess, because, when the former occurs, there are three possible cases: Retention of Possession, Loss of it *corpore*, and Loss *animo* (*i. e.* by an act of will). But both these cases (the above mentioned notice, and the *animus non possidendi*) agree in this, that they are alike impossible where the capacity of consciousness is wanting; so that, in this way, wards and lunatics cannot lose the possession of land by the acts of another (*e*); this similarity in practice

not at the same time acquire that, which requires, besides the existence of Possession, a special relation of succession, and therefore no *accessio possessionis*, and indeed this passage neither applies to the *civilis possessio* (*ad usucapionem*), nor to *naturalis possessio* (in the old *interdictum utrubi*); ne quidem (eam) possessionem *quæ est naturalis*. A like distinction between *omissio* and *alienatio* possessionis occurs in L. 4, § 1, 2, *de alien. jud. mut. cau.*, and a similar application was above made (p. 46) to the proposition " inter virum et uxorem nec possessionis *ulla donatio est.*" Glossa interlin. MS. Paris, No. 4483, on the words *quæ est naturalis* " amittere tamen eam poterit (civilem vere ne amittere quidem potest) nec sunt contraria hæc cum sit aliud possessionem alienare et aliud amittere." Muretus also, Epp. III. 81, Opp. vol. 1, p. 647 ; refers *alienatio* to

such a loss as is grounded on *animus*. Cuperus, p. 2, c. 38, conceives the contradiction between L. 11, *de adqu. rer. dom.*, and L. 21, *de poss.* to be irreconcileable.

(*e*) L. 29, *de poss.* (see the previous note). L. 27, *de poss.* " Si is qui animo possessionem retineret, furere cæpisset, non potest, dum fureret, ejus saltus possessionem amittere ; *quia furiosus non potest* desinere animo possidere." Cuperus, p. 1, c. 6, p. 66, asserts an exception to this rule, where the ward or lunatic sells anything, and the purchaser is *in bonâ fide*. L. 2, § 15, 16, *pro emt.*, but this passage only expresses that in such case, contrary to the rule, Usucaption is allowed —assuming that Possession generally existed ; but that in such a transaction the Possession would pass, (*corpore* namely, not *animo*), is the general rule, (see the last note), and the only exception is as to land: L. 27, 29, *de poss.*

may have caused the Roman Jurists to designate both by the same name (f), notwithstanding the distinction.

The rule, that Possession may be lost by a simple act of volition, has been now established and explained; it still remains to add something as to its application. Now it is just as clear, that an application of the rule arises beyond all doubt on the express declaration of the possessor, as that such declaration can very seldom decide the point, because, in every case in which it usually occurs—for instance, in delivery, the loss of Possession is generally determined in another manner, namely, *corpore* (§ 33). We must, therefore, in this case, as in many others, examine what is the proper construction of the whole conduct of the possessor, from which his intention may be inferred: several proofs of such construction have come down to us in the writings of the Roman Jurists, and they tend to throw much light upon the whole subject.

A construction of this sort lies at the bottom of the so-called *constitutum*. Whoever sells a subject, and, at the same time, hires it, does not in the least alter his physical relation in regard to it; but, as he nevertheless ceases to possess, the ground of this loss can only be sought for in an act of his will. The mode in which a *constitutum* generally may be recognized has been already discussed (§ 29), when *constitutum* was considered as a ground of acquisition; reference is made to it here as working the loss of a previous Possession, but the conditions both of that species of acquisition and of this loss are precisely the same.

A second case, in which a similar construction is made

only refer to the excepted cases, and L. 2, § 15, 16, *pro empt,* does not at all say, that what is there laid down does not apply to the first mentioned case also, for it does not speak of the existence of Possession, but assuming Possession only affirms the possibility of Usucaption. Even

where a lunatic, who is corporally present, is ejected by force, he does not lose Possession, because, on account of his state of mind he is considered as an absent person.

(*f*) "*Animo* desinere possidere."

use of, occurs with the *rei vindicatio*. It is an established rule that this action lies against the possessor (p. 11). If then, the possessor himself vindicates the subject, he appears by this to disclaim the Possession, so that the *interdictum uti possidetis* must be refused to him, if he should subsequently desire to resort to it. Nevertheless, the contrary is expressly laid down (*g*), the ground of which lies in the above sort of construction. For, whoever vindicates a subject, shews by the very act that he wishes to have it, and there is no doubt that he would desire to have the Possession immediately, which the form of action is to secure to him for ever, if such Possession were compatible with his character of plaintiff in a vindication-suit. Now it is true this compatibility is impossible, but still it is not necessary to assume a voluntary disclaimer of Possession, because the possessor may be either unaware of his Possession (*h*), or of the legal principle (*i*), upon which this incompatibility is founded. As now, in these two possible cases, the possessor undoubtedly had not the intention of giving up his Possession, so, generally, nothing has taken place from which this intention can be ascertained with certainty, consequently the Possession is not lost, and consequently the *interdictum uti possidetis* still lies.

Thirdly, the intention to give up Possession may be inferred from mere negligence. With land, the user of

(*g*) L. 12, § 1, *de poss.* ".... non denegatur ei interdictum uti possidetis, qui cæpit rem vindicare; non enim videtur possessioni renuntiasse, qui rem vindicavit." (P. 26). The words here left out can only be explained in the following book.

(*h*) The Gloss refers our passage in the text to this case, Glossa in L. cit. et in C. 5, X. de causa poss. Merenda, Controv. xii. 16, has supported this explanation with much force; it is not

incorrect, but partial.

(*i*) The *error juris* works no harm here, because, first, it is only *acquisition* generally that is prevented by it, L. 7, *de jur. et fact. ign.*, and here the question is as to *loss*; and, secondly, even the text cited merely means that an invalid legal form is not to be excused on the ground of error; but the present case is merely as to the construction of an act done, as to the mere proof of a factum.

it generally occurs at definite periods of the year, if then, for instance, a possessor allows his land to be unused for a series of years, we may fairly assume that he intended to give up the Possession; for it is highly improbable that this should be a mere act of forgetfulness, and whether his intention was generally not to keep it, or that he gave it up from mere negligence, or that a journey elsewhere was of more importance to him, is altogether immaterial here, as all this only applies to the motive of his determination, not to the determination itself; but as in all these cases the determination was freely, and with full consciousness, directed on something which made the exercise of Possession wholly impossible, a disclaimer of possession is necessarily involved in it (*j*). Supposing, however, that a possessor had, not from his own free will, but through fear, neglected the cultivation of his land, the above conclusion could not be drawn; no determination ever existed to give up the Possession, and the latter is, in fact, retained (*k*). Still more decided is the con-

---

(*j*) L. 37, § 1, *de usurp.* (Comp. § 7, I. *de usuc.*) "Fundi quoque alieni potest aliquis sine vi nancisi possessionem, quæ vel *ex negligentia domini vacet*, vel quia dominus sine successore decesserit, *vel longo tempore abfuerit*." That the subject must have been without a possessor, as opposed to the mere act of detention, by the owner's *absence*, or *negligence*, appears clearly not only from the term *vacans possessio*, but also from the consideration that otherwise the new occupation could not have given rise to Possession. Modern jurists (for instance, Cuperus, pp. 65, 66) have looked upon this conclusion as a piece of positive law, which it is not; indeed, some would even point out the period at which the Possession

was to be considered as lost.

(*k*) L. 4, C. *de poss.* "Licet possessio nudo animo adquiri non possit, tamen solo animo retineri possit. Si ergo prædiorum desertam ·possessionem *non derelinquendi affectione* transacto tempore non coluisti, sed *metus necessitate* culturam eorum distulisti, *præjudicium* tibi ex transmissi temporis injuria *generari non potest.*" Thus, the Possession would not be lost. It is evident, moreover, that no *dejectio* can have occurred, for then the Possession would have been lost *solo corpore.* We may conceive, therefore, a distant farm, which the possessor had been long prevented by the existence of war from cultivating.

tinuance of Possession, where the user is of such a nature, that it only recurs at certain periods: whoever during the interval omits to visit the subject, does not thereby manifest any intention of giving up the Possession. This explains why the Roman Jurists always selected the *saltus hiberni* and *æstivi* as an example to express the peculiar law as to land with respect to the preservation of Possession (*l*); namely, because these grounds remained unvisited for one-half of the year; but this circumstance, which was founded on the special character of such pastures, excludes the *animus dere-linquendi,* and consequently made it unnecessary to remark, in every individual case, that this *animus* must be conceived to be absent.

SECTION XXXV.

CONTINUATION OF POSSESSION THROUGH AN AGENT.

All that now remains to be inquired into, as to the continuance of Possession, is the relation of agency, by which Possession may be preserved as well as acquired.

In this species of continuing Possession the same three questions arise, which were discussed above (§. 28), with reference to acquisition, but they must be taken in a different order.

First, then; what is necessary for the preservation of Possession in the person of the possessor; and, conversely, how can Possession be lost in his person only ? It is clear, with reference to the physical relation to the subject, that

---

(*l*) L. 1, § 25, *de vi.* "Quod vulgo dicitur, æstivorum hiberno-rumque saltuum nòs possessiones animo retinere : id *exempli causa* didici Proculum dicere." (P. 260, n. (*a*)).

that alone could not work the loss of Possession. Thus, where a man demises his land, he does not lose the possession, even if a third party forcibly ejects him, because his dominion over the land is still fully secured to him by the tenant (*a*). It is quite otherwise with the *animus possidendi:* consequently, he who exercises his Possession through another, may lose his Possession by a mere act of will (*animus non possidendi*).

Secondly, the relation between possessor and agent may in this case, as with acquisition, be as well one of juridical authority (*b*) as a voluntary relation (*c*), and in the second case again, the *commission* on which it arises need not be constituted in any special juridical form. Moreover it is not peculiar to this continuance of Possession, although it happens to be more frequently the case than with acquisition, that this agency may be exercised through a succession of persons. Thus a tenant may underlet the subject-matter, the depositary may again deposit it, and still the previous Possession continues to run on (*d*). Just so, conversely, the landlord may sell his property to a third party,

(*a*) L. 1, § 45, *de vi.* " Si quis me vi dejecerit, meos non dejecerit, non posse me hoc interdicto experiri : quia *per eos retineo possessionem, qui dejecti non sunt.*"

(*b*) With slaves the special rule applies, that they preserve Possession for their master even against their will; for instance, when their intention is to steal the thing from him, L. 15, *de poss.* See a remarkable instance of this applied to the possession of a pledge, L. 33, § 6, *de usurp.;* L. 40, pr. *de poss.*

(*c*) L. 9, *de poss.* " Generaliter quisquis omnino nostro nomine sit in possessionem (possessione), veluti procurator, hospes, amicus, nos possidere videmur."

(*d*) L. 30, § 6, *de poss.* It is assumed of course, that the tenant on such underletting does not entertain the intention of appropriating the subject to himself; in that case the loss might undoubtedly take place; but this belongs to the third case. But if there is no such intention, the continuance of Possession is undoubted, although the underletting, &c., may be an unlawful act ; for instance, a breach of the contract, or even a *furtum usus;* to this latter case, L. 54, § 1, *de furtis* refers, and consequently, does not at all contradict the continuance of Possession.

T

and then hire it from him, so that thus the Possession exercised through an agent, may, like any other, be transferred by a *constitutum* (e). The mere cesser of the juridical relation of agency does not terminate the previous Possession (*f*).

Thirdly, (and this question is by far the most important), what is required in the person of the agent for this species of continuance of Possession, *i. e.*, how can Possession be lost in his person only? This loss may be conceived in two ways, either when the agent intends to acquire for himself the Possession, which he had previously merely exercised (loss *by* the agent), or when a third party, or even no one at all, acquires the Possession (loss *through* the agent). Why these cases are opposed in this manner, and no other, will appear from the following discussion.

Loss *by* the agent presents the lesser difficulty. The agent, as such, has not the *animus possidendi*, but he stands to the subject in the physical relation of possessor. For this reason, he cannot terminate the previous Possession *without* a new declaration of intention; *upon* this declaration the loss takes place immediately, and without any fresh act, just as it was laid down of the *traditio brevi manu* (§. 20). The first point is clear; so long, therefore, as the agent has no intention of possessing, no question arises as to this mode of loss, even if, upon other grounds, there is a refusal to restore the subject.

L. 20, *de poss.*

" Si quis rem, quam utendam dederat, vendiderit emptorique tradi jusserit, nec ille tradiderit; alias videbitur possessionem (*g*) domini intervertisse, alias contra. Nam nec tunc quidem semper dominus amittit possessionem, cum

(e) See above, § 29. This position nevertheless is denied by many, for instance, by Merenda, Contr. III. 21, which is to be explained by the mode in which the *Constitutum* is usually misunderstood.

(*f*) L. 60, § 1, *locati*.

(*g*) So read several Paris MSS. many MSS. of Gebauer, the edd. Rom. 1476, Nor. 1483, &c. Florent. "*possessione dominum.*"

reposcenti ei commodatum non redditur: quid enim si alia quæpiam fuit justa et rationabilis causa non reddendi? (*h*) non utique ejus rei possessionem intervertit" (*i*).

On the other hand, however, if only the general rule for acquisition were to be applied, the *animus possidendi* would be sufficient to constitute the agent possessor. But this rule can never be applied here strictly. Firstly, not as to land, because in this case, as in every other, Possession is not lost in land until the possessor has notice of his physical power to deal with it having been destroyed (p. 262). Here, also, the rule comes in, " nemo sibi causam possessionis mutare potest" (§. 7, p. 49), which otherwise would be violated; and one passage even refers to this rule (*j*). Secondly, not as to moveables. Here also the rule " nemo sibi causam " stands immediately in the way. For a reason, however, which can only be explained in the following Book, a rule was recognized as to moveables, that an agent was only there looked upon as a possessor, where he at the same time committed a *furtum;* but for such *furtum,* and, consequently, therefore, for this acquisition of Possessio, a *contrectatio* was necessary, that is, an actual handling of the subject, for the purpose of the theft (*k*). Now, it may

(*h*) Comp. *L.* 12, *in f. de vi.* Such a *justa causa* would be, for instance, the *jus retentionis* on the ground of the *actio commodati contraria.*

(*i*) Nor. 1483, Hal. So also, with a quite immaterial transposition, (*poss. ejus rei*), Ven. 1485. Florent. et ut. "*non utique ut possessionem ejus rei interverteret.*"

(*j*) L. 12, de vi. " .... quem dejecisse *tunc* videretur, eum emtori *possessionem non tradidit.*"

(*k*) L. 1, § 2, *de furtis.* "Sic is, qui depositum abnegat, non statim etiam furti tenetur; sed ita, si intercipiendi causa *occultaverit.*" L.

67,*pr. eod.* "Infitiando depositum, nemo facit furtum; nec enim furtum est ipsa infitiatio, licet prope furtum est. Sed si *possessionem ejus apiscatur intervertendi causa, facit furtum.* Nec refert, in digito habeat anulum, an dactyliotheca, quem cum deposito teneret, habere pro suo destinaverit." Thus, first, mere *infitiatio* does not amount to *furtum;* secondly, *furtum* and acquisition of Possession are inseparably connected: thus also, (on which all turns here), Possession is not acquired by mere *infitiatio*; thirdly, two examples are given, in which neither *furtum* nor Possession occur.

indeed be conceived that, although on this ground the agent
may not have begun to possess, still that the previous Possession would be lost, because the physical power to dispose
of the subject, would be evidently withdrawn from the
possessor by the simple intention of the agent; and in that
case, the subject would remain during the interval without
a possessor (*l*). But exactly for this last reason, it is easily
conceivable that the first departure from the rule was joined
to the second also, so that not only the commencement of
the new Possession (*viz.*, of the agent), but also the termination of the preceding, was defined by the same juridical
conditions which constituted *furtum* (*m*). This departure,

This is clear as to the *dactyliotheca*,
but as to the *anulus in digito* also
there is no doubt; for although
an actual handling takes place
there, still it was not with a *view
to stealing*, which view is denoted
in the former part of the passage
by "*occultaverit*." Averanius, Interpr. I. 28, § 12, has misunderstood these examples so completely, as to suppose that an
actual furtum is meant. So also
the Gloss before him, which even
notices the reading "*datus hypothecæ*."

(*l*) L. 47, *de poss.* proceeds on
this view, the contents of it are
shortly these; "Possession is lost
of a thing, so soon as the depositary has the intention of possessing
it for himself; it does not at all
contradict this, that the depositary does not at the same time
acquire the Possession, because in
many other cases it happens that
Possession is lost without any
body else acquiring it. This rule
undergoes an exception with
slaves only, on account of the
possible *animus revertendi*: there,

therefore, the possession of the
deponens continues up to the time
that the *depositarius* begins to
possess (by a true *furtum*)." That
upon such commencement the
preceding Possession is put an
end to, clearly follows from the
rule *plures eandem rem, &c.*

(*m*) L. 3, § 18, *de poss.* "Si
rem apud te depositam *furti fa-
ciendi causa contrectaveris*, desino
possidere: sed si eam loco non
moveris, et (*al etiamsi*) infitiandi
animum habeas, plerique veterum,
et Sabinus et Cassius recte responderunt possessorem me ma-
nere; quia furtum sine contrec-
tatione fieri non potest, nec animo
(*solo*) furtum admittatur (al. *com-
mittitur*)." This passage in itself
is clear, but how to reconcile it
with L. 47, de poss. (see the last
note)? Only thus, Papinian merely mentions (L. 47) that *responsa*
existed for the first doctrine
("responsum est") which also
appears from the present passage
("*plerique* ..... responderunt"):
he then endeavours to assign the
ground of this decision ("cujus

moreover, is not to be extended beyond the case to which it is here applied; *i. e.*, it is only true of a delegated Possession, which is put an end to by the fraud of the agent himself (*n*).

Thus, with respect to immoveables, the fraud of the agent can only divest the Possession, when such fraud is made known to the possessor; with respect to moveables, only when the fraud comprises a *furtum*.

We have hitherto spoken of loss *by* an agent; we must now inquire into loss *through* an agent, *i. e.*, the species of loss by which an end is put to the relation between the agent himself and the subject, which had previously secured our Possession. Many of the cases upon this point have been already subjected to so much controversy amongst the Roman lawyers, that, in order to arrive at clear conclusions, it is very desirable to limit, as much as possible, the true question in dispute. Now the case may be of such a nature, that the Possession would be lost, even if no agent had

rei *forsitan illa ratio est*), without giving his own opinion upon it. The usual mode of reconciling the passage is this: Papinian says, " *Si.. . tibi possidere .... consti-tueris .... confestim amississe me possessionem*," assuming, namely, that a *contrectatio* had also taken place. This explanation will do very well as a last resort for the commencement of the passage, but it makes all that follows insensible, (see the last note). It is to be found in the Gloss, and also in the following authors, Du-arenus in L. 3, § 18, de poss. Opp. p. 861; Merenda in Contr. L. 2, c. 21; Averanius, Interp. L. 1, c. 28, § 19, 20, T. 1, p. 323. This controversy, moreover, between the old lawyers belongs to the history of the two schools: the opinion quoted in L. 47, *de poss.* was that of the Proculians, that adopted in the Corpus (L. 3, § 18, *de poss.*) of the Sabinists. Hugo, Civilist. Magazin, B. 5, p. 123.

(*n*) Cuperus, p. 2, c. 33, has misunderstood this in a singular manner; he appears to consider the rule to be as follows : "when a *furtum* generally can be supposed, the conditions of it are at the same time conditions for the loss of Possession," and he deduces from this incorrect rule a proposition, which is quite true in all other respects, viz. that in L. 3, § 3, *de poss.* the allusion cannot be only to such treasure as may be in another person's ground.

interfered with it; in such case it would be always lost in the present instance also; and, therefore, this could not have been one of the disputed points. When, therefore, the tenant of land sells it, and the purchaser makes entry on the land, if the previous possessor does not attempt to disturb him (p. 263), undoubtedly from that moment the Possession is lost. Just so, when the agent loses a moveable, so that neither he nor the possessor can find it again (p. 256); or where he transfers the thing to a third party, by which the latter, in the same way as a thief, excludes the previous Possession, wholly without reference to the state of consciousness of the prior possessor. Besides, in many cases of this kind, the agent himself has already become possessor (p. 275), and then there is no doubt that he may alienate such Possession. Consequently, the present question may be stated thus: can Possession be lost *through* an agent, in cases where, without reference to agency, it would have been looked upon as continuing (*o*).

Now, the relation of natural Possession, which previously existed between the agent and the thing possessed, may be destroyed in two ways, *without* his will, and *with* his will.

As to the first case, again, there is no question. If the act of a wrongdoer dispossess the agent, undoubtedly the Possession is lost, and the knowledge of the prior possessor is immaterial (*p*). On the other hand, the Possession continues effective, if the agent, without any external aggression, becomes incapable of exercising our Possession, for instance, by death, or lunacy (*q*); and this applies to moveables as well as to immoveables.

(*o*) This question, therefore, will occur much less frequently with moveables, than with land.

(*p*) L. 1, § 22, *de vi.* " Quod servus vel procurator, vel colonus, tenent, dominus videtur possidere; et ideo his dejectis ipse dejici de possessione videtur, etiam si ignoret eos dejectos, per quos possidebat." For then also the interdict would at once arise, and the land as *fundus vi possessus* would be incapable of Usucaption, and thus the whole result is of little importance.

(*q*) L. 60, § 1, *locati.*; L. 25, § 1, *de poss.*; L. 40, § 1, *de poss.* It is only the exceptions in the

There is still another case to be inquired into, namely, where the relation of agent is put an end to by the will of the agent himself, and this case may be conceived possible in two ways:

1st. Where no one at all has obtained the physical Possession. Here, some jurists, perhaps, have considered the Possession as lost: proofs of the existence of such doctrine are not to be found, although it is generally looked upon as unquestionable, while, on the other hand, many passages assert the direct contrary without reference to any controversy on the point (*r*). The whole is contained in the following passage (*s*):

L. 40, §. 1, *de poss.*

" Si .... colonus .... decessisset........ non statim dicendum, eam (sc. possessionem) interpellare..... *Idem* (*t*) *existimandum* ait, si colonus sponte possessione discesserit. Sed hæc ita esse vera, si nemo extraneus eam rem interim possederit, sed semper in hereditate coloni manserit." If *" aliud"* is the right reading, the controversy is made out; if *" idem,"* all ground for it disappears. The whole context of the passage speaks for the latter reading, as the words *" Sed hæc ita esse vera"* apply to both the previous sentences, and it is only by a forced construction of the first reading, that they can be made to refer to the more distant

last passage, "cum dominus possessionem apisci neglexerit," and " si nemo extraneus," &c., which can raise any doubt: but the first exception may be well referred to certain analogous cases, (p. 271), and the second is closely connected with the following controversy.

(*r*) L. 3, § 8, L. 44, § 2, *de poss.*; L. 7, *pr. pro emtore;* L. 31, *de dolo.*

(*s*) The *argumentum a contrario,* by which another passage might be brought into the controversy,

L. 31, *de poss.* " .... si *non* deserendæ " is unserviceable, because there is no connection whatever between the passages.

(*t*) Glossa : " alias *aliud* .... alias *idem,*" Giphanius, in Lect. Alt. p. 535. Florent. *" aliud,"* and so the printed editions. Most of the Paris MSS. read "*aliud,*" six however read "*idem,*" and so likewise the MSS. at Metz, at Leipsic, and *penes me.* Gebauer here as usual contains no trace of a various reading.

proposition; the concluding words (*sed semper in hereditate*) speak for the first reading, but still they may be made operative according to the second also.

2nd. Where a third party has obtained the physical Possession. Delivery is only an instance of this kind, and the Roman jurists properly treat it as quite immaterial, whether the natural Possession is transferred to a third party immediately (by delivery), or mediately; as in the latter case the agent loses the thing in the first instance, without reference to the new possessor, and the latter subsequently obtains occupation of it. In this case, most of the authorities (*u*) consider the Possession as lost; but in the following passage, the contrary is just as distinctly laid down (*v*):

L. 3, §. 7, 8, 9, *de poss.*

" In amittenda quoque possessione affectio ejus, qui possidet, intuenda est. Igitur, &c. &c. Sed et si animo solo possideas, licet alius in fundo sit, adhuc tamen possides. Si quis nuntiet, domum a latronibus occupatam, et dominus timore conterritus, noluerit accedere; amississe eum possessionem placet. Quod si servus vel colonus, per quos corpore possidebam, *decesserint discesserenve*, animo (*w*), retinetis possessionem (*x*). Et si alii tradiderim (*y*) amitto

---

(*u*) L. 40, § 1, L. 44, § 2, *de poss.*; L. 33, § 4, *de usurp.*

(*v*) L. 32, § 1, *de poss.* cannot be made use of here, as it only contains the proposition that "an agent cannot transfer Possession *quasi ex Constituto,*" Cuperus, P. 2, C. 40. This important passage, which has also all analogy for it, is not opposed by L. 21, § 3, *de poss.* "Qui alienam rem precario rogavit, si eandem a domino conduxit: possessio ad dominum revertitur," because the *rogans* by the rule is himself possessor, (§ 27), and therefore not manager of another person's Possession.

(*w*) Cod. Rehd.; Edd. Rom. 1476, Ven. 1485, Lugd. 1509, 1513, Paris, 1536; "possidebam *decesserit vel animo.*" Nor. 1483, Hal. possidebam, *discesserit* (Hal. *discesserint*) vel animo." The MSS. have *decesserit,* or *decesserint,* or *discesserit,* or *discesserint,* but none of them the entire reading above of the Florence copy.

(*x*) Without distinction, whether another *occupatio* followed upon the *discessus* or not.

(*y*) Edd. Rom. 1476, Nor. 1483, Ven. 1485, Ven. 1494, Lugd. 1509, 1513, Hal. Paris, 1514, 1536. " *Sed si alii tradiderit,* (Hal. *tradiderint.*")

possessionem. Nam constat possidere nos, donec aut nostra voluntate *discesserimus*, aut vi dejecti *fuerimus* (*z*). Paulus is stating the modes of loss as to immoveables (he discusses moveables afterwards in § 13, &c.) " In these cases," he says, " the animus of the possessor is conclusive," and he then proceeds to confirm the rule by a variety of instances, 1st. By the mere *animus non possidendi* Possession is lost (*a*); 2nd. By simple occupation it is not lost; 3rd. But if notice is brought home to the possessor, and he does not venture to maintain his Possession forcibly, his Possession thereupon ceases ; 4th. If a slave or tenant, through whom we exercise Possession, dies or leaves the land voluntarily, our Possession nevertheless continues ; 5th. If the possessor himself delivers the land, the Possession ceases (*b*). All these particular instances, then, are comprised under the general rule, " We only lose Possession (of immoveables) by our own will, or by a *dejectio*." This conclusion demonstrates the propriety of the Florence reading, and, at the same time, the correctness of our explanation.

Thus the question only arises as to two cases : in the first, the agent had given up merely the natural Possession; in the second, in addition to this, a third party had occupied the Possession ; the opinions of the ancient lawyers were, *perhaps*, divided on the first case, they *undoubtedly* were on the second. Justinian, with express reference to a difference between the ancient jurists, laid down in one of his own constitutions (*c*), " That the fraud of the agent should not

---

(*z*) Hal. "*discesserint*"....*fuerint*. The result is not essentially different, but the passage loses in grammatical propriety.

(*a*) *Animus* denotes here, as usual, two distinct ideas (p. 269).

(*b*) Many have doubted the correctness of the reading "*tradiderim*," because then the position would be too clear for Paulus to enounce formally. But, firstly, the only object was to shew the conformity of several (in part well known) cases with a general rule ; and secondly, there were, in fact, cases of delivery, in which it was not at all superfluous to lay down and prove the loss of Possession, cf. L. 17, § 1, *de poss.* (§ 12).

(*c*) L. 12, C. *de poss.*

injure the possessor" (*d*), (and, consequently, should not put an end to his Possession); now, did this enactment refer to the first case *only*, or to the second *also* (*e*)?

I conceive to both cases, and for the following reasons:

1st. Because a difference among the old lawyers on the first point is not at all made out (see p. 278), and yet Justinian proposes to decide a disputed point.

2nd. On the other hand, the controversy as to the second case is fully established (p. 280), and this would most incomprehensibly remain unsolved, if it only applies to the first case.

3rd. Because the words, " definimus, ut sive servus, sive procurator, ... corporaliter nactam possessionem *dereliquerit, vel alii prodiderit*, desidia forte vel dolo, *ut locus aperiatur alii eandem possessionem detinere :* nihil penitus domino præjudicii generetur, &c.—evidently refer to each of these two cases specially, and they must receive a forced construction, and, indeed, are unmeaning and superfluous, if they do not connote (*f*) the opposition between them : more especially, as in this case, the old jurists made no distinction between occupancy and dereliction upon which occupancy followed.

4th. Lastly, from the general summing up—" Hoc enim tantum, sancimus, ut dominus, *nullo modo* aliquod discrimen sustineat *ab his quos transmisserit.........*"

According to the rival explanation, the loss could be founded only on an act of the agent, as the mere occupation of land, without the knowledge of the Possessor, cannot work the loss of Possession.

(*d*) Some have referred this merely to a right of reclaimer, but firstly, on general principles no such right ever existed, and a new remedy at law was undoubtedly not introduced here ; secondly, there would still be a *præjudicium* which could not be denied.

(*e*) For, that it relates to the first case, there can be no question: besides, the second case completely includes the first.

(*f*) For the definition and value of the word *connote* and its conjugates in philosophic language, see Mr. John Mill's admirable System of Logic, vol. 1. [Trans].

I. The interpretation of these passages was much contested even amongst the Glossers (*g*). Like the modern interpreters, they divide themselves into two great parties: the first, whose opinion has been here maintained, recognizes the continuance of Possession, without distinction, whether the agent merely leases the land, or transfers it to a third party (*h*); the second party only allows of the continuance of Possession in the first of these two cases (*i*).

Both of these views are to be found in the Glossers, as well as in later jurists, with numerous modifications, which generally are founded on an incomplete study of the Sources.

Lastly, this passage applies just as much to moveables as to immoveables (*possessionem cujuscunque rei*): only, as respects the former, the conditions of the application are nearly always wanting (p. 278, note (*o*)).

(*g*) Glossa in L. 12, C. *de poss.*; Azo in L. 12, C. de poss. Lectura, p. 570; Azo in Summa, *tit. de poss.* num. 15, fo. 135; Placentinus in Summa, *tit. de poss.* p. 332; Rogerius, de antinomicis Sententiis, p. 189, (after Placentinus, De Var. Act. ed. Mag. 1530, 8vo). Rofredus, Tract. Jud. Ord. p. 428-9; Odofredus in L. 3, et L. 40, ff. *de poss.* f. 56-65, et in L. *fin.* C. *eod.* f. 108. The jurists of the following period are cited in great number by Menoch., De Recup. Poss. remed. 14, Nos. 17-23.

(*h*) Giphanius in L. 12, *de poss.*, Lect. Alt. p. 536; he just before

had been of a different opinion, pp. 423-4. Merillius in 50 Decis. Opp. pp. 2, 130; Vinnius in § 5, I. *de interdictis*; Mylius, Diss. ad. L. f. C. *de poss.* Lips. 1690; Oppenritter, Decis. Imp. Syn. cont. 50, Imp. Justin. Decis. Viennæ, 1735-4, pp. 792-4.

(*i*) Cujacius in L. 3, § 8, 9, *de poss.*; Opp. VIII. 258, cf. V. 711, IX. 1018; A Faber de err. pragm. IV. 2; Ramos, De Poss. P. 2, C. 1, § 12, (Meirmann. T. 7, p. 97); Cuperus, De Poss. P. 2, C. 39; Fleck, De Poss. pp. 112, 113, De interd. unde vi, pp. 77-80; Thibaut, Ueber, Besitz. § 23.

BOOK IV.

INTERDICTS.

THE special Sources for this learning are the titles *de Interdictis*, in the Institutes, the Digest, and the Code; to which must now be added Gaius, lib. 4, §. 138, *et sqq*.

Authors:

Roffredi Tractatus Judiciarii Ordinis, Colon. 1591, f. Here belongs, Pars 2 *de Interdictis*, p. 62—109, and Pars 8 *de Constitutionibus quibus violentiæ puniuntur*, p. 397—435. Not so valuable as the other works of this period; rather a practical than a theoretical inquiry into the rules and forms of procedure.

Menochius, de adquirenda, retinenda et recuperanda possessione (the two first books, Colon. 1557; the whole, Colon. 1577, and afterwards frequently, for instance, Colon. 1624, f. I do not know the date of the impression of the original (Venetian edition.) A work for practitioners, that contains everything which has been written either good or bad on the subject. His own views may be sought in vain, but the arrangement is very tolerable, so that the work is not unserviceable as a collection of materials.

Donellus, XV. 32—8, et in Cod. VIII. 4, 5, 6, 9. See Introduction.

Friderus Mindanus, de Interdictis. See Introduction.

Retes, de Interdictis. See Introduction.

Haubold, Zeitschrift f. Geschicht. Rechtswiss. B, 3, s. 358, f. 9.

The most valuable work, however, is

Hollweg, Handbuch des Civilprozesses, B. 1, Bonn, 1834.

---◆---

SECTION XXXVI.

MEANING OF INTERDICTS.

Every Possession is protected by Interdicts; consequently, the notion of Interdicts must next be defined. The essence of an *actio* consisted in this, that the Prætor previously enounced in his Edicts that in such and such cases, not that he himself would do any thing, but that he would appoint and instruct a *Judex* to determine them (*judicium dabo*).

At the same time this only came into operation when some question of fact was in dispute; if, on the other hand, a point of law was in question, or one of the parties had committed an injury to the other, wilfully and without any probable cause, or even if the defendant yielded to the plaintiff's demand only in the presence of the Prætor (confessio), a *judex* was never given, but the Prætor himself settled the matter on the spot (*a*).

Wholly otherwise with Interdicts. As to these the Edict did not make mention of a *judex*, but of an immediate

---

(*a*) L. 3, § 1, 2, and L. 5, § 10, *de op. nov. nunt.*, apply to cases of manifest injury, to cases therefore which contained no contested facts, and which were ripe for immediate judgment. Comp. Tacitus, Ann. XI. 6. "Sui-lius et Cossutianus et ceteri qui *non judicium, quippe ut in manifestos*, sed pœnam statui videbant," etc. The *confessio* is treated of in Digest. 42, 2 Cod. 7, 59, Paul. II. 1, § 5.

order or prohibition of the Prætor; *veto, exhibeas, restituas* (*b*). If any case of this kind came before him, the
Prætor at once stated the law contained in the Edict, not
indeed upon evidence adduced, but still in the presence of
both parties (*c*), so that this proceeding had the closest
resemblance to our Mandate process (*d*). Now, two cases
might occur; either the defendant would confess the plaintiff's demand, and then the whole matter was at an end (*e*);
or the defendant traversed, or brought forward exceptions,
upon which a *judex* or *arbiter* was assigned (*f*), and that
which operated at the commencement as an order of the
Prætor was now converted into an instruction of the *Judex*
(*formula*) (*g*).

The main result, therefore, might be just the same in
Interdicts as in actions, and the distinction consisted rather
in the form and language than in substance; but such formal distinction had undoubtedly this practical bearing, that
a simple order much more frequently brought the matter to
a close in cases of Interdicts than of actions (*h*). From this

---

(*b*) Zeitschrift fuer geschichtliche Rechtswiss, B. 3, ss. 306-7.
The same thing also is meant by
Gaius, § 139, when he says, "præter aut perconcul principaliter
auctoritatem suam finiendis controversiis proponit," cf. Zeitschrift, B. 3, ss. 305-366.

(*c*) Hollweg. s. 384. (Add. to
6th ed.)

(*d*) The comparison to *Summariissimum* is less happy. Huber,
Prælect. lib. 43, epilog. [For an
explanation of Summariissimum,
see *post*].—Transl.

(*e*) L. 6, § 2, *de confessis*. This
does not mean, however, that
execution followed immediately;
other indirect remedies often
arose in the *periculum judicii* on
account of the bail, in the *jus juran-*

dum in litem, &c.; Hollweg. s. 389.
(Add. to 6th ed.)

(*f*) Gaius, Lib. 4, § 141.
"Nec tamen cum quia jusserit
fieri, aut fieri prohibuerit, statim
peractum est negotium, sed ad
judicem recuperatores vi itus et
ibi editis formulis quæritur an
aliquid adversus prætoris edictum
factum sit, vel an factum non sit
quod is fieri jusserit." Comp.
Theophilus, *ad pr. I. de Interdictis*.

(*g*) Here came in the "*editæ
formulæ*." (See the last note).
Comp. Aggerius in Goesius, p.
68, "interdicti formula litigatur,"
and Theophilus, loc. cit.

(*h*) (Add. to 4th ed.) This
view is in substance the same as
that brought forward by Hugo

substantial resemblance between Interdicts and actions it is now easily to be explained, why the former are constantly looked upon as *ordinaria* judicia (*i*), and that they are opposed to every other proceeding which takes place *extra ordinem*, whether the latter consists in an actual inquiry before the Prætor (without a *judex*) (*j*), or in immediate execution on a clear point of law (*k*); just as it has been observed on above, with actions.

From this also may be explained the disappearance of Interdicts proper with the whole *ordo judiciorum*. Indeed, it would appear that an order or a prohibition by the judicial authority must have been comprised in each form of process. But the old Interdicts were not framed on such general view. They were rather formal decrees, intended to serve as an introduction to the above described proceeding, and as instructions to the *judex*, and consequently had no longer any meaning after this sort of procedure and this *judex* had come to be disused.

They, therefore, subsequently grew up to be mere legal remedies or suits generally, and nothing then remained to

in the Goett. An. 3. 1804, and which I opposed in my first two editions by a comparison, stretched too far, between interdicts and actions. Gaius, § 139, 141, confirms it completely. To the above ground for the employment of interdicts there may be added the circumstance that the private interests of individuals were here much interwoven with questions of police. Hollweg. p. 387, cf., also the add. to § 6, *ante.* (Add. to 6th ed.)

(*i*) Frontinus in Goesius, p. 41, (cf. p. 56), "ad interdictum, hoc est jure ordinario, litigatur." (This passage however is not in point here, as it only refers to a distinction from the procedure before Agrimansors). L. 1, § 2, *si ventris nomine*, "si eum per interdictum ad jus ordinarium remiserit." To this also the *formula* mentioned in a previous note applies, the *formula* being always a token of *ordinarium judicium*, cf. Ulpian, XXV. 12.

(*j*) L. 3, § 3, *de lib. exhib.* " Ceterum *cessat interdictum*, et succedere poterit notio prætoris, *ut apud eum disceptetur*, utrum quis in potestate sit, an non sit."

(*k*) L. 1, § 1, de tat. exhib.; L. 1, § 2, de migrando; L. 3, *pr. ne vis fiat ei;* L. 5, § 27, *ut in poss. leg.;* L. 1, § 2, *si ventris nom.;* L. 1, § 1, *de inspic. vent.*

them of their original character but the name (*l*). They still occur in this form in the Compilations of Justinian, and so also they have come down to us, so that in this modern form they might as well be called *actiones* (*m*).

If now, besides the general relation between the parties here alluded to, we inquire further into the form of procedure, in Interdicts, in particular cases (which does not properly belong here), we learn from Gaius, that it often was extremely intricate; for, what with bail, restipilutations, and the like, a most extraordinary delay in reaping the benefit sought for might result, and the defendant had frequently not less than *five* judgments passed against him (*n*). When, therefore, most of the moderns assume, at all events tacitly, that Interdict-procedure was most summary, it is not only altogether groundless, but also is completely contradicted by the above facts. All that can be admitted is that Interdicts were most summary, where the defendant obeyed them forthwith, and thus gave no opportunity for further proceedings: if procedure had to go on, it was not more summary than in the case of actions (*o*). We have, indeed, in Cicero's speech, *pro Cæcinâ*, a specimen of Interdict-procedure, which does not appear a whit more

(*l*) L. 3, C. *de interdictis*. ".. .. Interdicta autem licet in extraordinariis judiciis proprie locum non habent, tamen ad exemplum eorum res agitur." Rubr. Digest. 43, 1, "de interdictis sive extraordinariis actionibus quæ pro his competunt." Cf. § 8, I. *de interdictis*; L. 2, 4, C. *unde vi*. According to these passages the change goes back, at least, as far as Diocletian, and there is not the slightest ground for supposing, with Giphanius, Explanat. Cod. P. 2, pp. 262-70, that these passages are interpolated, and that Justinian is the author of the

innovation. At the same time we must admit that interdicts still continued as mere forms for a long time after the thorough reformation of procedure. Hollweg, s. 393. (Add. to 6th ed.)

(*m*) The hearing and decision are erroneously ascribed to the Prætor himself by Sigonius, De Jud. I. 16; Cujacius, Paratit. Cod. VIII. 1, Vinnius, ad pr. I. de interd.

(*n*) Gaius, lib. 4, § 167.

(*o*) This concluding remark was added in the 4th ed., the proof from Cicero in the fifth.

summary, then the procedure in any other of his law speeches (*p*).

SECTION XXXVII.

POSSESSORY INTERDICTS.

Interdicts generally have only been made mention of here, because Possession is shielded by suits of this kind. Possessory suits therefore, are Interdicts, without having however, any other connection with other Interdicts than that of a common procedure, and this connection is wholly immaterial on the present subject. The notion of possessory suits, or (since all possessory suits are, at the same time, Interdicts), of possessory Interdicts has now to be defined.

This definition presents no difficulty upon the whole. *Rei vindicatio* means the suit which the plaintiff brings upon his property, *actio emti* that founded upon an *emtio*; just so possessory suits are those founded on the Possession of the plaintiff, *i. e.* they assume as their condition that the plaintiff has actually acquired a *jus possessionis.* The application of this notion to the *interdicta retinendæ* and *recuperandæ possessionis* is easily made; but in the *interdicta adipiscendæ possessionis*, the plaintiff neither alleges that he now has, nor that he ever had had Possession. Nevertheless, there are two modes conceivable, by which

---

(*p*) See on this question Savigny in the Zeitschrift f. geschichlt, Rechtswiss, B. 6, ss. 229—272. The passage quoted from Hollweg, s. 390, is particularly worth attention. Interdicts were summary in the sense that several penalties on plaintiffs (by rules of practice) were laid down to speed the determination of the cause, and also by many abbreviations introduced into more modern practice, but they were not summary in the more important sense, of not requiring full proof. (Add. to 6th ed.)

this Interdict may be connected with the other possessory
suits: first, by imagining a *fiction*, by which the Possession
may be considered as acquired, although we merely possess
the right to acquire it (*a*). But such a fiction cannot be
assumed arbitrarily, and not a single authority for it can be
brought forward, indeed it has all analogy against it, for in
the *interdict. retin.* and *recup. poss.* the ground of complaint,
comprises besides the Possession, the special kind of disturbance also, (violence, &c.); this is undoubtedly not
required in the *int. adipiscendæ poss.*, and consequently
a fictitious Possession would give rise to a more comprehensive right, than an actually acquired Possession.
Secondly, by considering the Possession of another person,
to whom the plaintiff was *successor*, as the condition. Thus,
for instance, the *int. quorum bonorum* would only lie where
the deceased had had juridical Possession of the thing, and
then by reference to such Possession it would become a
possessory remedy. But this very reference is unfounded;.
the *possessio* of the deceased is never put forward as the
foundation of this interdict (*b*), and it would be quite arbitrary
to limit the right of action of the heir in this manner. The
int. adipiscendæ possessionis stands therefore in no sort of
connection with the above notion of possessory suits.

Nevertheless, it is not to be denied that the Romans
themselves classed together the Interdicts, *adipiscendæ*,
recuperandæ and *retinendæ possessionis* (*c*); and from this

---

(*a*) Donellus puts forth this
view, Com. Jur. Civ. CIV. XV.
37, p. 814.

(*b*) *The only passage which
could throw a doubt for a moment upon this, is the following,
Paulus III. 5, 18. "In possessionem earum rerum, quas mortis
tempore testator *non possedit*,
heres scriptus, priusquam jure
ordinario experiatur, improbe
mitti desiderat." But this *missio*

of the testamentary heir, to which
the *Edictum D. Hadriani* refers,
is very different from the Interdict; indeed, it is even opposed
in this passage to an Interdict,
("jure ordinario"), see *ante*, (p.
287); so that, on the contrary,
this passage fully establishes my
assertion.

(*c*) L. 2, § 3, *de interdict.* § 2,
I. eod. Gaius, lib. 4, § 143.

classification all modern Jurists have framed their general
notion of possessory Interdicts. Possessory Interdicts according to them are those which had Possession for their
object. But this definition amounts to nothing, because
in all kinds of suits Possession may, or may not, be the
object, and it is evidently quite accidental. Thus, for
instance, the special.object of the *actio pigneratitia* is the
restitution of Possession, the same object occurs in the
actio emti and *locati*, and possibly in innumerable other
actions, and there would therefore be no ground for excluding all these suits from the above indefinite notion of
possessory suits. Indeed in the only passage, which speaks
pointedly of possessory remedies in the above indefinite
sense, Interdicts, actions, and exceptions are expressly
mentioned together (*d*); on the other hand the above three
classes are never mentioned as *possessoria* interdicta, but as
interdicta *rei familiaris* (*e*), or in such terms as would seem
to show that *all* Interdicts were comprised by them (*f*),
indeed one division of Interdicts, mentioned as the chief
division (*g*), expressly excludes the above classification.
Lastly, the most conclusive ground against the usual classification is this ; proper possessory Interdicts are founded on
torts (§§ 34—35); suppose now that the Prætor, instead of
an Interdict, had prescribed an *actio* for the case of a
dejectio, this actio *de vi* would undoubtedly have been
classed with the *actio vi bonorum raptorum*, &c., and no one
would then have thought of placing it in the same class
with the *int. quorum bonorum ;* consequently this ought not
to be done now either, since the prescribing of an Interdict
instead of an action, is wholly immaterial to us, and even

(*d*) L. 1, § 4, *uti poss.* "....
Omnis *de possessione controversia*
aut eo pertinet, ut quod non possidemus, nobis restituatur; aut
ad hoc, ut retinere nobis liceat
quod possidemus. Restitutæ (res-
tituendæ) possessionis ordo aut
interdicto expeditur, aut *per actio-*

nem. Retinendæ itaque possessionis duplex via est, aut *exceptio*,
aut *interdictum.*"
(*e*) L. 2, § 3, *de int.*
(*f*) L. 2, I. *de interdictis ;*
Gaius, Lib. 4, § 143.
(*g*) § 1, I. de int.; Gaius, Lib.
4, § 142.

according to the view of the Romans was accidental, *i. e.*, it did not affect the notion of the right of the action itself.

Thus, the Interdicts, *retinendæ et recuperandæ possessionis* are the only possessory suits, and the *int. adipiscendæ possessionis* have nothing in common with them. Moreover, these latter Interdicts have nothing in common even with one another, which may be easily shown by an enumeration of them, and this also appears from the fact of their being mentioned in such very different parts of the Sources. The *int. quorum bonorum* is not distinguished in Justinian's compilation from the *hereditatis petitio possessoria;* the *int. quod legatorum* refers, like all Possession, and so many other subjects, to a special principle of law, first laid down in the Edict., the int. *de glande leganda* is in substance an *actio ad exhibendum* for that special case; the *int. Salvianum,* another form of procedure for the *actio Serviana* (*h*), just as the *int. fraudatorium* (*i*) is for the *actio Pauliana.*

[Add. to 6th ed.] The view just given must now, in consequence of the late discovery of a fragment of Ulpian, be modified in the following manner.

When in the first instance, without reference to the language of the Sources, we consider only the purport of the legal remedies, it is evident that certain suits have no other destination than to protect *possessio* from particular kinds of disturbance, by which Possession is either defended from such disturbance, or is subsequently restored. Of this sort, are the *corporis possessio: Int. uti possidetis; utrub. unde vi* (*de clandestina possessione*), *de precario;* different Inter-

---

(*h*) Donellus, Comm. XV. 57, enumerates, besides the four first mentioned, two others also, the *int. de tabulis exhibendis,* and that which the *missus in possessionem* had. But neither of these had Possession for their object; they, therefore, do not belong here. The two Interdicts also, whose exist-ence we only ascertained through Gaius, § 145, 146, the *possessorium* and *sectorium* have no affinity at all with the *int. quorum bonorum.*

(*i*) L. 67, § 1, 2, ad *Sc. Trebell;* L. 96, *pr. de solut.;* L. 10, *per quæ in fraud. cred.*

dicts for the *juris quasi possessio*, which shall be mentioned in §§ 47, 48, 49. The close affinity of these remedies can be as little doubted as the essential difference from all other suits, when one looks at their origin and purport. But as, on account of the various effects of this close affinity, it becomes a pressing necessity to designate this class of cases by a technical phrase, I term them *possessory suits*, or (with reference to Roman procedure), *possessory Interdicts.* An historical value is not attributable to these terms. But the form of expression nevertheless recommends itself, as it in fact denotes those suits only which have juridical *possessio* as their condition and basis. These terms also are so far from being new fangled or arbitrary, that in fact they have been made use of by most Jurists in exactly the same sense, and it was only owing to a special circumstance that the latter were induced to comprehend under the terms other suits also, viz., the *int. adipiscendæ possessionis.*

But it is a wholly different question whether this classification is to be found in the ancient Jurists; and I must now state that, according to my present conviction, it is not to be found there, but, on the other hand, another and very different one. And that is, the three classes of Interdicts, *adiscipendæ, recuperandæ,* and *retinendæ possessionis* are grouped together. I thought in my earlier editions, that these classes might be referred to the above given notion of possessory Interdicts, by merely excluding the first class; but it is clear, from the newly discovered fragment of Ulpian, that, even by this bold step, nothing would be gained. For there two Interdicts are mentioned, *Quem fundum* and *Quam hereditatem,* which are called *duplicia,* that is, either *adipiscendæ* or *recuperandæ* possessionis, according to circumstances (*j*). Now, as these Interdicts could not relate in their form to any *possessio,* and its particular sort of disturbance, but only to a duty unperformed, it is clear that even the class of *Int. recuperandæ possessionis* must be

(*j*) Rudorft, Zeitschr. f. geschichtl. Rechtswiss. B. 9, S. 18.

excluded from our notion of possessory Interdicts. It follows, consequently, that the three classes of the Romans stand in no relation to our notion, but it also follows, that they are useless in a scientific point of view, because they merely regard the external *object* (which is quite immaterial to the essence of the suit), whether Possession is to be newly acquired, or recovered, or maintained.

Lastly, there is a third question, distinct from the two others, as to the propriety of the above technical expression. The Romans call the suits belonging to an inheritance *possessoriæ actiones*, when they are not given to a *heres*, but to a *bonorum possessor* as fictitious actions (*k*). So, also, the *hereditatis petitio* is called *possessoria* in its extended application to the *bonorum possessor* (*l*). On the other hand, the three above mentioned classes are never termed *possessoria interdicta*, although we might especially expect to find the name as a connotation of their common species. The term only occurs in one passage in connection with our notion, and then quite incidentally (*m*). Thus, in fact, our terminology has no foundation in the Sources; but, as no confusion of ideas is to be dreaded from its use, I do not consider it necessary to displace it from its ancient employment with respect to Possession: those who desire to proceed more strictly in this matter, may make use of the German term Besitzklagen (Possession-suits).

The principle which has been laid down, that possessory Interdicts always require juridical Possession in the plaintiff, determines also the amount of evidence which is required for them; it is the business of the plaintiff, therefore, to prove the existence of Possession in his own person. Hereupon arises, however, the following question (*n*). The

---

(*k*) L. 50, *de bonis libert.* L. 4, *de Carbon. ed.*

(*l*) Heading of the title in Digest, Lib. 5, tit. 5.

(*m*) L. 20, *de servitut.* "Ego puto usum ejus juris pro traditione possessionis accipiendum esse, Ideoque et *interdicta veluti possessoria* constituta sunt."

(*n*) This discussion upon evidence was introduced in the 4th edition.

plaintiff's statement is necessarily directed to the existence
of Possession at a particular period, for instance, in the *int.
uti possidetis*, to Possession at the time of action brought;
in the *int. de vi*, at the time of the ejectment. Now, must
the existence of Possession at these precise periods be made
out, or is it sufficient to prove that the plaintiff, or his heir,
had once *acquired* Possession, and so the continuance of it
is to be presumed, until the defendant shews that this Possession has been subsequently lost? The same question,
it is well known, occurred in the *vindicatio rei*, and there it
was expressly laid down, that it was sufficient to prove the
property at any previous period, and the *onus* was then thrown
upon the defendant, if he wished to maintain that it had been
divested (*o*). The analogy of this rule would seem to make
it apply to possessory suits also ; nevertheless, I conceive the
contrary to be the case. The distinction between property and
Possession, in this respect, consists in this, that continuance
with the former does not depend on any continuing facts;
it, consequently, cannot be presumed, and, consequently, is
not only difficult, but absolutely impossible, to prove. It is
otherwise with Possession, the continuance of which depends
on a constantly enduring relation of facts to the subject-
matter, and which, therefore, is always a matter for presumption and proof. All that can be said for the opposite doctrine is this ; the above mentioned relation of fact has no
distinct character (§ 19). The Judge, therefore, in considering the evidence, must look to all the circumstances,
and he will look back to the time when Possession was
acquired, in order to form a presumption as to its continuance up to the present moment; this presumption will have
more or less weight, according to the length of time which
has passed since the acquisition. But if it be asserted,

(*o*) L. 16, C. *de probationibus.*
Voetius ad Pandectas VI. 1, § 24.
Krazer ueber den Beweis des
Eigenthums, Vienna, 1810. This
point arises principally on the *ex-* ceptio rei venditæ et traditæ, at least
in the form in which this occurs
in Justinian's Code, though not
in the earlier law.

that the proof of *acquisition* only is necessary in Possession, as well as in property, the distinction must be admitted in every case, that acquisition of property may take place in the person of the heir, while for Possession, on the other hand, acquisition in the plaintiff's own person is required, as property passes by inheritance, but not Possession (§. 30). The question here discussed occurs with Usucaption, as well as with Interdicts; so that with the former also, the proof of the commencement of Possession is nowise sufficient. This question gave the older Jurists a great deal of trouble, though in modern times it has not been much discussed. Placentinus and Hugolinus transferred the presumption from the prior Possession to the present; Johannes objects to this, on the ground of Possession being so much easier lost than property (*p*). Later jurists have for the most part adopted the presumption, but with so many limitations and exceptions, that the result of the whole amounts very much to what I venture to assert (*q*). Thus, for instance, many state, that the presumption falls to the ground, when the Possession had only been proved to exist ten years previously; others say more correctly, an old Possession affords less probability than a recent one, and, therefore, the whole must be left to the decision of the Judge (*r*). They were more united on the point, that if Possession had been established at two different periods, a presumption arose as to its continuance during the interval, and this rule has been introduced into the French code (*s*).

(*p*) Glossa in L. 16, C. *de probat.*

(*q*) This point has been discussed thoroughly by Alciatus, De præsumptionibus, req. 2, præs. 21, and Mascard, De Probationibus, vol. 1; Conclus. 170, vol. 3, concl. 1202.

(*r*) Mascard. Cor. cit. concl. 170, No. 22-3. This also is the true meaning of the passage, C. 9,

X. *de prob.* &c., § 51.

(*s*) Code Civil, art. 22, 34. Malville, T. 4, pp. 366, 367, objects to the rule *olim possessor, hodie possessor,* but mentions as the general doctrine, that Possession may last ten years *solo animo,* which is as much as to say, that after ten years no such presumption arises.

SECTION XXXVIII.

POSSESSORY INTERDICTS.— *Continued.*

The notion of possessory Interdicts has now been completely defined; but there is still an objection to be answered,
which is of the greatest importance to the whole discussion.
Most modern practitioners, namely, have, more or less distinctly, treated Interdicts as *provisional vindications,* i. e., as
provisional remedies in reference to property (*a*): this view
shall be now examined.

Provisional remedies are those which only decide the controversy for the time, as another (peremptory) inquiry and
decision may be made. Thus, for instance, in the *missio
heredis scripti* on an apparently valid will, the hereditary
right of the plaintiff is specially inquired into and examined;
but the same point may be afterwards again inquired into in
the *hereditatis petitio.* These two inquiries, therefore, stand
to each other in like relation, as a suit before a Court of
original jurisdiction, and before a Court of Appeal.

If, then, possessory suits are to be considered in fact as
such provisional remedies in reference to property, the law
as to these suits must be thus conceived; whoever possesses
is to be looked upon, for the time, on a general presumption, as
owner, but this decision on the provisional vindication (of
the *possessorii*) may be either reversed or confirmed in a

(*a*) See above, § 2, and for
the origin of this doctrine, see
Bartolus and Cujacius, § 11.
The opposition between *petitorius*
and *possessorius* is usually regarded in this view. Perhaps,
amongst others, the passage of
Isidore has led to this doctrine,
wherein Interdicts generally are
defined to be provisional deci-

sions: Orig. V. 25, in Gothofred,
p. 932. "Interdictum est, quod
a judice non in perpetuum, sed
pro reformando momento ad tempus interim dicitur: salva pro-
positione actionis ejus." So also
Interpr. Goth. in Paul, V. 6, § 1,
from which the passage of Isidore
may have been taken.

subsequent suit (of the *petitiorii*). That this is an incorrect
view, as the right of Interdicts depends on grounds which
have no reference whatever to property, is a proposition
which was first of all assumed at the commencement of this
treatise (§. 2), and subsequently was completely established,
by its being proved that the right of Interdicts was considered by the Romans as the only right belonging to mere
Possession (§ 7), and that the acquisition of Possession itself
was of such a nature that Possession did not stand in connection with property, or with any other right (Book 2,
particularly §. 28). It is now necessary to remove the
grounds of the above error, which, as it concerns Interdicts
only, could not be touched on before.

Interdicta retinendæ possessionis are stated to be necessary
preliminaries of vindication, it is even said, that the latter
was the occasion of their introduction (*b*); in another passage, the owner is advised always to use an Interdict where
possible, and not vindication (*c*). But this preliminary relation is evidently very different from a provisional remedy,
because the essence of the latter (namely, the inquiry into
the same legal question), is quite unimportant in the former,
so that even a civil suit may serve as a preliminary to a criminal inquiry. Besides, further; the above preliminary relation to
vindication may occur in several other actions (for instance,
on contracts), and there is no doubt, that every lawyer would
advise an owner, who besides his vindication had a remedy
on his contract, to select the latter, although it undoubtedly
is not a provisional vindication. Lastly, and chiefly, this
preliminary relation is in itself quite accidental as respects
Interdicts; for as the right to Interdicts is completely established on simple Possession, they undoubtedly may be
made use of even where neither of the contesting parties
claims the property.

(*b*) L. 1, § 2, 3, *uti possidetis*   Festus, *v. possessio* (Gothofred,
(§ 4, I. *de interdictis*) ; L. 35, *de*   p. 372), and Simplicius in Goe-
poss.   sius, p. 79.
    (*c*) L. 24, *de rei vind.* ; Comp.

Therefore, although the use of Interdicts may be very frequent in practice as preliminary to vindication (*d*), still this circumstance is wholly accidental, and it cannot be relied upon at all, when the question turns upon the definition of the juridical nature of such Interdicts (*e*). This last observation is chiefly established by a passage of Ulpian, already frequently quoted in this treatise (*f*). For the question being whether the possessor, by making use of vindication, would lose his Possession, and, consequently,

(*d*) Ulpian, L. 1, § 2, 3, *uti poss.* assigns this as the reason for introducing the *int. retinendæ possessionis*, because without such interdict the state of Possession during a suit upon property could not be determined. Now indeed, as Ulpian says, in every suit as to the property, it must be inquired in the first instance, which of the two parties is to be considered as plaintiff, (*petitor*), which as defendant (*possessor*); but there already existed, from the earliest period, a particular form of procedure for this inquiry, viz. the *manus consertæ*, which was used even so late as Aullus Gellius, (Noct. Att. XX. 10, "verba.... quæ.... dici *nunc quoque* apud Prætorem solent"), and therefore long after the introduction of Interdicts. Now, there were indeed cases in which the complaint was *in rem* without Roman vindication, namely, when a *peregrinus* was a party, when lands in the provinces were in question, and in the *publiciana actio*. But the two first cases did not come within the interdict of the *prætor urbanus*, and as to the *publiciana actio*, it must be first proved that it is older than

the Edict. But there appears to me, generally, such a close resemblance of possessory interdicts amongst themselves in their forms and legal principles, that it seems rash to attribute to them such different origins and various objects. The most decisive ground against Ulpian, from the words of the Edict itself, can be best established in the following chapter. Albert, Ueber das *int. uti possidetis*, § 127, opposes the above explanation of the passage in Ulpian, and considers § 3 as a wholly unconnected sentence with § 2; both paragraphs, however, appear to me to be so inseparably connected in their language, that § 3 can only be looked on as the continuation and development of § 2.

(*e*) Least of all can I admit that the Interdict assumes a different character, according as it is used as a preliminary to vindication, or for other purposes. By this latter view, which Albert, Ueber das *int. uti poss.* § 131, puts forward, there would be two different Interdicts *uti poss.*

(*f*) L. 12, § 1, *de poss.* See *ante*, § 6, and more especially p. 270.

his *interdictum uti possidetis :* it was answered in the negative. Now had the *int. uti possidetis* been, not merely
casually and in the generality of cases, but, in its very essence,
a preliminary to vindication, *i. e.*, the commencement of a
vindication suit, that would have been the most conclusive
ground for considering the actual employment of vindication
as a renunciation of the Interdict; for this reason, Ulpian
prefaces his decision of the question by the remark, that the
contest as to property, and the contest as to Possession, were,
in their nature, independent of each other, from which he
draws the conclusion, that Interdicts were not renounced by
the use of a vindication (*g*):

"*Nihil commune habet proprietas cum possessione: et
ideo* non denegatur ei interdictum uti possidetis, qui cæpit
rem vindicare; non enim videtur possessioni renuntiasse,
qui rem vindicavit."

Thus, possessory Interdicts are suits which are founded on
mere Possession (p. 289), and this notion is established by
the proof that they stand in no necessary connection with
vindication. But it is not every violation of Possession generally, but a violation in a definite form, which gives a possessor the right of Interdicts, and the several Interdicts are
distinguished from one another according to these forms of
disturbance. For all Interdicts are founded *either* on violence,
or clandestinicity, *or* abuse of a *precarium;* but violence
may amount either to a disturbance, or to a deprivation, of
Possession; and, again, for a mere disturbance there are
different Interdicts, according as land, or a moveable, may
be the object of Possession. Therefore we have to treat
here of the following Interdicts:

    I. Interdicta retinendæ possessionis.

        1st. In general, §. 39.

        2nd. *Uti possidetis,* §. 40.

        3rd. *Utrubi,* §. 41.

(*g*) Undoubtedly the renunciation might be established on
another ground (p. 270), which Ulpian does not expressly mention here.

II. Interdictum de violenta possessione, §. 42.
III. Interdictum de clandestina possessione, §. 43.
IV. Interdictum de precaria possessione, §. 44.
V. Constitutions of the Emperors on possessory Inter-
dicts, §. 45.

———

SECTION XXXIX.

INTERDICTA RETINENDÆ POSSESSIONIS.

Verginii de Boccatüs a Cingulo, Ic. Romani, Tract.
de int. uti poss. s. de manutenen. in poss.
Colon. 1581–8, also in Tract. Tom. III., p. 2,
Ven. 1584 f.
(All *interdicta retinendæ possessionis* (even those for
quasi *possessio*) are jumbled together in this work, which is
ill done and useless).

———

The *interdicta retinendæ poss.* protect the person in
possession against all violent attacks upon his Possession.
To assist us in stating the above proposition more
precisely, it is necessary to mention the different cases, in
which these Interdicts may be used in practice:
1st. When the possessor has sustained damage by the
disturbance of the Possession, for which he seeks compensation.
2nd. When a future disturbance of the Possession is
dreaded, against which the possessor wishes to protect
himself.
3rd. When the proceedings in a suit respecting property
are to be governed by a previous inquiry as to the state of
Possession, whether or not any violent disturbance of the
Possession shall have taken place, or be merely anticipated.
In all these cases the above Interdicts were unquestionably
available. It is just as clear that exactly the *same* Interdict

was applicable to all these different cases, and that the *same* passage in the edict is the source from which all sprung. How then are these different cases logically and historically connected with the employment of the *same* Interdict.

The first case is expressly mentioned in the Edict, and indeed the limitation for the employment of the Interdict has no meaning in any other case (*a*). There is also, no doubt, that an *obligatio ex maleficio* lay at the bottom of this case.

The second case also is mentioned in the edict (*b*), and this too can be reduced to an *obligatio ex maleficio*, except that the *maleficium* must not be looked upon as committed, but merely as inchoate. For it is evident, that the (anticipated) *maleficium* is the only ground of the Interdict in this case, and that therein *no* other right comes into play. So that thus, this case also does not contradict the classification adopted above (§. 6). The first and second case coincide in this, that they protect the *existing* possessor against disturbance, so that the principal question is whether the plaintiff is possessor. On the other hand, the distinction between them is not essential, juridically considered, so that their juxta position in the edict cannot be urged as an objection.

The second case especially will frequently occur in a suit as to property, when it is desired to guard against this sort of intrusion during the progress of the suit. But this must not be confounded with the third case. For the actual state of the Possession *may* be quite clear at the time, and yet a violation of it may be dreaded from an active opponent; in such case the Interdict would be needed, on occasion, it is true, of the *rei vindicatio*, but on no account for the purpose of regulating the proceedings of the suit (No. 3), but merely to prevent violence (No. 2). But the state of Possession may also be at the same time a matter of doubt,

---

(*a*) "Neque pluris quam quanti res erit intra annum, quo primum experiendi potestas fuerit, agere permittam."

(*b*) "Uti possidetis . . . . . quominus ita possideatis vim fieri veto."

and then it must be at once decided upon, according to the above given rule.

' It now becomes easy to explain the third case also. In every suit as to property, the state of the Possession must be first of all determined if it is a matter in controversy. For this purpose, the ceremony of the *manus consertæ* was introduced into the ancient law in respect to *vindicatio*. But the great difficulty then was that the Prætor must always decide the matter himself without a *Judex*, although the inquiry might be a very complicated one. Consequently this form was not used in many real actions (see *ante*, p. 299) (*c*). And on the other hand a ready expedient presented itself. For if in such case, any hostile proceedings were dreaded at the time of action brought, an Interdict was made use of, which in itself raised exactly the same question that had to be decided as to the property, and for this purpose not only a *judex* was introduced, but also the proceeding was not restricted to the *vindicatio ex jure Quiritium*. It then became usual to treat every case of contest as to the Possession, as if hostile proceedings were anticipated, so that by aid of this fiction, the *interdictum retinendæ possessionis* became the juridical form, which completely supplied all the above wants.

But this fiction was quite unimportant, as it did not at all influence the result of the preliminary inquiry in essentials, and consequently it worked no injury to either party. In this manner the third of the above mentioned cases of *interdicta retinendæ possessionis* was introduced. This case was not comprised by the words of the Edict itself, for the *vim fieri veto* cannot be brought to bear upon it (*d*), but it

(*c*) The form ceased finally as a rule after the abolition of the *legis actiones*, and only continued as a sort of exception in proceedings for contumacy. (Add. to 6th ed.)

(*d*) As this case is not even mentioned in the terms of the Edict, it is impossible that it can have given rise to the Interdict, which shews that the historical remark of Ulpian (p. 299, n. (*d*)), is wholly groundless. It appears presumptuous to contradict a Roman jurist on such a point; but, *first*, the Edict is of greater

was brought within the province of the Edict by a wholly innocent fiction. By means of this fiction, the third case becomes, in a theoretical view, quite similar to the second, and therefore affords no more ground than the latter for an objection to the classification of these Interdicts given above (§ 6). Now as to the conditions for the employment of the *int. ret. poss.*

The *first* condition, for this as for every other possessory Interdict (pp. 56-58) is, that Possession should have been actually acquired; not indeed *civilis* possessio, but still juridical *possessio* as opposed to the natural relation of detention (*e*). The *second* condition is a *forcible* disturbance (*f*), which is to be understood thus. The term *vis* is applied generally to every act, which takes place against the will of another. Therefore in the Int. *quod vi aut clam* it is necessary, that this will should be known in fact to the party committing the act, or that he himself should have prevented its being so made known to him (*g*). But this repugnance of the will to any disturbance is contained in the very fact of Possession, so long as the disturbance is not specially permitted (*h*). Therefore in the meaning of

---

authority than Ulpian, *i. e.* I would rather assume that Ulpian is incorrect in an historical explanation, than· that the Edict means to say something different to what it aotually does say. Besides, the confusion here is comparatively slight, for it will be readily remarked that the *third* case, which in an historical point of view, and as part of the system is so subordinate, is, when practically considered, far the most important and most frequent. Added to which, Ulpian lived many hundred years after the Interdict was introduced; secondly, we don't know how much of the passage of Ulpian was left

out, or added, by the compilers; thirdly, there are many similar cases, where the historical explanations of the old Jurists are demonstrably incorrect.

(*e*) On this point see Klepe, Diss. de Nat. et ind. possessionis, ad int. uti poss. et utrubi necess. Lips. 1794. (See Introduction, No. 34). The objections to this proposition may be best answered as each Interdict of the class comes in question.

(*f*) "Vim fieri veto," L. 1, *pr. uti poss.*; L. 1, *pr. utrubi.*

(*g*) L. 1, § 5, 7; L. 20, pr. § 1, *quod vi*; L. 73, § 2, *de Reg. Jur.*

(*h*) L. 5, *de serv. præd. urb.*

this Interdict, violence is present, whenever our free user of the subject is impeded, even if this take place by means of the property belonging to a neighbour, for instance, by an adjoining wall (*i*); for although such party may not have erected it, and perhaps even knows nothing about it, still he possesses the erection in such manner as to incommode me, and this amounts to the notion of violence. These Interdicts therefore are here exactly parallel to negative suits, and this parrallelism is expressly recognized (*j*). In what manner this forcible disturbance may be considered, either as an act done, or as an act anticipated, or lastly as a mere fiction, has been already explained. *Thirdly*, the forcible disturbance of the Possession must not have put an end to the Possession itself, and this condition clearly appears by the very name (*retinendæ* possessionis) of this class of possessory Interdicts (*k*). A more detailed account of this · merely negative condition has been already presented in the third book of this work, where all the cases generally were described, in which Possession is to be considered as lost. It need not be stated that the condition only arises in the case of a bygone disturbance of Possession, in which case the possessor may acquire his right to the Interdict in two modes: first, by the obstruction offered to his own dealing at will with the subject (*l*): second, by the other party exercising acts of Possession, without having driven him out of Possession (*m*).

(*i*) L. 14, § 1; L. 17, *pr. si serv.*

(*j*) L. 8, § 5, *si serv.* The whole of this passage has been introduced into the text in the 6th edition, and is owing to a communication from Hollweg.

(*k*) The Gloss terms this kind of violence "vis *inquietativa*," and opposes it to "vis *expulsiva*," Gl. in § 4, I. *de interd.* et in L. 1, § 9, *uti* poss.

(*l*) Examples; the possessor is prevented from cultivating his land, L. 3, § 4, *uti poss.*, or from erecting or altering a building, L. 3, § 2, 3, *uti poss.* L. 52, § 1, *de poss.* L. 12, *comm. div.*, or from digging up his treasure in another person's land, L. 15, *ad exhibendam.*

(*m*) L. 11, *de vi.* " *Vim* facit, qui non sinit possidentem eo, quod possidebat, uti arbitrio suo; sive

x

Any one may be a defendant, to whom we can bring
home the disturbance, consequently, amongst others, our
own agent for the Possession; for instance, the hirer of our
house, who wishes to build or pull down anything contrary
to the will of his landlord. Doubt might be entertained on
this point, because the latter might bring his *actio locati;*
but this only shows that he would have the choice of two
suits. He would have even, in this case, the choice of a
third remedy, by which analogy our statement as to possessory Interdicts is again confirmed. So also in cases
where the tenant ousts his landlord from the Possession, the
latter unquestionably has his choice between the *actio locati*
and the *int. de vi* (*n*).

The object of these Interdicts is threefold:

1st. In the case of a disturbance—Recovery of damages.

2nd. In the case of a threatened disturbance (and this
may also be presumed from a preceding disturbance, so
that both objects may coincide).—Prevention of the dreaded
unlawful act. Whether such act can be prevented by the
mere decree of the Judge, or whether actual execution of
such decree is necessary, or whether quiet enjoyment is to
be secured by bail, are questions quite beside the general
object of these Interdicts.

3rd. In the user of these Interdicts in a suit on property
—Decision of the question as to which of the two parties
actually has the present Possession. This object may also
coincide with the two preceding.

For the carrying out of these Interdicts there is still
another rule established, which must be here explained.

inserendo, sive fodiendo, sive
arando, sive quid ædificando, sive
quid omnino faciendo, *per quod
liberam possessionem adversarii
non relinquit.*" It appears most
clearly, as well from the last
words as from the first, ("vim
facit" in reference to vim *fieri
veto*), that a mere disturbance of
Possession, not an actual ouster,
is spoken of; Donellus XV. 33,
p. 804. Many jurists have been
induced by the place in which
this passage is inserted (tit. ff. *de
vi*) to refer it to the interdictum
de vi.

(*n*) Namely, the Int. *quod vi
aut clam.* L. 25, § 5, *locati.*

These Interdicts are considered as *duplicia* (*o*), or *mixtæ actiones* (*p*), and thereby two consequences follow; first, either party may institute the suit, or come forward as plaintiff (*q*); second, both parties enjoy the same privileges in the proceedings, and are not, as in most suits, opposed to one another by distinct functions (*r*). The most important practical consequence of this rule is that the plaintiff as well as the defendant may be *condemned* (*s*). This may be

(*o*) If the *interdicta retinendæ possessionis* are to be considered as essentially the preliminary steps in vindication (§ 38), we must consider this third, as the main object, and the two first as merely subordinate, and this is what most of the defenders of that view in fact assert. Lately, however, Wiederhold has gone so far, as wholly to deny every other object, except that of regulating a suit claiming property. See *ante*, the addition at the end of § 11. (Add. to 6th ed.)

(*p*) From a lately discovered fragment of Ulpian, it has been made clear that the Romans used the technical term *duplex* in another and wholly different sense, viz. in reference to such Interdicts as might be, according to circumstances, either *recuperendæ* or *adipiscendæ possessionis*, &c.; and from this newly disclosed signification we are now first enabled to understand the hitherto inexplicable passage, L. 2, § 3, *de interd.* Cf. Rudorff, Zeitschrift f. geschichtl. Rechtsw. B. 9, ss. 11, 18. (Add to 6th ed.)

(*q*) For both interdicts; Gaius, Lib. 4, § 160; Lib. 37, § 1, de O. et A.; Lib. 7, I. *de interd.* For

the *int. uti possidetis* only, L. 2, pr. de interd.; L. 3, § 1, *uti poss.*

(*r*) In my two first editions (pp. 346, 406) I was wrong in denying this proposition, on the ground that the possessor only could succeed. But in *rei vindicatio* also, the owner only can succeed, still the non-owner may institute the suit, because the result above demonstrates which of the two is owner. Just so with our Interdicts in reference to Possession. The distinction however is, that in suits on property, a continuing qualification ascertained beforehand, is prescribed as the condition for a plaintiff, viz. non-possession; no such qualification is required in the *int. retinendæ possessionis*, and therefore they are called *duplicia*. Besides, it is well known that partition suits are *duplices*; the *actio confessoria* and *actio negatoria* are not so, but still they have this in common with the above, that in both of them either party may sue as plaintiff.

(*s*) § 7, I. de interd. "duplicia vocantur, quia *par utriusque litigatoris in his conditio est*, nec quisquam præcipue reus vel actor intelligitur; sed unus quisque *tam*

x 2

conceived in two ways; first, where the defendant and not the plaintiff, has in fact the Possession, and in this case there is no doubt that the defendant, who might himself have sued as plaintiff (*t*), may recover in the suit, just as if he had brought it himself: second, it may be conceived that the plaintiff has the Possession in fact, but still that he must have judgment against him on the ground of the defendant's exceptions. The defendant in this case could not have sued as plaintiff, and yet the Possession must be assigned to him (*u*), and this apparent inconsistency may easily be justified. For if, as in the case assumed, the plaintiff fails in his proofs, the Court must either give no decision on the Possession, or constitute the defendant possessor. But by the first course it would be left open to either party to exercise violence against the other at pleasure; now as this never could be allowed to be the result of a judicial decree, nothing but the second course remains, *i. e.*

rei, quam actoris partes sustinet." Gaius, lib. 4, § 160. Still clearer is L. 10, *fin. regund.* "Judicium comm. div. fam. ercisc., fin. reg. tate est, ut in eo *singulæ personæ duplex jus habeant;* agentis, et eo cum quo agetur."

(*t*) In most instances this is the defendant's case, and the question in dispute; and this explains the form " *uti possidetis*," i. e. "whichsoever of you two, who both claim the Possession, *does in fact possess.*" The glossators have started many suggestions as to this formula, amongst others, that the Prætor out of politeness addressed the possessor in the second person plural. Another explanation has very important results; for it refers " uti *possidetis* " to the possessio plurium in solidum, which latter therefore is proved partly

as a general rule, and secondly, is admitted only in the case of thé int. *uti possidetis;* since, in this Interdict the *dejectus* also might nevertheless come forward as possessor. (See *post,* p. 311). Glossa in rubr. Tit. C. *uti poss.;* Azo in Summa, h. t. No. 19, et in Lecturâ hoc tit. p. 622 ; Placentin in Summa, h. t. p. 376-7 ; Donellus in Cod. h. t. No. 6, 7, 8, p. 288-9. (The objection, which Albert, Ueber das Int. uti poss. § 116—121, has lately brought against the view in the text, appears to me to be ill-founded).

(*u*) That this was so, follows not only from the notion of the int. *duplex,* but also from L. 3, *pr. uti poss.* "Si *a me possides, superior sum interdicto,*" i. e. I shall gain the suit, which can't be imagined in any other way.

the Interdict must be considered as *duplex*, and the defend-ant must be put in possession, although he never could succeed as plaintiff on this Interdict (*v*).

At the same time however, this similarity of condition between the parties, as respects procedure, must not be extended too far. For in reference to the *onus probandi* the same rules prevail as in all other suits, and on this subject that party is undoubtedly to be looked upon as plaintiff who first comes to the Court (*w*). Now the first rule as to evidence is that which has been laid down above, (p. 291), as to possessory suits generally. But then there arises the following special point, if the defendant admits the plaintiff's Possession generally, but asserts a joint Possession, (p. 113), on whom does the burthen of proof fall. This might be looked upon as an exceptional case, and for this reason the *onus* might be cast on the de-fendant; I think, however, that it does not shift the burthen from the plaintiff. For, in fact, the plaintiff asserts his Possession as to every portion of the subject, as to part this is admitted, but as to other parts it is denied; it is therefore a partial negative litis contestation, which calls upon the plaintiff for evidence. In support of this it may be added that otherwise, in every case of undoubted joint Possession, either party might improperly sue, and so cast the burthen of proof on his opponent as the defendant (*x*).

(*v*) In most cases, it is true, he might avail himself of *another* In-terdict, as plaintiff; for instance, the int. *de vi*, where he had been ousted from his possession by force, and the ejecting party had then brought an Interdict *uti pos-sidetis* against him, which he had answered by an exception, L. 1, § 5, *uti poss.*

(*w*) L. 2, § 1, *comm. div.*; L. 13, *de jud.* Both these passages, it is true, refer to partition suits, but the analogy of the latter must apply to our Interdicts also.

(*x*) This concluding remark was introduced into the 4th edi-tion.

310

SECTION XL.

INTERDICTUM UTI POSSIDETIS.

Special Sources for the *interdictum uti possidetis.*
§ 4, I., *de interd.*
Digest Lib. 43, tit. 17.　} See the Introduction.
Cod. lib. 8, tit. 6.
Carl Albert Ueber das Interdictum uti possidetis of the
Romans, Halle, 1824, 8vo., (a profound and valuable
work).
Wiederhold, Das Interdictum uti possidetis, and die
Novi Operis Nuntiatio, Hanau, 1831, 8vo. (See
ante, add. to conclusion of § 10).

The rules which have been laid down generally in the
last section as to the Int. *retinendæ possessionis,* have now to
be applied to the possession of land, and consequently to
the Int. *uti possidetis* (*a*).
The general conditions of this Interdict are; first,
simple Possession; secondly, a forcible disturbance; and
thirdly, a disturbance of such a nature that it does not put
an end to the Possession. The first and third of these
conditions have been disputed in the application of the
Interdict *uti possidetis.* As respects the first point, Cuperus
requires that the *possessio* should be *civilis* also, in order
to give rise to the Interdict, this position is a simple consequence of his incorrect notion of *civilis* possessio, and

---

(*a*) The passage from the Edict
is to be found in L. 1, *pr. uti possidetis,* and with slightly varying
expressions; in Festus *v. posses-*
sio apud Gothofred, p. m. 372.
Compare the remark *ante,* at the
end of § 13.

therefore is answered by the refutation of the latter. But Cuperus cites a special proof of his position as to this Interdict, and this proof comes in question now. Ulpian, namely, says in a well known passage, that in the Int. *unde vi* the *possessio* need not necessarily be *civilis*, consequently, argues Cuperus, it must always be so in the Interdict *uti possidetis* (*b*). The third condition that the plaintiff must still be the actual possessor, is so clearly laid down as to this very Int. *uti possidetis* (*c*), that it is the last case as to which any doubt should have arisen. The *first* ground for this doubt is founded on the erroneous explanation of *civilis* possessio as a possessio quæ animo *retinetur* (pp. 98-9), and p. 307); this mode of continuing Possession is open to a *dejectus* also, consequently such party may have his choice between the Int. *de vi* (on account of his lost *naturalis* possessio), and *uti possidetis* (on account of his continuing *civilis* possessio) (*d*). A *second* ground lies in the incorrect explanation of L. 11 *de vi* (p. 305): in this passage the Int. *de vi* is permitted on a simple disturbance of Possession, consequently the *dejectus* must, conversely, also be allowed to use the Int. *uti possidetis*. Thirdly, say some, as the *dejectus* may undoubtedly succeed in the cause as defendant, it follows that he may also have the Interdict as a plaintiff (*e*): this is an instance of the resemblance between the parties in an interdictum *duplex*, being carried out too

(*b*) De Nat. Poss. P. 2, c. 8, and in L. 1, § 9, *de vi*, scribit Ulpianus de Interdicto *unde vi, Nam et naturalis possessio* ad hoc Interdictum pertinet ; aperto indicio, eam non pertinere ad Interdictum uti possidetis, aut Utrubi."

(*c*) L. 1, § 4, *uti possidetis.* ".... interdictum..... uti possidetis.... redditur, ne vis fiat ei, *qui possidet*.... hoc interdictum tuetur, *ne amittatur possessio*, de-

nique Prætor *possidenti* vim fieri vetat," &c.

(*d*) Azo in Summa Cod. *tit. uti poss.* Nos. 16, 17, p. 145. Menoch. De Retinend. Poss. rem. 3, Nos. 35, 36, 37. Giphanius, Antinom. Lib. 4, Disp. 48, pp. 24—30.

(*e*) Both these last grounds are to be found together in Busius, Subtit.-Jur. Lib. 6, c. 8; and Giphanius, loc. cit. (See the last note).

far, against which error warning has already been given, (p. 309).

The results of this Interdict coincide entirely with what has been above laid down generally as to the *Int. retinendæ possessionis.* The first result then, is, to prevent any act by which the Possession may be disturbed. This end is usually fully attained by the mere order of the Court forbidding the disturbance; independent of which, there is no doubt that this decree, like all others, must be carried into execution, and such execution may consist in the Court, amongst other things, requiring security from the party decreed against, from whom disturbance of the Possession is apprehended. The right therefore of obtaining such security is comprised in the general right of execution, and requires no positive proof here, although such proof has been brought forward simply by aid of an incorrect interpretation (*f*). For a previous disturbance of Possession, the

(*f*) L. *un.* C. *uti possidetis.* "Ut possidetis fundum, de quo agitur, cum ab altero nec vi, nec clam, nec precario possidetis, Rector provinciæ vim fieri prohibebit: ac *satisdationis,* vel *transferendæ possessionis* Edicti perpetui forma servata, de proprietate cognoscet." For either, it has been said, the defendant is not in possession, and then he must give security; or he is in possession, and then the Possession is taken from him by this Interdict. (See above, p. 311). Duarenus in *tit. uti poss.* et in Disp. Anniv. I. 21, Opp. p. 944 and 386. But all that refers to the Interdict ends with the words "*vim fieri prohibuit;*" what follows has reference to vindication, in which it was a universal rule that the defendant should

either give security *de judicato,* or give up Possession, (*satis dationis,* vel *transferendæ possessionis*), which rule was afterwards repealed. As to the old law, see Gaius, IV. 91, as to the later, § 2, I. *de satisd.* The correct explanation is to be found in Glossa in L. *cit.;* Azo in Summa Cod. hoc. tit. No. 23; Baro in Manual in Dig. pp. 6, 184; Cujacius in Paulum I. 11, § 1 (a sharp attack on Duarenus); Donellus in Cod. h. tit. n. 25—28, (who nevertheless introduces other errors into his interpretation), but better than all, in C. F. Conradi in Diss. Cautio de non ampl. turb. in jud. poss. usu fori recepta, Helmst. 1737; where, besides the interpretation of this passage, the subject of security generally is

possessor recovered damages, and in the assessment of such damages, consideration was paid as to what the possessor had actually lost, or had been prevented from acquiring, by the disturbance (*g*).

So much for the conditions and for the operation of these Interdicts generally. But there were certain special cases excepted, in which the Interdict was either disallowed altogether, or allowed only in part: the exceptions of the defendant, which apply to these cases, have now then to be stated. The first of these exceptions relates to the mode in which the Possession of the plaintiff arose; if this Possession itself commenced by violence, or clandestinely, or by a *precarium*, the defendant would succeed in the suit, and not the plaintiff (*h*): still this illegal act must have taken place between the actual parties to the suit; consequently the exception did not avail, if the *dejectio*, &c., &c., had been effected, either by the *auctor* of the plaintiff (*i*), or against any other person than the defendant (*j*). The ground of the above exception consisted wholly in this, that the defendant might simultaneously maintain his Int. *recuperandæ* possessionis (*k*); instead then of deciding against the defendant, who certainly was

excellently treated. See a late article of Rudorff's in the Zeitschrift fuer geschichtl. Rechtsw. B. 9, s. 27, who has shewn the connection between the passages in the lately discovered Sources and this passage.

(*g*) L. 3, § 11, *uti possidetis.*

(*h*) L. 1, *pr.* § 5; L. 3, *pr. uti. poss.* (See above, p. 122).

(*i*) L. 3, § 10, *uti poss.* "Non videor vi possidere, qui ab eo, quem scirem vi in possessione esse, fundum accipiam."

(*j*) L. 1, § 9. "…. Ut, si quis possidet vi, aut clam, aut precario, si quidem ab alio : prosit ei

possessio : *si vero ab adversario suo*, non debet eum propter hoc, quod ab eo possidet, vincere," cf. L. 2, *eod.* ; L. 53, *de poss.* ; § 4, I. *de interd.* ; L. 17, *de prec.*

(*k*) I said, in the 5th edition, that this would be so *in most cases*, and I founded that expression on the view I then entertained, that *clandestina possessio* required a different and more extensive signification with an exception than with an Interdict. The correction of this view is contained in the addition to § 43. (Add. to 6th ed.)

not possessor, in the Int. *uti possidetis*, and then leaving
him to succeed in another suit, to shorten proceedings
and avoid circuity of action, the plaintiff was cast, and
then on a special ground (p. 311), the Possession was given
over to the defendant. The second exception relates to the
limitation of time for the Interdict. For if a year had expired after the Possession had been disturbed, no use could
be made of this Interdict for the recovery of damages (*l*);
for then by the loss of the possessor the disturber would at
the same time have succeeded (*m*). No other exceptions
besides the above named can be admitted (*n*).

SECTION XLI.

INTERDICTUM UTRUBI.

Special Sources for the *Interdictum utrubi.*
§. 4, I. de interd.
Digest, lib. 43, tit. 31.   } See the Introduction.
Cod. Theodos., lib. 4, tit. 23.

As land was protected by the Interdict *uti possidetis*,
so also were moveables by the Interdict *utrubi*, although

(*l*) L. 1, *pr. uti possidetis.* "Intra annum, quo primum experi-
undi potestas fuerit, agere permittam."

(*m*). L. 4, *de interd.* "Ex quibus causis annua interdicta sunt,
ex his *de eo, quod ad eum, cum
quo agitur, pervenit,* post annum
judicium dandum Sabinus respondit."

(*n*) Not, for instance, the exceptio possessionis *nullæ,* which
Albert, § 94, contends for. This,
in fact, only amounts to a negative
litis-contestation, the nature of
which is in no way altered, whether the defendant limit himself
to a simple denial, or claim for
himself the Possession. (Add. to
5th ed.)

the wording of the latter in the edict mentioned slaves
only (a).

The first condition for this, as for the Int. *uti possidetis*,
was juridical Possession, without distinction whether it was
civilis possessio or not (b). But Possession simply was,
however, not in itself sufficient, as the Possession must have
been exercised during the current year for a longer period
than that of the adversary (c); in this period, the Possession
of the vendor, &c. was naturally included, so that in this
case, as with Usucaption, and the limitation of many other
suits, the *accessio* possessionis was of great importance (d).
The more modern law repealed this limitation, and completely assimilated the Int. *utrubi* to the Int. *uti possidetis* (e) without doubt, this alteration may be ascribed to
Justinian, and the passage of Ulpian wherein it occurs (f)
is an interpolation, for no trace of the innovation is to be
found in Paulus (g), or in Gaius (h), or in the constitution of
Diocletian (i). The second condition is a forcible attack

(a) L. 1, *pr.* § 1, *de utrubi.*
" Prætor ait, *utrubi hic homo, quo
de agitur, majore parte hujusce anni fuit: quo minus is eum ducat,
vim fieri veto.* Hoc interdictum
de possessione *rerum mobilium* locum habet." Gaius, Lib. 4, §
149, 150.

(b) Cuperus II. 8, affirms the
contrary in this case also : one of
his reasons has already been cited
on the Int. *uti possidetis* (p. 311):
a second reason is founded on L.
46, *de don. int. vir et ux.*, which
passage has been already explained.

(c) The *major pars* anni therefore is to be taken relatively. L.
156, de verb. sign. Gaius, Lib. 4,
§ 152.

(d) Cuperus, II. 8, in part following Schulting, makes the ap-
posite remark, that L. 46, *de don.*

int. vir et ux. (see above, p. 48),
L. 13, *de poss.* and L. 1, *de utrubi*,
are all connected together as
being extracts from the same
work, and therefore, probably,
accessio possessionis was treated
of on occasion of this edict. See
also L. 14, § 3, *de div. temp. præs.*
(Klepe, De Nat. et Ind. Poss. p.
27) ; L. 11, *de adq. rer. dom.* (see
ante, p. 267 and p. 268) ; lastly,
Gaius, Lib. 4, § 151.
(e) § 4, I. *de Int.*
(f) L. 1, § 1, *de utrubi.*
(g) Rec. Sent. V. 6, § 1. "..
.. In altero vero (si in Int. utrubi)
potior est, qui majore parte anni
retrorsum numerati.... possedit."
(h) Gaius, Lib. 4, § 150.
(i) Fragmenta Vaticana, §
293. A passage of Paulus, Fragm.
Vat. § 311, refers to the same
point, only less expressly. Pos-

on the Possession, as to which nothing special occurs for remark. Lastly, the Possession must be still continuing, and, therefore, must not have been put an end to by the disturbance. In Justinian's code this proposition does not admit of doubt, and all that has been said thereupon above, with reference to the Int. *uti possidetis,* might be repeated here. But how was it with the older law, before the uniformity of the two Interdicts? Was it then also a *pure* Int. retinendæ possessiones, *i. e.,* was a *present* Possession also necessary besides *possessio majoris partis anni,* or was the fact of present Possession immaterial? I am now of opinion that the latter is the correct view, although on quite different grounds to those generally adduced in its support. For,it has been usual to rely on the following passages, which, taken altogether, prove nothing:

1. L. 3, §. 5, *ad exhibendum.*

" Sed et si quis *interdicturus, rem exhiberi desideret,* audietur."

2. L. 3, §. 12, *ad exhibendum (j).*

" Pomponius scribit, ejusdem hominis recte plures ad exhibendum agere posse: forte, si homo primi sit, secundi in eo ususfructus sit, tertius *possessionem suam contendat,* quartus pigneratus sibi eum adfirmet. Omnibus igitur ad exhibendum actio competit: quia omnium interest exhiberi hominem."

Both these passages, it is said, shew that the Int. *utrubi* was preceded by an *actio ad exhibendum,* therefore the former must have lain for a lost Possession. But, *first,* it is not at all necessary to refer these passages to the Int. *utrubi,* and, *secondly,* the conclusion from such reference is incorrect. First, because § 5 may be just as well applied to any

---

sibly also L. 11, § 13, *de act. emti vend.,* which at all events presents the clearest meaning in reference to the old Int. utrubi. (Add. to 6th ed.)

(*j*) Both passages are brought forward by A. Pagenstecher, Admonitor, ad Pandect. Lib. 43, Tit. 31, ed. Goning, 1715, 8vo, p. 775, and before him by Cujacius, Obs. V. 23, and Paratit. in Dig. tit. utrubi.

Int. *adipiscendæ* possessionis, and §. 12 does not assume that any suit as to the *possessio* is necessary: and, indeed, from other passages it is clear, that the *actio ad exhibendum* may be employed without reference to another suit, provided only that *justa causa* and *interest* are present (*k*); with these conditions, *possessio* itself might be obtained in such a suit (*l*). Secondly, the conclusion is incorrect; for if, in fact, the *actio ad exhibendum* may form a first step towards the Int. *utrubi*, still it is not necessary for this Interdict, that the Possession should be lost. For as the *commodans*, &c., does not lose his Possession, when the *commodatarius* merely refuses to restore it, but without committing actual *furtum* by *contrectatio*, the Int. *utrubi* may, in this case, as an Int. *retinendæ* possessionis, be preceded by an *actio ad exhibendum :* the same may be said of the case in L. 14, C. *de agricolis*, which is now to be explained.

3. L. 14, C. *de agricolis*, (cf. Cod. Theodos. IV. 23) (*m*).

" Si coloni quos bona fide quisque *possidet* (*n*), ad alios fugæ vitio transeuntes necessitatem propriæ conditionis declinare tentaverint, bonæ fidei *possessori* primum oportet ceteri reformatione succurri: et tunc causam originis et proprietatis agitari."

The reading "*possidet*," which undoubtedly is taken from manuscripts, as it has for it the testimony of most trustworthy editors, is confirmed by the "*possessori*" following, as this

(*k*) L. 3, § 9, 10, 11, 14, *ad exhib.*
(*l*) L. 5, § 1, *ad exhib.*
(*m*) I. Gothofred in L. cit., Klepe De Nat. et Ind. Poss. p. 25.
(*n*) "*Possedit*" in seven Paris MSS. of the *Volumen*, the Goetingen MS., Edd. Mag. 1477; ap. Schoeffer, Basil. 1478; ap. Wenster, Ven. 1491; ap. Arrivabene, Ven. 1498; ap. Tortis, Lugduni,

1508; ap. Nicol de Benedictis, Lugd. 1512, f.; ap. Fradin., Paris, 1511, 1515; ap. Boncardum et I. Parvum, Hal. Cont. I. (Paris, 1559), Cont. II. (Paris, 1562), Russard. So also Cod. Theodos. (but from the Breviarium). "Possidet," Cont. III. (Paris, 1566), Cont. IV. (Lugd. 1571), Charondas Cont. V. (Paris, 1576), and all the editions of Gothofred, and from these Gebauer also.

word, according to its ordinary meaning, signifies nothing but " *ei qui possessor* EST." The contents of the passage itself afford a still stronger ground for this reading. For the bondsmen (*coloni*), who are treated here, as in many other respects, exactly like slaves (*o*), had run away, and had put themselves as *freemen* under the protection of a third party; the suit must have been brought against this third party. Thus, this third party was not the possessor of these bondsmen, because he did not entertain any desire to be so: they, on the other hand, were considered as *servi fugitivi*, and, as such (p. 256, n.), were still possessed by their former master (*p*). Consequently, the Int. *utrubi* in fact is spoken of in this passage, which also appears from the heading of the title in the Theodosian code, and to which Interdict the expression *bonæ fidei* possessor has reference, in order to call attention to the exceptions by which this Interdict, like the Int. *uti possidetis*, may be excluded; but the Interdict itself is here, as in every other case, an Int. *retinendæ* possessionis.

4. Petronius, c. 13 (*q*). See *ante*, p. 43.

Petronius relates, that a cloak having been lost, which another party had carried off, an *Interdict* should be brought against this person. This passage would indeed prove the position, if Petronius is to be looked upon as a competent authority on such a very special point in the civil law.

All these grounds, therefore, fail to establish the position; on the other hand, the following are quite conclusive (*r*):

1. Theophilus (*s*), who must have been well acquainted with the ancient form of the Interdict, expressly uses the following example to explain it, "if I possess a thing for

---

(*o*) Gothofredi Paratit. in Cod. Theodos. V. 9.

(*p*) Wenck Cod. Theod. Libri V. priores, p. 268, defends the reading *possedit*, being governed by his false notion of *civilis possessio*. (Add. to 6th ed.)

(*q*) Pagenstecher loc. cit.

(*r*) Hugo first called my attention to these grounds.

(*s*) Theophilus in § 4, I. de interdictis. In Gaius, Lib. 4, § 152, the converse of this case is laid down.

seven months, and the other party possess it for the five following months, I must succeed in the suit, and the other party must give up Possession."

2. Otherwise, in many cases (for instance, the one mentioned by Theophilus), the question could not have been determined.

The rule of law in practice, therefore, was quite clear; but the question is, how is it to be explained on theoretical grounds; Does it shew that the Int. *utrubi* is to be considered as an Int. *recuperandæ* possessionis? This point is of the greatest importance in my view of possessory Interdicts, as the *formal* disturbance on which I found them, undoubtedly does not occur in the Int. *utrubi*, if it is an Int. *recuperandæ* possessionis. But it can be proved by distinct evidence, that the Romans never considered this Interdict as one *recuperandæ* possessionis. Both Gaius and Paulus, neither of whom knew anything of the new form of this Interdict, mention it expressly as an Int. *retinendæ* possessionis, together with the Int. *uti possidetis* (*t*); Paulus speaks immediately after of the Int. *de vi*, cites the well known rule that it can not be used for moveables, and mentions another suit applicable for such cases; and just there, where the Int. *utrubi* must have suggested itself in preference to everything else, if it were ever applicable to a case of lost Possession, he does not say one word of it (*u*).

Now the whole matter may be summed up thus. The Int.

(*t*) Gaius, Lib. IV. § 148; Paulus V. 6, § 1. "Retinendæ possessionis gratia comparata sunt interdicta, per quæ eam possessionem, quam jam habemus, retinere volumus : quale est uti possessionis de rebus soli, et utrubi de re mobili." Perhaps, in this view, the reading "*possidet*" in Gaius, Lib. 4, § 150, p. 238, lin. 15, may be defended, which was altered in the edition on my suggestion into *possedit*.

(*u*) Paulus V. 6, § 5. "De navi vi dejectus hoc interdicto (de vi) experiri non potest: *sed utilis ei actio de rebus recuperandis, exemplo de vi bonorum raptorum datur.* Itemque de eo dicendum est, qui carruca, aut equo dejicitur." A similar passage in Ulpian, L. 1, § 6, *de vi*, is less conclusive, because some interpolation may have been made there.

utrubi is *retinendæ possessionis*, but by a special fiction (*v*), the possession of the *major anni pars* is looked upon as present Possession (*w*). Should the plaintiff not be the actual possessor at the time, the precedent disturbance consists in the immediate refusal to restore the subject. Whether the defendant had previously taken Possession by force, or whether he had obtained it in any unobjectionable manner, is, in this point of view, immaterial. Both of these (I mean the *major pars anni* and the forcible occupancy,) may coincide, but such coincidence is merely accidental (*x*), which makes the essential difference between this Interdict and the interdicts *recuperandæ* possessionis clearly visible (*y*). At the same time, it cannot be denied that this coincidence, though in itself accidental, is likely to occur in the majority of cases, so that this Interdict may serve the same practical purpose as if it were an Interdict *recuperandæ* possessionis. This may be seen particularly on the following ground. If the Possession of a moveable is actually taken from me by force, and I bring this Interdict within the year, I must necessarily succeed, on account of the *exceptiones vitiosæ possessionis* thereupon arising. No more than a theoretic value can be ascribed to the above strenuous advocacy of the Int. *utrubi*, as merely an Int. retinendæ possessionis, because

---

(*v*) This fiction, and consequently the whole peculiarity of the old Int. *utrubi*, would probably appear very simple to us, if we knew the whole of the Roman procedure in all its bearings.

(*w*) I find this view in Wieling, Fragment. Edicti Perpetui Francequ. 1733, pp. 325-6. "Duplex fuisse hoc interdictum videtur ; unum prohibitorium cujus verba hoc tit. referuntur : alterum restitutorium quod omittitur. . . . ceterum retinendæ magis possessionis hoc Interdictum fuisse, quam recuperandæ, si propiæ et

ex arte loquamur; possessio enim, quæ hoc interdicto retinere dicitur, non est præsens, verum majoris anni partis ; ita ut vere retineatur possessio, illa nempe majoris anni partis, quam dixi ; sed recuperetur tantum præsens, si tempore interdicti mutata adpareat."

(*x*) This explains why Paulus *loc. cit.* does not mention the Int. *utrubi* in the case of a violent abstraction of Possession.

(*y*) The remark, which now follows in the text, was first introduced in the 4th ed.

it will be seen hereafter (§. 42), that this Interdict, in its
practical results was, and with justice, made use of as a substitute for the Int. *unde vi* (*z*). We have spoken hitherto of
the conditions for this Interdict; its operation has nothing
peculiar about it. Thus, here also, the disturbance of the
Possession must be prevented (*a*), besides which, damages
must be granted for the time gone by (mesne profits).

Lastly, we have still to mention the exceptions to this
Interdict. The first is founded, as in the Int. *uti possidetis*,
on the *vitiosa* possessio of the plaintiff (*b*), and to make the
exception prevail here also, the force, &c., must have been
exerted against the present defendant. In the later law,
this position does not admit of a doubt (*c*), and even in the
older law, it has only been denied from an odd conceit of
Cuperus (*d*). His reasons are these: 1st. Paulus does not
expressly repeat the words " *ab adversario* " (*e*), but in the
same way this proof might be applied to the later law also;
for even in the Pandects, and in a passage, indeed, which is
probably interpolated, the above words are wanting (*f*).

(*z*) It would be quite consistent with this view, that the Romans, although they treat the
Interdict, especially as *retinendæ
possessionis*, should nevertheless
designate it as an Interdictum
duplex, *i. e.* as one which might
serve, according to circumstances,
either retinendæ or recuperandæ
possessionis. I think it indeed
probable that this form of expression was used by them. Compare
the additions in the 6th ed. *ante*,
to § 37, 39. (Add. to 6th ed.)

(*a*) L. 1, *pr. de utrubi.* " Vim
fieri veto."

(*b*) We may lay down in this
case also, as well as with the Int.
uti possidetis, and indeed still more
confidently, that the defendant

relying on this exception might
succeed in the Int. *utrubi* just
like a plaintiff; compare § 43, *post.*
(Add. to 5th ed. modified in the
6th).

(*c*) § 4, in fin. I. *de interd.*

(*d*) De Nat. Poss. p. 2, c. 7.
With later writers this conceit
passes for an historical certainty.

(*e*) Paulus V. 6, § 1. "Et in
priore quidem (*uti poss.*) is potior
est, qui redditi interdicti tempore
nec vi, nec clam, nec precario ab
adversario possidet. In altero
vero (*utrubi*) potior est, qui majore parte anni retrorsum numerati, nec vi, nec clam, nec precario
possedit."

(*f*) L. 1, § 1, *de utrubi.*

Y

2nd. The *argumentum a contrario* (*g*), which is evidently still weaker than his first reason. On the other hand, the express testimony of the Institutes, which specially refers to the earlier law (*h*), is wholly overlooked, and no possible reason can be assigned, why this testimony should not be received as complete proof. The point is wholly put at rest by Gaius (*i*). The second exception with the Int. *uti possidetis* had reference to the limitation of suits (p. 314); this exception does not seem to have prevailed here, as it is neither mentioned in the Edict itself (*j*), nor in the Institutes (*k*); in fact, however, it was included in the older law in the special period of time mentioned in the Interdict, and in the later law, its validity followed from the absolute identity of both Interdicts (*l*).

SECTION XLII.

INTERDICTUM DE VI.

Special Sources for the Int. *de vi.*
　　Cicero pro A. Cæcina.
　　Cicero pro Tullio (Ciceronis Orat. Frag. ed. Peyron, Stuttgard, 1824, p. 96—109).
　　Gaius, lib. 4, §§. 154, 155.

(*g*) L. 2, *uti poss.* "Justa enim an injusta adversus ceteros possessio sit, *in hoc interdicto* nihil refert." Therefore (concludes Cuperus) it does make a difference in the Int. *utrubi.*

(*h*) § 4, *de interd.* "Utrubi vero Interdicto is *vincebat*, qui majore parte ejus anni nec vi, nec clam, nec precario *ab adversario* possidebat. *Hodie tamen. . . .*"

(*i*) Gaius, Lib. 4, § 150. "Si vero de re mobili, tunc eum potiorem esse jubet, qui majore parte ejus anni nec vi, nec clam, nec precario ab adversario possedit."

(*j*) L. 1, *pr.* § 1, *de utrubi.*
(*k*) § 4, I. *de interd.*
(*l*) This remark was first introduced in the 4th ed.

§. 6, I. *de Interdictis.*
Dig., lib. 43, tit. 16.
Cod. Inst., lib. 8, tit. 45.   } See Introduction.
Cod. Theod., lib. 4, tit. 22.
Writers :

For the explanation of Cicero's oration, pro Cæcina, besides the editions of Grævius and of Naples, *cum notis variorum,* some of the special editors and commentators on this speech alone are valuable: Jac. Omphalius (Paris, 1535, 8vo.), Barth. Latomus (Argent. 1539, 8vo.), and Pet. Pelittarius (Paris, 1540, 4to.).

But the following Essay is far the most important and useful:

> Henr. Const. Cras. Diss. qua Spec. jpr. Ciceron. exhib., s. Ciceronem justam pro A. Cæcina causam dixisse contenditur. Lugd. Bat. 1769. (A profound treatise, which not only treats of the speech of Cicero, but extends itself to the whole Interdict. That Cicero, however, defended the right side is not made more apparent by this Essay).

> Ferd. Gottl. Fleck, Comm. binæ de Interd. unde vi et Remediis Spolii. Lips. 1797, 8vo. (See Introduction). Only the first part of this work applies here, and this part is copied from Cras, with the exception of a few unimportant passages.

Whoever lost his Possession by violence, might recover it back in different ways, according as this violence occurred with, or without, arms. Two different Interdicts, therefore, are usually stated to exist, *de vi quotidiana* and *de vi armata.* At bottom, however, there was but one single Interdict, which was either used in the regular way (Int. *de vi* simply, without addition), or with more precise qualifications to the prejudice of the defendant (Int. *de vi armata*) (*a*). The ordinary everyday violence, in which the case prescribed by

(*a*) Both cases may be com-   and *sine clausulâ.*
pared to a *mandatum cum clausulâ*

the rule was comprehended, bore, for this reason, no particular name; Cicero called it once, for the purpose of more
accurate distinction, *vis quotidiana,* and the Interdict, in
such cases, *Interdictum quotidianum* (*b*), which, however,
must only be understood as a descriptive denomination, and
not as a technical expression. Nothing could be more
different from this than the old introduction to the complete
vindication-suit, the form of which turned principally on
symbolical violence, viz., on the *deductio quæ moribus fit,* and
the *manus consertæ,* which are termed by Gellius *vis civilis*
and *festucaria* (*c*). In this case all was mere show, not
earnest, whereas in every Int. *de vi* a case of real violence
occurred, whether it was performed with arms or without (*d*).
Modern Jurists have nearly always confounded this *vis civilis*
with the *vis quotidiana* in one way or other, and have considered the Int. *de vi* either as a portion of the *manus consertæ,* or the *deductio quæ moribus fit* conversely as a
ceremony belonging to Interdicts, by which mistakes, the
correct view as to these proceedings must be necessarily
impeded. The distinction between the two degrees of
violence in the Int. *de vi* was still observed in the times of

(*b*) Cicero pro Cæcina, cap. 31,
32.

(*c*) Gellius, Lib. 20, cap. 10,
ad fin.

(*d*) I have discussed this point
in a distinct article : Zeitschrift
f. geschichtl. Rechtsw. B. 3, s. 421,
in which however I constantly
used the expression *lis vindiciarum*
to denote the symbolical procedure at the commencement of a
vindication-suit, which I now
consider, according to Gaius, Lib.
4, § 16, 91, 94, to be altogether
improper. In support of the
above objections in the text to
the confusion referred to, it may
be said, that in fact the Interdict
and the *manus consertæ might*

occasionally be used for similar
purposes. For, if a man wished
to vindicate a piece of land, from
which he had been ousted, he
might at once by the *manus consertæ* obtain a decision on the
Possession for the purpose of regulating the suit as to the property, and he would probably
thereby be put immediately into
possession ; but he might also
commence with an Interdict, and
then the still following symbolical
act would be a mere formality,
as every thing would have been
already decided in the proceedings on the Interdict which served
to commence the suit on property.

the classical Jurists, but as Justinian no longer recognizes it (*e*), we should have been unable to distinguish with certainty even the traces of the older law in the Extracts from the Jurists (*f*), if tolerably precise information had not been furnished us on the subject by Cicero. In the modern law, therefore, there exists one rule only for the Int. *de vi* (*g*), and this points partly to vis *armata,* and partly to what was called vis *quotidiana* in the earlier law; but as even in the earlier law the distinction involved only particular legal rules, it will be sufficient, in an exposition of the modern law, to observe upon these special differences only.

The *first* condition of this Interdict is, that the plaintiff must actually have had juridical Possession at the time of the ouster (*h*). No doubt can be raised as to the correctness of this position as respects the later law, as our Law Sources expressly lay down that Possession generally is necessary, but not *civilis* possessio, for the purpose of using this Interdict (*i*). The question is a more difficult one as to the older

(*e*) One distinction only occurs in the Digest; children and freedmen might maintain the Int. *de vi armata* against their parents and patrons, but not the common Int. *de vi*, and in its place only an actio in factum, L. 2, § 1, L. 7, § 2, *de obsequ.,* and indeed, in Justinian's time, the distinction between an Interdict and an *actio* was obsolete.

(*f*) L. 1, *de vi*, refers to the case of *vis quotidiana,* and L. 3, *de vi* (Cujac. in Paul. V. 6, § 3) to *vis armata.* This also explains the heading in the Digest, De vi et de vi armata. The traces of the respective legal principles are mentioned *post.*

(*g*) This Int. *de vi* still turns upon the simple rule in the Edict, ' *unde illum vi dejecisti, id illi restituas.*" The language of the

defendant's answer has reference to this formula in the Interdict. The defendant might deny the *factum* of the plaintiff, for instance, the *dejectio,* or rely upon an exception, but his answer always was "se illum restituisse." Cicero, Pro Cæcina, cap. 8, cf. cap. 19, 21, 28, 29, 32. In the Digest, out of the *restituas* of the Edict, was made "judicium dabo." See Zeitschrift f. geschichtl. Rechtsw. B. 3, s. 306.

(*h*) The principle above laid down (p. 291), in reference to possessory suits generally, applies to the proof of this fact also.

(*i*) L. 1, § 9, 10, 23, *de vi;* L. 4, § 28, *de usurp.* It should nevertheless be remarked here, that in recent times it has been contended on various grounds that for the Int. *de vi*, a different and

law. Cicero says expressly, that for the Int. *de vi armata,*
no Possession at all was required *(j)*, and this statement is
well worth a closer consideration. The case in which Cicero
was counsel for the defendant was shortly this; Cæcina
claimed a piece of land by inheritance, Æbulius claimed it
on other grounds; Cæcina was about to make entry on the
land, but was forcibly resisted by Æbulius, and a posse of
armed men *(k)*. Most probably Cæcina had never been in
Possession at all, for although Cicero affirms that he had
the Possession, this statement, which went to the very root
of the matter, is only contained in a couple of words, at the
end of the speech, and is thrown in as a sort of makeweight,
so that it evidently was his intention to keep the fact in the
back ground as much as possible; nevertheless, in these few
words more than one trace is to be found, from which the
exactly opposite conclusion is to be drawn *(l)*. If now
Cæcina had never, in fact, had Possession, he could not win
his cause except by the Court holding that Possession was
not necessary for this Interdict; it consequently was the task
of his advocate to make this false view as plausible as possible; Cicero, in fact, adopted this course, and therefore
he is not to be depended upon as an historical authority *(m)*.

simpler Possession was sufficient
than for the Int. *uti possidetis:*
because, for instance, the mere detention of a hirer, of a borrower,
&c. gave rise to the right of an
Int. *de vi.* See *ante,* the addition
at end of § 10. (Add. to 6th ed.)

(j) Pro Cæcina, cap. 31, 32.

(k) Pro Cæcina, cap. 32.

(l) The following words are
especially remarkable : " Cæsenniam possedisse *propter usumfructum* non negas." (See *ante,*
§ 24). For they make the following passage quite unimportant :
"Cæcina..... *venit* in istum fundum, *rationes a colono accepit,* sunt
in eam rem testimonia," as they

do not denote any prehension of
the Possession, since the *account-
ing* merely referred to the period
preceding. Cras himself (p. 30)
considers the words "*propter
usumfructum*" so conclusive, that
he strikes them out, following the
example, it is true, of many editors, but without the authority
of any manuscripts. (See Beck's
note, Opp. Vol. 2, T. 2, p. 308,
ed. Lips. 1800-8.)

(m) Even Cras (p. 35) does not
venture, on the strength of this
solitary passage, to defend the
orator, and he contents himself
with an elaborate demonstration
that the whole cause ought not

One expression, however, in that passage requires some further examination, " Cui ergo aut in illud quotidianum Interdictum, *unde ille me vi dejecit*, additur, *cum ego possiderem*, si dejici nemo potest, qui non possidet ; aut in hoc Interdictum, *de hominibus armatis* non additur, si oportet quæri, possederit, necne ?" Cicero prays in aid here the language of the judicial writs ; this was universally recognized, consequently, there must have been some general foundation for it, but as to what it was, he gives a somewhat incorrect explanation. Perhaps, the matter may be explained thus : the Int. *de vi* was usually, *i. e.*, when arms were not used, demanded in this form, "unde ille me vi dejecit, cum ego *nec vi, nec clam, nec precario ab illo* possiderem " (*n*). The whole of the second sentence, therefore, contains merely the three known exceptions, and the "cum ego possiderem" was inserted on account of the exceptions, and not to signify the fact of Possession, which was already plainly enough expressed by the " unde me dejicisti "(*o*). If arms had been used, the exceptions did not avail, in the formula, therefore, the whole of the second sentence, " cum ego .... possiderem " was left out, although Possession was not less necessary for the foundation of this right of suit. It is, therefore, very probable, that Cicero availed himself of this omission, to found upon it a conclusion, which was not less indispensable for the cause of Cæcina, than it was unfounded in law. Modern Jurists have generally looked upon the state-

to be given up as bad on account of one bad argument. Giphanius had previously put forth the same opinion on this passage. Giphanius in Cod. *tit. unde vi*, Expt. Cod. P. 2, p. 276.

(*n*) This follows, 1st, from Cicero, Pro Cæc. C. 32. "....Ne id quidem satis est, nisi docet ita se possedisse, ut *nec vi, nec clam, nec precario possederit*." 2nd, from a passage in the Lex Thoria in Sigon. De Ant. Jur. Italiæ, II.

2 : "Quod ejus is quei ejectus est possederit, *quod neque vi neque clam neque precario possederit ab eo, quei cum ea possessione is ejecerit.*"

(*o*) A proof of this view is to be found in Cicero, Pro Tullio, c. 44 : "Deinde additur illius causa quicum agitur *cum ille possideret*, et hoc amplius, quod nec vi nec clam nec precario possideret." (Add. to 5th ed.)

ment of Cicero as true, and have explained it to mean as if
in the case of arms, *detention*, without any juridical Possession, was sufficient ground for the Interdict (*p*); but this
distinction is not only not made by Cicero in terms, but it
is impossible that he can have had it in view, for Cæcina was
not in any way a tenant to whom merely *juridical* Possession
of the subject could be denied, for he either had juridical
Possession, or not even detention, so that nothing could
turn upon this distinction. Now as the passage from Cicero
gives us the only information upon the whole matter, it is,
consequently, altogether arbitrary to found the above distinction upon it. Westphal (*q*) conveniently avoids all these
difficulties; he considers Cicero's statement as true, takes
it literally, and, consequently, explains the Int. *de vi armata*
as an Interdict both *adipiscendæ* and *recuperandæ* possessionis.

The *second* condition for this Interdict is *forcible* disturbance of Possession. Here also, as with the previous Interdicts, every act of violence is not sufficient, but it must be
atrox vis (*r*). But *atrox vis* does not denote an outrageous
act of violence, such as beating or wounding (*s*), but merely
such violence as makes the continuance of Possession impossible (*t*). This, therefore, must be directed more completely

---

(*p*) For instance, Cujacius in
Paul. V. 6, § 3, and in L. 18, de
vi. (Lib. 20, Quæst. Papin. Opp.
IV. p. 652. The position appears
to be treated here as existing
law).

(*q*) Arten der Sachen, &c. §
245.

(*r*) L. 1, § 3, de vi. "Ad solam autem atrocem vim pertinet
hoc interdictum." Westphal. §
275, translates this, "a seemly
violence:" he had better have
said "an unseemly violence."

(*s*) Consequently, the following
passage in Cicero, Pro Cæc. c. 16,

does not at all clash with the
above rule: "Cum de jure et
legitimis hominum controversiis
loquimur, et in his rebus *vim*
nominamur, *pertenuis vis intelligi
debet.*"

(*t*) L. 1, § 29, de vi. "Pomponius ait, vim (sc. in hoc interdicto) sine *corporali vi* locum non
habere." (See *ante*, p. 259).
Ulpian does not deny this proposition, but he only defines the
application of it. Namely, whether the *corporalis* vis be actually
exerted, or merely *threatened*, and
so *avoided*, makes no difference:

and more immediately against the person, than the disquiet-
ing violence required for the Int. retinendæ possessionis (§.39),
and in so far, we may always look upon it as a greater
degree of violence, although both species of violence have
this in common, that they exert an external restraint on
the will of the possessor, and thus interfere with the liberty
of the person (*u*). *Immediate personal violence*, therefore,
is the condition by which this Interdict is distinguished
from the Int. retinendæ possessionis. Whether arms were
or were not used in the violent disturbance of Possession,
was quite immaterial in the later law.

Third condition : the violence must have been committed
by the defendant himself. This rule has, however, several
exceptions : 1st. He by whose will the act takes place, for
instance, by giving orders to another person, is just as
responsible as the party committing the act (*v*). The history
of this proposition is as follows : originally the Interdict ran
thus, " unde tu .... dejecisti." Many defendants, however, abused this construction, by affirming that the ejectment was not made by themselves, but by other parties
(although under their orders). To meet this chicanery, the
Prætors adopted another form of expression in the Edict,
" unde dolo malo tuo ...... vi detrusus est," which expressly
included the above case, and the plaintiff now had his
choice between the two forms (*w*). But, subsequently, the

with the Int. *uti possidetis* the latter was never once required. A
second proof of the above interpretation of *atrox vis* is contained
in L. 3, § 1, *quod metus*, ... *Vim
uccipimus atrocem*, namely, in the
Edict *quod metus causa ;* but in
other passages the force which is
spoken of in this Edict (*i. e.* vis
atrox) is explained thus : "vis
enim fiebat mentio, *propter necessitatem impositam contrariam volun-
tati*," (L. 1, *eod.*), and "Vis autem
est majoris rei impetus, *qui re-*

pelli non potest." (L. 2, *eod.*)

(*u*) The view here given in
the text was introduced in the
6th edition.

(*v*) This addition was made in
the 5th edition.

(*w*) The whole of this appears
by Cicero, Pro Tullio, cap. 29,
30, 44, 46. The earlier form is
in cap. 44, the later in cap. 29 ;
it is repeated by him in c. 46,
where however an *hiatus* exists in
the manuscript. Cap. 46, is thus a
mere repetition of cap. 29, and it

original *dejecisti* was construed as if it also meant *dejici fecisti,* so that the provision mentioned became superfluous, and the older form was all-sufficient (*x*). 2nd. The heir is only so far liable where he himself has got something by virtue of the proceeding (in id quod ad eum pervenit) (*y*), or where he would have got something except for his dolus (*z*). Not so with him called the *singularis successor;* for instance, the purchaser of a house, which had been subjected to a *dejectio:* for this party is not in any way liable (*a*). 3rd. When the act of violence was committed by slaves, even without the will of their master (see 1st exception), the master was responsible in two ways, he must, *firstly,* submit to the Interdict itself, as to every other *actio* ex delicto, like a *noxalis actio;* and, secondly, he must restore whatever he might have acquired by the wrongful acts of his slaves (id quod ad eum pervenerat) (*b*). This second liability extended itself, however, still further, namely, to all such cases in which we may have immediately acquired anything by force, which another person had exerted in our name, or even if he were only simply dependent upon us (*c*).

Fourthly. The Possession must be lost by the act of violence (*d*), *i. e.,* the act itself must be capable of being considered a *dejectio* (*e*). In what cases, generally, a corporal

is quite erroneous to attempt to refer the latter to the Int. *de vi* ARMATA.

(*x*) L. 1, § 12, 15 ; L. 3, § 10, 12, *de vi.*

(*y*) L. 1, § 48 ; L. 3, *pr.;* L. 9, *pr. de vi;* L. 11, C. *de poss.*

(*z*) L. 2, *de vi.*

(*a*) L. 3, § 10, *uti possidetis.*

(*b*) L. 1, § 11, 15—19, 21, *de vi.*

(*c*) Instances, 1st, L. 4, *de vi.* " Si vi me dejecerit qui nomine municipum, in municipes mihi interdictum reddendum Pomponius scribit ; *si quid ad eos per-*

venit." 2nd, L. 1, § 20, *de vi.* " Si filius familias vel mercenarius vi dejecerit, *utile interdictum competit."* (Namely, against the *conductor* of the slaves, or against the father, only indeed *in id quod pervenit,* for this had been spoken of in the preceding words. L. 16, *de vi,* is not in point here).

(*d*) L. 1, § 45, *de vi.* (See *ante*).

(*e*) *Dejicere* was the technical term even in Cicero's time ; before then *detrudere,* Pro Cæc. cap. 17, which word also occurs in L. 4, § 27, *de usurp.*

act (*corpore*) put an end to the Possession, has been above inquired into. In all these cases, therefore, the simple question is, whether *external violence* is the cause of the loss, and this, generally, is a matter easily ascertainable. Thus, for instance, it is immaterial whether the violence is actually committed, or whether it is avoided on a well-grounded alarm, it being assumed that the danger is immediate and not prospective (*f*); so also, whether the possessor is turned out of his house, or is prevented from entering (*g*); and, taking these two rules together, it is clear that the possessor, whose house is taken Possession of during his absence, may bring the Interdict as *dejectus*, even when he does not make the attempt to assert his Possession by force (*h*). On the other hand, the Interdict does not lie, where the Possession is transferred by delivery; even if the delivery is caused by fear, though other actions may be brought (*i*), the Interdict cannot (*j*). In most cases, therefore, the application of the term *dejectio* presents no difficulty; one case, however, must be expressly mentioned. Whoever loses Possession through an act of violence, and immediately thereupon repossesses himself by violence, never actually loses the Possession (*k*). This, therefore, is

(*f*) In this way the apparently contradictory passages may be reconciled. (See *ante*, p. 259).

(*g*) *Ex* aliquo loco, and *ab* aliquo loco dejicere : both expressed at once by "*unde* dejicisti," Cic., Pro Cæc. cap. 30, 31.

(*h*) See above, p. 260, note (*z*), and particularly L. 3, § 8, 9, *de poss*. (See above, p. 280).

(*i*) L. 9, *pr. quod metus*, (Ulp. lib. 11, ad Edict.) "Sed et si per vim possessionem tradidero ; dicit Pomponius hoc (huic) Edicto (sc. *quod metus*) locum esse."

(*j*) L. 5, *de vi*, (Ulp. lib. 11, ad Edict.) "Si rerum (Accurs. al. incipit, *si metu* et al. *si rerum*)

"tibi possessionem tradidero, dicit Pomponius, unde vi interdictum cessare : quoniam *non est vi dejectus, qui compulsus est in possessionem inducere*." Cras, p. 18, not. 1, suggests with much probability, that this and the previous passage (L. 9, *quod metus*) formed only one passage, and consequently the present one must be read "Si *per vim*." Compare Dirksen, Abhandlungen I. 451.

(*k*) L. 17, *de vi*. "Qui possessionem vi ereptam, vi in ipso congressu recuperat, *in pristinam causam reverti potius quam vi possidere intelligendus est*: ideoque si te vi dejecero, ilico tu me, not to be considered as a double *dejectio*, but only as one indivisible transaction, in which the previous possessor defended his Possession by force. The practical bearing of this view is important; if the transaction contained a double *dejectio*, the legality of the second *dejectio* could only be supported by an exception against the Interdict of the other party, and this exception was no longer held good in the modern law (*l*); but on the above view the exception was unnecessary, because the *factum* (*dejectio*) was wanting, on which alone the Interdict could be founded, and the legality of the act would be a simple consequence of the general right of self-defence (*m*). An important application of this rule occurs as to the Possession of land, which is occupied in the absence of the possessor (p. 261). For if the possessor is prevented by force from re-entering, he then only loses the Possession, and that by an actual *dejectio* (*n*): if, conversely, he succeeds in ejecting his opponent, no *dejectio* at all has taken place, and the previous Possession is not lost, so that no doubt can arise on the legality of this act.

The *fifth* condition for the Interdict concerns the subject of Possession; it must be an *immoveable* to give rise to the Interdict (*o*). But as the same grounds for protecting the naked Possession exist with respect to moveables, as with immoveables, it would be inconsistent if no Interdict, or other suit, were available for the former, by which the Int.

deinde ego te; unde vi interdictum tibi utile erit." The application of the last words can only be explained when exceptions are discussed.

(*l*) L. 3, § 9, *de vi*, does not expressly say any thing, except that "such act of the previous possessor is lawful," which legality might also be made to appear in that case by an exception, so that we cannot draw any conclusion from this as to the rule. But as, in respect of *vis armata*, which is

spoken of in this passage, the exception did not avail, and as the limitation "sed hoc *confestim*, non *ex intervallo*" were altogether incorrect in reference to an exception, the passage nevertheless is only to be explained by the above rule, so that it contains, as well as L. 17, *de vi*, the proof of the rule.

(*m*) L. 1, § 27, 28, *de vi*.

(*n*) L. 6, § 1, *de poss.*

(*o*) L. 1, § 3—8, *de vi*; Paulus, V. 6, § 5.

de vi might be represented. Ulpian mentions three other suits, which might be substituted for the Int. *de vi* in the case of moveables; the *actio furti, actio vi bonorum raptorum,* and the *actio ad exhibendum* (*p*).

But the *actio furti,* like the *furtum* itself, on the existence of which it was founded, prescribes conditions, which never come in question in simple Possession, namely, the *tueri animus,* the *contrectatio,* and an *interest* in the person of the plaintiff himself (*q*), which is founded on another *right:* the same also is true as to *condictio* furtiva, which is not mentioned in the passage in question. The *actio vi bonorum raptorum* is also founded on a similar legal interest (*r*), and, at the same time, on the intention of the robber to violate such right independent of the mere Possession (*s*). Lastly, *the actio ad exhibendum* might, indeed, be brought without reference to another suit, but the same *interest* was also required here as in the previous actions (*t*). Therefore, every one of these actions contains conditions which are not comprised in the right of Possession, and cases, consequently, may be conceived, in which the right of simple Possession is forcibly violated, without any remedy being available, although if

(*p*) L. 1, § 6, *de vi.* "Illud utique in dubium non venit, interdictum hoc ad res mobiles non pertinere. Nam *ex causa furti,* vel vi *bonorum raptorum* competit; potest et *ad exhibendum* agi." (Add. to 6th ed.) I am indebted to a communication of Hugo's, part of which appeared in Goett. Anz. 1818, p. 1556, for the following interpretation of the passages. Ex causa means "according to circumstances," (L. 28, § 1, ad L. Aquil.), and must not be construed with *furti;* the whole meaning therefore is "according to circumstances the actio furti lies, or vi bon. raptorum, or even the actio ad exhib-

endum." That the actio furti is not rei persecutoria is no objection, because, as affording compensation to the amount of the interest, it was more than sufficient. The enumeration however is incomplete according to any interpretation.

(*q*) L. 53, § 4; L. 71, § 1, *de furtis.*

(*r*) L. § 22—24, *vi bon. rapt.;* § 2, I. *eod.* Only it was not so strictly insisted upon as in *furtum.*

(*s*) L. 2, § 18, *vi bon. rapt.;* § 1, I. *eod.*

(*t*) L. 3, § 9, 10, 11, *ad exhibendum* (p. 317).

the subject of Possession had been land, the Int. *de vi* would
clearly have sufficed. To explain this omission, the above
attempted derivation of Interdicts from the history of Possession (§ 13) will, above all, be serviceable. But at the
same time, this hypothesis may, perhaps, not be generally
received, and others again may consider that it does not
explain every thing, as, at least, on the transfer of Possession
in its present form, all the accompanying wants connected
with it must have been provided for. For these reasons, an
attempt shall be made to explain this omission from our
known Law Sources. The three actions, which Ulpian mentions as substitutes for the Int. *de vi* in the case of moveables,
are older than Interdicts, consequently, most cases of lost
Possession of moveables were already provided for by them,
at the time that Interdicts were introduced. But Interdicts,
like the whole of the Edict, were not founded on theoretic
grounds, but on the wants of the day, and it was, therefore,
very natural that a special Int. *recuperandæ* possessionis
should not have been framed for some particular case in
respect of moveables, although in strict logic it ought to
have been extended to it, in order to protect the right of
naked Possession. The correctness of this view is confirmed
by the following statement. Whoever exercises the Possession of another as his agent, may be untrue to him, and
even acquire the Possession of the subject; but the Roman
law expressly lays down, that this acquisition and loss of
Possession could only occur by means of such an act, on the
part of the agent, as amounted to a *furtum* (*u*). One reason
for this exception might be, that the Possession was not lost
until the subject, as *res furtiva,* became incapable of Usucaption; but a second reason, which is still more general,
appears to have presented itself in this case. The possessor,
namely, would not lose his Possession (and, consequently,
the Int. *utrubi*), until on occasion of the *furtum* of the
agent, he had acquired a new right of action, so that the
above rule was framed with a view of limiting the cases in

(*u*) L. 4, § 18, *de poss.*

which the right of Possession in a moveable was lost, without the previous possessor being able to complain of this disturbance. Thus the matter may be explained, if we are to construe strictly the view presented by Ulpian, in the passage cited. But if we turn from the contents of that passage to the undeniable systematic coherence of the earlier law, a much more complete and satisfactory explanation may be afforded by the older form of the Int. *utrubi ;* for by means of that Interdict, the same object was actually attained for which we now find an Interdict wanting (p. 320). For in that Interdict, the party would succeed who had had *longer* Possession than his *opponent* during the current year; but in comparing their two periods of Possession, a *vitiosa* possessio counted for nothing (*v*). Whoever, therefore, was forcibly ejected from the Possession of a moveable, would only have to sue within the year, and then he was sure to succeed, because his Possession would be longer than that of his opponent, who would not be able to reckon *his* Possession, on account of its violent commencement. Thus, in fact, the above Interdict completely performed the office as to moveables, which the Int. de vi discharged as to land, if attention were only paid to the period of limitation. This view, moreover, cannot be objected to on the ground that Ulpian does not mention the Int. *utrubi* in the above passage, although his subject so expressly called for it; for, in the Justinian law, this Interdict had acquired a wholly different character, and thus it was very natural that the above reference of the older Jurists to its earlier form should disappear in the Digest (*w*). On these grounds, it would appear that the above-mentioned omission did not, in fact, occur in the older law; but, in truth, arose in the Justinian Code through the altered character of the Int.

(*v*) Gaius, Lib. 4, § 150. " Si vero de re mobili, tunc *eum potiorem esse* jubet, qui majore parte ejus anni *nec vi, nec clam, nec precario* ab adversario possedit (possidet)."

(*w*) This explanation, founded on the Int. *utrubi,* was introduced into the 4th edition.

utrubi. But even so much cannot be affirmed, since long before Justinian, the same object had been provided for in another way; for the Int. *de vi* itself had been long set free from its original limitation to land, and, therefore, in the Justinian Code it must be construed to apply to moveables and immoveables indiscriminately.

Valentinian, namely, ordained, that all forcible takings of Possession of any subject whatever should be visited with two results: 1st. Restitution of Possession; 2nd. Loss of the property (as a penalty for the disturbance), or if the disturbant was not proprietor, payment of damages equivalent to the value of the subject (*x*).

Only the first of these two obligations is in point here, and this contains a clear extension of the Int. *de vi* to *moveables.* That the legislators themselves entertained this view, *i. e.,* that it was a simple modification of the old Int. *de vi,* is not only shewn by the position of this rule with respect to the Interdict in the Sources (*y*), but also more especially by the circumstance, that the conditions of its application are not more closely defined, as, from the importance of the rule, and from the other consequences bound up with it, undoubtedly would have been the case, if it had not contained a tacit reference to all the well-known conditions of the Int. *de vi.*

[Addition to the 4th edition]. The above detailed view

(*x*) L. 3, C. Theod. *unde* vi; L. 7, C. I. *eod.* (The occasion of the law was indeed an individual case, but the law itself was general from its commencement). § 1, I. *de vi bon. rapt.; § 6, I. de interd.* Simple applications of it are to be seen in L. 10, C. *unde vi.;* Nov. Theod. (Valent.) Tit. 19 (in Ritter, p. 56). Legal principles in connection with it, L. 12, § 2, L. 13, *quod metus causa; L. 7, ad L. Jul. de vi priv.* An earlier trace of the

same principle, L. 2, C. Theod. *fin. req.; L. 4, C. I. eod.* Principal author on the historical explanation, I. Gothofred, on the passages cited above from the Cod. Theod.

(*y*) L. 3, C. Theod. *unde vi.* L. 7, C. I. *eod.* On the connection between the right of Possession and the right of self-protection, compare the addition to the end of § 6, above, pp. 33-4, where Rudorff's opinion is mentioned.

of the influence of the laws against self-defence on the Int. *de vi* has been retained unaltered from the three first editions. This view has been lately combatted by Thibaut in a special treatise (*z*), it therefore becomes necessary to investigate the subject anew, and to give a more complete justification of the steps in the investigation. Thibaut says, in substance, as follows: " On the one hand, it is laid down expressly in the Digest, that the Int. *de vi* applies only to land; on the other hand, the penalties against self-protection are connected with that Interdict in the Institutes and Code. But, from the careless construction of the compilations of Justinian, this latter circumstance is of little importance, and consequently he concludes that the Interdict always retained its old nature unaltered, and the penalties on self-protection were only introduced accidentally in connection with the Interdict. From this he deduces the conclusion, that in cases of violent abstraction of the possession of moveables, actions only could be brought, *i. e.* ordinary procedure, and not Interdicts, *i. e.* summary procedure."—First of all we must establish what the precise question in dispute is. Now I cannot admit the question to be, whether the procedure in these cases was ordinary or summary. For the special character of interdict-procedure had wholly disappeared in the Justinian code; previously, without doubt, there had existed a distinction between Interdicts and Actions, without however the least distinction between ordinary and summary procedure, (see *ante*, p. 288), but at all periods the distinction was a subordinate one, and quite unimportant in comparison with the question, whether a right of action existed or not. The true nature of the dispute therefore does not, as I conceive, turn upon the form of procedure which was to be adopted on the occasion of an usurped possession of moveables, but rather upon the following point. In the Interdicts *de vi*, *uti possidetis*, and *utrubi*, a party may unquestionably succeed, who has no right to the subject,

(*z*) Gensler's Archiv. B. 1, Heid. 1818, 8, s. 105—111.

z

who does not claim to have any right, nay, even, who has obtained possession in the most unlawful manner; for instance, by violence against a third party, and who openly confesses it. So far there is no dispute, and this constitutes the peculiarity of possessory suits, which would have been exactly the same, if such suits had been, from the beginning, actions and not Interdicts. Wherever, then, we are deprived of the possession of a moveable by force, the question arises as to the mode of dealing with the case. If the principles which govern possessory suits are applied to it, I must recover back the Possession, even if I possessed without any right, or even without any claim. If, on the other hand, those principles do not apply, I do not recover the Possession, either by summary or by ordinary procedure. Then, if I desire to *vindicate* the subject-matter, I must have the property; to maintain the *actio furti* and *vi bonorum raptorum* I must likewise have the property or some right to the thing, or at least must be responsible for it to some one so entitled (for instance, as a hirer): so also, the actio ad exhibendum demands a legal interest in the subject: thus in all these suits there is required, as an indispensable condition, an actual independent right in reference to the subject, to which naked Possession in no wise can be said to amount. It is this latter proposition which I understand Thibaut to contend for, so that a mere possessor has no right of action at all. My view, on the other hand, is concisely this. In the case supposed, I derive from my naked Possession, and without any independent right, an undoubted right of action. Up to Justinian's time, as I have shewn, the Int. *utrubi* served for this purpose, although afterwards indeed it could no longer be so used. But, on the other hand, another suit .was afforded me springing out of the laws against self-protection, and this statement shall now be established. The L. 7, C. *unde vi* unquestionably comprises both moveables and immoveables without distinction; this appears, first, from the generality of the language used, and secondly, from the application of the rule in § 1, I. *vi bon.*

rapt. The contents of the law are, shortly, as follows: whoever deprives me forcibly of Possession shall first of all restore the Possession, and secondly, pay a penalty equal to the value of the subject; *i. e.* he shall deliver the property to me, if he is proprietor, or if not proprietor, shall pay the value in damages. Therefore, in such case, (independent of the penalty), restitution of the Possession is ordered in every instance of self-protection, without distinction as to moveables or immoveables, and especially without distinction, whether the possessor had any right or not to the subject. Consequently, naked Possession accompanied by a formal disturbance constituted the only title to the above claim, just as in the case of the old Interdicts, or in other words, the old principle of the Int. *de vi* is here extended to the possession of moveables. Properly speaking, however, it should not be termed an extension, because at the period of this constitution the naked possessor could already have procured restitution by the Int. *utrubi.* The whole of this view therefore proceeds, not upon the fact that in the Code and Institutes the penalty on self-protection is introduced under the Int. *de vi,* nor upon a strict literal construction of the words in L. 7, C. *unde vi,* "*possessionem quam abstulit, restituat possessori,*" but upon a strict deduction from the unquestionable tenor of this passage in the Codex. The main question arising upon it is, may the above described naked possessor of a moveable, who has lost possession by violence, have an action for restitution or not? I affirm that he may, and whoever concedes this to me, agrees with me in the main. The second question, whether this very peculiar right of suit (wholly distinct from the actio furti, vi bon. rapt. &c.) should be an Interdict, or an Action, I consider to be, so far as the Justinian code is concerned, pure logomachy. Undoubtedly, however, there is still a third question remaining—according to what principles is the suit of the mere possessor to be decided in detail? As I conceive, it is an extension of the Int. *de vi,* and the whole theory of that interdict becomes applicable.

One of the most important consequences arising from this is, that the above right is not afforded to mere detention, but only to true juridical Possession. And I find the following proofs of this statement: 1st, in the words *possessionem*.......restituat *possessori;* 2nd, in the constitution being inserted under the title *unde vi ;* 3rd, in the circumstance that otherwise there would be an absence of all defined rules for the new right of action, a reproach to the legislator, which disappears if he considered the new right as an extension of the Int. *de vi.* Thibaut objects to this, that in the Digest this Interdict is notwithstanding always restricted to land. But a similar relation with reference to gradually modified rules of law is to be found in many cases which no one observes upon; for instance, when it is said, that only the owner may maintain the actio legis Aquiliæ (*a*), and presently afterwards that the fructuary may maintain an actio utilis (*b*). In conclusion I would only add what follows in support of my view. In the old law the Int. *utrubi* afforded the possessor the protection which we are now speaking of. This ceased on the establishment of Justinian's Code, so that here a great omission must have arisen in reference to practical law. Now, it is not impossible that this may have occurred through the carelessness of the compilers; but it is much more natural to suppose that the alteration in respect to the Int. *utrubi* was introduced expressly because it was perceived that the objects previously accomplished by it had long been provided for in another way.

The operation of the Interdict may be stated simply thus: the *dejectus* must be restored to the same condition in which he was before the *dejectio.* 1st. The first thing therefore is, restitution of the lost Possession itself. If the defendant is still in Possession, the restitution proceeds without question ; but even if he had never had it, or had again lost it, he is still not the less bound to restitution,

(*a*) L. 11, § 6, ad L. Aquil.   (*b*) L. 11, § 10, eod.

that is to say, to pay (c) the value of it (d). 2nd. Besides the lost Possession itself, compensation must be paid for all damage caused by the *dejectio* (e). Some of the most important consequences of the rule are as follows; 1st. When other things were lost at the same time by means of the *dejectio*, they must be restored, or the value of them paid. In this respect the Interdict might apply, even in the older law, to moveables, and this case was even specially mentioned in the words of the Edict (f); juridical possession of such things is never once prescribed (g), and as to them as well as to the principal subject, it was quite

---

(c) L. 1, § 42, *de vi.* "Ex Int. unde vi etiam is, qui non possidet, restituere cogetur." L. 15, *eod.* " Si vi me dejeceris . . . . . . quamvis sine dolo et culpa amiseris possessionem, tamen damnandus es, quanti mea intersit; quia in eo ipso culpa tua præcessit, quod omnino vi dejecisti." (Cf. L. 1, § 36, *eod.*) The passage immediately following (L. 16) contains a remarkable application of the rule; where, namely, a filius familias commits the *dejectio,* his father is liable *in id quod pervenit* (p. 330); thus it would seem as if the son were not bound to make restitution in such cases, because he no longer had possession of the subject; but according to our rule it is quite otherwise, for by this the son also must answer for such subject. " Interdicto unde vi uti potes, si a filiofamilias dejectus es, *ut et ejus causa quod ad patrem pervenit* ipse teneatur." Thus read several Paris MSS., Edd. Ven. 1485; Lugd. 1509, 1513; Paris, 1514, 1536; so also (only with a second *et* before *ad patrem*) Rom. 1476;

Nor. 1483; Ven. 1494. The Florence reading is extraordinarily divaricating, and is evidently corrupt; that of Holoander is compiled from several others.

(d) The value of this Possession is to be carefully distinguished from the value of the subject, *i. e.* of the property, and nothing turns here upon the latter. L. 6, *de vi.* The Gloss states wholly incorrectly that the value of the subject must always be paid, and that the special interest in the Possession would only raise this value.

(e) L. 1, § 41, (cf. § 31), *de vi.* " . . . . Vivianus refert, in hoc int. omnia, quæcunque habiturus vel adsecuturus erat is qui dejectus est, si vi dejectus non esset, restitui, aut eorum litem a judice æstimari debere: eumque tantum consecuturum, quanti sua interesset, se vi dejectum non esse."

(f) L. 1, *pr. de vi:* " *quæque tunc ibi habuit.*" Commentary upon these words, L. 1, § 32, 33, 34, 37, 38, *eod.*

(g) L. 1, § 33, *de vi.*

immaterial whether the defendant retained the possession of them or not (*h*). 2nd. The *profits* also of the things lost by the *dejectio* must be restored; they are calculated from the time of the *dejectio* (*i*), and it does not signify whether the defendant had actually perceived them, but merely whether the *dejectus* was prevented from obtaining them (*j*). 3rd. If the subject-matter has been damaged by the *dejectio* (the house burnt, for instance), this loss must be made good, even if it occurred without any *culpa* in the defendant; still the damage must be of such a nature that it would not have taken place without the *dejectio* (*k*). 4th. Lastly, it was a very important question whether, if the possessor at the time was acquiring Usucaption, damages were recoverable for the interrupted Usucaption (*l*)? According to the general rule, that the *dejectus* must be borne *harmless*, this question should be answered in the affirmative, and even the passage in the Digest which affirms the contrary, as to *furtum*, may be relied upon as an authority for this conclusion (*m*). For the only ground which it brings for-

---

(*h*) L. 1, § 34; L. 19, *devi* Paulus, V. 6, § 8.

(*i*) L. 1, § 40, *de vi.*

(*j*) L. 4, C. *unde vi.*

(*k*) L. 1, § 35, *de vi.* Paulus, V. 6, § 8. L. 14, § 11, *quod metus causa.*

(*l*) Another question is, what does this damage amount to? Supposing that only a few days were wanting to complete the Usucaption, the value of the property itself might be properly taken as the measure, as the acquisition of it was so near at hand. Except in this case no other way could be conceived for deciding upon the matter with certainty, except by taking security; if, after that, the owner should bring vindication before the pe-

riod for the first Usucaption had expired, the Usucaption would have availed nothing, and therefore no damages were payable, if at least it were proved that the owner would have brought vindication at all events, and that he had not had his attention called to it by the wrongful act towards the subject.

(*m*) L. 71, § 1, *de furtis*: "Ejus rei, quæ pro herede possidetur, furti actio ad possessorem non pertinet, quamvis usucapere quis possit: quia furti agere potest is, cujus interest rem non subripi: *interesse autem ejus videtur, qui damnum passurus est: non ejus qui lucrum facturus esset.*" (In my first three editions I understood this passage to apply

ward is, that in that case no interest exists which can be referred to another already acquired right; and it is precisely by this reference to a *legal interest* that the *obligatio furti* is to be distinguished from the right of naked Possession. (P. 333). When no evidence could be brought as to the particular articles which had been lost in the *dejectio*, the loss itself and the value were decided by the oath of the plaintiff; but the Judge must previously have fixed a *maximum*, according to circumstances, which the plaintiff was not permitted to exceed (*n*).

The *conditions* and the *operation* of the Interdict have been now stated, and nothing remains but to describe the *exceptions* by which this Interdict was restrained (*o*). The

generally to every case of Usucaption; but now I am convinced that it only refers to the *improba pro herede usucapio* of the old law (Gaius II. 55, 56), and that it has crept into the Digest through an oversight. For in the law of Justinian, no one could have Usucaption but a *bonæ fidei possessor*, but this party actually had the *actio furti*, (L. 12, § 1, *de furtis*; § 15, I. de obl. quæ ex del.), and indeed quite consistently, because the *bonæ fidei possessio* itself was already an acquired immediate right, and is recognized as an integral portion of property (D. 49, de V. S.), and indeed in most cases was protected by an appropriate suit, the actio Publiciana. Consequently, the *lucrum facere* in the above passage is not to be understood as of profits generally in the case of donations, but it denotes, as in Gaius, the illegality of this particular profit, and consequently a malæ *fidei possessio*. (Add. to 4th ed.)

(*n*) L. 9, C. *unde vi* (*Juramentum Zenonianum*). The distinction from the ordinary *jus jurandum in litem* is usually considered to consist in this latter being merely relative to the value of the article demanded, and assuming that everything else is proved. A. Faber, Conject. XVI. 13, No. 21, XVI. 17, n.36. Others consider it as merely an application of the ordinary jus jurandum in litem : Cujacius in L. Opp. T. 9, p. 1160. (In my three first editions I held to the first opinion ; I now consider the second to be the correct one. For the *dejectio* from the land as the substantial ground of complaint must in this case also be proved *aliunde*, and if only the loss of moveables were sworn to, this oath would merely apply to the amount of the damage which arose out of the *dejectio*.

(*o*) We may observe at once here, that the Int. de vi *armata* was free from *all* exceptions : Cic. pro Cæc. c. 8. "P. Dolabella præ-tor interdixit, ut est consuetudo,

first exception here, as with the Int. *retinendæ* possessionis, had reference to the *origin* of the Possession, from which the plaintiff had been ousted. If this Possession itself had commenced *vi, clam,* or *precario,* provided indeed that such violence had been exerted against the present defendant, (*ab adversario* vi possidere), the Interdict was excluded (*p*); except that the exception did not avail against the Int. de vi *armata* (*q*). The reason why the exception was permitted (except in this latter case), rested on this general ground (*r*); the defendant had as to the same matter a special Int. recuperandæ possessionis, which he might have brought with success after losing the first suit, and it was, therefore, merely for the purpose of shortening proceedings, that an exception against the first, the Interdict, was granted instead of a new Edict. A party, however, who had used vis armata

---

de vi, *hominibus armatis,* sine ulla exceptione." C. 22, "Vim, quæ ad caput et vitam pertinet, restitui sine ulla exceptione voluerunt." C. 32. "…. ut qui armatus de possessione contendisset, inermis plane de sponsione certaret."

(*p*) Cic. pro Tullio, c. 44, (see *ante,* p. 327). Cic. pro Cæcina, c. 32: "In illa vi quotidiana…. ne id quidem satis est, nisi docet, ita se possedisse, ut nec vi, nec clam, nec precario possederit." Cic. Epist. ad Fam. VII. 13, (p. 390, ed. Græv.) "Neque est quod illam exceptionem in interdicto pertimescas, *Quod tu prior vi hominibus armatis non veneris.*" (The "*non*" which Manutius interprets so oddly, and which many others wish to strike out, belonged to the usual form of the exception, in which both the defendant and the Prætor addressed the plaintiff; compare L. 1, § 7, *de*

cloacis. "…. Non esse in interdicto addendum: quod *non vi, non clam, non precario, ab illo usus,*" (al. *usus es*); where the *non* is used for *nisi.* The meaning of this negation is given in Gaius, IV. 119. Paulus, V. 6, § 7. "Qui vi aut clam, aut precario possidet, ab adversario impune dejicitur." (*Impune*—namely, so that no Interdict was to be dreaded, which alone was spoken of. It might nevertheless amount to a trespass). Fragm. Legis Thoriæ, (Haubold Monumenta Legalia, p. 15). "Qui…. ex possessione …. vi ejectus est quod ejus is, quei ejectus est possederit, *quod neque vi, neque clam, neque precario possederit,* ab eo quei *eum* ea possessione vi *ejecerit,*" rel.

(*q*) Cic. pro Tullio, c. 44. (See *ante,* p. 343). Cic. pro Cæc. c. 32 ; Gaius, IV. § 154, 155.

(*r*) Compare *ante,* p. 313, note (*h*).

was not allowed this advantage. Justinian rejects this exception generally, and even treats its invalidity as a well-known
matter (s): modern Jurists have all sorts of opinions upon it.
According to some, Justinian must have changed the old
law tacitly, others hold the alteration must have been introduced in some lost constitution, and, again, Tribonian must
have been wholly ignorant of the old law (t): the last of
these opinions, which is defended strenuously by Hotman,
should rather pass for a piece of ignorance. The whole
subject required no new law, since it was quite clear in
itself, as the result of another very familiar modern rule
of law.

For, according to the constitution, even the property
would be lost by the *dejectio* if it had previously belonged
to the disturbant; *a fortiori*, therefore, all right to the
naked Possession, if he had previously been possessor of the
subject. Now, the above exception was founded on the
previous *jus possessionis*, which had been theretofore forcibly
disturbed; it was, therefore, very natural, that after the
above constitution the exception should no longer avail,
without any new law being required on the point (u). That

(s) § 6, I. *de interd.* "Nam ei
(sc. dejecto) proponitur interdictum unde vi, per quod is, qui
dejecit, cogitur ei restituere
possessionem, *licet is ab eo, qui
dejecit vi, vel clam, vel precario
possidebat.*"

(t) Duarenus, Disp. Anniv. I.
20. Hotomanus, Obs. VII. 620;
Cujacius et Schulting in Paulum,
V. 6, § 7.

(u) Schulting (see the last
note) indeed had supposed that
this new principle arose out of
this constitution: but he does not
seem to have conceived clearly
the whole bearing of the case, or
otherwise he would have rejected
the other doctrines, which he

nevertheless allows to stand. It
may perhaps be urged as an objection to the above view, that in
the Edictum Theodorici, c. 76,
the Interdict is mentioned *with*
the exceptions. " Illi res occu ·
pata per violentiam. . . . reddetur,
qui. . . . *nec violenter, nec abscon-
dite, nec precario* possidet ;" although in his time the laws
against self-protection were already in existence. But it is
quite comprehensible that the
accurate logical conclusion should
have been recognized in the
legislation of Justinian, although
wholly overlooked in the careless
Edict.

the Jurists of Justinian's time viewed the matter in this
light, not only follows from the passage cited from the Institutes, which is scarcely to be explained in any other way (v),
but more particularly from the circumstance, that several
traces of the old law are to be found in the Digest, and yet
everything is very skilfully omitted by which any departure
from the old law can be proved directly, $i. e.$, in any other
way than by an *argumentum a contrario*. The following
passages may be cited as authorities for this statement (w):

L. 1, § 30, *de vi.*

" Qui *a me* vi possidebat, *si ab alio* dejiciatur habet
interdictum."

L. 18, *pr. de vi.*

" .... emptorem quoque ... . interdicto teneri:
non enim ab ipso, sed a venditore, per vim fundum esse
possessum ......"

L. 17, *de vi.*

" .... ideoque si te vi dejecero, *ilico* tu me, *deinde*
ego te; unde vi interdictum *utile tibi erit*" (x).

L. 14, *de vi.*

" Sed si vi *armata* dejectus es, sicut ipsum fundum recipis,

---

(v) For it is no proof against
this, that this section from the
Institutes first of all mentions the
Interdict itself with a connotation of the above modification,
(and so the *rei persecutio* generally), and then cites the *penalty*
of the constitution, as to which
latter only the constitution is
mentioned as the source.

(w) From the simple fact, that
in L. 1, *pr. de vi,* the *exception*
was omitted, although it undoubtedly occurred in the Edict,
it follows most clearly that the
mode in which the subject is
treated in Justinian's Code could
not have arisen from mere inat-
tention in the compilers.

(x) The first part of the passage runs thus : " Whoever *in
continenti* turns the *dejector* himself out of possession, never actually loses the Possession" (p.
331). Thereupon the conclusion
is drawn, " if I take your Possession by force, and am immediately
thereupon (*ilico*) ejected by you,
but subsequently (*deinde*) again
occupy the Possession forcibly,
the Interdict lies (*utile tibi erit*)
against me," *i. e.* it is not excluded
by an exception, which without
doubt might have been maintained if the second *dejectio* (*ilico
tu me*) had been a true *dejectio,*
and not rather a mere defence of
Possession.

etiam si vi, aut clam, aut precario eum possideres (*y*): ita
res quoque mobiles omnimodo recipies."

The *second* exception against the Interdict was founded
on the *limitation* of suit. After expiration of a year, the
Interdict was excluded by this exception (*z*), but this rule
again is limited by the following exceptions: 1st. Whenever the defendant had acquired anything by means of the
dejectio (*in id quod ad eum pervenit*), he had no right to this
exception (*a*). Therefore no use could be made of the
exception in the chief and most important case of the Interdict, viz., where the defendant still retained Possession, and
the plaintiff was demanding the Possession itself, and not
damages (*b*). 2nd. In vis *armata*, the exception did not
avail (*c*), but no trace remains of this exception in Justinian's compilation. 3rd. Lastly, by a constitution of Con-
stantine (*d*), the exception was taken away, in cases where,

(*y*) And this universally, without distinction, whether the Possession had been obtained *ab
adversario* or *ab alio* vi, clam,
precario.

(*z*) L. 1, *pr. de vi.* "*.... De
eo.... tantummodo intra annum..*
judicium dabo.*" (L. 1, § 39, *eod.*
" Annus in hoc Interdicto *utilis*
est." Cf. L. 2, C. *eod.*)

(*a*) L. 1, *pr. de vi.* "*.... Post
annum de eo, quod ad eum, qui vi
dejecit pervenerit,* judicium dabo."
L. 7, § 5, *comm. div.* "*.... Placuit, etiam post annum in eum,
qui vi dejecit, interdictum reddi ;
(that is to say, under the above
assumption, which did not require
to be expressed, because it was
evident *per se* in the case in question). Cf. L. 3, § 1, *de vi.* L. 2,
C. *unde vi.*

(*b*) It is impossible to produce
more errors as to this exception than Domat brings together

in a few words; Lois Civiles III.
7, s. 1, § 18, and s. 2, § 30.
" Whoever is turned out of Possession by force, still retains Possession for a year, and by means
of that, this Interdict ; after that
period he loses both his Possession
and the Interdict, and nothing is
left to him but vindication." He
is here describing the *praxis* of
the French law, and relies on the
Ordonnances, but this does not
excuse him, as he at the same
time grounds it all on the Roman
law.

(*c*) Cic. Ep. ad Fam. XV. 16,
p. 415, ed. Græv. " Postulabi-
musque ex qua hæresi, *vi hominibus armatis* dejectus sis, in eam
restituare. In hoc interdicto non
solet addi, *In hoc anno.* Quare
si jam biennium, aut triennium
est.. . in integro res nobis est."

(*d*) L. 1, C. *si per vim.* (L. 1,
C. Th. *unde vi*).

during the absence (*e*) of the possessor, his people had been turned out of Possession. In such case, the Interdict was not limited to any time at all, whether the possessor chose to sue after his return, or whether his people brought the suit previously; for the constitution gave these latter the privilege of maintaining the Interdict without any express authority, and yet as procurators of the possessor.

Both of these exceptions have a peculiar character in reference to this Interdict; and of the other exceptions which may be used in this as in all other suits generally, one only needs to be particularly mentioned, on the ground of its application being limited. The *exceptio pacti* is forbidden in this case, as in other illegal transactions, where the *pactum* has *preceded* the illegal act itself.

L. 27, §. 4, *de pactis.*

" Pacta, quæ turpem causam continent, non sunt observanda: veluti si paciscar, ne furti agam, vel injuriarum, si feceris: *expedit enim timere, (timeri) furti vel injuriarum pœnam.* Sed post admissa hæc, pacisci possumus. *Item, ne experiar interdicto unde vi, quatenus publicam causam contingit (f), pacisci non possumus.*"

SECTION XLIII.

INTERDICTUM DE CLANDESTINA POSSESSIONE.

The Interdictum de *clandestina* possessione appears to be wholly similar to the Int. *de vi.* Like the latter, it requires,

(*e*) The *absence* itself however in this case is to be defined somewhat differently to that in the loss of Possession, for here only a protracted absence is meant.

(*f*) That is, " because the State itself is interested that no violence should take place, the prevention of it should be caused by dread of the Interdict." See

in the first place, according to all analogy, juridical *Posses-sion;* next, the Possession must be lost, and the right to redemand Possession by this Interdict founds itself on the illegal form of the act by which the loss was occasioned. Now, *clandestina possessio* means a Possession which has been taken behind the back of the party from whom oppo-sition was to be apprehended (*a*). All, therefore, turns upon the commencement of the Possession ; if by this commence-ment, the Possession amounts to *clandestina possessio,* it does not cease to be so upon the previous possessor subse-quently acquiring notice of it (*b*): so also, conversely, the Possession is not converted into a *clandestina possessio,* by the possessor's proceeding, after the acquisition, to conceal it (*c*). There was a special exception in the case of an owner, who, although his Possession may have had such commencement in fact, is, nevertheless, not to be looked upon as a *clandestinus possessor* (*d*). This general notion of *clandestina possessio,* however, has no juridical meaning, except when it is associated with a violation of Possession. Many, indeed, have conceived that even without such vio-lation, and thus merely in reference to property, the above

ante, the addition at the end of § 6, where Rudorff's Essay is spoken of.

(*a*) L. 6, *pr. de poss.* " Clam possidere eum dicimus, qui fur-tive ingressus est possessionem ignorante eo, quem sibi contro-versiam facturum suspicabatur, et, ne faceret, timebat."

(*b*) L. 40, § 2, *de poss.* ".... Si sciens tuum servum non a domino emerim, et tum (al. *cum*) clam eum possidere cæpissem, postea certiorem te fecerim : non ideo desinere mec clam possidere."

(*c*) L. 6, *pr. de poss.* " Is au-tem, qui cum possideret non clam se celavit, in ea causa est, ut non videatur clam possidere : non enim

ratio obtinendæ possessionis sed origo nanciscendæ exquirenda est." On the other hand : L. 4, *pr. pro suo.* (".... Tum enim clam possedisse videberis ") ; but this passage has reference to the peculiar right as to the *ancilla furtiva,* as to which several special points were laid down. Cujacius in L. 40, § 2, de poss. (African. Tr. 7, afterwards differently and not so well in L. 6, de poss., Opp. VIII. 268). Others consider this case as an exception in *furtum* generally. Glossa in L. 6, *de poss.;* Duaren. L. 6, *de poss.* Opp. p. 865.

(*d*) L. 40, § 3, *de poss.* Cuja-cius in hoc. loc. (Afric. Tr. 7).

Possession might arise, so that Usucaption would be prevented by it (*e*). But the *res clam possessa,* as such is, in fact, not withdrawn from Usucaption, but only the *res furtiva,* which is generally, indeed, though not always, identical with the former. The above view was founded on the passages where a *clandestina possessio* is spoken of in cases where the possessor had purchased the subject from a third party, and in which cases, it is said, no violation of Possession can be conceived (*f*). But in these cases also the possessor would be worsted in the old Int. *utrubi,* which did not give the victory to the party disturbed in his Possession, but to him who had had the longest Possession, in suchwise, nevertheless, that in the comparison of the two Possessions, the *violenta, clandestina,* and *precaria* possessio were reckoned as nothing. If then there is only one sort of *clandestina possessio,* it always is of the same nature, whether it is to be regarded as the ground of an Interdict, or of an exception. Indeed, even those who recognize a *clandestina possessio* of two sorts, must still admit that the clandestinity is of the same nature in an *exception* as in an *Interdict,* namely, an act violating the Possession, and this both on the ground of the close connection between the exception and the Interdict, and also because the exception in all cases could only exclude that party who possesses clam *ab altero,* which is only to be conceived where the secrecy was a violation of the Possession.

(*e*) Albert, § 57, and the authors there cited. I myself was substantially of the same opinion in the 5th edition, p. 501-2, although I objected to the form in which it was put. The whole of the opposite view, which I now present, is here given for the first time.

(*f*) L. 40, § 2, de poss.; L. 4, *pr. suo.* No doubt can arise as to my present explanation from the first passage. In the second undoubtedly a conclusion is drawn from the *clam possidere* against the possibility of Usucaption, but only on the ground that the sole title for Usucaption there conceivable, *pro suo,* was excluded by it. Besides which, according to the jurist's view, the subject was undoubtedly *furtivum,* so that both coincided.

Thus, the Possession which is lost must be juridical, and from the mode in which this took place, the new Possession must be capable of being looked upon as *clandestina possessio*, in order to give rise to the Interdict. To these conditions, finally, it must be added that the object of Possession must be an immoveable. This proposition is not supported by any direct evidence, but by such strong analogy, that any other proof is almost superfluous. For the Int. *de vi* was inapplicable to moveables, on the ground that other suits were already available as to them, when Interdicts generally were introduced (p. 334). These other suits (with the exception of the actio *vi bonorum raptorum*) applied in like manner to the *clandestina possessio* of moveables; and it is therefore much more improbable that a special Interdict should have been given in such case, when there was none such in *violenta* possessio, which undoubtedly must have been considered a much more important case (*g*).

The conditions for this Interdict have now been fully stated, but a wholly different question remains to be answered; and this question is, is there, in fact, such an Interdict as this? (*h*) Why this question is only raised now will immediately appear.

(*g*) L. 1, *pr.* L. 3, *pr. uti poss.*; Gaius IV. § 151. I laid down erroneously in the 5th edition that *clandestina possessio* was different in an exception to what it was in the Interdict. This inconsistency had been previously objected to with reason by Albert, § 71.

(*h*) It also must be added that the Int. utrubi in its earlier form must have afforded exactly the same protection against the clandestine as against the forcible abstraction of Possession. If, for instance, a party deprives me secretly of a moveable, the Interdict utrubi would give me an undoubted re-medy, because the defendant could not bring his *clandestina possessio* into account, and therefore I should have the longest possession of the two. If this view is correct, it must then be acknowledged that a *casus omissus* here occurs in the Justinian Code as to moveables. For the laws against self-protection, which are wholly sufficient in cases of violence, do not extend to clandestine Possession. Thus the party from whom an article has been stolen, and who cannot establish a *furtum* by any *right to the thing*, has in fact no suit at all against the thief, and

Only one testimony is to be found for the existence of this Interdict, and even that is very ambiguous. For Ulpian says, on a widely different occasion, "Julianus speaks of a special Interdict for *clandestina possessio:*" and he does not give his own opinion on the point (*i*). On the other hand, this Interdict is not only not even mentioned in the whole description of Interdicts in the Institutes and Digest, but there is no case remaining in which it could be employed, as in all the instances in which it would formerly have availed, the Possession now is either not lost, or the Int. *de vi* is applicable. All this is clearly to be explained by the historical investigation which was made above on occasion of the loss of Possession. Land continued to be possessed so long as the possessor had no notice of the new occupation, from which it follows that *clandestina possessio,* which is only conceivable generally as a clandestine act in reference to the previour possessor (p. 351), was no longer possible as to land (p. 262). But this Interdict had only reference to land (p. 351), consequently, from that period the Interdict was untenable. Now, the above proposition, with all its consequences, was not altogether established in the time of Labeo, and, consequently, at the still earlier period when Interdicts were introduced (*j*), such an Interdict might un-

for this case the Int. de clandestinæ possessione would still be an actual desideratum. (Add. to 6th ed.)

(*i*) L. 7, § 5, *comm. div.* (The question here is as to the right of the possessor to call for a *judicium communi dividundo*). "Julianus scribit, si alter possessor provocet, alter dicat eum *vi* possidere, non debere hoc judicium dari, nec post annum quidem: quia placuit etiam post annum in eum, qui vi dejecit, interdictum reddi; et si *precario,* inquit, dicat eum possidere, adhuc cessabit hoc judicium: quia et de precario interdictum datur. *Sed et si clam dicatur possidere qui provocat, dicendum esse ait, cessare hoc judicium: nam (al. nam et) de clandestina possessione competere interdictum inquit.*"

(*j*) The existence of this Interdict at an earlier period indeed is supported by an important testimony in the following passage of Cicero, In Rullum III. 3. "Hæc tribunus plebis promulgare ausus est, ut quod quisque post Marium et Carbonem possidet,

doubtedly have been assigned: in the time of Papinian, Ulpian, and Paulus, the proposition was universally recognised, these Jurists accordingly could not any longer look upon the Interdict as valid, and it could, with still less propriety, be admitted into the Digest. At the commencement, and in the middle of the second century, the proposition itself was not altogether established, and was certainly not extended to all its consequences, and therefore Julianus might still mention the Interdict as existing law. In the *exceptio* clandestinæ possessionis, some little difference is to be observed from the case of the Interdict. If a party occupies my land clandestinely, and then immediately brings the Int. uti possidetis against me, so that I first hear of his occupation by this suit, no opportunity arises for me to make use of the alternative allowed by the law of attempting to reinstate myself (p. 351), and, therefore, the whole issue in the case could not be raised more simply and satisfactorily than by calling in aid the old *exceptio clandestinæ possessionis*.

Modern Jurists have generally passed over this Interdict in silence, which is objectionable, not only on account of the cursory notice of it by Julianus, but also on the ground of the constant connection in which *clandestina* and *violenta possessio* are always mentioned. The author of the ancient statutes of Pisa, which Grandi ascribes to the twelfth century, has mentioned the Interdict in this very connection (*k*).

ideo jure teneret, quo qui optimo privatum. Etiamne *si vi ejecit?* etiamne si *clam,* si *precario venit in possessionem?* Ergo hac lege jus civile, causæ possessionum, *prætorum* interdicta tollentur." This means, up to that time the Interdicts recuperandæ possessionis would have availed, but they were now taken away from the previous possessor by this iniquitous law. (Add. to 6th ed.)

(*k*) Grandi Epist. de Pand. ed.

2 Flor. 1727, 4, p. 224. " Hac Saluberrima Constitutione sancimus, quod si aliquis fuerit possessor. . . . . .aliquo tempore prius illo qui nunc invenitur in possessione, *licet non probetur quod vi, vel clam, vel precario possideat,* ab adversario tamen in possessione recuperanda semper potior sit prior possessor; nisi, etc." That is, the prior Possession in itself, as a rule, is to give a right against the actual possessor, although *none of the three Roman*

Cujacius not only speaks of the Interdict, but lays down that it is still applicable; but the exposition which he gives of the case where it may be applied, is very unsatisfactory (*l*).

———◆———

SECTION XLIV.

INTERDICTUM DE PRECARIO.

Special Sources for the *Precarium*.
Paulus, lib. 5, tit. 6, § 10-12.
Digest, lib. 43, tit. 26.
Cod. lib. 8, tit. 9.

Authors :
Christ. Rau. s. Aug. Corn. Stockmann, Dissertatio de Precario, Lips. 1774.
J. G. Vogel, Dissertatio de Precario, Gott. 1786.
Neither of these very remarkable.

————

When the mere *enjoyment* of a right is transferred to another, it may be effected in a variety of juridical forms. The contract of demise, the *commodatum*, &c., are merely forms of this sort, by which the simple enjoyment of the property is severed, usually for a definite period, from the property itself. In all these cases provision is made, in such legal form itself, for the right of restitution; not so, when the transaction takes place without any juridical form, for instance, by a mere *pactum*. But for two cases of this

Interdicts recuperandæ possessionis would lie.

L. 40, § 2, de poss. (African. Tr. 7), et in L. 6, § 1, *pr. de poss.*

(*l*) Cujacius, Obss. IX. 33, in Opp. VIII. 267—8.

kind, the Roman Law established a special right of restitution. Whoever permits another to enjoy *property* (*i. e.* natural possession), or to enjoy an *easement*, he retains to himself the right of recalling this permission at will, and has the above-mentioned special right, and the juridical relation which arises thereupon, is called *precarium* (*a*). This name had its origin in the fact of the permission itself being usually obtained by a *prayer;* this prayer, however, is not essential, and even a tacit permission is sufficient (*b*). We have now only to deal with the *first* of these two cases, which relates to the enjoyment of property.

Whenever, therefore, *detention* is transferred in this way, the rule is that juridical possession passes with it, and to prevent this rule from operating, the contrary must be specially expressed (p. 222). In both cases, however, the permission may be recalled at will; but should the subject not be restored, the Possession becomes illegal (*vitiosa, injusta* possessio) (*c*), and may be claimed by an

(*a*) L. 2, § 3, *de prec.* "Habere precario videtur, qui possessionem vel *corporis* vel *juris* adeptus est, *ex hac solummodo causa*, quod preces adhibuit, et impetravit, ut sibi *possidere* aut *uti* liceat."

(*b*) Paulus V. 6. s. 11. "Precario possidere videtur non tantum qui per epistolam, vel quacunque alia ratione hoc sibi concedi postulavit, sed et is, *qui nullo voluntatis indicio, patiente tamen domino possidet.*" Cujacius (in a note to the above passage), confines it to a continuance of a previous *precarium*, without any ground indeed, unless such ground is contained in the following section of Paulus, ".... magis dicendum est, clam videri possidere, (thus not *precario*), *nullæ enim preces*

ejus videntur adhibitæ." But these very last words are wanting in the editio princeps, (see Hugo's note).

(*c*) Some passages call precaria possessio, *justa*, others, *injusta*, evidently because each is possible, though at different periods; it commences to be *injusta* when restitution is refused. This abuse of good will and confidence has the same operation here, as force in *violenta possessio.* Cuperus, II. 7, objects to this very natural reconciliation of the passages, which was long ago suggested and acquiesced in : his principal argument is that in no case is a *revocatum* precarium mentioned, but a *precarium* simply which is associated with the exceptions *vi*

A A 2

interdict in a similar way, as forcible Possession. Therefore, the *precarium* arises in this case, and only in this case,
because *vitiosa* possessio alone gives rise here to the juridical relation, and it is never treated as a contract (*d*). One
consequence of this is, that the right of demanding the
thing back at will is not destroyed, even if the party who
gave the permission has renounced such right (*e*); whereas
a suit founded on a contract would be barred by an
exceptio *pacti*.

The Int. *de precario* applied originally to land only, as
appears, first from its analogy to the Int. *de vi*, and secondly,
from express evidence; but so early as the time of the
Classical Jurists it had been extended to moveables (*f*).

and *clam* as a ground of *injusta
possessio*; but, if an exception is
used, it is self evident that the
permission is withdrawn. The
view of Cuperus is carried out
further, and defended by Albert,
§ 58—61.

(*d*) All this is very clearly laid
down in L. 14, L. 22, § 1, *de prec.*,
L. 14, § 11 *de furtis*, and it is also
proved by the circumstance, that
the Interdict even falls to the
ground, if any other suit arising
out of a juridical transaction is
available.   L. 2, § 3, *de prec.*
("*ex hac solummodo causa*"),
L. 15, § 3, *eod.*   The above
proposition, however, might be
doubted on two grounds; 1st,
in L. 23, *de Reg. Jur. precarium*
is termed *contractus;* but that
word is evidently used there for
any possible ground of obligation,
for even *tutela* and *negotiorum
gestio* are comprehended by it.
2nd. In later times, besides the
Interdict, an action also (*præ-*

scriptis verbis) was given, L. 2,
§ 2, L. 19, § 2, *de prec.*, Paulus,
V. 6, § 10. This shall be discussed at the end of the section.
For the practical right, this latter
only amounted to the plaintiff
having his choice between two
modes of procedure. The nature
of the *obligatio* itself was not at
all altered by it.

(*e*) L. 12, *pr. de prec.* G. F.
Kraus, Diss. de precario ad
certum tempus dato. Viteb. 1750.
A limitation of the right to demand restitution so completely
contradicts the nature of a *precarium*, that, if an agreement of
this kind is clearly shewn to
exist, it must be treated, not as
a restrictive contract, but as a
mere memorandum to the receiver
as to the time for making re-
delivery.

(*f*) Isidori Orig. V. 25. " Precarium est dum prece creditor
rogatus permittit debitorem in
possessione *fundi* sibi obligati

The *obligatio* only affects the party who had received the Possession by a *precarium*, and it is immaterial whether he had made the request himself, or through another (*g*). An heir does not possess the subject properly as a *precarium* (*h*); but whether the Interdict could be brought against him was a very contested point amongst the Roman Jurists. Some denied it absolutely, and saw in it rather a *clandestina possessio*, and therefore undoubtedly the ground for an Int. *de clandestina possessione* (*i*). Others allowed of the Interdict against the heir absolutely (*j*). This last view must be considered as the prevailing one in our Law Books, as the passages which mention it are most decisive, whereas for the other opinion there can only be brought forward one hesitating passage, which is referable indeed to other matters. The Interdict cannot be used against the *owner* of the subject, because in such a case no *precarium* could exist.

demorari et ex eo fructus capere." This appears to be taken from ancient sources. L. 4, *pr. de prec.* " In rebus etiam mobilibus precarii rogatio *constitit,*" which appears to shew that this rule of law had been only lately adopted. This is the reading of the Florence MS. and of Haloander; other MSS., and old editions, it is true, read *consistit,* by which all reference to such an alteration disappears.

(*g*) L. 4, § 2, L. 6, § 1, L. 13, *de prec.*

(*h*) L. 12, § 1, *de prec.* An important consequence of which is that the *accessio possessionis* thereupon fails.

(*i*) L. 11, *de div. temp. præscr.* " Quamvis precarium heredem ignorantem non teneat, nec Inter-dicto recte contineatur." This passage, taken by itself alone, is however not conclusive, because the term introduced, *ignorantem*,

may mean that *precarium and the Interdict* would not avail, so long as the heir had no notice, and that upon his having such notice, his share in the *precarium* would arise, which sense is supported by L. 12, § 1, de precario (see last note). But Paulus, V. 6, § 12, is quite clear; " Heres ejus, qui precariam possessionem tenebat, si in ea manserit magis, dicendum est, *clam videri possidere :* nullæ enim preces ejus videntur adhi-bitæ. Et ideo persecutio ejus rei semper manebit, *nec interdicto locus est.*" (That is, interdicto de precario).

(*j*) L. 8, § 8, *de prec.* " Hoc interdicto heres ejus, qui precario rogavit, tenetur, quemadmodum, ipse," &c. L. 2, C. eod. " Habi-tantis precario heredes ad res-tituendum habitaculum teneri contra eos interdicto proposito, manifeste declaratur."

The examination of this rule in detail has already been made (see *ante*, p. 223).

The *obligatio* itself, upon which this Interdict is founded, requires, in the first place, restitution of the subject, not compensation for its value (even if lost or destroyed), unless *dolus* or *lata culpa* can be established against the defendant (*k*). But the defendant is *in mora* from the time of instituting the suit, and from thenceforward, as in the other Interdicts, he is answerable for every *culpa*, he must give up the profits, in short, he must place the plaintiff in the same condition in which he would have been if there had been no refusal to make voluntary restitution (*l*).

There are no special exceptions with respect to this Interdict, none namely founded on limitation of suit (*m*); and even the general limitation, which the latter law introduced, can only be applied in the cases where the Possession after a refusal to restore has endured for thirty years.

I have thus described the *precarium*, as it is to be found in the Law Sources, but it cannot be denied that there is something very perplexing in this legal institute. First, how was it that the Romans, who were by no means a generous or present-making people by nature, were so early driven to the necessity of such a special legal remedy, from which we may infer that a constant demand for it arose in daily life? And when the demand arose, why did they not treat the case exactly like a *real* (realis) contract, namely, either as a *commodatum*, or at least as an innominate contract in the form *do ut des* (*n*)? For the original delivery,

---

(*k*) L. 2, *pr. de poss.* "Ait prætor, *quod precario ab illo habes, aut dolo malo fecisti ut desineres habere, quâ de re agitur illi restituas.*" L. 8, § 6, *eod.* "Et generaliter erit dicendum, in restitutionem venire dolum et culpam latam dumtaxat, cetera non venire." Cf. L. 8, § 3, 5, eod. L. 23, *de Reg. Jur.*

(*l*) L. 8, §§ 4. 6, *de prec.*

(*m*) L. 8, § 7, *de prec.*

(*n*) [Add. to 4th ed.] That a *commodatum* was not adopted, is to be explained by the fact that in the earlier times *precarium* only applied to land (p. 356), and *commodatum* only to moveables. L. 1. § 1, *commod.* L. 17, *pr. de præscrip. verb.*

and the agreement to re-deliver undoubtedly existed, and nothing more was required for the existence of a real contract. Further, how could the Romans entertain different opinions even upon this point, for some of them deny the existence of a *civilis obligatio,* and thence deduce the necessity for an Interdict, whilst others prescribe the *actio præscriptis verbis* (p. 356)? Why did a different rule prevail here as to *culpa* to that which general principles warranted (p. 358)? Lastly, how could the liability of heirs be disputed (p. 357)?

All these doubts are soluble, when we call to mind the origin of *precarium* indicated above (§ 13). It was originally a sort of feudal relation between the patron and his client, arising upon demised land belonging to the ager publicus. Such lands were granted at will, and the *Int. de precario* lay against the client who would not give them up on demand (*o*). But as there existed between the patron and the client a sort of family relation, like a father's to his children (*p*), no proper *obligatio,* no contract, could be recognised, although in similar cases between third parties a contract would undoubtedly have arisen. That this relation did not extend to heirs, that the usual principles as to *culpa* in contracts did not apply, that it only had reference to land—all this no longer presents any difficulty. That it did not cease at the same time with the *ager publicus,* depended on similar grounds, as applied to *possessio* generally (§ 13). For, although it was devised and moulded for this particular purpose, still it was capable of being applied in its original character to other objects also, for which it was not devised in the first instance: and, when the old ager publicus ceased to exist, this extension was all that remained of the ancient *precarium.* It was now therefore

(*o*) Niebuhr Roemische Geschichte, Th. 2, S. 187, 2nd ed., chiefly from Festus v. patres, ".... quique agrorum partes adtribuerint tenuioribus perinde ac *liberis,*" like a *peculium* therefore, in which also the right of recalling the permission at will existed.

(*p*) Festus *loc. cit.*

made use of as to moveables also, and thereupon the above noticed controversy arose amongst the Roman lawyers, some of whom adhered to the strict letter of the ancient *precarium*, whilst others desired to found new rules upon its wholly altered condition, and this last view, as might be supposed, appears to have obtained the preference in our Law Books.

Perhaps, however, the *precarium* would have altogether disappeared as superfluous, if it had not accidentally become important for another legal case. According to the earliest form of the law of pledge the subject was immediately *mancipated* to the creditor with a trust for future remancipation (*fiducia*) (p. 216). It was not usually intended in such case to deprive the debtor of the use of the subject, and the question thereupon arose, under what form of right this user might be permitted to the non-owner. The *precarium* undoubtedly served for this purpose most effectually, and therefore it may perhaps have continued to be of importance down to the time of the classical Jurists (*q*). In the Law of Justinian this application of it had disappeared.

SECTION XLV.

NEW RIGHT OF THE CONSTITUTIONS.

The whole right of possessory Interdicts, which has hitherto been set forth, depends upon a definite form of violation of Possession, upon which only the *obligatio* arose,

(*q*) Interpr. PAULI, V. 6, § 7. ".... precario (possidet) qui per precem postulat, ut ei in possessione permissu domini *vel creditoris fiduciam* commorari liceat." Schulting suggests the emenda- tion *fiduciarii* with great probability : my manuscript however reads *fidutia*. Compare also Isidori Orig. V. 25 (see ante, p. 356, n. (*f*),) but especially Gaius II., § 60.

which was enforced by Interdicts. Many Jurists consider all this learning as wholly obsolete : they conceive that the constitutions introduced a general legal remedy, the *actio momentariæ possessionis*, by which every sort of lost Possession could be immediately recovered, without reference to the mode in which it had been lost: and that by this universal right of action, the old Interdicts were not so much put an end to, as rendered superfluous (*a*). According to this view the new right to possessory suits was just as indefinite and arbitrary, as the old right was defined and consistent, and it is therefore the more necessary to investigate the historical correctness of the doctrine minutely.

The new right it is said, is not so much expressly laid down in any single law, as *assumed* to be undoubted in several constitutions. But, even without closely examining these constitutions, this new right may be distinctly contradicted. For Justinian has not only imported the old law into the Digest, but it is even brought forward in the Institutes, and indeed with all the later modifications, which in part had been introduced by himself, a most undoubted proof therefore that the right there treated of was not obsolete but a practical Institute. Indeed, what is still more conclusive, in one of the latest constitutions, which is cited to prove the new right (*b*), the old right is expressly referred to as existing law, for a new suit is given in a very special case, *merely because the old Interdicts did not provide for it*. It is thus, therefore, sufficiently proved that the above new right is not contained in the constitutions, the exposition of which shall be now given.

I. L. 5, C. unde vi (*c*).

(*a*) Cujacius especially has maintained this proposition, Obss. 1, 20, XIX. 16. Paratit. in Cod. *tit. unde vi;* Comm. in Cod. *tit. unde vi*; App. T. 9, p. 1148. 1153—9, and several others have followed him. On the other side are, Giphanius, Proleg. Lib. 8, Cod., Westphal, § 320, Fleck, De Interd. p. 66—71.

(*b*) L. 11, C. *unde vi*.

(*c*) Comp. L. 1, C. Th. *fin. reg.*—Cujac. Obss. XIX. 18. J. Gothofred, in L. cit. C. Th.,

" Invasor locorum pœna teneatur legitima: si tamen vi loca eadem invasisse constiterit. Nam si per errorem aut incuriam *domini* loca ab aliis possessa sunt: sine pœna *possessio restitui debet.*"

Thus—" possession is recoverable even in cases where it had not been lost by violence." But the owner also demands possession in vindication, and that this was the point in question is clearly enough shewn by the expression " *domini*" (*d*). The whole passage, therefore, like many others, is inserted by Tribonian in a wrong place.

     II. L. 8, C. *unde vi* (*e*).

" Momentariæ possessionis interdictum, *quod non semper ad vim publicam pertinet, vel privatam,* mox audiri, interdum etiam sine inscriptione meretur." Thus there were cases which allowed of an Interdict, although no *accusatio ex Lege Julia,* would lie. Such cases may easily be conceived : if, for instance, during the absence of the possessor his land had been occupied without any particular violence, and he does not venture to return back, no *crimen vis* occurs, but still there is ground for the Interdict (p. 331).

     III. L. 11, C. *unde vi.*

" Cum quærebatur inter Illyricianam advocationem, quid fieri oporteret propter eos, qui vacuam possessionem (*f*), absentium sine judiciali sententia detinuerunt, quia veteres leges nec

---

Goesius in Notis ad scr. rei agr., p. 183, (also in Ritter at the passage of the Cod. Th.), Westphal, § 320, Fleck De Interd. p. 67.

(*d*) Cujacius himself, Opp. IX. 1016, explains the *restitutio possessionis* in a very similar passage, L. 6, C. *de poss.* in the same way, without recollecting his explanation in this place.

(*e*) L. 8, C. Th. *de jurisd.*— Cujac. Obss. I. 20, Giphanius, in h. L. (Expl. Cod. P. 2, p. 288).

(*f*) *Vacua possessio* may be said either of a subject which has no possessor, or of a possession, which at the moment is not corporally enjoyed (for inst. possessio fundi quæ animo retinetur.) The expression is here used in the first sense, which moreover is the technical one : the reasons shall be given at length, *post.* Azo in Summa, h. tit. no. 31, fo. 146, et in Lectur. in h. L. p. 619. ; Glossa in h. L. ; Giphanius, in h. L. (Expl. Cod. P. 2, p. 295).

unde vi interdictum, nec *quod vi aut clam,* vel aliam quandam actionem ad recipiendam talem possessionem definiebant, violentia in ablatam possessionem minime præcedente, nisi domino tantummodo in rem exercere permittentes (*g*): nos non concedentes aliquem alienas res, vel possessiones (*h*), per suam auctoritatem usurpare, sancimus, talem possessorem, uti prædonem intelligi, et generali jurisdictione ea teneri, quæ pro restituenda possessione contra hujusmodi personas veteribus declarata sunt legibus (*i*) ...... si non ex die, ex quo possessio detenta est, triginta annorum excesserint curricula" (*j*). The case alluded to in this law must be taken to be this : the Possession of the subject had been lost by mere absence (p. 271), and this *vacua possessio* had been occupied by another (*k*). Now, in this case, none of the previous possessory suits applied, indeed no suit at all

(*g*) This part of the passage makes the whole most clear. For the case must of necessity be conceived to be one in which no personal action would lie according to the old law.

(*h*) *Res,* when opposed to *possessiones,* (p. 68), mean moveables, the new law, therefore, embraces both, which was very natural, as the Int. *de vi* had been long extended to moveables.

(*i*) That is, by the extension of the Int. recuperandæ possessionis (sc. *de vi*) to this case, all the rules are to be observed, which prevailed according to the old law with the Int. *de vi* " quæ .... contra hujusmodi personas (sc. prædones) veteribus declarata sunt legibus."

(*j*) That the suit would not avail after thirty years, is a consequence of the general thirty-years' limitation ; that it was not

limited to one year is explained by the assumption that the defendant himself still retained the possession, in which case also the Int. *de vi* was not restricted to one year. Consequently, this provision contains nothing special, and it must be carefully distinguished from a similar provision in L. 1, C. *si per vim,* which does in fact provide for an excepted case.

(*k*) That this is the only way of supposing the case has been already suggested, and is now capable of proof. For, if the previous possession had only first ceased upon the occupation of the present possessor, the Int. *de vi* would have availed for land (p. 331), and the *condictio furtiva* for moveables. But according to Justinian's own showing the case was such that the old law afforded no remedy.

except vindication. Justinian enacts, that the Int. *de vi* should be applied to such case; undoubtedly something new is contained in the law; but, first, this new enactment only had reference to a single, expressly defined, case; and, secondly, no rule, which had previously prevailed as to possessory suits in other respects, was thereby modified. For, as the Possession had been already lost prior to the occupation, no disturbance of Possession came in question, so that even the determination of this special case bears no resemblance to the rule, which, as a general rule, is sought to be established by it.

IV. L. 12, C. *de poss.*

The passage itself has been explained above (p. 281-2). It enacts, that in certain cases the Possession should not be lost by the breach of faith of the agent; no special right of suit is there spoken of, and, least of all, a new *actio recuperandæ possessionis*, as the precise object of the law is, the *continuance* of Possession.

V. Lastly, the mere *heading* of one of the titles (*l*) has still to be reckoned here, and it may, perhaps, have contributed much to the above incorrect view. It runs thus: " si *per vim* vel *alio modo* perturbata sit possessio." What is to result upon these two cases of a *perturbata possessio* (*per vim* vel *alio modo*), is not said; the result, therefore, can only be ascertained by what is stated in the constitutions of the title itself. The *first* of these constitutions speaks merely of a possessio *per vim* perturbata. The contents of the second are as follows:—" The state of Possession shall not be altered in a lawsuit, either by a rescript of the Emperor, or by a decree of the Judge, if one of the parties is absent." This enactment refers evidently to *procedure* only, and it is merely introduced in an improper place by the compilers. Thus, the disturbance of Possession against which the law is directed (possessio

---

(*l*) Cod Just. Lib. 8, Tit. 5.

alio modo quam per vim perturbata), is a case of inter-locutory proceedings, and has not the smallest affinity with the disturbance, which gave rise to an Interdict.

Therefore, the old right of Interdicts was in no degree taken away or rendered superfluous by the constitutions, and the doctrine as to Possession, which formed the basis of those Interdicts, remained unaltered in the Code of Justinian.

BOOK V.

JURIS QUASI POSSESSIO.

———◆———

SECTION XLVI.

INTRODUCTION.

THE right of Possession consists in the protection given to the mere exercise of property against certain forms of disturbance. These forms of disturbance, and the above protection, may be conceived in a similar manner as to such rights also, which, as individual elements of property, have been severed from the property itself (*jura in re*), and the Roman Law has, in fact, adopted this idea. The relation of this *juris quasi possessio* to true Possession, has been developed above (§ 12). The same three questions arise in this case as with Possession itself, that is, the acquisition, loss, and protection by Interdicts, of the *juris quasi possessio,* have to be determined. But this inquiry must be especially directed to each class of the above rights, and therefore this Book divides itself into three parts:—

1. Personal Easements, § 47.
2. Real Easements, § 48.
3. *Jura in re,* which can not be classed under Easements, § 49.

One general remark, however, may be made at once as to these three classes. In these cases, as with Possession proper, the acquisition and continuance of the right depend upon a corporal relation, jointly with *animus*. The second of these conditions is to be defined, in compliance with the rule, exactly in the same way, as to all these rights, as with Possession itself. Thus no *juris quasi possessio* can be acquired without *animus possidendi*, and the right of Possession never arises upon a mere *animus possidendi*. This general observation, therefore, may suffice, and the *animus possidendi* will only be mentioned in the cases of the several rights themselves, when its occurrence assumes any special character (*a*).

The most important, and the greatest number of, Easements, were protected in their Possession by Interdicts: some, by the same Interdicts which have been already described with respect to Possession proper; others, by peculiar Interdicts. In opposition to the former, the *corporis possessor* might protect his Possession of freedom by the Interdict *uti possidetis* or *utrubi;* and, on the other hand, the possessor of an easement might always make his Interdict avail in the shape of an exception. [Add. to 6th Ed.]

SECTION XLVII.

PERSONAL EASEMENTS.

(*Easements in Gross.*)

Personal Easements (*i. e.* principally *ususfructus* and *usus*), have this peculiarity about them, that the enjoyment of them is always bound up with the natural Possession of the subject itself. Accordingly, the *quasi possessio* of them has more resemblance to Possession proper than that of the

---

(*a*) *Bona fides* is necessary in the Int. *de aqua* only (§ 48), in other cases not.

other rights, and this resemblance manifests itself not only with respect to acquisition and loss, but also with respect to Interdicts.

Thus, this sort of Possession is *acquired* by the same acts as the Possession of the subject itself; namely, by delivery of the subject, or by the owner taking the *fructuarius* to the land, or by allowing him to take Possession by himself(*a*); assuming, of course, that all this takes place in express reference to *ususfructus*.

This Possession is *continued*, like every other Possession, by the uninterrupted power to reproduce the original dominion (*b*), and it is lost, therefore, by the ceasing of this power. Besides this, however, another mode of loss has to be noticed; for, as the easement itself becomes lost by mere *non usus* after a certain length of time, so in the whole interval the Possession must be taken to have been lost, although the reproduction spoken of might have been possible at any moment. On the other hand, it cannot be maintained that every non-user, however short, puts an end in fact to the Possession, because then no limits whatever would exist, and both preservation of Possession, and, more especially, prescription, would become impossible. For this reason, nothing else remains but to consider the Possession during a mere non-user (and where there is no occupancy by a third party), as *in suspenso*, and that it is only on a

(*a*) L. 3, *pr. de usurp.* "Omnium prædiorum jure legati potest constitui ususfructus, ut heres jubeatur dare alicui usumfructum. *Dare autem intelligitur, si induxerit in fundum legatarium, eumve patiatur uti frui.* Et sine testamento autem si quis velit usumfructum constituere, pactionibus et stipulationibus id efficere potest." The ' pactiones et stipulationes' do not refer to the Possession, but to the right itself, which at an earlier period would be acquired by the *in jure cessio*, but in the later law was acquired by simple contract. The first is proved by Ulpian XIX. 11, and the latter by § 4, I. *de serv. præd.* § I., *de usufructu.*

(*b*) Even the special right of Possession in a *servus fugitivus* avails here also, and it is laid down as to this case under still more advantageous terms, L. 12, §§ 3, 4, *de usufructu.*

renewal of the user, or on the expiration of the whole period, that it is to be ascertained whether the Possession had existed during this interval or not (*c*). But on the very ground of this preliminary state of suspense, such mode of loss is wholly without operation upon Interdicts (*d*).

This Possession agrees with every other in being capable of being continued through an agent, for instance by a tenant, and in the application of this rule it is only necessary to mention especially a few cases :

1st. The right of these easements inheres in a person definite, and is consequently inalienable, consequently the alienation (by sale, gift, &c.) has, in substance, no other effect than as a mere demise ; a mere personal right arises against the *fructuarius*, and the form only of this *obligatio* is different. It results from this position as to Possession, that in all the cases in which the possession of the subject is usually transferred, the possession of the *ususfructus, etc.* is unaltered, so that the *fructuarius* retains the right of possession in like manner whether he lets the *ususfructus*, or sells or gives it away, or transfers it to another on a *precarium* (*e*). 2nd. The *ususfructus* may be let even to the

(*c*) A similar case of suspense occasionally occurs with usus-fructus also as to the property in the profits.

(*d*) A somewhat similar relation exists with the continuance of Possession, in so far as this may lead to acquisition through prescription. Unterholzner, Verjaehrungslehre, § 214, lays down that, in this case, the Possession runs on, although ordinary interruptions of the enjoyment occur, but that on the other hand it is broken by the enjoyment being neglected for any extraordinarily long period. This doctrine undoubtedly gives a wide discretion to the judge,

but it seems correct. (Add. to 6th ed.).

(*e*) L. 12, § 2, *de usufructu :* " Usufructuarius vel ipse frui ea re, vel alii fruendam concedere," (examples are given of this latter) vel locare, vel vendere potest : *nam et qui locat utitur : et qui vendit, utitur. Sed et si alii precario concedat vel donet, puto eum uti :* atque ideo retineri usumfructum. The last words indicate that by *non usus* after a certain period, the *ususfructus* itself is lost. So that the continuance of Possession is thus necessary here for the preservation of the right itself.

owner of the subject, so that in this case the Possession is continued through the owner. But, if the owner sells the subject without reference to the *ususfructus* (i. e. without reserving it) or lets it in his own name (thus equally without reference to the *ususfructus*) the Possession is thereby put an end to (*f*).

Interdicts, lastly, are just the same in this case as in possession proper, and this circumstance may have chiefly led to these two rights being confounded with one another (*g*). For as the enjoyment of these easements, like that of property, depends on the natural possession of the subject itself, the mode of disturbance in both cases is exactly the same also, and so also the protection against such disturbance is laid down in the same way for both cases:

I. If the subject is an immoveable, the Int. *uti possidetis* is applicable, when the Juris quasi possessio is violated, but not put an end to. This Interdict therefore is applicable in the following cases, 1st. Where several parties have the *ususfructus* of the same thing (i. e. in *partibus indivisis*), and mutually disturb each other; 2nd. Where the *fructuarius* wishes to protect himself against the inroads of the owner, or conversely ; 3rd. Where a third party, *i. e.* a wrong-doer, disturbs the possession of the *fructuarius;* 4th. Where different rights such as *usus* and *usus fructus*

(*f*) L. 29, *pr. quib. mod. ususfr.* This passage must not be made use of in the controversy which was touched upon above (§ 35) as to Possession itself. For first, the *juris quasi possessio* generally is not at all identical with Possession proper, and secondly, every thing in this case turns upon the special relation between the *fructuarius* and the owner, which has nothing similar in the case of Possession proper.

(*g*) It is only from the Fragm.

Vat. §§ 90, 91, 92, 93, that we learn that in these cases each Interdict was merely employed as a *utile interdictum*. The principal passage, § 90, must be amended thus : " Si usufructu legato legatarius fundum nanctus sit, competit *utile* interdictum adversus eum, quia non possidet legatum, sed potius fruitur. *Inde et* interdictum uti possidetis utile hoc nomine proponitur, *et* unde vi, quia non possidet," etc. [Add. to 5th ed.]

co-exist as to the same subject, and the enjoyment of them is to be secured against mutual encroachments (*h*).

II. The Interdict *utrubi* must be applied as to this *Juris quasi possessio* in the case of moveables, exactly as the Int. *uti possidetis* in the case of immoveables; it is easily conceivable that this application should not be expressly mentioned in the Law Sources, when we recollect how little the Interdict *utrubi* generally is spoken of.

III. When the possession is not merely disturbed, but put an end to by violence, the Interdict *de vi* lies (*i*). By the old law, it was excluded in the case of moveables, except when they happened to be lost simultaneously with the land (*quæ ille tunc ibi habuit*) (*j*); the extension of this *obligatio* to moveables by the constitutions, must apply here also. The first object of the suit is the recovery of the subject, because the ability to exercise the right depends upon having physical possession; the second object is complete compensation (*k*). In many cases this compensation will even form the sole object of the suit, when for instance, the right to the easement itself has in the mean time ceased either by the death of the *fructuarius*, or by *capitis diminutio*, or by *non usus :* in the two first cases the compensation has reference only to the period gone by, because even

---

(*h*) L. 4, *uti possidetis*. "In summa puto dicendum, et *inter fructuarios* hoc interdictum reddendum, et si alter *usumfructum, alter possessionem* sibi defendat. Idem erit probandum, et *si usus-fructus quis sibi defendat possessionem :* et ita Pomponius scribit. Proinde et si *alter usum, alter fructum* sibi tueatur, et his interdictum erit dandum." Wiederhold, p. 51, gives a most confused exposition of this passage according to his view of the Interdict. [Add. to 6th ed.]

(*i*) L. 3, § 13, 14 de vi; L. 60, pr de usufructu (upon ususfructu) ; L. 3, § 16, *de vi ;* L. 27, de donat. (upon *usus*) ; Huenerer, Diss. de Restitutione usufructuarii ex int. unde vi, Arg. 1631. G. A. Struv. Diss. De Int. unde vi, Jen. 1658.

(*j*) L. 3, § 15, *de vi.*

(*k*) L. 9, § 1, *de vi.* "Dejectum ab usufructu in eandem causam Prætor restitui jubet : id est, in qua futurus esset, si dejectus non esset."

B B 2

without the *dejectio* the loss would have occurred (*l*); when on the other hand the right becomes lost by *non usus,* the *dejectio* itself contains the cause of the loss, and consequently the damages must extend to the future also (*m*).

IV. No question arises, naturally enough, as to the Int. *de clandestina possessione,* as, even with respect to possession proper, its name is only casually mentioned.

V. Lastly, the enjoyment of such an easement may be transferred to a third party *precario* (*n*), and then the restitution of the subject is demanded back according to the words of the Edict by the Int. *de precario* (*o*).

SECTION XLVIII.

REAL EASEMENTS.

The possession of real easements (easements appurtenant) cannot be defined so simply as personal easements. Several cases under this head have to be accurately distinguished, some of which have given rise to much controversy (*a*).

All real easements form special exceptions to the general rule respecting property belonging to another, for either the party who possesses the right of easement may himself do something, which otherwise would be forbidden him (servitus quæ in patiendo consistit), or the owner must

---

(*l*) L. 60, *pr. de usufructu;* L. 3, § 17, *de vi.*

(*m*) L. 9, § 1; L. 10, *de vi.*

(*n*) L. 12, § 2, *de usufructu.*

(*o*) L. 2, *per de prec.* "...: Quod *precario* ab illo *habes....* id illi restituas." L. 2, § 3, *eod.*

"*Habere precario* videtur, qui possessionem vel corporis *vel juris* adeptus est....."

(*a*) Oppenritter, Summa Poss. P. 1, c. 5, *de acquisitione quasi possessionis;* almost entirely on real easements.

refrain from doing something which otherwise would be lawful to him (servitus quæ in non faciendo consistit) (*b*). We call the first kind of easements *positive*, or *affirmative*; the second *negative* or prohibitory rights. With positive easements, that which may be done by virtue of the easement, may be an independent act in itself, and only indirectly relate to the land of another (such as *jus itineris*), or it may be inseparably connected with the land of another (such as *jus tigni immittendi*). These three classes of real easements must be now carefully distinguished (*c*).

First Class. Positive easements (servitudines quæ in patiendo consistunt), the enjoyment of which consists in a distinct independent act. In general, the acquisition of this *juris quasi possessio* may be stated thus: the act which constitutes the subject of the right must be exercised in fact, and be exercised *as a right* (*d*). Whoever, then, goes into his neighbour's field to speak to him, does not establish thereby any *jus itineris;* whoever, on the other hand,

---

(*b*) This distinction does not apply to personal easements because they are all essentially positive.

(*c*) This division almost entirely agrees with another one, which however is merely accidental, and therefore not universally true : the first class contains jura prædiorum *rusticorum*, the second and third jura prædiorum *urbanorum*.

(*d*) L. 25, *quemadm. serv.* "Servitute usus non videtur, nisi is, qui *suo jure uti* se credidit : ideoque si quis pro via publica vel pro alterius servitute usus sit, nec interdictum, nec actio utiliter competit." From this antithesis it appears, that the *credidit* in the first sentence, ambiguous when taken by itself, does not refer to

bona fiaes but to the actual *animus possidendi.* L. 7, *de itinere.* "Si per fundum tuum nec vi, nec clam nec precario commeavit aliquis, non tamen *tanquam id suo jure faceret*, sed, si prohiberetur, non facturus : inutile est ei Interdictum de itinere actuque : nam ut hoc Interdictum competet, *jus fundi possedisse* oportet." Comp. L. 1, p. 6, *de itinere.* This important condition of such quasi possession is only to be regarded as the special form which the *animus possidendi* assumes on this occasion. For the entry upon land to speak to the possessor, would be an act incapable *per se* of denoting any *animus possidendi*, whatever the secret intention of the party might have been [Add. to 6th ed.]

intends to exert such a right, and performs it forcibly, in spite of the owner's opposition, undoubtedly acquires the Possession, so that the *patientia* of the owner is not at all necessary for the acquisition of this Possession (*e*). The same observations apply here respecting the loss of this Possession as were made above (p. 368), with respect to personal easements. It need only be added here, that the Possession may be acquired through the act of any third party (without any relation of agency), provided only that this act is done *nomine fundi* : L. 5, L. 6, *pr.* L. 24, *quem admodum serv.* L. 1, § 7, L. 3, § 4, *de itinere.* With respect to Interdicts, the loss of possession here is very important in consequence of several peculiar rules. Interdicts, lastly, of an entirely special kind were established here, and the usual possessory suits could not be made use of at all (*f*). The Int. *de vi* is not applicable, because no proper *dejectio* can be conceived in this case (*g*). The Int.

(*e*) L. 20, *de serv.* " Ego puto, *usum* ejus juris (*jus fundi* was in question) pro traditione possessionis accipiendum esse." *Usus* therefore, without any other distinct qualification constitutes prehension. The same conclusion may be drawn from the exceptions to the several Interdicts, which exceptions (*vi, clam, precario,*) would have had no meaning in these cases, as with possession proper, unless prehension itself could be predicated as to them. The passages which have led to a contrary opinion being asserted (L. 11, § 1, *de public. in rem acta.* L. 1, § 2, *de serv. pr. rust.*) do not speak of the acquisition of Possession, but of the right itself, as to which the case stands thus, 1st, *cessio* and *mancipatio* founded this right in point of fact (Ulpian XIX. 1. 11); 2nd, *traditio* did

not give the right itself, but only the *publiciana actio* (LL. cit.) : and in that case as in every case of delivery, the will of the *tradens* was required, and this made *patientia* always necessary.

(*f*) Many Jurists however have admitted them, for instance, Busius in Subtil. Juris VII. 5, and quite recently Thibaut, Archiv. B. 1, S. 111—116, B. 18, S. 325; Pandekten, § 769, 8th ed. On the other side, see Giphanius in Cod. tit. *uti poss.* P. 2, p. 302.

(*g*) L. 4, 27, *de usurpatione.* "Si viam habeam per tuum fundum, et tu me ab ea *vi expulseris:* per longum tempus non utendo omittam viam : quia nec possideri intelligitur jus incorporale, *nec de via quis, id est mero jure detruditur.*

de precario is at least superfluous: for whoever permits another *precario* to go over his land, and then withdraws the permission, can enforce this prohibition by the Int. *uti possidetis* (*h*), besides which, the very words of the Int. *de precario* contemplate the restoration of something given, which cannot be in any way conceived in this case (*i*). The Int. *uti possidetis*, therefore, would be the only one which might be conceived possible here, but still this Interdict was not allowed, but special Interdicts were given for the most important cases of this kind (*j*); therefore a right of action availed in these specific cases only (*k*), and only in

(*h*) The whole relation may be stated thus; the owner by virtue of his mere possession has the Int. *uti possidetis*; if the defendant possesses the easement, he may avail himself of the Int. *de itinere* even as an exception; but if the possession of the easement is founded on a *precarium*, the plaintiff may admit the Possession itself, and yet get over the exception by a replication. Properly, the application of the Int. *de precario* might be conceived to occur in a case where the possessor of the easement had permitted another *precario* to use it, and afterwards demanded it back; but this sort of transfer had no place with easements. (Add. to 6th ed.)

(*i*) For the *habere* precario may be conceived in every *jus in re* (L. 2, § 3, *de prec.*), and particularly in easements of this first class (L. 3, L. 15, § 1, *de prec.*) but not the *restituere* precario upon which alone the Interdict is founded (L. 2, pr. *de prec.*). Nevertheless it is not unimportant, even, with these easements, to as-

certain whether they are founded on a *precarium* or not, because exceptions at all events depend upon the latter (L. 1, pr. *de itinere*).

(*j*) L. 20, in f. *de serv.* " . . . . Ideoque et *interdicta veluti possessoria* constituta sunt." Thibaut, S. 116, expounds this indefinite expression as a universal one, but quite arbitrarily. For the sentence may just as well mean "For this reason, in (most or many) cases of this kind there are possessory remedies."

(*k*) As all possessory Interdicts are wholly positive in their nature, the Int. *uti possidetis* cannot be allowed in these unnamed cases, because the employment of it would require, not the application of a general principle to a particular case, but rather, an extension of the principle to wholly new cases, and because then the more unimportant easements of this kind would be favoured above the older and more important ones (via, actus, iter, aquæductus). Nor is an extension by analogy of the special Interdicts

the forms which were expressly provided, and which shall now be explained. But, although in this case special Interdicts were required by the peculiar character of the subject-matter, still they were closely allied to the Int. *uti possidetis*, and, like it, they depend upon the same foundation. For they are, in like manner, prohibitory, and they rest upon an *obligatio ex maleficio*, which latter point is placed beyond doubt by the words contained in every formula, *vim fieri veto* (*l*).

of this class to the remaining unmentioned cases more conceivable, because the positive conditions of the above special Interdicts are far too diversified (Add. to 4th ed). In this *vexata quæstio* it is especially to be remarked, that it is by no means an accidental circumstance, that special and not the general Interdicts should have been given for several of these cases, for the ground lies in the special nature of these easements, which consist in acts of an intermittent character, to which therefore the general Interdicts could not be made applicable. It would require a more minute discussion as to what quantity of enjoyment entitles to a possessory remedy. In rights of way this was laid down at thirty days in the past year, in rights of watercourse any one act of exercise in the year. These cases exhausted all that was of importance with the Romans, and in the less important cases, wherein the general Interdicts were equally inapplicable as in the more important, resort must be had to the *petitorium* suit. With respect to the right of common, it appears to me most

probable, from the slight and indistinct mention of it, that this right was of rare occurrence as an easement among the Romans, and therefore of little importance, which explains the total want of any possessory remedy for this case historically (although not very satisfactorily for our practical wants). Lastly, I conceive that in the present day this question, so important for the theory, has no interest in practice, as the action of waste (spoliatorium) is applicable to this easement. Comp. *post*, the addition to § 52. (Add. to 6th ed.)

(*l*) Albert, Besitz unkoerperlicher Sachen, § 140, strives most incomprehensibly to contradict this proposition, for he lays down that the *vim fieri veto* has quite a different meaning in this easement, from what it bears in the Int. *uti possidetis* (§ 145); what this different meaning is he has in vain attempted to show. If these words had only been casually used once by a Jurist in the course of interpretation, some question might have been raised; but they occur expressly in the formula of each of these

I. *Jus itineris, Actus, Viæ.*

Sources:

Digest, Lib. 43, tit. 19.

C. Albert, ueber den Besitz unkoerperlicher Sachen.

N. T. Darstellung des possessorischen int. de itinere actuque privato. Leipzig, 1826.

T. C. Althof, Das. Int. de itinere actuque privato. Riegel, 1846.

The *first* condition for this Interdict is *possession* of the easement, and this Possession must be now precisely defined. It coincides with every Juris quasi possessio of this class in this, that the right must have been exercised by the plaintiff himself, or by some one in his name (*m*), and exercised as a right: whoever, therefore, makes a path over another's land on any other ground, for instance, because the old road is under water, does not thereby exercise the act of a possessor, and his relation is very precisely distinguished even from a *precaria possessio* (*n*). But exercise of the easement is not in itself sufficient; there must also exist a defined amount of it to comply with the prescribed condition for the Interdict. For whoever wishes to use the Interdict must, during the current year (reckoning from the commencement of the suit), have exercised the right, on at least thirty different days (*o*). Still substitution may be made, even in opposition .

Interdicts, just as in the formula *uti possidetis*, and yet they are to have a different meaning! (The sentence in the text, to which this note refers, was introduced in the 6th edition).

(*m*) L. 1, § 7, 8, 11 ; L. § 3, 4, *de itin.*

(*n*) L. 1, § 6; L. 7, *de itin.* (see *ante*, p. 373).

(*o*) L. 1, § 2, 3, *de itin.* Albert's Essay is almost wholly dedicated to the task of discovering another meaning for this rule (§1—39). He requires, namely, only a *frequent* user, so however that the acts of enjoyment should include at least a month. Thus twenty-nine days following one another would be insufficient, but two days, with three months between them, would be sufficient, the decision as to the effect of the latter however being left to the Judge. If this had been the intention it would have been much better to mention no number at all. His principal argument is that in most cases it would rarely happen that a cart

to this mode of reckoning: if, for instance, the enjoyment is prevented during the past year by force or other sufficient cause, by substitution the previous year may be taken into the reckoning (*p*). Lastly, with this condition the *accessio possessionis* has to be noticed, as it is quite immaterial whether the plaintiff himself, or his *auctor* (testator, vendor, &c.), or both together, shall have exercised the right during thirty days of the last year.(*q*). In cases where the right had been exercised by the *auctor*, the remedy for the actual plaintiff is an Int. *adipiscendæ* possessionis (*r*). The *second* condition for the Interdict is a violent disturbance, the notion of which is to be defined exactly in the same way as with the Int. *uti possidetis*. The Interdict lies against every disturber, without distinction, whether he be the proprietor, bound by the easement, or any other person, and therefore the Interdict does not wholly turn on the relation between the easement and the property (*s*).

The plaintiff demands by this Interdict, first, that the disturbance of his Possession should be put an end to (*t*) ; secondly, that complete compensation should be paid him (*u*). The operation of the Interdict, therefore, is exactly like that of the Int. *uti possidetis*.

Finally, exceptions are founded merely on the mode in which the easement has been enjoyed, for no special exception, founded on limitation of suit, is required, because in the very *factum* which the plaintiff has to establish a limi-

---

should be driven thirty days in the year to a particular plot of ground. But it is not required that all the species of user should occur on each day. Whoever proves therefore that he walked ten days, rode ten days, and drove ten days on the way in question would entitle himself to the Interdict for the *actus servitus* [Add. to 6th ed.]

(*p*) L. 1, § 9, *de itin.*

(*q*) L. 3, § 6—10; L. 6, *de itin.*

(*r*) L. 2, § 3, *interdictis*. "Apiscendæ possessionis sunt Interdicta. ... ex hoc genere est et : *quo itinere venditor usus est, quominus emptor utatur, vim fieri veto*."

(*s*) L. 3, § 5, *de itin.*

(*t*) L. 1, *pr. de itin.* ".... vim fieri veto."

(*u*) L. 3, § 3, *de itin.*

tation of time is comprised. The rules, therefore, which govern these exceptions are as follows: The days on which exercise has been made of the right by violence, clandestinely, or by a *precarium*, are not calculated in the thirty days (*v*). This is the only effect of the exceptions: if, therefore, the easement has been exercised for thirty clear days without such defects, no exception lies on the ground that on other days besides these thirty the easement has been exercised with violence, or clandestinely, or by *precarium* (*w*). On the other hand, it is quite immaterial whether the violence, &c., upon which the enjoyment of the easement for thirty days founded itself, should have been exerted against the present defendant, or against his agent, or against a previous possessor: thus, also, whoever buys or inherits land, succeeds at the same time to the exceptions which his predecessor, to whom he is the legal *successor*, might have made use of.

L. 3, § 2, *de itinere.*

" Si quis ab *auctore meo*(*x*) vi aut clam, aut precario usus est: recte a me via uti prohibetur, et interdictum ei inutile est: quia a me videtur vi, vel clam, vel precario, possidere, qui *ab* actore (*y*) *meo* vitiose possidet. Nam et Pedius scribit, si vi aut clam, aut precario ab eo sit usus in cujus

(*v*) L. 1, *pr.*; L. 3, *pr.* § 1, *de itin.*
(*w*) L. 1, § 12; L. 2; L. 6, *de itin.*
(*x*) So read four Paris MSS. (No. 4455, 4486, 4487, and 4456) and (perhaps the only printed edition); Paris, 1536, 4. Glossa anon. interlin. (MS. Paris, 4479), "id est administratore," (this Gloss assumes the reading *actore*, and is therefore taken from a manuscript where it must have occurred). Odofred. in h. L. fo. 102, " alii habent, *ab actore* id est a

castaldione." Florent. " ab *auctore* vi ;" Rom. 1476, etc., and even two earlier editions from the same press as the above mentioned Paris edition, (Paris, 1510 and 1514, 4to.), ab *auctore meo* vi. The *meo* is also to be found in very many MSS. For the indiscriminate use of actor or auctor, actio or auctio, see Cujacius, Obss. XXIV. 8.

(*y*) So reads again: Paris, 1536, 4to., and so also the three first MSS. (the fourth has here *auctore*).

locum (z) hereditate vel emptione, aliove quo jure successi, *idem esse dicendum.*" . . . . The Florence reading is highly improbable, because it makes Ulpian say the same thing twice over, and yet the language used indicates that a further proposition is affirmed, as appears particularly by the words, " *idem* esse dicendum," which could only be used in respect to a different case, to which, however, the same rule was applicable as to the previous one. The reading here adopted fully removes the difficulty. In the first case a forcible act is spoken of against my *actor* (*i. e.* the slave who had the charge of my estate); in the second, an act exercised against my *auctor* (testator, vendor, &c.) In the first case, I may have the exception which is founded on the act of violence, and in the second also the same law applies (*idem* esse dicendum).

The difficulty is also removed by Hervag's reading, but quite in another way. In the first case a juridical *successor* (" ab auctore") is spoken of; in the second case a non-juridical (non cujus in locum . . . . *jure* successi); but the second sentence would then not only be very ill expressed, but would be contrary to all analogy.

II. There is another Interdict in respect to this easement, but it relates to the *repair* of the way, the user of which is protected by the previous Interdict.

     Sources: Digest. Lib. 43, tit. 19, (L. 3, § 11, etc.)

The complainant, therefore, demands by this Interdict, that the owner shall not prevent him from putting the way in good repair.

(z) So read the old editions, with the exception of Haloander's and of Paris, 1536, 4, " *Non* in cujus locum," is in the text of Basil, 1541, f. (ap. Hervag). As a various reading merely, Lugd. 1551, 1557, 4, Portanæ. As the various reading of a *Cod. Medic.* the edition of Vintimilli, Paris, 1548, 8, and many others following it, Lugd. 1551, 12 ; Paris, 1552, 8 ; Russord., Charond., Paciana., Baudoz. ; this Medici manuscript however is not to be confounded with the celebrated Florence copy, see Brenckmann, Hist. Pandect. p. 254. I have not found the *non* in any manuscript.

This Interdict, however, on easily understood grounds, is more restricted than the preceding one; for the plaintiff must give security to meet the damage which may ensue upon his repairs (a); he must, besides, prove (and here this Interdict is distinguishable from all other Possessory suits,) his *jus* reficiendi, and, in addition to this, his possession also, just as it would have to be proved as a preliminary step in the foregoing Interdict. The *jus* reficiendi, however, is admitted as the consequence of the easement itself, whenever no special exception can be proved against it; consequently, the plaintiff must prove, besides his possession, his *right* also to the easement (b).

Here, therefore, the right to the easement is not only the condition, but is the object also, of the Interdict, so that the plaintiff may not only obtain protection by it against all interference with his repairs, but the right to the easement itself, just as in the *confessoria actio*, must be decreed to him if he establishes his case (c). The relation of the Interdict to the *confessoria actio* may, therefore, be stated thus: Whoever can prove the right to the easement may protect each exercise of the right by the *confessoria actio:* but in this particular case he may have his choice between an *actio* and an Interdict; still, if he adopts the latter, he must prove, not only his right to the easement, but possession also. As, therefore, this Interdict is nothing but an actio confessoria in the form of an Interdict, nothing more need be said of it since the form of procedure has ceased, by which alone it was distinguished from the above action.

(a) L. 3, § 11; L. 5, § 4, *de itin.*

(b) L. 3, § 11, 13, 14, *de itin.*

(c) L. 2, § 2, *de interdictis.* " Quædam interdicta *rei persecutionem continent*, veluti de itinere actuque privato (sc. reficiendo); nam *proprietatis causam continet* hoc interdictum." The limitation of this passage to the Int. de itinere *reficiendo* becomes undoubted by comparing it with the L. 3, § 13, *de itin.*; Costa in pr. *I. de interd.* The incorrect exposition which Hasse has given of this passage, arising out of his general view, has been already noticed in the addition at the end of § 6.

III. Jus aquæ quotidianæ vel æstivæ ducendæ (*d*).

Source: Digest. Lib. 43, Tit. 20.

The condition for this Interdict, first of all, is, possession of the easement. The easement, at the same time, must be exercised with the conviction that the right itself exists (*bonæ fidei possessio*) (*e*). It must, lastly, have been exercised during the current year, or if the water course were used during winter only, or during summer only, it must have been exercised within the last year and a half (*f*).

In this case, also, besides Possession, forcible disturbance is required, and it is immaterial whether this is effected by the act of the owner, or of a third party (*g*). If several persons make claim to the same water course, this suit avails, like the Int. *uti possidetis*, as Int. *duplex* (*h*).

The object of the suit is, first, the quiet enjoyment of Possession (*i*): next, compensation for damage sustained, which in this, as in all easements, may consist in the loss of the right itself by *non usus* (*j*).

Exceptions are framed, confessing that the easement has been exercised in point of fact, but alleging the mode to have been unlawful, viz., *vi, clam, precario* (*k*).

IV. A special Interdict (*de rivis*) also applies to the repairs of a water course.

Source: Dig. Lib. 43, Tit. 21.

(*d*) Originally this Interdict applied only to agriculture; it was subsequently extended to all water courses; L. 1, § 11, 13, 14; L. 3, *pr. de aquâ.* Indeed it was carried so far that it applied also to water courses, which were not prædial easements at all, but were merely permitted as a personal right and for personal use, L. 1, § 12, 24, *eod.*

(*e*) L. 1, § 10—19, *de aquâ.*

(*f*) L. 1, § 31—36; L. 6, *de aquâ.*

(*g*) L. 1, § 25, *de aquâ.*

(*h*) L. 1, § 26, *de aquâ.* "Si inter *rivales, id est, qui per eundem rivum aquam ducunt,* sit contentio de aquæ usu, utroque suum usum esse contendente: duplex interdictum utrique competit." (For the definition of *rivalis*, see Glossa, c. 18, C. 32, q. 5), Comp. L. 4, de aqua. Paulus, V. 6, § 9.

(*i*) L. 1, pr. de aquâ. "Vim fieri veto." L. 1, § 27, *eod.*

(*j*) L. 1, §. 23, *de aquâ.*

(*k*) L. 1, pr. § 10, 20, *de aquâ.*

This Interdict has precisely the same conditions as the preceding one (*l*); the right to the easement, therefore, does not come in question here, but only the Possession (*m*). But security must also be given in this case in respect of the damage which may be occasioned by the repairs (*n*).

V. In a similar manner, and with like conditions to the two last Interdicts, two other Interdicts are mentioned, to protect the jus aquæ *hauriendæ* against aggression.

Source: Digest. Lib. 43, Tit. 22.

Whoever, then, has not made use of this right forcibly, &c., during the current year, may bring the first of these Interdicts, in order to secure the future enjoyment; and the second Interdict in order to enable him to reinstate the wells, &c., to which the easement attached.

Second class of real easements: positive easements which stand in immediate connection with the Possession of land. The acquisition and preservation of their Possession is very easily defined, as they always consist in the continuing form, by the existence of which the right is actually exercised. If, for instance, a *jus tigni immittendi* is in question, the *juris quasi possessio* depends upon the fact, whether the *immissio* actually has place or not (*o*). The Interdicts can only be explained under the third class.

Third class: Negative easements.

Whoever possesses one of these rights, may require the owner of property to abstain from some act that, as owner, he would be justified in exercising. Now, how is the possession of such a right to be acquired?

This question is generally referred, in the first place, though erroneously, to the acquisition of the right itself. For it is affirmed, that delivery is required in this case as

(*l*) L. 3, § 7, *de rivis.*
(*m*) L. 1, § 9 ; L. 4, *de rivis.*
(*n*) L. 3, § 9, *de rivis.*
(*o*) L. 20, *pr. de serv. præd. urb.* " Servitutes, quæ in super-ficie consistunt, *possessione* retinentur . . . " namely by virtue of the Possession of the subject-matter (of the *corpus*), by which the right is exercised.

well as in property, although the *in jure cessio* of the old law, and mere contract by the Code of Justinian, were fully sufficient for this acquisition (*p*). But the question is important—1st. For the right to Interdicts; 2nd. For title by prescription; 3rd. For the *publiciana actio*, which in this case also only arises upon a delivery, the latter, however, only being required when the easement was not given by the ascertained owner (*q*).

One case of acquisition of this sort of Possession is undisputed, namely, when an attempt has been made to oppose the user of the easement, but has been prevented, either by the opposition of the other party, or by force, or by the decree of the Court (*r*). But, except in this case, the mode of acquisition has been a very contested point. Some require that, according to the analogy of the above case, a similar attempt to prevent the user should be made, illusively, and that an illusory prohibition should also be given (*s*). But this sort of symbolical procedure does not at all agree with the nature of Possession; we cannot cite any positive evidence for it, and it has only been suggested out of necessity, and from the want of any better information. Others affirm, on the other hand, that the mere passiveness of the opposite party by itself constitutes the Possession of negative easements; so that, for instance, every owner of a house would have against all his neighbours the Possession of a *jus altius non tollendi*, as respects the present height of their houses (*t*). This view, again, was only adopted out of necessity, as it is highly improbable

---

(*p*) Ulpian XIX. 11; § 4. I, *de serv. præ.*

(*q*) L. 11, § 1, *de public. in rem act.*

(*r*) L. 15, *de op. novi nunt.* L. 45, *de damno inf.*

(*s*) Heisler, Untersuchung des Satzes, dass die Verneinenden Diensbarkeiten, &c., (Abhand-lungen, Halle, 1733), § 14—16; Thibaut Ueber Besitz, § 16.

(*t*) I also maintained this opinion in my two first editions, influenced principally by L. 6, § 1, *si serv. vindic.*; " Si forte non habeam ædificatum altius in meo, adversarius meus possessor est." But *possessor* does not relate here

that every landowner should actually possess at any moment innumerable easements against all his neighbours.—I conceive that the true conclusion depends on the same principle which was applied above (p. 373), with respect to affirmative easements. The Possession of the latter is not founded on every act of user, but only on a user *as of right* (tanquam id suo jure faceret). A distinction is thus made between the accidental user in fact, and the user grounded on juridical conditions, and on a kind of necessity; and the ground of this distinction consists here, as with the above-mentioned easements, solely in this, that otherwise the *animus possidendi* would be wanting in the first state of facts.

If we apply this distinction to negative easements, it gets rid of the second of the above views; for, if my neighbour has built his house to a certain height only, I enjoy the benefit of it merely casually and as a matter of fact, and I have, therefore, no Possession. On the other hand, it is clear on this principle why the getting the better of an attempt to prevent the user should give the Possession, because immediately thereupon the forbearance becomes no longer merely accidental, but is produced by the party's opposition. The mere title in law, however, must have the same operation; for, if my neighbour has given me either by agreement or by devise, the *jus non altius tollendi*, from that moment the forbearance to raise the house is no longer accidental, but necessary, being founded on the agreement or will: consequently, the same act which is capable of conferring on me the right itself, passes the Possession at the same time, without its being necessary for

to Possession, but to the character of defendant, "the adversary is he who (if he chooses) may be the defendant in a suit." The words following corroborate this exposition. For, if Possession were meant, nothing would have been more natural than to ascribe possessory interdicts to the adversary. This however is not the case, and all that he has is the Int. quod vi aut clam, which may be used without any Possession.

C C

the above-mentioned illusory prohibition to intervene. The distinction between the acquisition of the right itself and of the Possession, only amounts to this, that the former can only be conferred by the actual owner of the neighbouring land, whereas the Possession may be undoubtedly granted by the mere possessor of it.

It follows from the above, that the Possession of negative easements may be acquired in two ways,—by adverse user, and by legal title; *i. e.*, 1st, by resistance to the attempt to obstruct the user; 2nd, by any juridical proceeding, which in its form is capable of transferring the right of easement, whether in the given case it be actually transferred or not.

The Possession of negative easements is lost when the opposite party is able effectually to obstruct the user; thus where a neighbouring house, as to which I assert a jus altius non tollendi, is in fact raised higher, I necessarily lose my Possession of the easement.

Lastly, the Interdicts have to be defined, by which the enjoyment of the second and third class of easements is protected. Each of these easements, properly speaking, is only an attribute of the Possession of the principal; whoever, for instance, possesses the jus tigni immittendi, or altius non tollendi, has strictly nothing but the Possession of a house, modified in one way or another. For this reason, it were quite unnecessary to introduce special Interdicts for the possession of these easements, as every violation of them must have equally violated the Possession of the principal. The suit, therefore, which alone was applicable to the Possession of these easements, was the Interdict *uti possidetis* (*u*),

---

(*u*) L. 8, § 5, *si serv. vind.* ".... agi poterit, *jus esse fumum immittere*, quod et ispum videtur Aristo probare. *Sed et interdictum uti possidetis poterit locum habere, si quis prohibeatur, qualiter velit, suo uti.*" Here an affirmative easement (one indeed of the second class) is only spoken of, but there is no doubt that the same holds good as to negative easements also. At the same time a special ground arose why the use of possessory suits should be less frequent as to the latter rights, namely, that with them it was not

for the Int. *de vi* would not lie, because the most violent disturbance of this kind could not put an end to the Possession of the land. This rule is clearly shewn by an exception to it, namely, it was found necessary for the *jus cloacæ* to define the possessory suits somewhat differently to what they had actually been defined in the Int. *uti possidetis;* accordingly, not only was a special Interdict given (*v*), but also the Interdict *uti possidetis* is specially excluded (*w*). This view becomes still more clear by the contrast of the first class of real easements (which consist in independent acts). These easements, also, are attributes of the land, *i. e.*, the right to them is an attribute of the property in the land (*x*); but not so their Possession. For as the latter depends upon acts, which are quite independent of the Possession of the principal, it cannot be said that the easements themselves are possessed together with the principal, or that the violation of them violates the Possession at the same time. Therefore special Interdicts were framed for the most important

only sought to prevent an obstruction, and to recover damages, but also to cause the new erection to be pulled down, &c. But for this object, there was an appropriate Interdict (*quod vi aut clam*) which does not belong to possessory suits, and was even more beneficial, as its conditions were different and more simple than the preceding.

(*v*) Digest, Lib. 43; Tit. 23, *de cloacis* (sc. *purgandis, reficiendis*). The distinguishing character of this Interdict consists in the exclusion of the ordinary exceptions (L. 1, § 7, de cloacis), and the ground of this exclusion is easily ascertained. The state is interested ("ad publicam utilitatem spectare videtur") in no obstruction being offered to the

cleansing, &c.; the inquiry as to the right itself, or even to the *justa possessio* may be raised on another occasion.

(*w*) L. 1, *pr. uti possidetis:* ".... de cloacis hoc interdictum non dabo."

(*x*) L. 86, *de Verb. sign.* "Quid aliud sunt jura prædiorum, quam *prædia qualiter se habentia,* ut bonitas, salubritas, amplitudo?" *i. e.* easements are just as much qualities of the land, as a good soil, a healthy situation, &c. which have nothing juridical in them. The proposition moreover is laid down generally, and applies therefore to easements of the first class also: something similar is expressed as to the latter only in L. 12, *quemadm. serv. amitt.*

rights of this class, without its being found necessary to exclude them expressly from the Int. *uti possidetis;* and therefore we were required to affirm above that these easements, except in the cases mentioned, could not be protected by Interdicts.

SECTION XLIX.

SUPERFICIES.

The last case of *juris quasi possessio* relates to superficies (§ 25), as the only *jus in re*, except easements, to which a *quasi possessio* can be ascribed (*a*).

Special source for *superficies.*

Digest, Lib. 43, Tit. 18.

Every building is considered merely as a portion of the soil on which it stands, and the property, as well as the Possession of it, are inseparably connected with the property and possession of the soil. The only severance which is possible in this case consists in a particular kind of *jus in re*, which may be transferred to another by the owner. Whoever has this *jus in re*, is no more the possessor than he is

---

(*a*) Some perhaps would refer a quasi possessio to the following cases also, in which nevertheless it is excluded, and rendered superfluous by a true *corporis possessio;* 1st, Provincial-lands (§ 9), as to which a very indistinct mention of Interdicts occurs in Simplicius (Goesius, p. 76). See on this obscure passage, Trekell, Kleine deutsche Aufsaetze, Leipzig, 1817, S. 39 : 2nd, Pledge-right (§ 24) : 3rd, Emphyteusis (§ 13, § 24, § 26). For this case indeed a special Interdict was introduced, the Int. de loco publico fruendo, Dig. 43, 9, L 1, § 7, *ut in flum pub.;* L. 13, § 7, *de injur.* But this Interdict was not in any way founded on Possession : the *conductio* was alone sufficient, if Possession also occurred, the Interdict then coincided with a possessory remedy.

the owner of the house, but he has a *juris quasi possessio,* and through the latter, possessory suits also. This *juris quasi possessio* has the greatest resemblance to the Possession of personal easements, because they both depend on the natural Possession of the subject. In the acquisition and loss of the Possession, there is no distinction at all, and even in Interdicts none of any practical consequence.

I. Violent disturbance of Possession does not give rise, as in *ususfructus,* &c., to the Int. *uti possidetis,* but to a special Interdict (*b*), which has, however, all the advantages of the Int. *uti possidetis* (*c*). The distinction, therefore, is only in the name, and it may be safely so explained: *superficies* was merely an Institute of the Prætor, and therefore its juridical existence must have been due to a special passage of the edict. That this passage should have been introduced amongst Interdicts rather than amongst real actions, was only mere accident. It is quite otherwise with *ususfructus :* all easements were already founded on the *jus civile,* and it only required, therefore, in *ususfructus,* the simple application of the ordinary possessory Interdicts.

II. If the natural Possession was actually put an end to by *dejectio,* the Int. *de vi* applied in this case just as in Possession proper (*d*).

III. Lastly, if the *superficiarius* permitted the exercise of his right to another *precario,* and the latter then refused to make restitution, the Int. *de precario* might be employed, as this Interdict availed for all *jura,* as to which restitution was applicable (p. 375), and *superficies* must be included, just like easements (p. 366), amongst jura (in re).

(*b*) L. 1, *pr. de superfic;* L. 3, § 7, *uti possid.*
(*c*) L. 1, § 2, *de superfic.*
(*d*) L. 1, § 5, *de vi.* " Proinde

et si superficiaria insula fuerit, qua quis dejectus est, apparet interdicto fore locum."

BOOK VI.

MODIFICATIONS OF THE ROMAN LAW.

———◆———

SECTION L.

THE theory of Possession has been discussed in the first five Books of this Work, without any reference whatever to anything that may have been incorporated into the Roman Law in modern times; and this mode of inquiry is always necessary, where we do not desire, by confounding the old law with the new, to misunderstand both together.

But this inquiry being now concluded, it is permitted to inquire into the modifications which the Roman Law has undergone in modern times. And a special reason also occurs why this question should not be passed over. For, of all the important errors which are commonly entertained as to the Roman view of Possession, there is perhaps not one which has not also been raised in the Canon and German Law. On this ground, therefore, little would have been done for practical purposes, if the doctrines above alluded to were merely refuted by principles of Roman Law. The refutation might be assented to, yet still it may be conceived that an erroneous deduction from the above correct view had been made. To entitle, therefore, a civil theory of Possession to make any claim to be serviceable in practice, it is necessary to inquire into and describe the relation which the theory bears to the provisions of modern law: the purpose of the following Sections is to notice this relation; to discuss it thoroughly does not lie within the limits of this Work, as for that object an entirely different historical position would have to be taken up.

There are three points to which this inquiry must be directed: the first is as to the notion of Possession itself (§ 51); the two last have for their object possessory suits, *spoliatory* suits (§ 52), and possessorium *summarium*, or *summariissimum* (§ 53).

———◆———

SECTION LI.

NOTION OF POSSESSION.

The first inquiry, then, which is to be made now, relates to the notion of Possession.   Possession, in the Roman Law, refers only to *property* and *jura in re:* subsequently (and especially by the Canon Law) it was extended to every possible right.

Now the whole right of Possession consists in the protection against certain kinds of disturbance given to the mere exercise of the right, without any reference to the existence of the right itself.   This protection, therefore, can only extend to such rights as allow of these kinds of disturbances being conceived, and, except property and *jus in re*, no such rights existed.   But by the constitution of the Christian Church, and of the European States, rights were created, and were bound up with the possession and enjoyment of the *soil*, such as the Romans either knew nothing of, or never contemplated as the special rights of individuals.   Thus, the exercise of episcopal jurisdiction depends on the Possession of the See and its temporalities, and a similar relation of State-jurisdiction, or of individual branches of it, occurs both in the palatinate authority of princes, and the jurisdiction of certain owners of estates.   The same relation

exists with the real charges established by the German
Law, such as tithes, ground-rents, and services. For all
these rights a similar protection to that afforded to property
may be conceived, and the Possession of these rights, which
have been established in the above manner, may be resolved
in the most frequent and important cases into the Possession
of land, i. e. into the exercise of property. In many cases
the correctness of this reference is very manifest: where,
for instance, a bishop is forcibly ejected from his See by an
opponent, the violation of Possession in the soil is mixed up
inseparably with the violation of episcopal rights, and the
same necessary connection exists also in every protection
against this disturbance. But, even in the cases where the
exercise of only one of these rights, jurisdiction for instance,
is prevented by violence, although the above reference to
the soil does not then exist, still something analogous to it
is conceivable, just as in the case of the Roman *Juris quasi
possessio*. For forcible disturbance is just as well conceivable, as to these rights, as with respect to easements, and
therefore the same protection for the mere exercise of them
which the Roman Law has laid down for the latter, is
strictly consequential.

The application of Possession here described is, however,
not merely conceivable, but was long ago actually employed.
Mention is constantly made in the Canon Law of diocesan
and other ecclesiastical rights, and of the tithes bound up
with them: and so, also, no one has ever doubted that
jurisdiction and other public rights of a like nature may be
protected in their exercise against forcible attacks, exactly
like property, although as to all these rights no Roman
lawyer would ever have contemplated a right of Possession.
This view is confirmed by a very remarkable limitation
which the Canon Law affixed to this new species of Possession. Where, namely, spiritual persons possess tithes in
another person's parish, and are ejected from their Possession
by the *parochus* thereof, they are not allowed to avail themselves of the protection to their Possession, but must prove

their right itself, because the *jus commune*, i. e. the principle of the constitution of the Church makes against them (*a*).

Now, what is the relation between this species of Possession and that of the Roman Law? It is not a case of direct application of the latter right, because the subjects for this application were unknown to the Roman Law; but it all turns on a very simple and consistent carrying out of its principles. The view, therefore, of Possession is in no respect altered; it is only applied to objects where the Romans would probably have applied them, if they had recognised the objects themselves (*b*).

But, besides these rights, as to which an extension of the Roman Law in its strict spirit cannot be denied, there are two other classes of rights specially enumerated to which Possession is referred, rights of personal *status* and obligations. In the examination of this doctrine, the general notion of Possession, by which the very distinct Roman notion has been supplanted, shall be completely refuted.

First, then, a right of Possession is laid down in the case of family rights, and this doctrine, in respect to the most important case of the class, marriage, appears to be supported by express passages of the Canon Law (*c*). To compare this with a case of proper Possession will put the matter in a clear light. If a question arises as to *property* in a close, the suit may undoubtedly be decided without anything at all being said as to the right of the mere possessor; but even then it would be competent, indeed it might be necessary, for the Judge to make some provisional regulation as to the state of the Possession, still this provisional arrangement would be very different from a protection to the Possession as a special right in itself. In order to put

---

(*a*) C. 2, *de restit. spoliat.* in VI. ".... cum .... sit.. . manifestum (nisi aliud ostendatur) eas *de jure communi* ad eamdem ecclesiam pertinere."

(*b*) It is very remarkable that even the Glossers appear to have entertained the same view. Roffredi Tract. Jud. Ord. p. 81—83.

(*c*) C. 8, 10, 13, X. *de restit. spoliat.*

this protection in distinct opposition to the above arrangement, let us suppose that neither of the parties has the property in point of fact, but that one of them had been turned out of possession forcibly by the other; the provisional arrangement could make no alteration in the case, as at that moment the Possession was quiet and decided, although by the *obligatio,* which constitutes the only right of Possession, there would be a demand for the restitution of Possession, which had been put an end to by force at a previous period. Let us now return to family rights, the Possession of which is to receive protection from the Court. This protection is evidently nothing more than a provisional arrangement as to the state of Possession, which stands in immediate connection with the final decision of the right itself. The form of the marriage, for instance, is not disputed, but other grounds against its validity are brought forward; these grounds have then to be inquired into, but, in the mean time, says the Canon Law, the marriage relation shall continue, unless on some special grounds, this very continuance were sinful (*d*). In all this, therefore, no right of simple Possession is contained, *i. e.* no *jus obligationis,* by which the exercise of another right is secured without reference to the existence of this other right itself.

All that has been observed against the possession of family rights applies still more strongly to the possession of obligations. In most cases of this species Possession cannot be conceived at all, and it is only by accident that even in one case it should be spoken of. Whoever, namely, has received interest for his capital, by this receipt is said to have acquired *Possession* of the right to the capital, and to the future interest. Now that in such case no true right of Possession is created any more than in family rights, requires no special proof at all. But even the provisional arrangement, as to the state of the Possession, which must be affirmed in cases of family rights, is neither necessary here,

---

(*d*) C. 10, 13, X. *de restit. spoliat.*

nor actually prescribed, although the contrary has been frequently maintained on the strength of certain passages in the Roman Law, which contain no such doctrine at all.

It has now been shewn, that the view in which Possession was treated of in the Roman Law itself, has been not so much altered as expanded on logical principles, and extended to new objects. It still remains to be inquired how far suits for Possession, *i. e.* the forms, by which Possession is protected against outrage, have been modified.

———◆———

SECTION LII.

SPOLIATORY SUITS (*a*).

Writers upon Spoliatory Suits :—

C. Ziegler, Ad Can. redintegranda, last edition, with notes in Woltaer's Observ. ad Jus Civ. et Brand. fasc. 2, Hal. 1779, Obs. 35.

J. H. Boehmer, in J. Eccles, Prot. Lib. 2, Tit. 13. Ejusd. Notæ in c. 3, C. 3, q. 1, ed. Corpus. Juris Can., Hal. 1744.

Fleck, De Interdictis unde vi, et remedio spolii, p. 83—136.

————

Amongst the spurious decretals by which the pseudo collection of Isidore undermined the authority of archbishops

(*a*) *Spolium* ex mente juris canonici est iniqua privatio possessionis vel quasi, quomodocumque facta .. . *Spoliatus* itaque dicitur, qui qualicumque possessione vel quasi inique est privatus, ... Si per modum actionis *spolium* in judicio deducitur, summarie utique agitur. Vicat Vocab. ad voc. Spolium [Transl.]

and provincial synods (b), a whole column is to be found to the following effect (c) :—" A bishop who has been ejected from his see, or robbed of his property, shall not be chargeable before the synod for any offence until he is restored to the possession of his lost estate." No one undoubtedly imagined less than the impostor himself who fabricated these Briefs of Roman Bishops, that from one of their passages an entirely new system of possessory remedies, and, indeed, of Possession itself, would be deduced. The passage which has obtained this accidental honor is as follows (d):—

" Redintegranda sunt omnia exspoliatis, vel ejectis episcopis præsentialiter ordinatione pontificum, et in eo loco, unde abscesserunt, funditus revocanda quacunque conditione temporis aut captivitate, aut dolo, aut violentia malorum (e), aut per quascunque injustas causas, res ecclesiæ,

(b) Spittler, Geschichte des Kanonischen Rechts, Halle, 1778. S. 261—272.

(c) C. 3, 4, 5, 6 ; C. 2, q. 2, c. 1, 2, 3, 4 ; C. 3, q. i.

(d) C. 3, C. 3, q. i. This passage is to be found in the following different places, 1st, in a Decretal of John ; 2nd, in a Decretal of Eusebius ; 3rd, in the fifth Synod of Symmachus (anno 504). That this Synod in particular is just as fabulous as the above two Decretals is shown expressly by Ballerin, p. 532, p. 551—3, ed. 1790. It is therefore completely groundless to assert, as has been lately, that the passage in substance may nevertheless be genuine, as it belongs to this Synod, for the Synod itself is not less supposititious than the Decretals. The passage moreover agrees word for word with a portion of a

passage to be found amongst the acts of a suit instituted at Aix-la-Chapelle, A. D. 838, and which itself appears to have arisen out of the interpretation of the Breviarum. See Savigny's Geschicte des Roemischen Rechts, &c., B. 2, § 41. (Add to 5th ed. from a suggestion of Biener's.) It is not however affirmed by this, that the above rules, even in their wording, were pure invention: they were rather founded on some older Canon law, but their form, and the special moulding of the older rules contained in them were forgeries. Car. Blascus, De Collect. Isidori, Cap. 8, § 5, T. 2, p. 59, of Galland. (Add. to 6th ed., suggestion of Biener).

(e) This reading of an old Berlin MS. is justly conceived by Boehmer to be more probable than the ordinary ones, violentia

vel proprias, id est˙ substantias (*f*) suas perdidisse nos-
cuntur (*g*), *ante accusationem, aut regularem ad synodum
vocationem eorum,*" et rel.

If what so many Practitioners assert be true, this passage
makes all, that the Roman Law has established with respect
to Possession, wholly superfluous; for it is said to contain
all the following propositions:—

1st. The right of action lies without any reference to
juridical Possession in the plaintiff.

2nd. It lies for moveables also. This has been discussed
above with respect to the Roman Law (§ 42).

3rd. It lies also for incorporeal subjects, *i. e.*, as a protection for the exercise of all rights generally. See § 51.

4th. It is not founded on forcible disturbance of Possession, but it lies in like manner on every loss of Possession
without lawful cause.

5th. It lies against a third party in possession.

6th. It is not limited to a year. See § 42.

The first, fourth, and fifth of these propositions chiefly
deserve remark: if they were actually contained in the
above passage, it would signify little, that bishops only are
immediately spoken of; bishops might be mentioned by
way of example, or we might extend by mere analogy that

*majorum, violentia majore, virtute
majorum.* The correct reading is
also to be found in a beautiful
MS. of the Decretum in the
University Library at Marburg.
It must be confessed however
that *virtute majorum* occurs in the
sources cited by Gratian: *virtus*
in the sense of the middle ages
for violence. (Add to 6th ed.).

(*f*) Thus read the four MSS.
which Boehmer made use of.
MS. Marburg, " i. suas substantias " al. *aut substantias.*

(*g*) These concluding words

are wanting in the MSS. and old
editions of Gratian, and the
Correctores remark thereupon;
" hæc addita sunt ex originali
etc." *i. e.* from the sources used
by Gratian. That he himself did
not intend to alter the sense by
omitting them, is shown by his
additio at the end of the whole
quæstio, in which he sums up the
contents shortly thus, " Patet
ergo quod exspoliati prius sunt
præsentialiter restituendi, *antequam ad causam sint vocandi.*"
(Add to 6th ed.)

which the author of the above passage, and Gratian after him, only applied to bishops.

But from the earliest times all well grounded Jurists have refused to allow themselves to be deluded, or at all events very slightly, by suppositions like the above: they have been unanimous in maintaining that the passage introduces no new right of action, and that the author had in his eye the Roman Law, and consequently the Int. *de vi*, although several even profound lawyers have not been indisposed to admit some slight modifications of the Interdict by this passage of the Decretal.

But the whole of these suppositions may be refuted in a much more satisfactory manner. Not one word in the passage expresses that restitution is to be made to a bishop who has been robbed, but only that he shall not be indictable so long as restitution is withheld. It does not say, " *Redintegranda sunt* omnia episcopis, but redintegranda sunt omnia episcopis ...... *ante accusationem, aut regularem ad synodum vocationem eorum.*" If the passage had been expressed as follows (and it is mere accident that it was not so), " Nullus episcopus exspoliatus debet accusari priusquam integerrime restauretur" (*h*), no one could have well contended that a special right of action was contained in it. In the whole paragraph, therefore, no question is made of a right of action, but only of an exception to an indictment before the Synod, and hereupon we may gather two results. First, that the extension, mentioned slightly above, of this enactment, which was passed in reference to bishops, to all other persons whatever, is out of the question; for, although a right of action in respect of a lost Possession may be just as well conceived in respect of such other persons also, the above exception has no meaning except in the definite relation of a bishop to the Synod. Second, that in the above passage a right of action is undoubtedly not intro-

(*h*) *C.* 2, C. 2, *q.* 2.

duced, but at most is only assumed as existing. Everything, therefore, which can be proved out of this passage as to possessory suits, must be referred to such assumption.

Now there are three new cases which it is said the right of action here comprises ; the right, namely, without *juridical* Possession, without violent disturbance, and against any third party in Possession. The first of these cases has nothing whatever in the passage itself to warrant it, but some foundation appears to occur in it for the two latter. As to the second case, because the words " aut captivitate, aut dolo, aut violentia malorum, aut per quascunque injustas causas," seem expressly to provide that the enactment shall not be confined to the case of violent disturbance. As to the third case, because the general words " redintegranda sunt" do not make any distinction between the different persons who may happen to have the possession at the time. It is therefore probable that the author of the passage, and Gratian likewise, assumed that even without these two conditions a right of action might be allowed. But a right of action on naked Possession? Of this the whole passage does not contain a single trace. The bishop who, through *injusta causa*, is not in possession of the bishopric, is still bishop in fact; the property, which he may have lost through *injusta causa*, is still his property in fact ; and in these cases no question could arise as to his (petitory) right of action, although perhaps he might not be able to maintain a possessory suit.

To resume shortly the whole of this exposition. A right of action is not founded here, but assumed. This suit in most cases would be a Roman Interdict (*i*), and in other cases (*j*) a vindication. Thus the right of suit, which the

---

(*i*) " *Exspoliatis* vel *ejectis* epis-copis.... *captivitate* .... aut *vio-lentia*." It is well worth noticing that Gratian in his remarks at the end of the whole question when he gives the final result, contemplates this case only.

(*j*) " *Aut per quascunque injus-tas causas.*"

passage assumes, is wholly explainable out of the Roman Law, and it is unnecessary, even for the sake of this assumption, to suppose a new species of action.

If then a new right of possession is not contained in the words of the passage, and if its author Gratian had still less any idea of introducing a new right by it, how has the exposition been arrived at, which is not the mere suggestion of an individual Jurist, but the universal doctrine of prac-titioners? Upon this point there is only one supposition possible, but it is a very probable supposition. The Roman law of Possession was not thoroughly understood, and consequently in many cases a right of suit for a lost Possession was found wanting, when a complete knowledge of the Roman right would have afforded the remedy. On this ground the readiest course was to devise some new remedy which by its general and undefined character was well adapted to render a laborious study of Roman law superfluous. Now is it wonderful that practitioners should have adopted this invention with the greatest alacrity? that far from doubting of its genuineness they should have striven to perfect this invention more and more? But an authority also was required in the matter, and it was by a singular accident a passage was selected for the purpose out of the pseudo-collection of Isidore: upon a text which was itself spurious, the most arbitrary interpretation had nothing to be ashamed of!

Besides these important innovations which are *not contained* in the Canon law, there are however two others, less important, but actually contained in it, both of which have reference to the right of forcibly disturbed Possession (*k*).

The first of these innovations respects the right of action itself. The Roman law did not allow the action against a third party in possession even when he had received pos-

---

(*k*) A third case which the C. 9, X. de probat. is said to contain will be best explained in the following section.

session from the party who had exercised violence, with full knowledge how the possession of his *auctor* had commenced (*l*).

But Innocent III. perceived that the soul of this third party stood in just as much danger as that of the disturbant himself, and he therefore allowed the action against the former also (*m*). This therefore constitutes a true (though otherwise not a very important) extension of the Int. *de vi*.

The second innovation relates to the *exceptio spolii*. Thus an exception, which originally only applied in the indictment of bishops, appears to have been adopted by customary law in all suits generally, and it was finally established by positive law (*n*). Every party who had been robbed might have this exception, by which he might postpone all the civil suits, which the *spoliator* could bring against him, until restitution had been made: the exception however was excluded when the suit related to a right or to property of a church, and the right of a private individual was brought forward as an exception, or conversely. In a criminal suit the exception might be made use of, even when the indictment was not preferred by the *spoliator*, but by a third party; but in this case the *spolium* must consist of more than half of the entire property, and the prosecutor might also demand that a certain term should be assigned to the

(*l*) L. 3, § 10, *uti possidetis* (*ante*, p. 330). Boehmer shows by a note on C. 18, X. *de rest. spol.* that he was a much better Canonist than Civilian; he considers that the Decretals contain no new provision.

(*m*) C. 18, X. *de restit. spoliat.* Ziegler l. c. p. 246, makes the very just remark that as this law contains a new provision, the right of suit against the third party could not have been already given by the previous Canon, c. 3, C. 3, *q.* 1. Woltaer's objections in

answer are more learned than convincing (p. 250); they do not besides apply so much to the Canon itself, as to the usual exposition of it, which had long prevailed. Woltaer maintains further (p. 252) that the C. 18, X. *de rest. spol.* even applies to every third party in possession who only has notice of the *spolium* by the suit, because he also is one *scienter detinens*. But it is said expressly " si quis .... scienter rem talem *receperit*."

(*n*) C. 1, *de restit. spol. in* 6.

D D

defendant within which the Interdict should be used; after the expiration of which period the operation of the exception ceases (*o*). In civil suits as well as in criminal the *spolium* itself, upon which the exception was founded, must be proved within fifteen days at farthest.

The meaning then, shortly, of the *exceptio spolii* has only reference to procedure : but what is its relation to the Int. *de vi* when this is the suit brought by the other party ? The suit and the exception must relate either to the same or to different matters. In the first case the Interdict, like all other suits, is stopped for a time by the above dilatory exception; but the defendant in its stead may also bring forward his Interdict as a reconvention, and then the result is that both suits proceed, and are decided together (*p*). In the second case, if the plaintiff, who demands back a lost Possession, had previously ousted the possessor from the same Possession, the above exception cannot be conceived of as a dilatory exception, which it always is in the Canon law ; but as a peremptory exception it is invalid according to Roman law (p. 345), and this invalidity must consequently be affirmed here also.

(Addition to 6th edition). Hitherto we have shown how little solid the basis is for spoliatory suits in the written Law Sources. Nevertheless it is not to be denied, that for centuries past they have established a firm footing in practice, and it is necessary now to lay down their nature and limits precisely, according to their practical operation, in order that all may not be left here to the dominion of chance.

Now it has been already shown that the middle ages have bequeathed to us several important legal institutes, to which a protection of Possession would have been afforded by the

---

(*o*) It need not be observed that this exception in criminal causes applies, only where pure accusa-torial procedure avails, *i. e.* that it is almost entirely out of use.

(*p*) C. 2—4, **X.** *de ord. cogn.*

Roman law, if they had been known to the latter (§ 51).
To this class belong especially, besides the numerous juris-
dictionary and ecclesiastical rights, the widely extended
servitudes on land of the German Empire. In this latter
case the application of the above remedy introduced in
practice raises no question, indeed it is the true form in
which the above important extension of the whole right of
Possession was introduced into daily life.

Moreover, in those institutes also, which the Roman law
recognised, but to which it did not extend the protection
of Possession simply because of their rare occurrence, I consider that the spoliatory suits are applicable. I mean those
prædial easements, to which the Int. *uti possidetis* did not
apply, and for which nevertheless no special Interdicts were
introduced. If this is conceded, the spoliatory suits operate
in this respect as an extension of the Roman law according
to its true spirit, and they furnish at the same time the
practical solution of the question whether Roman Interdicts
might or might not be applied to such easements (*q*).

But further than this I do not conceive that spoliatory
suits can be carried. Not for instance to those legal institutes, which in their nature do not contain any necessity,
or even a capability, for any logical or sound application of
the protection of Possession; I mean family rights and obligations (§ 48). But I consider the application of spoliatory
suits to the province, already fully occupied by the possessory Interdicts of the Roman law, to be equally unfounded.
There is neither room nor necessity for their application in
this case, and if nevertheless it be sought to employ them

(*q*) It may be objected that in
other prædial easements the Roman law only permits the Int. *uti
possidetis* or a substitute of that
Int. (§ 48), but that spoliatory
suits are *recuperandæ poss.*, and
therefore an extension of the Int.
de vi. But in these rights the
disturbance of Possession cannot
be so accurately distinguished
from the termination of it, as in
property and personal easements,
and therefore a precise division of
the Interdicts for the former is
neither possible nor required.

indiscriminately with Interdicts, an incurable and endless confusion is the inevitable result. I am not alluding to the disturbance of all the necessary logical consequences which such a confused procedure introduces, because merely theoretic considerations must give way to the actual wants of daily life, but even this latter practical interest undoubtedly gains nothing by a procedure, which renders all fixed principles uncertain, and at last leaves the knot to be cut on mere arbitrary grounds, as the decisions will at one time be founded on this system of law and next day upon another. Such a condition of practical law can only be desirable to suit the convenience and ignorance of certain Judges, and the interests of those practitioners, who have the length of a suit more at heart than the good of their clients. Should we merely attempt then to carry out logically spoliatory suits to the above given endless extent defended by so many, we shall soon find cases in which even the defenders of them will shrink from the application. They must therefore tacitly admit that in such instances the application can not be made, by which it is rendered quite clear that this whole doctrine depends only on blind discretion. If this view is correct, then the hirer and the borrower, to whom Interdicts are refused, must also be denied the use of spoliatory suits also. But in the province in which spoliatory suits are actually applicable, the question arises as to the rules by which they are to be governed. The written law affords us no direct instruction on this point, and in practice we may seek in vain for distinct and uniform rules, although writers do not willingly neglect to rest themselves upon practice to prop up their views, however contradictory this practice may be with itself. I conceive that here also it is only in the analogy of the Roman law that a firm footing can be found, so that the new institute must be treated even in individual cases as the logical extension of Roman law, with continued reference indeed to the peculiar character of each legal institute, and the especial wants arising therefrom.

An empty cry is often raised against the endeavours of

what is called the historical school, to clothe every right exclusively with Roman forms, and thereby to do injustice to the original inventions of practice, and to the development of modern scientific intelligence. Many, without doubt, will cast the above-mentioned reproach on the view which I have here presented of spoliatory suits. I rejoice, therefore, to think that I can bring forward Muehlenbruch, whom many (I know not why) class amongst the opponents of the historical school, as the defender of the above view. He also considers the Int. *de vi*, in its genuine Roman form, as the only suit of modern law for the restoration of Possession; and he also sees nothing in spoliatory suits but the extension of that Interdict to a third *mala fide possessor* (*r*). In the last half of the eighteenth century, there appeared in Rome, with the *Imprimatur* of all the authorities, a copious work on spoliatory suits (*s*). From a modern Roman one un-doubtedly expects all respect for Canon law, and for the practice founded on it! The author, however, treats the Canon *Redintreganda* with the most sovereign contempt (cap. 3). But the spoliatory suit itself, which he describes, is nothing but the Roman Int. *de vi*, explained throughout by passages from the Digest, and elucidated only in a few points by passages from the Canon law. He thus lays down, quite decidedly, as existing law, that the hirer and tenant may not have spoliatory suits, and proves this propo-sition by L. 1, § 10, 22, L. 20, *de vi* (cap. 5, § 4, 5). Could this author have been a prophetic disciple of the German historical school ?

(*r*) Muehlenbruch, Doctrina Pandectarum § 244, 134.
(*s*) Franc. Mazzei, De Legi-timo actionis spolii usu comment-arius, Romæ 1773, 4to.

SECTION LIII.

POSSESSORIUM SUMMARIISSIMUM.

From the thirteenth century downwards an entirely new suit has been used for Possession in Italy, Spain, France and Germany, which is called *Possessorium summarium*, or *Summariissimum* (*a*), in distinction to the possessory suits which the Roman law had already introduced. The Gloss does not mention this remedy, but the substance of it, though not the name, is to be found so early as Durantis and Johannes Andreæ (*b*). The origin of this institute is to be explained by the mode in which the use of it is described generally by the older writers (*c*). The course of procedure in question

---

(*a*) In the older writers it bears very different names : In Italy it is called *Mandatum de manutenendo*, in Spain *Inecio* de Interim, in France *Recredentia* (probably Récréance), &c.

(*b*) Durantis, Lib. 4, Part. 1, Tit. de libell. concept. § 9, No. 22, first cited in Hollweg's Grundriss, § 213. In a dispute about the possession of a wood the parties were so envenomed against each other that neither of them would come forward with a libel as plaintiff, and a hostile collision was dreaded. The Judge prohibited both parties in the first instance from going to the wood, called upon them *ex officio* for their respective evidence, and decreed the possession to one of them only. Jacob Balduini, and Bagarottus were the advocates.

The same case is mentioned again but more briefly, Lib. 2, P. 1, tit. de petit. et poss., § 1, No. 38. The substance of this case therefore is, a procedure and decision without libel, which is more than the mere inhibition of violence, and we may therefore undoubtedly assert that the first trace of the new remedy is to be found here. Boyer assents to this, Summ. Prozess, S. 177. (Add. to 6th ed.)

(*c*) It will be readily conceived that no pains have been spared in the endeavour to derive this Institute from the Roman Law. Budæus, L. 2, de O. T., annot, in ff., p. 90—1, Lugd. 1546, and many others after him, affirm that the form of the *manus consertæ* was exactly the same. But that form was nothing but the opening of a vindication, and was

on Possession had become most protracted, instead of being, as it ought, expeditious, in order to restrain the universal practice of recourse to self-protection; a lawsuit upon simple Possession accordingly, which would not have lasted probably more than a few days in ancient Rome, might be spun out for years, and the parties in the meantime usually endeavour to obtain by force what they otherwise hoped to obtain, only later, by the decree of the Court. The same practice of resorting to self-protection might also occur in vindication, or in a suit on a contract; but to ward off the evil in these cases, no special legal provision was required; the state of Possession was there quite ascertained, and it was precisely from the uncertainty as to the state of Possession that the strongest inducement to violent proceedings existed, because these latter could always be adopted under the plea of self-defence. The same occurred with the Int. *de vi* as with vindication, &c.; the state of Possession, according to the plaintiff's own shewing, was determinate, for the plaintiff only claimed the restitution of Possession upon an *obligatio*. It was quite different with the Int. *uti possidetis;* in this case the actual state of the Possession was nearly always the question in dispute, and consequently the very object of the suit formed the greatest inducement to acts of violence, and a special legal provision was required, in order to prevent all violence in the interim, *i. e.* until the final decision of the question. This provision was the *Summariissimum*, the object of which it is now easy to describe. It only applies in the case of an

---

never used, as Budæus supposes, as the preliminary in a suit on mere Possession (§ 36). To have expressed himself correctly he should have said, the *manus consertæ* stand in a similar relation to vindication, as the *summariissimum* does to the *ordinarium*, *i. e.* to the Int. *uti possidetis.* Others find the *summariissimum* in L. 1, § 3, *uti poss.* Retes apud

Meerm. VII. p. 507, or in L. 13, § 3, *de usurp.*, I. Grav. de jud. poss. summ. Tueb. 1672, § 6—8; others again in Cicero, Pro Cæcina, cap. 12, "Nondum de Cæcinæ causâ (sc. *principali*) disputo, nondum de jure possessionis (sc. *ordinario*) nostræ loquor." Peller, De Summariis. poss. Altorph. 1665, § 13.

Int. *uti possidetis*, upon which no decision had been yet given : it is only necessary when the danger of open violence is so imminent that it cannot be warded off except by an immediate order of the Court(*d*); it avails in this case as an interlocutory Int. *uti possidetis* itself, that is, it raises and decides the same legal question as the Int. *uti possidetis*, and the only difference between them is, that in the former every consideration, and even a moral certainty on the state of facts, must give way to the necessity for an immediate decision. The first condition which was required for the user of Summariissimum in the Int. *uti possidetis* was a present juridical Possession. The assertion of several writers is quite groundless, that mere detention only, and not Possession, properly so called, was required for it. The party, indeed, who has detention only, will oftner succeed in this case than in the Int. *uti possidetis* in persuading the Court to allow his detention to enure as Possession ; but the object of the inquiry, and the ground of decision is still always juridical Possession, and no reason whatever can be suggested why any other rule should prevail here than in the Int. *uti possidetis* itself; for the peculiar end for which *Summariissimum* was established (to prevent breaches of the peace), is attained by any settlement of the present state of the Possession, and except for this end no other ground of decision can possibly be conceived, except those which would arise in the Int. *uti possidetis* also. But it was not every Possession that was sufficient to maintain the Int. *uti possidetis*, as by the three well-known exceptions, every *injusta possessio* was excluded. These three exceptions, therefore, must in the other case also govern the decision, except that the application of this rule cannot easily be made, because such an expeditious proof of these exceptions, as would be

---

(*d*) It is clear that it is open to the Court to join to this remedy other precautionary measures even speedier in their operation, to prevent violence, such as sequestration, fines, &c. [Add. to 6th ed.]

here required, could scarcely be brought forward in the generality of cases.

It is shewn, therefore, by this exposition, that the proper end of the above institute is to prevent breaches of the peace, and we may look upon it as a measure of police, which it had been thought good to introduce under the form of a judicial institute. This view is confirmed by the distinct form in which it was introduced by the Legislature into Germany, and, although this provision was not laid down as a general law for all Germany, there cannot be a doubt that it contains substantially the safest rule for decision in all those states where it is not established as positive law, but only occurs amongst the general undefined practice of the Court. The contents of the law are as follows (*e*): Where immediate subjects of the empire have a dispute as to Possession, and the present state of Possession is doubtful, and the case so " that serious disturbance, tumult, or outrage (breach of the peace therefore) may be apprehended," the Chamber of Justice shall be entitled, either on application of the parties or *ex officio*, to sequestrate the Possession, and immediately thereupon, " without any judicial forms or other protracted examination of the matter, to decide which party shall have the *momentaria possessio vel quasi*, or, it may be, to inhibit the parties to restrain themselves until the final decision of the whole case, *in possessorio* and *petitorio*, provided that in such case no prejudice shall arise to either party, as to his right to the holding or Possession."

This law makes it easy to ascertain the mode of applying the above institute. The first ground for establishing it by this law evidently arose from the fact that even the (ordinary) *possessorium* could not be sufficiently quickly decided; but it was not the length of the suit alone which gave rise to the provision, but the danger to the public security, which was brought about by the above lengthened procedure (*f*).

(*e*) *Ord. Cam.* 1555, P. 2,   P. 2, Tit. 22, § 4, 5.
Tit. 21, § 3; *Conc. Ord. Cam.*   (*f*) Frider, De Interdictis

Whenever, therefore, such danger can not be proved, there is no ground for the *summariissimum*, merely because one of the parties wishes, on account of the dilatoriness of the ordinary possessory procedure, to be put into Possession in the interim. If the *summariissimum* were founded on this latter ground alone, there is no reason why a similar interlocutory decision should not be made in every other law suit, for instance, in one on property, as delay in all litigation is equally oppressive. Indeed it is very natural that, from the constant use which is made of the above institute, the dispute as to Possession should continually become more and more protracted, and that soon a second *summariissimum* were necessary in order to escape the length of the first. If, on the other hand, this institute is only applied according to its original object and the provision of the law, it is clear that the demand for it in the different countries of Germany would be exceedingly small; for wilful disturbance of the public peace is the only case to which it would be then applicable, and this is no longer to be feared in the several German States (*g*).

If now the case is of the nature prescribed by the law of the empire, there is no doubt upon this law, that all, which has been asserted above as necessary for proceedings in *summariisimum*, is required. For as the law does not decide to which party the Possession is to be delivered, this question can be determined only upon general grounds, and upon the principles stated above. The law lays down very

Comm. 13, will not allow of a complete division into *ordinarium* and *summarium*, and he lays great stress upon his new doctrine. The *summarium* he says is the only *possessorium*, and the *ordinarium* which is spoken of elsewhere, and even in the laws of the Empire, is nothing but the *petitorium*, because it contains also the *possessionis causa* (*i. e.* the

final determination of the state of Possession). At the end of the chapter he himself mentions, however, a couple of exceptions, and it just happens that in these very exceptions all the cases are comprised in which the *summarium* avails as a rule.

(*g*) Bayer, Summ. Proz. S. 178, lays down that the regulation of the Chamber of Justice treats of two expressly, what the operation of *summariissimum* is; namely, it is to work no prejudice even to juridical Possession. Should it afterwards appear in the *possessorium ordinarium* that, not the successful party in the *summariissimum*, but the opposite side, had juridical Possession, such Possession is not lost by the decision in the *summariissimum*, and the Possession thereby transferred is to be looked upon as mere detention, by means of which the juridical Possession of another had been exercised in the interim (*h*).

Hitherto we have only discussed the possessorium *summarium* without even mentioning the *ordinarium*; for this latter is only so designated for the sake of distinction, being nothing but the old Int. *uti possidetis*, and it is easily comprehensible, that the institution of police, by which the public peace was to be preserved in the interim (*summariissimum*), should have had no influence upon it (*i*). Some Jurists have supposed exactly the converse of this relation (*j*); special applications of these views are to be found

different cases; breaches of the peace, and violence of individuals; the former only has become rare and improbable, not the latter. But the law contains merely two different means to an end, sequestration, and an interlocutory judgment; the *case*, for which these means are prescribed, is a solitary one, a threatened disturbance of the public peace and security. [Add. to 6th ed.]

(*h*) Compare the essay of Kober, p. 24, cited at the end of this section.

(*i*) The different names are to be explained thus. The newly introduced remedy was entitled *summarium* in opposition to *ordinarium*, and *summariissimum*, because (according to the general opinion at least), summary procedure already prevailed in *ordinarium*. *Summariissimum* is in truth a most barbarous word, but it is all the better for that, as it cannot leave any room for misconception. [Add. to 6th ed.]

(*j*) F. A. Hommel, Dissertatio de processa poss. Summ. quæst. 12, Lips, 1748, Qu. 1—3; Klepe, De nat. et ind. poss. ad interd. cap. 3, p. 35, 36. Klepe holds both *possesoria* to be, properly, innovations; the *ordinarium* by the Canon Law, the *summarium* by the regulation of the Chamber of Justice; but Interdicts also are still available. How he makes all these to stand in relation to one another, is quite inconceivable.

in numerous writers; the *summarium*, namely, is said to be the old Interdict, with certain modifications merely, and the *ordinarium* is an institute not differing from *possessorium* or *petititorium*, which the Canon Law introduced between the two. That this view is historically false, appears by the first glance at the older writers, and the above law of the empire. Those writers, without exception, treat *summariis-simum* (the *Recredentia*, the *Interim*, &c.), as something new, which the practice of the Court had added to the Roman Law, and the regulation of the Chamber of Justice, which defines precisely the conditions for the employment of this Interdict, expressly says that this previous decision shall have no influence in the final judgment as to the right itself, or as to the Possession (p. 409), which can only mean that these latter are to be governed by the provisions already laid down by the Roman law as to property and Possession. The passage in Canon law which led to the above incorrect view of a new possessorium *ordinarium*, is C. 9, X. *de probat.*, and there are two peculiarities by which this remedy is distinguished from the Roman. First, the Possession, upon which the *ordinarium* is founded, must be a *justa* possessio. If it is only meant by this that the *possessio* must not be *injusta* (*i. e.*, acquired neither violently, nor clandestinely, nor *precario*), the proposition is true; but that is saying no more than what was already clear by the Roman law, viz., that the Interdict is excluded by the three well known exceptions. But the *justa* possessio here meant, is a Possession arising out of a juridical transaction (*justus titulus*) (*k*). Secondly, the Possession must be more than a year old to enable the *ordinarium* to be brought (*l*):

(*k*) Hommel, loc. cit., p. 15, 56. A satisfactory proof is furnished here as to the correctness of the observation made above, (p. 391), as to the genealogy of this class of errors. The connection of the above doctrine with another on the notion of Possession (p. 101—4), and with a third upon the nature of Interdicts (p. 297) is not to be mistaken.

(*l*) Hommel, loc. cit. qu. 1, 2 ; Klepe loc. cit. The same rule was recognized in practice in

in contrast to this condition, therefore, the Possession in *summariissimum* is called the youngest Possession. But the passage cited from the Decretals establishes no new remedy, but in reference to the Int. *uti possidetis*, decides in a particular case according to the evidence brought. This view is made highly probable by two general observations. First, by the passage being introduced under the title *de probationibus;* second, because, otherwise, there would be a most important contrast and distinction between two possessory remedies in the Canon law, of which the Canon law itself was wholly ignorant. This view is established beyond all doubt by the contents of the passage itself. The case which Innocent III. had to decide, referred to the possession of a district with jurisdictory and other rights. Both parties had brought forward a host of witnesses ; each had proved that for many years past he had exercised such rights, and the *factum* of Possession was consequently a matter of great doubt. In this difficulty the Pope decided thus: as one party had possessed the territory for sixty years with all palatinate rights, and at the same time had shewn a legal title to Possession, but the other party had only exercised certain of such rights for fifty years, and could not prove any title for such exercise, the first party was entitled to be protected in his Possession by the Int. *uti possidetis.* Both grounds of the decision may be made to conform exceedingly well to the Roman theory of the Interdict. The Interdict required, 1st, actual Possession.

France so early as the 16th century. Cujacius in Paratit. ad Cod. tit. uti possidetis. So also the present French code requires two things in a possessory suit, 1st, Possession for a year at least ; 2nd, institution of the suit within a year of the trespass. Code de Procedure, art. 23. [Add. to 6th ed.] According to Hommel the *ordinarium* is a Remedium *recu-* *perandæ* possessionis; but this makes the whole confusion so complete, that one does not know where to commence the refutation and set it all right. This very widely diffused opinion amongst the older practitioners was generally expressed thus ; the *Ordinarium* is not founded on a present, but on an earlier Possession. Leyser, Spec. 499.

This was doubtful, on account of the contradictory evidence; but it was clear that one party had had Possession ten years before the other. Now as the loss of this former Possession was not proved, and as no other Possession was possible *co-existent* with the former one (*duo in solidum,* etc.), it was presumed, in the absence of any other evidence, that the first Possession still continued. 2nd. Possessio *non vitiosa.* As one party brought forward grants from Emperors and Popes, and the other was unable to adduce any such proofs of title, it became highly probable that the first had a possessio *non vitiosa,* and the other, if he had Possession at all, a possessio *vitiosa,* so that in this case also the latter would fail on the ground of exceptions, which the other side had nothing to fear from; in this view it was that *titulus* was mentioned. That this, in fact, was the meaning of the Pope, appears very clear from the following words, which contain the pith of the decision:—" Nos recognoscentes in hoc casu non sic locum esse interdicto uti possidetis, ut dicere debeamus: uti possidetis, ita possideatis (*m*); cum probationes Ecclesiæ longe sint potiores, *et ideo sit in interdicto superior.* Commune Faventiæ sibi condemnamus ...... quod possessorium judicium, quo tantummodo actum est, ut neque per se, neque per alios super his præsumat Ravenn. Ecclesiam ...... molestare (*n*).

[Addition to the 6th ed.] Here again many will exclaim, all this may be very fine, if reference is only made to the old written law, but practice has moulded it all differently.

(*m*) That is, although the Int. *uti poss.* is brought here, still the decree will be of little avail, if it merely contains the general words of the Edict, it must therefore specify the person who is to be protected in his Possession.

(*n*) The view which I have here given as to *possessorium ordinarium,* and the cap. 9, X. *de*

probat is also fully developed in the following treatise. Kober (præs. Jac. Frid. Kees) De Judicio possessorio ordinario, Spec. 1, Lips. 1805. This treatise is very useful, both from its profound and clear treatment of the subject, and from its abundance of extracts from writers.

We will therefore consult here the most approved writers on procedure, men, whom no one has ever yet ventured to reproach with prejudices in favour of Roman law. Their doctrine is as follows:

The *Summariissimum* is a provisional remedy for the defence of Possession. It enables a decision to be made upon the most summary procedure at the earliest possible period, in order to prevent violence from taking place. Therefore mere probability is admitted in place of full proof, but the facts which must be sworn to, and on which the decision is founded, must be the same as in the *ordinarium*. Thus here, also, *possessio* is required, and if perhaps in some cases mere detention is given effect to, this only happens from the Judge being liable to be misled from the insufficiency of the evidence, so as to treat detention as *possessio*. So also when regard is had to the *youngest* (most recent) Possession, this must not be understood as if Possession of a different nature were required to that in *ordinarium*, but when both parties set out individual acts of Possession on affidavits, the latest acts of Possession are looked upon as presumptive evidence of preceding acts, and therefore consequently of a continuing Possession. The exceptions available in *ordinarium* are scarcely ever attended to here, because such facts are put in question, as can be made to appear clear at the moment, and without any lengthened examination of evidence. Above all no written pleadings are allowed, but every thing if possible is decided in a single term, and on vivâ voice discussion (o).

This wholly practical description of *Summariissimum* agrees entirely with the view 1 have presented above, and it is clear that the length of a procedure so conducted could only be reckoned by days, or at most by weeks. There is only one point in which I do not quite agree with those

(o) Dantz, Summarischer Pro- scientific); Martin, § 259, 11th
zess, § 16; Bayer, Summ. Pro- ed. Comp. Mevius, P. 1, Dec. 39;
zess, § 65, 66 (comprehensive and P. 3, Dec. 132.

writers: namely, they allow an appeal against the decision, although they do not admit it to be a stay of proceedings. But even with such limitation, an appeal appears to me to be quite opposed to the nature of the proceedings. First, because the suit is thereby protracted to an indefinite length of time, and thus an immediate decision is rendered impossible, although the above writers admit it to be essentially necessary. Secondly, because the allowance of appeals frustrates the special object of *Summariissimum*. For this proceeding should only lie, when violence is to be anticipated from the undecided state of the Possession. But a decision has been already made upon the Possession, and this decision in every case is carried into effect, on account of the stay of proceedings being denied. Therefore all uncertainty as to the state of facts is put an end to, from which alone any special apprehension of violence proceeded, and which apprehension alone the *Summariissimum* was intended to provide for. Undoubtedly it is possible that the decision of the Judge, proceeding upon summary evidence, may work injustice to the unsuccessful party; but in answer to that, the *ordinarium* which still remains, provides a complete remedy. The passage of the Roman law which has been cited as an authority for the appeal (only without a stay of proceedings) (*p*) evidently proves nothing, because *Summariissimum* was altogether unknown to the Roman law: the passage undoubtedly refers to the ordinary Interdicts, and indeed according to the better opinion to the *uti possidetis* as well as to the *unde vi* (*q*).

It is quite another question whether the *Summariissimum* is actually so conducted in Courts of Justice as these writers describe. This must be positively denied. I myself remember a case which I helped to decide as Judge. The *sum-*

(*p*) L. un. C. si de momentanea poss.

(*q*) Comp. Albert, Int. uti possidetis, § 139—144.

mariissimum had here lasted about twelve years, it had been before several tribunals, and the termination of the suit was still not to be reckoned upon. Now if this suit should have lasted in the whole for twenty years, the *ordinarium* follow‑ing it might easily last for fifty, and the *petitorium* for a hundred years. Are we then to consider this absurd and vexatious procedure as a contradiction to the views previously set forth, and should we endeavour to honor this folly by adopting it into the theory? This were indeed a piece of idolatry in favour of practice, whose defenders are con‑tinually calling out in behalf of common sense and expedi‑ency. No constant and uniform practice, moreover on this point is to be found, as the passages already cited from Mevius fully show, and it would not be difficult to cite similar evidence to a considerable amount. According to my conviction, every Judge who sees the evils of this prac‑tice, should use his authority to oppose it. In most cases the very wide discretion which the Judge has in all cases of undefined summary procedure, will be sufficient for this purpose. As regards appeals, it lies of course with the higher tribunals to deny their application, so soon as they shall arrive at a sounder conclusion upon the subject.

SECTION LIV.

The results of this inquiry as to the state of modern law are as follows: In modern times undoubtedly legal rules have been adopted which were unknown to the Roman law: but the whole Roman theory is so far from being broken in upon by the above rules, that on the contrary they can not be understood except by treating them as additions to the above theory, the validity of which is thereby clearly recog‑nised.

INDEX.

———

A.

ABSENCE, does not put an end to possession, 171, 261.
ACQUISITION, of possession, rule, 127.
    See Prehension, *Animus*, 142.
    symbolical, unsound doctrine, 146.
    based on one physical act, *ib.*
    delivery at house sufficient, 160.
    and on state of will, *animus*, 170.
    exception to general rule, 177.
    animus defined, *ib.*
        who are incapable of it, 179.
    of individual parts of a whole, 189.
        rules as to, 190—2.
    through an agent, 224.
        exceptions as to *animus*, 235.
    peculiar rules for, as to possession, 241.
    may be by tortious acts, 242.
    or informal acts, 243.
ACTIO EMTI, suit founded on purchase, 289.
    actio, what meaning of, 285.
ACTIO FURTI, not maintainable by thief, 35.
    lies by creditor to obtain possession, *ib.*
ACTIO, momentariæ possessionis, 361.
ACTIO PUBLICIANA, founded on possession, 5.
    what, 9.
ADVERSE POSSESSION, 385—6.
AGENT, acquisition through, 224.
    requisites for, 226.
    relations of, 228, 230.
    custody by, does not amount to possession, 72, 206.
    divests possession of principal by fraud, 277.
AGER PUBLICUS, origin of special possession, 136.

AGER VECTIGALIS, what, 77.

AGREEMENT, sufficient to pass possession, 237.

ANIMALS, possession in, 256.

ANIMUS, must be combined with physical act to enure as prehension, 158.

required to acquire possession, 171.

ANIMUS POSSIDENDI, meaning of, 72.

exceptions as to, 235.

See Acquisition, 177.

ANOMALOUS cases of possession, 90.

AUSTIN, views on customs, 41, n.

B.

BENTHAM, views on customs, 41, n.

BONA FIDES, necessary to give title to profits, 10.

required for usucaption-possession, 59.

meaning of *bonæ fidei* possessor, 67.

BONITARIAN. *See* Ownership, 75.

BONORUM POSSESSIO, does not mean possession, but special property, 137—8.

BASILICA, classification of profession, 14.

C.

CANON LAW, passage in as to spoliatory suits, 396.

CAUSÆ POSSESSIONIS, rule as to explained, 49.

See Justa Causa.

CHILD, possession of, 229.

See Parent.

CICERO'S speech in possessory suit pro Cæcinâ, 43.

example of interdict-procedure, 288, 326.

CIVILIANS, opinions of on Possession, 97.

CIVIL LAW, technical meaning of, 40—1.

other meanings of, 42.

CIVILIS POSSESSIO, erroneous views of, 99.

meaning of, 39.

CIVILIS, explanation of term, 39.

CLAM, one of the *vitia possessionis, see Vi.*

CLANDESTINE POSSESSION, 262.

See Interdicts, 349.

CLASSIFICATION of *jus possessionis*, 21.

difficulties of civilians, 21—4.

Roman, of interdicts, 290.

CODE, place of possession in, 14.

COMMERCIUM, things not in, incapable of being possessed, 84.

COMMISSION, to receive possession, 228. *See* Acquisition.

COMMODA POSSESSIONIS, 5—16.

COMMODATUM, 206. *See* Owner, Hiring.

COMPOSSESSIO, what, 113.

Roman jurists divided upon, 115.

CONDITION, gifts on, do not pass possession, 176.

CONTINUANCE, of possession, 246.
 conditions for, 171, 247.
 through agent, 273.
 rule as to, 125.
CONSTRUCTIVE POSSESSION, 18, 144.
CONSTITUTUM POSSESSORIUM, 237.
CORPORALIS POSSESSIO, 54, 56.
CORPORATIONS incapable of *animus possidendi,* 179.
CORPOREAL act, required in possession, 169. *See* Prehension.
CUJAS, his view of possession, 103.
CULPA lata, and *levis,* meaning of, 39, n.
CUPER, excellent commentary on possession, 105.
 but erroneous in parts, 106.
CUSTODY. *See* Detention, 2.
 not indispensable for continuing possession, 255.
CUSTOM. *See* Customary law.
CUSTOMARY law, notions of the civilians on, 41,

D,

DAMAGES, recovered by interdicts, 306,
DEFENDANT, often meant by term possessor, 69.
 privilege of, in possessory suits, 10.
 may defend his possession by force, 11.
 in possessory suits, who may be, 306.
DELIVERY or traditio, a title to property as well as to possessio, 9, 16.
 sufficient to transfer possession, 152.
 essential to pass property, 237.
DENIQUE, special meaning of in Digest, 45.
DEPOSIT, does not pass the possession, 221.
 exception, 222.
DERIVATIVE possession, 80.
 erroneous view of, 82, n.
 includes anomalous cases, 90.
 peculiarity of, 205.
 through an agent, 228.
 constitutum possessorium, 236.
DETENTION, definition of, 2.
 the same protection not given to, as to possessio, 30.
 is called technically, *naturalis possessio,* 39.
 not to be confounded with possession, 63.
 generally meant by term *possessio,* 64.
 to enure as possession, requires *animus possidendi,* 72.
DE VI, Interdict. *See* Interdicts.
DIGEST, arrangement of, 13.
 plan of possession in, 13.
DOMAT, misconception of the Roman possession, 25.
DOMINION, exercised in fact over property by possession, 27.
DOMINIUM, what, as opposed to *jus in re,* 76, n.
DONELLUS, true views of possession, 24, 108.
DUO in solidum possidere non possunt, rule of, 88.
DUPLEX, meaning of, in Roman law, 307, *ib.* n.

E.

EASEMENTS, personal (in gross), 367.
    possession of, 369.
    real (appurtenant), 372.
    conditions for, 377.
    negative, 384.
    mode of acquiring possession of, 383—6.
    through third party, 374.
    amount of enjoyment necessary, 376, n.
EDICT, arrangement of, 14.
EMPHYTEUSIS, what, 77.
EMPHYTEUTORY, has possession, 215.
ESSE IN POSSESSIONE, meaning of, 55, n.
EVIDENCE. *See* Onus probandi, Non user.
    amount required in Interdicts, 294.
    as to easements, 376, n.
    presumption of possession continuing, 295.
    possession not evidence of property, 298.
EXCEPTIONS to interdicts, *vi, clam, precario,* 313.
    limitation, 314.
    to interdict *utrubi,* 321.
    to int. *de vi,* 344.
EXCLUSIVE possession, rule as to, 113.
    See Joint Possession, 117.
EXTRA ORDINEM, proceedings, 287.

F.

FACT, possession in, distinguished from legal possession, 54.
FACTUM, the act required in taking possession, 151.
FERÆ NATURÆ, 169.
FICTION, in taking possession denied, 144—5.
    none necessary for *int. adipisc. poss.*, 290.
    nor for act of taking possession. *See* Prehension.
FICTITIOUS POSSESSION, 144.
FORCE. *See Vis.*
    may be exerted by Possessor in defence, 11.
FORM, defects in, do not vitiate possession, 243.
FRAUD, by agere when it divests possession, 277.
FRUCTUARY, who is, 87—8.
    has no true possession, 210—11.
FRUCTUUM PERCEPTIO, see Profits, 10.
    belongs to bonæ fidei possessor, 201.
    but a distinction as to possession in, 202.
    and to mortgagee, 204.
FRUITS of possession, 8.
FURTUM POSSESSIONIS, where it lies, 63.

G.

GAIUS, light thrown by his work on possession, 49.
GAME, rule as to possession of, 169.
GANS, view of possession, 31.
GIFTS, between husband and wife, effect of on possession, 48,
GUARDIAN, may acquire possession for infant, 181.
    may acquire possession for ward, 235.

H.

HEIR, liability for violence of ancestor, 330.
HIRING, possession remains in the lessor, 206.
HISTORICAL origin of Interdicts, 135.
    school, view of possession by, 31.
HOBBES, views on customs, 41, n.
HOUSE, delivery at house passes possession, 160.
    provided the house is in actual use by party, 161.
HUSBAND and wife, donations between, 47.
    effect of, on possession, *ib.*, 48.

I.

IGNORANTIA, how it affects the acquisition of possession, 227, 235.
INCORPOREAL things, *quasi* possession of, 130.
INFANTS, cannot acquire possession, 180.
    disputed passage respecting, 181—5.
INHERITANCE, entry required to vest possession, 241.
INSTITUTES, place of possession in Justinian's, 13.
INTENTION. *See* Animus.
INTERDICTS, belong to the law of obligations, 21.
    not so classed in the Roman law, 23.
    sometimes treated as provisional remedies for property, 227.
    this view refuted, 298.
    all founded on tortious acts, 300.
    on violence, clandestinicity, or abuse of a precarium, *ib.*
    retinendæ poss. to protect possession from violent acts, 301.
        conditions for, (1) juridical possession, and (2) forcible dis-
            turbance, 304.
        (3) possession must be put an end to, 305.
        judgment, gives damages, and possession, 306.
        the interdicts *duplicia, i. e.*, both parties actors, 307.
    uti possidetis, 310.
        conditions for this interdict, *ib.*
        cases of possession not protected, 313.
        limitation of suit, 314.
    authorities on, 284.
    explanation of, 286.
    often equivalent to actions, 287.
    and in the later law not distinguishable, 288.
    procedure in, not summary, *ib.*

INTERDICTS—*continued.*
   possessory interdicts assume a jus possessionis, 289.
   but interdicts *adipiscendæ possessionis* not founded on such
     claim, 290.
   Roman classification of interdicts erroneous, *ib.*
   the only possessory interdicts are *retinendæ* et *recuperandæ* pos-
     sessionis, 292.
   and the int. adipiscendæ possessionis distinct, *ib.*
   the above view modified by a new passage of Ulpian, 293.
   amount of proof required of possession, 295.
   difference between proof of property and proof of possession, 296.
   utrubi, 314.
      lies for possession of moveables, 315.
      conditions for, *ib.*
      not an interdict for recovering possession, 319.
      exceptions to this interdict, 321.
   de vi, lies in cases of violence, 323.
      conditions for, 325.
      does not lie for moveables, 333.
      Thibaut's view of this interdict, 337.
      exceptions to, 343—7.
   de clandestina possessione, 348.
      conditions for, 349.
   de precario, 354.
      where the possessio becomes injusta, 355.
      whether it lies against heirs, query, 357.
   possessory, not superseded by the actio momentariæ possessionis,
     361.
   not available to party having simple custody, 30.
   fruit of possession.   *See* Interdict, 6.
   for personal easements, 370.
      real easements, 372.
      negative easements, 386.
ISIDORE, Pseudo-Decretals of, 395.

                 J.

JOINT POSSESSION, what, 113.
   See Compossessio.
   rule in Roman law explained, 117.
   exceptions to rule, 118.
JUDGMENT, effect of in interdicts, 306.
JURIDICAL, precise meaning of, 2, n.
   possession, two kinds of, 59.
   but only one genus, 60.
JURIS QUASI POSSESSIO, 130—1.
JURISTS, passages of, on *possessio civilis,* 44, 194.
JUS CIVILE, meaning of, 40.
JUS IN RE, different kinds of, 24.
   what, 76, n.
JUSTA CAUSA, necessary to give title to profits, 10.
   required for usucaption-possession, 59.
JUSTUM, meaning of in Roman law, 65.   *See Justa Causa.*

L.

LAND, when it ceases to be capable of being possessed, 85.
    only recoverable by interdicts, *recup. poss.*, why, 139.
    what act necessary for taking possession of, 149. *See* Prehension.
    when the possession of ceases, 258, 260.
    possession of, how recovered, 310. *See* Interdicts.
LAW, distinction into public and private, 11, n.
    interdicts connected with both public and private law, 33.
LEGAL POSSESSION. *See* Juridical, 59.
LESSOR, possession belongs to him not to lessee, 89.
    possession in, custody in tenant, 206.
LIMITATION, of suit,
    in *uti possidetis*, 314.
    in *utrubi*, 315.
    in *int. de vi*, 347.
LOSS OF POSSESSION,
    exception to general rule, 177.
    distinction between acquisition and loss in rule as to parts of
      a whole, 197.
    corresponds with continuance, 245.
    by external events, (corpore) 254.
    occurs when the physical power ceases or is obstructed, 254,
      258.
    notice where required, 262, 266.
    by act of mind, (*animo*) 266—7.
    nonuser, 271.
    by act of agent, 274.
    fraud, 277.
    controversy of Roman lawyers, 281.
LOAN, a borrower has no legal possession, 57, 223. *See* Precarium.
LUCRATIVA POSSESSIO, meaning of, 51.

M.

MASTER, acquires through slave, 229.
MATTER AND FORM, philosophical distinction, 3, n.
MATRIMONIUM, distinction as to, 59, n.
MERENDA, views on possession, 24.
MESNE PROFITS, right to by possessor, 29.
MISSUS IN POSSESSIONEM, has no legal possessionem, 57.
MISSIO IN POSSESSIONEM, what, 208.
MODIFICATIONS, of Roman law, 391.
    doctrine of possession not altered, 394.
MODUS ADQUIRENDI, of property, 9, 16.
MORTGAGE, anomalous case of possession, 90.
MOVEABLES, possession protected by *int utrubi*, 314.

N.

NAKED POSSESSION, what, 11.

NATURAL POSSESSION, meaning of, 39.
  has two meanings, both negative, 61.
  but sometimes includes legal possession, 61—2.
  though generally, only means detention, 62.
NATURALIS possessio, opposed to *possessio*, 54.
NEGATIVE EASEMENTS. *See* Easements.
NEMO, sibi causam possessionis mutare potest, meaning of rule, 49.
NIEBUHR'S explanation of possession among the Romans, 136.
NONUSER, evidence of possession given up, 271.
NOTICE, when necessary to previous possessor, 151.
  of loss of possession, 262.
  See Ignorantia, 227.
OBLIGATIONS, law of, includes possession, 21.
  possession part of the law of, 129.
OCCUPANCY, a title to property, 9.
  what act required to obtain possession, 172. *See* Prehension.
ONUS PROBANDI, does not lie on possessor, 10, 309.
ORDINARIA, judicia, what are, 287.
OWNER may hire, or borrow possession, 19.
  chargeable with theft of *possession* of his own property, 63.
OWNERSHIP, pledgee has not the property, 79.

                        P.

PAULUS, his treatment of possession, 14.
  rule as to joint possession, 116.
PARENT, acquires through his child, 229.
PAWNEE, has possession, 215.
PECULIUM, rule as to possession in, 229.
PERPETUAL leases, anomalous case of possession, 90.
PERSON, the protection given to possession founded on the rights
  of persons, 27, 301.
PERSONAL presence, the only *factum* required for taking pos-
  session, 157.
PETRONIUS, no authority on technical law, 43.
PETITOR, possessor, equivalent to plaintiff and defendant, 69.
PETITORIUM, suit founded on property, 27.
PHYSICAL POSSESSION. *See* Detention, 66.
PLEDGEE, his right to possessory suits, even where he has not the
  custody, 35.
  had no civil possession in Roman law, 45—6.
  but had juridical possession, 46.
PLEDGE, property in where, 79.
  possession in, 215.
  special rules respecting, 216—18.
POLICE, protection of possession belongs to, 409.
POSSESSIO, several meanings of term, 39.
  possessio simply, 39.
  naturalis, 40.
  civilis, 41.
  technical reference to *ager publicus*, 136, n. (*e*)
  also denotes relation of defendant, 69.
  requisites for juridical possession, 71.

POSSESSIO—continued.
animus possidendi, to a physical act, 72.
derivative possession, what, 80.
different kinds of possession, classified, 83.
things not capable of being possessed, 84.
possession always exclusive, 113.
joint possession, (*compossessio*) what, *ib.*
continuance of possession, 125.
vacant possession, 127.
quasi possession of incorporeal things, 130.
historical meaning of possessio in Roman law, 136.
no true property in ager publicus, 136.
its *possession* made over to individuals, 136.
and this possessio equivalent to property, 138.
physical act necessary for possession, 143.
fictitious prehension not recognized in Roman law, 146.
ficta, interpretiva, 18, n.
quasi possessio, 213.
POSSESSION, founded on physical holding, 2.
definition of, 80.
rights of possession different from right to possess, 3.
usucaption and interdicts the only rights ascribable to posses-
      sion, 5, 8.
false theory of possession, 7.
rights falsely ascribed to it:
      (1) perception of profits, 10.
      (2) onus probandi on adversary, 10, 29.
      (3) right of self defence, 11.
      (4) right of retainer, 12, 29.
where classed in Roman system, 13.
partly a right, partly a fact, 17.
asserted by some to be a right, 34.
originally a mere fact, 18.
sometimes the fact absent, 18, n.
as a right belongs to the law of obligations, 21.
it only gives a right to bring interdicts, 23.
difficulties of classifying possession, 25.
possession distinct from property, 26.
remedies given to protect possession in respect of person of
      possessor, 27—8.
refutation of erroneous views, 31—8.
different meanings of possessio :
      possessio civiles, 39.
      possessio naturalis, *ib.*
      possessio simply, 40.
passages of classical jurists, 44, *et seq.*
      possessio, and possessio naturalis opposed to each other, 54.
      possessio justa, 65.
      possessio bonæ fidei, 67.
act of taking, with respect to land, 149.
personal presence only required, 151.
      with respect to moveables, 152.
      by personal presence, 158—60.
      by deposit in house, 160.

POSSESSION—_continued._
of treasure trove, 162.
nature of prehension, 172.
how possession is to be taken of estate consisting of outlying farms, 173.
where no new act of prehension is requisite, 174.
detention converted into possession, 175.
mental act requisite (animus possidendi), 177.
corporations, lunatics, infants incapable of acquiring possession, 179.
parts of a whole, how possessed, 189.
where detention is transferred without possession, 206.
when possession accompanies detention, 215.
case of a pledge-holder, _ib._
possession passes to pledgee, 217.
special possession remaining in debtor, 218.
may be let out, locatio possessionis, 219.
detention, where possession sometimes passes, sometimes not, 222.
case of deposits, and loans, 223.
acquisition by an agent, 224.
constitutum possessorium, 237.
continuance of possession till lost, 245.
continuance requires a corporeal relation and animus, 246.
what physical act puts an end to possession, 254.
loss by animus, 266.
continuance preserved by agent, 272.
derivative, what, 205.
of easements, _see_ Easements.
doctrine of, extended by modern law, 390.
not altered, 417.
POSSESSORIUM suit founded on possession, 27.
POSSESSOR'S right to be protected against disturbance, _ib._
POSSESSORY INTERDICTS founded on a wrongful act, 6.
POSSESSORY SUITS, 289.
PRÆTOR, his proceedings in with an _actio,_ 285.
in Interdicts, 285—6.
PRECARIO, _see Vi,_ Interdicts, 354.
PRECARIUM, anomalous case of possession, 90.
inconsistency of Digest as to possession in, 123.
original meaning of, 139.
passes the possession, 223.
exception, _ib._
PREHENSION, erroneous definitions of, 143.
consists of will and physical power, 147.
passage of Paulus on, 148.
what act is necessary for immoveables, 149.
exception, 151.
what necessary for moveables, 152.
examples of, 156.
delivery at house sufficient, 160.
of treasure trove, 162.
of game, 169.
in case of occupancy, 172.

PREHENSION—*continued.*
of outlying farms, 173.
when not necessary, 174.
of profits, 200.
　　See Fructuum.
PRESUMPTION, possession does not presume property, 28, 295.
PRESCRIPTION. See Usucaption.
PRINCIPAL, may possess through an agent, 72, 206.
liable for violence of agent, 329.
PRIVATE LAW, 11, and n.
PROCEDURE, in interdicts not summary, 288.
PROCTOR. See Agent.
PROFITS, right of possessor to, when, 10.
PRO HEREDE, singular rule allowing any one to occupy a vacant
　　possession, 50.
PROOF. See Evidence.
PROPERTY, definition of, 3.
wholly distinct from possession, 26.
possession not primâ facie evidence of, *ib.*, 298.
often called familiarly *possessio*, 68.
generally so used as to lands only, 68.
analogous case of term in English, *ib.*, n.
bonitarian property also termed possessio, *ib.*
and all property not recognized in *jus civile*, so called, 137.
matters, not subject of property, incapable of being possessed, 85.
PROVINCIAL lands, not subject of true property *in old law*, 75.
distinction abolished by Justinian, 76.
PROVISIONAL VINDICATIONS, what are, 297.
suits for property not possession, *ib.*

Q.

QUASI POSSESSIO, what, 88.
protection of, 366—7.
of incorporeal things, 130.
relation to possessio, 213.
QUIRITARIAN RIGHT, *jus Quiritium, see* Ownership, 75.

R.

RECAPTURE, immediate, maintains former possession, 331.
REI VINDICATIO, suit founded on property, 289.
RENTING of possession by owner, 19.
RES FURTIVA, could not be *possessed* for usucaption, 59.
RES PUBLICÆ and res sacræ, incapable of being possessed, 85.
RESTITUTION, where given, *see* Interdicts.
RETAINER, right of belongs to possessor, 12.
RIGHT of way, *see* Way.
of watercourse, *see* Watercourse.
possession of easement must be exercised as of right, 377.
of possession, distinguished from the right to possess, 3.
question whether possession is a right or mere fact, 17.

RIGHT—*continued.*
    new rights created by modern law, 391.
    protected by possessory suits, 393.
ROBBER. *See* Thief.
ROMANS, their peculiar views as to possession, 136.
RUDORFF, view of possession, 33.

S.

SELF DEFENCE. *See* Self protection.
SELF PROTECTION, prohibited by Roman law, 33.
SERVITUDES. *See* Easements.
SEQUESTRATION, anomalous case of possession, 90.
SLAVES, not capable of possession, 52, 85.
SONS, under paternal control cannot possess, 85.
SPOLIATORY suits, 396, 402.
SPOLIUM, what, 395, n.
SUI JURIS, persons not, incapable of being possessors, 85.
SUMMARIISSIMUM, a new possessory suit, 406.
SUMMARY procedure, required in possessory suits, 407.
SUPERFICIES, a *jus in re,* 77.
    passage respecting explained, 212.
    right of a *jus in re,* 388.
SYMBOLICAL taking of possession, 144.
SYSTEM, place of possession in Roman, 30.

T.

TABLE of different kinds of possession, 83.
TAKING. *See* Prehension, 143.
TENANT, disclaimer by of landlord's title gives him possession, 49.
    has no legal possession, 57.
    possession not vested in, 206.
    supposed exceptions, 207.
TERMINOLOGY, as to *possessio, poss. civilis,* 39, *et seq.*
THADEN'S view of possession, 34.
THEFT, may be made of the possession independent of the property, 63.
THIBAUT'S views on possessio civilis, 44, n.
    correct view on derivative possession, 96.
    erroneous views on possession, 105, 108.
    views on int. *de vi,* 337.
THIEF, may have possession, 73.
TITLE, possession with, 67.
TORT, possession acquired by force sufficient for interdicts, 59.
    possession may be gained by, 242.
    all interdicts founded on, 300.
    species of, *ib.*
    violence, what is, 304—5.

TRANSFER of possession, 80—1.
    sometimes by act of will only, 81.
TREASURE TROVE, rule as to possession of, 162.
    exposition of controverted passage in Roman law, L. 3, § 3, *de poss.,* 164.

U.

ULPIAN, important passage of, on possession, 57.
    new passage of, on Interdicts, 292.
UNDIVIDED parts of whole, capable of being possessed, 190.
USUCAPTION, definition of, 5.
    springs out of possession, *ib.*
    and possessory interdicts the only rights of possession, 8.
    other rights ascribed by Authors, *ib.*
    closely connected with possession, 17.
    not founded on possession only, 129.
    interruption of, 199, n.
    different rule as to moveables and immoveables, 202.
    requisites for, 203—4.
USURPATIO, what it is, 199, n.
USUS, 211.
    See Ususfructus.
USUSFRUCTUS, quasi possession of, 131.
    does not give possession, 209.
UTERQUE, different meanings of, 249.
UTI POSSIDETIS, special interdict for land, 310.
    where not allowed, 313.
UTRUBI, interdict to protect moveables, 314.
    conditions for, 315.
    See Interdicts.

V.

VACANT possession, first condition for acquisition, 127.
    rule with respect to, 50.
VI, clam, precario, the foundation of interdicts, 6, 67, 301, 313.
VINDICATION, suit in lay against possessor in fact, 58.
VIOLENCE. *See Vis.*
    as to lands guarded against by int. *de vi,* 332.
    as to goods by int. *utrubi,* 335.
    subsequently by int. *de vi,* 336.
    Thibaut's views controverted, 336.
VIS, meaning of, 304.
    atrox vis, 328.
    protection against, 323.
VITIA possessionis, vi, clam, precario, 6, 66, 355.

W.

WARD. *See* Guardian, 235.
WATERCOURSE, protection to right of, 382.
WAY, protection to right of, 377.
WIFE. *See* Husband and Wife, 47, *et seq.*

Z.

ZACHARIÆ'S erroneous view of derivative possession, 82, n.

THE END.

LONDON:
PRINTED BY RAYNER AND HODGES,
109, Fetter Lane, Fleet Street.

www.ingramcontent.com/pod-product-compliance
Lightning Source LLC
Chambersburg PA
CBHW021428180326
41458CB00001B/175